Autoethnographic Tactics to Closing the Gap on Educational Attainment

Anika Chanell Thrower
Borough of Manhattan Community College, CUNY, USA

Alex Evangelista
Borough of Manhattan Community College, CUNY, USA

Ruth Baker-Gardner
University of the West Indies, Jamaica

Hammed Mogaji
Federal University of Bahia, Brazil

A volume in the Advances
in Educational Marketing,
Administration, and Leadership
(AEMAL) Book Series

Published in the United States of America by
    IGI Global
    Information Science Reference (an imprint of IGI Global)
    701 E. Chocolate Avenue
    Hershey PA, USA 17033
    Tel: 717-533-8845
    Fax: 717-533-8661
    E-mail: cust@igi-global.com
    Web site: http://www.igi-global.com

Copyright © 2024 by IGI Global. All rights reserved. No part of this publication may be reproduced, stored or distributed in any form or by any means, electronic or mechanical, including photocopying, without written permission from the publisher.

Product or company names used in this set are for identification purposes only. Inclusion of the names of the products or companies does not indicate a claim of ownership by IGI Global of the trademark or registered trademark.

                Library of Congress Cataloging-in-Publication Data

Names: Thrower, Anika Chanell, 1973- editor. | Evangelista, Alex James,
   1984- editor.
Title: Autoethnographic tactics to closing the gap on educational
   attainment / Edited by Anika Thrower, Alex Evangelista.
Description: Hershey, PA : Information Science Reference, [2024] | Includes
   bibliographical references and index. | Summary: "Nontraditional and
   underrepresented students can rarely emerge themselves in their studies
   because of competing priorities off campus. College graduations from
   different levels of degree attainment must step forward to share their
   journeys to assist in addressing the enrollment crisis"-- Provided by
   publisher.
Identifiers: LCCN 2023035020 | ISBN 9798369310748 (hardcover) | ISBN
   9798369310755 (ebook)
Subjects: LCSH: Minorities in higher education--United States. |
   Educational attainment--United States. | College attendance--United
   States. | African American college students--Social conditions. |
   Universities and colleges--United States--Admission.
Classification: LCC LC212.42 .A92 2023 | DDC
   378.1/9820973--dc23/eng/20230814
LC record available at https://lccn.loc.gov/2023035020

This book is published in the IGI Global book series Advances in Educational Marketing, Administration, and Leadership (AEMAL) (ISSN: 2326-9022; eISSN: 2326-9030)

British Cataloguing in Publication Data
A Cataloguing in Publication record for this book is available from the British Library.

All work contributed to this book is new, previously-unpublished material.
The views expressed in this book are those of the authors, but not necessarily of the publisher.
For electronic access to this publication, please contact: eresources@igi-global.com.

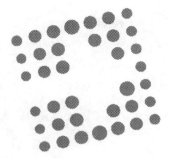

Advances in Educational Marketing, Administration, and Leadership (AEMAL) Book Series

ISSN:2326-9022
EISSN:2326-9030

Editor-in-Chief: Siran Mukerji, IGNOU, India, Purnendu Tripathi, IGNOU, India

MISSION

With more educational institutions entering into public, higher, and professional education, the educational environment has grown increasingly competitive. With this increase in competitiveness has come the need for a greater focus on leadership within the institutions, on administrative handling of educational matters, and on the marketing of the services offered.

The **Advances in Educational Marketing, Administration, & Leadership (AEMAL) Book Series** strives to provide publications that address all these areas and present trending, current research to assist professionals, administrators, and others involved in the education sector in making their decisions.

COVERAGE

- Marketing Theories within Education
- Educational Marketing Campaigns
- Academic Administration
- Governance in P-12 and Higher Education
- Educational Finance
- Educational Leadership
- Enrollment Management
- Advertising and Promotion of Academic Programs and Institutions
- Consumer Behavior
- Academic Pricing

IGI Global is currently accepting manuscripts for publication within this series. To submit a proposal for a volume in this series, please contact our Acquisition Editors at Acquisitions@igi-global.com or visit: http://www.igi-global.com/publish/.

The Advances in Educational Marketing, Administration, and Leadership (AEMAL) Book Series (ISSN 2326-9022) is published by IGI Global, 701 E. Chocolate Avenue, Hershey, PA 17033-1240, USA, www.igi-global.com. This series is composed of titles available for purchase individually; each title is edited to be contextually exclusive from any other title within the series. For pricing and ordering information please visit http://www.igi-global.com/book-series/advances-educational-marketing-administration-leadership/73677. Postmaster: Send all address changes to above address. Copyright © 2024 IGI Global. All rights, including translation in other languages reserved by the publisher. No part of this series may be reproduced or used in any form or by any means – graphics, electronic, or mechanical, including photocopying, recording, taping, or information and retrieval systems – without written permission from the publisher, except for non commercial, educational use, including classroom teaching purposes. The views expressed in this series are those of the authors, but not necessarily of IGI Global.

Titles in this Series

For a list of additional titles in this series, please visit:
http://www.igi-global.com/book-series/advances-educational-marketing-administration-leadership/73677

History and Educational Philosophy for Social Justice and Human Rights
Jahid Siraz Chowdhury (Lincoln University College, Malaysia) Kumarashwaran Vadevalu (University of Malaya, Malaysia) A.F.M. Zakaria (Shahjalal University of Science and Technology, Bangladesh) Sajib Ahmed (Universiti Malaya, Malaysia) and Abdullah Al-Mamun (Sunway University, Malaysia)
Information Science Reference • © 2024 • 300pp • H/C (ISBN: 9781668499535) • US $235.00

Promoting Crisis Management and Creative Problem-Solving Skills in Educational Leadership
Afzal Sayed Munna (University of Sunderland in London, UK) Uzoechi Nwagbara (University of Sunderland in London, UK) and Yahaya Alhassan (University of Sunderland in London, UK)
Information Science Reference • © 2024 • 321pp • H/C (ISBN: 9781668483329) • US $215.00

Strategic Opportunities for Bridging the University-Employer Divide
William E. Donald (University of Southampton, UK & Ronin Institute, USA)
Information Science Reference • © 2024 • 329pp • H/C (ISBN: 9781668498279) • US $225.00

Enrollment and Retention Strategies for 21st Century Higher Education
Rayshawn L. Eastman (Mount St. Joseph University, USA)
Information Science Reference • © 2024 • 300pp • H/C (ISBN: 9781668474778) • US $215.00

Interrogating Race and Racism in Postsecondary Language Classrooms
Xiangying Huo (University of Toronto, Canada) and Clayton Smith (University of Windsor, Canada)
Information Science Reference • © 2024 • 370pp • H/C (ISBN: 9781668490297) • US $215.00

For an entire list of titles in this series, please visit:
http://www.igi-global.com/book-series/advances-educational-marketing-administration-leadership/73677

701 East Chocolate Avenue, Hershey, PA 17033, USA
Tel: 717-533-8845 x100 • Fax: 717-533-8661
E-Mail: cust@igi-global.com • www.igi-global.com

I sit on life's bleachers, cheering for you-Dr. Blanche Eloise Jackson Glimps, 1942–2023

List of Reviewers

Rob Eirich, *Southern Alberta Institute of Technology, Canada*
Animat Fakunle, *Borough of Manhattan Community College, CUNY, USA*
Mounia Ghalmat, *Ministry of National Education, Preschool, and Sport, Morocco*
Kia A. Glimps-Smith, *The University of Virgin Islands, US Virgin Islands*
Pratima Gurung, *Kathmandu University, Nepal*
Iqra Iqbal, *University of Central Punjab, Pakistan*
Taisha Johnson, *University of LaVerne, USA*
Lina Kurchenko, *Kyiv National Economics University, Ukraine*
Felicia Mayfield, *Clark Atlanta University, USA*
Meghry Nazarian, *United Arab Emirates University, UAE*
Şenol Orakcı, *Aksaray University, Turkey*
Johanna Reyes, *Universidad Católica de Cuenca, Ecuador*
Melony Smith-Wellington, *Arkansas State University, USA*
Robin Throne, *University of the Cumberlands, USA*
Junell Trim, *University at Albany, SUNY, USA*
Nishi Tyagi, *Sharda University, India*
Christina Walker, *University of Kentucky, USA*

Table of Contents

Preface xiii

Acknowledgment xxii

Section 1
Raising Unlikely Scholars

Chapter 1
Human Agency: My Story 1
    Taisha Johnson, University of LaVerne, USA

Chapter 2
Out of the Shadows: An Unexpected College Journey 15
    Venesta Poleon, Independent Researcher, USA
    Musiki G. Glover, Independent Researcher, USA

Section 2
The Academic Trek

Chapter 3
Navigating Unfamiliar Terrain to J.D./Ph.D. 35
    Christina S. Walker, University of Kentucky, USA

Chapter 4
Empowering Persistence: Autoethnography Unveiling the Path of Non-
Traditional Doctoral Attainment 57
    Kia A. Glimps-Smith, The University of Virgin Islands, US Virgin
      Islands

Chapter 5
Schooled in Black Hair 138
    Melony Smith, Arkansas State University, USA

Chapter 6
Life Begins at 40: An Investigation Into the Educational Journey of Selected
Undergraduate Students in the Caribbean 155
    Ruth Baker-Gardner, University of the West Indies, Jamaica
    Suzette S. Brown, University of the West Indies, Jamaica
    Nicoleen Saunders-Grant, HEART Trust, Jamaica

Section 3
Dearth of Positive Ethnic Representation in the Comic Realm

Chapter 7
An Autoethnographic Approach to Adaptations and Limitations in Comics 189
    Jason D. DeHart, The University of Tennessee, Knoxville, USA

Compilation of References 208

Related References 230

About the Contributors 252

Index 257

Detailed Table of Contents

Preface xiii

Acknowledgment xxii

Section 1
Raising Unlikely Scholars

Chapter 1
Human Agency: My Story 1
    Taisha Johnson, University of LaVerne, USA

Human agency encompasses intentionality, forethought, ownership, purpose, and self-efficacy. This chapter explores these elements at various stages of Dr. Taisha Johnson's life. Dr. Johnson shares her humble beginnings. Dr. Johnson's journey was profoundly shaped by an absentee father, and her supportive mother, Barbara Blackwell. Her mother's unwavering support and inspiration laid the foundation for her success. Her narrative aims to inspire others to stay focused on their quest for purpose and meaning in their lives. While encouraging them to take the time to seek their natural talents as early as possible. Most importantly, her life's work exemplifies the significance of changing one's professional focus as needed and then sharing one's gifts with the world.

Chapter 2
Out of the Shadows: An Unexpected College Journey 15
    Venesta Poleon, Independent Researcher, USA
    Musiki G. Glover, Independent Researcher, USA

This chapter presents an ethnography of the subject V. Poleon's journey and experiences towards gaining higher education. Utilizing story-telling methods including her private voice recordings telling and searching for memories of her schooling as well as one-on-one interviews, the authors delve through 40 years of life. Through the lens of addressing the low rates of minority enrollment in college, they examine Venesta's unique story and the barriers she faced including her undocumented status, denied access to financial resources, her impoverished upbringing, and the lack of educational empowerment within her home and community. Utilizing escapism, Ms. Poleon imagined routes to immigrate off the island and network survival to begin her steep mountain climb to success in the United States.

Section 2
The Academic Trek

Chapter 3
Navigating Unfamiliar Terrain to J.D./Ph.D. 35
    Christina S. Walker, University of Kentucky, USA

Nontraditional and underrepresented students face immense stressors in their pursuit of higher education. Their ability to fully realize their potential and capability to pursue higher education may be inhibited simply by the ways they've learned to perceive the world and themselves during childhood. These students' paths to attaining higher education are often more arduous as they counter unique and separate obstacles than their more privileged peers. Such challenges may include being the first in their families to pursue higher education or having little experience navigating higher education, being of lower socioeconomic status, balancing familial and work roles and obligations, and experiencing ostracism and invisibility. From poverty to military service, to stumbling blocks, to achieving undergraduate and graduate education, this chapter details a student's unconventional and arduous journey to attaining higher education and her successful pursuit of two doctoral degrees. The hope is that students experiencing similar struggles may be empowered.

Chapter 4
Empowering Persistence: Autoethnography Unveiling the Path of Non-
Traditional Doctoral Attainment 57
    Kia A. Glimps-Smith, The University of Virgin Islands, US Virgin
    * Islands*

Autoethnography melds autobiography and ethnography, dissecting personal experiences for cultural insight. It challenges conventional research methods, emphasizing political and social justice. This research delves into transformative learning for non-traditional Black women in doctoral programs, amplifying their narratives amid often overlooked voices. Emphasizing determination and resilience, the research aims to offer critical insights, enhance academic support, create a successful environment, and improve graduation rates. It contributes to discussions on adult education, highlighting transformative learning's impact on inclusion, reflective thinking, and emotional flexibility. The research, which is dedicated to Dr. Blanche Jackson Glimps, helps shape policies, improve support systems, and direct the development of curriculum.

Chapter 5
Schooled in Black Hair 138
    Melony Smith, Arkansas State University, USA

This chapter narrates the journey of three women through their early education into the unfamiliar realm of college, while fitting together their educational and professional pursuits within the context of their hairstyle choices. The telling of these women's stories is layered in deeply rooted connections to the socio-cultural history and experiences of Black people in American society. Each segment of the chapter begins with an overview of the history of a Black hair style and then moves on to chronicle pivotal common episodes and experiences across all three women's lives. Within the chapter, the women explore: how they felt about education early on, when and why they realized college was the next step, their college experiences, their pursuit of advanced degrees, and finally their professional lives. This exploration is narrowly focused on commonalities across the women's experiences allowing for an account of the inequities, microaggression, and racism that complicated their journey and making their triumphs all the richer.

Chapter 6
Life Begins at 40: An Investigation Into the Educational Journey of Selected Undergraduate Students in the Caribbean.. 155
    Ruth Baker-Gardner, University of the West Indies, Jamaica
    Suzette S. Brown, University of the West Indies, Jamaica
    Nicoleen Saunders-Grant, HEART Trust, Jamaica

Colleges have traditionally recruited from among high school graduates to meet their enrolment targets, ignoring the possibility of exploiting the interest of older working adults who desire to enter tertiary institutions. This chapter details the experiences of 10 undergraduate students 40 and over who are currently enrolled in undergraduate programs. It explores the reasons for their late entry into tertiary education, their motivations for choosing to continue their education, the challenges they experienced, and how they overcame these challenges. This sample was chosen using purposive sampling, and data was collected using the interview method. The findings indicate that participants were unable to continue their education earlier due to financial constraints but enrolled in tertiary studies for several reasons including financial gains to be achieved and self-actualization. They experienced significant challenges while pursuing their degrees, chief among which was the difficulty of balancing school, work, and family obligations.

Section 3
Dearth of Positive Ethnic Representation in the Comic Realm

Chapter 7
An Autoethnographic Approach to Adaptations and Limitations in Comics 189
Jason D. DeHart, The University of Tennessee, Knoxville, USA

This chapter explores the experiences of a White male educator in an Appalachian fringe rural setting. Using an Emic perspective, he draws upon autoethnography to explore pedagogy and positionality. In particular, the author focuses on graphic novels and how visual texts can engage readers from underrepresented populations. The medium's limitations are explored, including the lack of some positive representation of minoritized students. Particular texts are named and explored, and the implications of this project include a framing of classroom practice that is both welcoming and text-centered. Further implications point to the necessity for writing and composing with the underrepresented students in mind.

Compilation of References 208

Related References 230

About the Contributors 252

Index 257

Preface

OVERVIEW

The flexibility of degree attainment through online education resulted in an influx of nontraditional students into higher education in the United States. According to the National Center for Education Statistics (n.d.), a nontraditional college student can include the following demographics: 25 years of age and older, part-time student, full-time job, from a single-parent home, and possessing GED or high school completion certificate. Nontraditional college students are likely to be underrepresented or belong to marginalized populations (National Center for Education Statistics, n.d.). Over the last few decades, attainment of college degrees within the United States by students from underrepresented groups has been lower than their White counterparts.

For context within this book, underrepresented, minority, and marginalized populations refer to individuals not identified as White. This reference is applicable as it speaks to racial relations in the United States. The enrollment, retention, and graduation issues among said groups have morphed into societal problems. Research and governmental data showed unwavering correlations between lower educational attainment and minority group status. Between 1976 and 2013, higher educational attainment increased among Hispanics from 4% to 16%, Asian/Pacific Islanders rose from 2% to 6%, Blacks increased from 10% to 15%, and American Indian/Alaska Native students increased from 0.7 to 0.8%. In recent times, the National Center for Education Statistics (NCES) asserted college student enrollment rates were highest for Asians, Whites, and Hispanics, with Blacks lagging (NCES, 2019). Sustainably tackling the college enrollment crisis will require a collective effort and an examination of the demographic distribution. Utilizing an autoethnographic approach, this publication intends to open up conversations about college enrolment and nontraditional students authentically.

Higher education is important as it has a significant positive impact on the lives of individuals, with lack leading to dire consequences. Higher education is an investment, as more education beyond high school usually leads to higher socioeconomic status (SES) (Tompsett, J., & Knoester, C. 2023). Higher education should be a human right as without it non-White individuals have daunting outlooks on prosperity in life. Lack of education within families has a potential domino effect for future generations. Low SES means lessened career opportunities, income, and educational attainment (Binkley and the Associated Press, 2023). In turn, this hinders populations' prosperity and economic freedom. In such instances, quality of life increases generationally and beyond. Utilizing comparable ages, in 2019, nearly 40% of nontraditional Black adults had at least a two-year college degree, an increase from 26% in 2000 (Postsecondary National Policy Institute, 2021). Furthermore, their White counterparts saw increases from 44% to 56% (PNPI, 2021). Individuals from a lower SES with less monetary resources and education have a heightened probability of experiencing morbidity (Alder, 1994, Marmont et al. 1997 & Marmont & Shipley 1996) and mortality (Marmont et al. 1997 & Marmont & Shipley 1996). Research affirms correlations between a lack of higher education and poor health outcomes (CDC, 2012; Thrower, 2013).

Unsurprisingly the more education one acquires, the more opportunities one has to expose themselves to heightened quality of association or social capital accompanied by a broader range of options. In 2017, individuals with at least a bachelor's degree experienced less poverty (United States Census Bureau, 2019). The stress of lessened job opportunities because of lack of degree attainment is a significant stressor that has cruel consequences to increasing poor health outcomes. It is the editor's assertion that limited employment opportunities experienced by many underrepresented populations mean individuals are overworked and underpaid and acquire jobs that compromise personal safety and health. For example, Blacks are more likely to be exploited. The underrepresented nontraditional college student who aspires to a higher quality of life and recognizes the value of an advanced education must tolerate inequalities structurally, institutionally, interpersonally, and individually. Such experiences exacerbate poor outcomes induced by chronic stress. Viewing the enrollment, retention, and graduation crisis as a societal responsibility may move the pendulum from contemplation to action for the unlikely scholars of tomorrow.

To this end, this book will explore enrollment, retention, and graduation issues among nontraditional underrepresented students through autoethnographic writing. Topics include higher education attainment challenges for individuals 40 and over residing in a third-world country, overwhelming stressors including risking deportation, enduring socioeconomic problems in formative years, imposter syndrome, mattering, microaggressions in campus climates, and of course, subtle influences that dim positive outlooks on oneself. Such narratives embedded in this publication have the potential to help improve the enrollment, retention, and graduation outcomes for the most vulnerable populations.

Preface

Target Audience

This publication represents reflections from underrepresented individuals who earned college degrees at various levels. Consequently, it provides a rich collection of narratives from their lens to be shared with

- Instructors teaching stress management courses or stress management components, social justice, equalities, minority psychology, and cultural perspective in higher education

Nontraditional students
- Diversity and inclusion departments and their staff
- Diversity training
- Campus sustainability departments and those professionals responsible for student engagement and enrollment
- Higher education cultural competency training programming
- Cultural awareness platforms
- College-based conferences
- Interventions and preventive workshop training at predominately White colleges and universities.
- Institutions to complement annual training
- Cultural diversity education and training for department heads (i.e., deans and chairs).
- First Year Education (FYE) programming
- Campus bookstores and within departments for adoption

ORGANIZATION OF THE BOOK

This publication is organized into three sections with seven chapters. The following are brief descriptions of each:

Section 1 (Chapters 1-2) highlights the plights of students from backgrounds lacking higher education roots. However, because of their life experience and the fortitude to see beyond the challenges, they would not be denied the opportunity to pursue higher education. These chapters take readers into the trenches where they are able to witness the rise of pioneers.

Chapter 1, "Human Agency: My Story" by Taisha Johnson, is an autoethnographic depiction of a once young lady whose family came from lack and humble beginnings. Despite an absent father, her mother provided the love and mortal support for her to realize her ultimate purpose in life. The chapter details the ebbs and flows of the pursuit of her life's calling. Her reluctance to settle led to her calling in psychology as a mentor and a college instructor. This chapter aims to inspire those lacking the fortitude to see past their current situations, showing them that higher education has the propensity to break generational curses.

Chapter 2, "Out of the Shadows: An Unexpected College Journey" by Venesta Poleon and Musiki G Glover, is an inside look into lengthy interview-style dialogues between two women. Artifacts, including voice recordings, in-person interviews, and virtual connections, were collected over several months. Candidly, one shares her life challenges to the other individual. She depicts her plight from St. Lucia to the United States with immigrant status and her climb to demanding access to her life's desires—economic freedom through higher education. When she exposed herself to the forbidding university experience, life began to take shape. Both individuals provided insights in their own words. The chapter concludes with both individuals' insights about risk-tasking being the ultimate price for freedom.

Section 2 (Chapters 3-6) highlights the plights of the nontraditional college student offering narratives from different lenses around the United States and in the Caribbean. Moreover, the chapters identify the need for mentorship and strategic retention processes with underrepresented individuals' life barriers in mind. Most importantly, these chapters exemplify the need for scholars who "make it" to reach back.

Chapter 3, "Navigating Unfamiliar Terrain to J.D./Ph.D." by Christina S. Walker, describes the life of an individual who learned difficult survival lessons as a young child. Being a quick study, she applied those lessons as she joined the United States Army, serving on the battlefield in Kuwait and Iraq. As a result, she won several honors. Later, she pivoted to college and moved forward to become an attorney. Currently, she is on her doctoral journey. This Army vet talks directly to the nontraditional students about exposing themselves to life's unknowns. Lastly, it sends a call to action for those positioned to assist the nontraditional student on the trajectory of higher education attainment.

Chapter 4, "Empowering Persistence: Autoethnography Unveiling the Path of Nontraditional Doctoral Attainment" by Kia A. Glimps-Smith, offers a well-curated narrative that illustrates such topics such as social-emotional skills, persistence theory, transformative learning, "Doctoratal," attrition, achievement Motivation, and Mezirow's framework. Through her transparency, she demonstrates what it means to remain a "lifelong scholar" even during crucial junctures in her life, along with the benefits and challenges. In conclusion, following in the footsteps of her last mother, she demonstrated the resiliency required to close the education gap. She provides a blueprint for future scholars to leave a legacy in their respective families."

Chapter 5, "Schooled in Black Hair" by Melony Smith, provides a narrative of three Black women's experiences and relationships from primary grades through advanced degrees, then into the professional realm. This narrative is intertwined

Preface

with the relationships with their Black hair. This chapter explores the complications of their relationships while simultaneously addressing challenges with their hair. Readers are schooled in historical hair trends, including hot comb usage, Jheri curls, weaves, natural hair, braids, and wigs. This chapter aims to explain the intersection of race, microaggressions, and black hair Black women's experiences to provide insights for diversity-based initiatives.

Chapter 6, "Life Begins at 40: An Investigation Into the Educational Journey of Selected Undergraduate Students in the Caribbean" by Ruth Baker-Gardner, Suzette S. Brown, and Nicoleen Saunders-Grant, details the experiences of nontraditional students in Jamaica, an island in the Caribbean. Data was collected from ten undergraduate students forty years old and over enrolled in undergraduate degree programs using the semi-structured interview method. The light was shed on their reason for late college enrollment, which include competing responsibilities and priorities, financial support, and lack of institutions to heighten successful outcomes. This chapter aims to bring awareness of economic freedom's importance through degree attainment. Institutions must mobilize needs assessments to inform the implementation of recruitment activities intended to attract nontraditional students.

Section 3 (Chapter 7) steps back from the direct issues affecting the nontraditional student in the previous chapters and sheds light on the indirect undertones in society. More specifically, the subtle impact comic creators potentially inflict on the future minority college.

Chapter 7, "An Autoethnographic Approach to Adaptations and Limitations in Comics" by Jason D. DeHart, a White male educator, raises awareness of comic book readership and viewing from his emic perspective. In his formative years, he took joy in this popular pastime. Conversely, in his later years, he calls out the medium's lack of positive representation of marginalized groups, which the marginalized student could internalize. From the contributing authors' stance, comic characters who are non-white have often been depicted as problematic in mainstream comics over the past decade and beyond. A call to action is needed to make available comic content, which ensures marginalized students can see themselves in ways that advocate inclusiveness and positivity.

CONCLUSION

Through autoethnographic narratives, the nontraditional and underrepresented college graduates represented in this publication articulated their experiences to inform strategies needed to positively change the trajectory of enrollment, retention, and graduation rates for the most vulnerable populations in higher education. Early in life, many of these individuals were counted out by society (and sometimes by themselves) based on circumstances beyond their control. To be clear, their resilience to persevere came at a substantial cost. Their accounts of unsurmountable stressors and willingness to give it all up in pursuing college degrees are commendable.

Notable first in higher education attainment in American history:

1876-Edward Alexander Bouchet was the first Black man to earn a Ph.D. from Yale University.

1921-Georgiana Simpson, Sadie Mossell Alexander, and Eva Dykes were the first Black women to earn their Ph. D.s from the University of Chicago, University of Pennsylvania, and Radcliffe College, respectively.

1953-Carlos Albizu was the first Hispanic to earn his Ph.D. from Purdue University

1931-Martha Bernal was the first Hispanic woman to earn a Ph.D. from Indiana University

In solidary,

Anika Chanell Thrower
Borough of Manhattan Community College, CUNY, USA

Alex Evangelista
Borough of Manhattan Community College, CUNY, USA

Ruth Baker-Gardner
University of the West Indies, Jamaica

Hammed Mogaji
Federal University of Bahia, Brazil

REFERENCES

Allen, W. R. (1992). The Color of Success: African-American College Student Outcomes at predominantly White and Historically Black Public Colleges and Universities. *Harvard Educational Review*, *62*, 26–44.

Beckles, H., & Richards-Kennedy, S. (2021). Accelerating the Future into the Present: Re-imagining Higher Education in the Caribbean. In H. van't Land, A. Corcoran, & D. C. Iancu (Eds.), *The Promise of Higher Education*. Springer. doi:10.1007/978-3-030-67245-4_54

Preface

Binkley, C., & Associated Press. (2023). *The labor shortage is pushing American colleges into crisis, with the plunge in enrollment the worst ever recorded*. Retrieved February 5, 2024 from https://fortune.com/2023/03/09/american-skipping-college-huge-numbers-pandemic-turned-them-off-education/

Center for Disease Control and Protection. (2012). *Higher education and income levels keys to better health, according to annual report on nation's health*. Retrieved February 04, 2023 from https://www.cdc.gov/media/releases/2012/p0516_higher_education.html

Marmot, M., Ryff, C. D., Bumpass, L. L., Shipley, M., & Marks, N. F. (1997). Social inequalities in health: next questions and converging evidence. *Social Science & Medicine (1982), 44*(6), 901–910. https://doi.org/ doi:10.1016/s0277-9536(96)00194-3

Marmot, M. G., & Shipley, M. J. (1996). Do socioeconomic differences in mortality persist after retirement? 25 year follow up of civil servants from the first Whitehall study. BMJ (Clinical Research Ed.), 313(7066), 1177–1180. https://doi.org/10.1136/bmj.313.7066.1177

National Center for Education Statistics. (2019). *Immediate College Enrollment rates*. Retrieved February 04, 2024 from: https://nces.ed.gov/programs/coe/indicator/cpa

National Center for Education Statistics (n.d.) *Nontraditional Undergraduates / Definitions and Data* Retrieved February 04, 2024 from: https://nces.ed.gov/pubs/web/97578e.asp

Postsecondary National Policy Institute. (2021). *Indicator 23: Postsecondary Graduation Rates*. Retrieved February 04, 2024 from: https://nces.ed.gov/programs/raceindicators/indicator_red.asp

Thrower, A. C., Danawi, H., & Lockett, C. (2013). Determinants of High Pre-pregnancy BMI of U.S. Puerto Rican WIC Participants. *The International Journal of Childbirth Education, 28*(4), 55–61.

Tompsett, J., & Knoester, C. (2023). Family socioeconomic status and college attendance: A consideration of individual-level and school-level pathways. *PLoS One, 18*(4), e0284188. doi:10.1371/journal.pone.0284188

United States Census Bureau. (2019). *Reports Nearly 77 Million Students Enrolled in U.S. Schools*. Retrieved from https://www.census.gov/newsroom/press-releases/2019/school-enrollment.html

United States Census Bureau. (2022). Improved Race and Ethnicity Measures Reveal U.S. Population Is Much More Multiracial. Retrieved February 04, 2023, from. https://www.census.gov/library/stories/2021/08/improved-race-ethnicity-measures-reveal-united-states-population-much-more-multiracial.html

SUGGESTED READINGS

Allen, W. R. (2008). Foreword. In M. Gasman, B. Baez, & C. S. V. Turner (Eds.), *Understanding minority-serving institutions* (pp. xv–xviii). SUNY Publishers.

Berry, A., & Kitchen, J. (2020). The role of self-study in times of radical change. *Studying Teacher Education*, *16*(2), 123–126. doi:10.1080/17425964.2020.1777763

Brown, B. (2017). *Braving the wilderness: the quest for true belonging and the courage to stand alone* (1st ed.). Random House.

Cokley, K., McClain, S., Enciso, A., & Martinez, M. (2013). An examination of the impact of minority status stress and impostor feelings on the mental health of diverse ethnic minority college students. *Journal of Multicultural Counseling and Development*, *41*(2), 82–95. https://doi.org/10.1002/j.2161-1912.2013.00029.x

Grand Rapids Community College. (2022). Seven dimensions of wellness | grand rapids community college. https://www.grcc.edu/faculty-staff/human-resources/professional-development/employee-wellness/seven-dimensions-wellness

Hancock, S. (2015). *Autoethnography as a lighthouse: Illuminating race, research, and the politics of schooling*. Information Age Publishing.

Hollies, L. H. (1999). Mother Goose meets a woman called Wisdom: A short course in the art of self-determination. Pilgrim Press, The/United Church Press.

Jones, M. C., & Shorter-Gooden, K. (2009). *Shifting: The double lives of Black women in America*. Harper Collins.

Morgan, D. L., & Davis, C. H. III, (Eds.). (2019). *Student activism, politics, and campus climate in higher education*. Routledge., doi:10.4324/9780429449178

Nadal, K. L. (2008). Preventing racial, ethnic, gender, sexual minority, disability, and religious microaggressions: Recommendations for promoting positive mental health. Prevention in Counseling Psychology: Theory, Research. *Practice and Training*, *2*, 22–27.

Nagoski, E., & Nagoski, A. (2020). *Burnout: the secret to unlocking the stress cycle*. Ballantine Books.

Pieterse, A. L., Todd, N. R., & Evans, S. T. (2010). An exploratory examination of the association among racial and ethnic discrimination, racial climate, and trauma related symptoms in a college student population. *Journal of Counseling Psychology*, 57(3), 255–263. doi:10.1037/a0020040

Roland, E., Hughes, T. N., & Simmons, F. (2021). Imagine paying for a course, then you end up teaching: Black woman doctoral students in equity, social justice, and diversity courses. *Journal of Diversity in Higher Education*, 1–12. doi:10.1037/Dhe0000368

Shavers, M. C., & Moore, J. L. (2014a). The double-edged sword: Coping and resiliency strategies of African American women enrolled in doctoral programs at predominately white institutions. *Frontiers*, 35(3), 15–38. doi:10.5250/fronjwomestud.35.3.0015

Sue, D. W., Alsaidi, S., Awad, M. N., Glaeser, E., Calle, C. Z., & Mendez, N. (2019). Disarming racial microaggressions: Microintervention strategies for targets, white allies, and bystanders. *The American Psychologist*, 74(1), 128–142.

Sue, D. W., Capodilupo, C. M., Torino, G. C., Bucceri, J. M., Holder, A. M. B., Nadal, K. L., & Esquilin, M. (2007). Racial microaggressions in everyday life:

Sensoy, O., & DiAngelo, R. (2017). *Is everyone really equal?: An introduction to key concepts in social justice education*. Teachers College Press.

Tatum, B. D. (2017). Why are all the black kids sitting together in the cafeteria?: And other conversations about race (Third trade paperback edition.). New York: Basic Books.

U.S. Department of Education, National Center for Education Statistics. (2020). The Condition of Education 2020 (NCES 2020-144).

Van der Kolk, B. A. (2014). *The body keeps the score: Brain, mind, and body in the healing of trauma*. Penguin.

Wise, T. (2011). *White like me: Reflections on race from a privileged son*. Soft Skull Press.

Acknowledgment

In the stillest moments, clarity has the opportunity to flourish.

In those moments, individuals have the prospect of creating synergies that help them pivot as needed, align themselves with other trailblazers, and thrive. Higher education provides access to opportunities. It is daunting to know that once upon a time, access to knowledge through books and formal education was forbidden for people who resembled most of the authors in the publication.

Still I Rise-Maya Angelou

The co-editors of this publication would like to acknowledge the sacrifices it took to break down barriers, generational curses, and personal challenges to earn their education. Striving for better through higher education attainment is rarely easy, as everyone has a story full of moments of truth. Projecting voices through their rich narratives took courage. As movers and shakers, they proudly take their places in history as laying the foundation for tomorrow's college graduates.

Lastly, the co-editors humbly extend gratitude to those reading this publication. Continue to do the work consistently.

I hustle for my last name, not my first-Dam Dash

Section 1
Raising Unlikely Scholars

Chapter 1
Human Agency:
My Story

Taisha Johnson
University of LaVerne, USA

ABSTRACT

Human agency encompasses intentionality, forethought, ownership, purpose, and self-efficacy. This chapter explores these elements at various stages of Dr. Taisha Johnson's life. Dr. Johnson shares her humble beginnings. Dr. Johnson's journey was profoundly shaped by an absentee father, and her supportive mother, Barbara Blackwell. Her mother's unwavering support and inspiration laid the foundation for her success. Her narrative aims to inspire others to stay focused on their quest for purpose and meaning in their lives. While encouraging them to take the time to seek their natural talents as early as possible. Most importantly, her life's work exemplifies the significance of changing one's professional focus as needed and then sharing one's gifts with the world.

INTRODUCTION

Human agency encompasses intentionality, forethought, ownership, purpose, and self-efficacy. This chapter explores these elements at various stages of Dr. Taisha Johnson's life. Dr. Johnson shares her humble beginnings. Dr. Johnson's journey was profoundly shaped by an absentee father, and her supportive mother, Barbara Blackwell. Her mother's unwavering support and inspiration laid the foundation for her success. Through her narrative, her goal is to inspire others to stay focused on their quest for purpose and meaning in their lives. While encouraging them to take the time to seek their natural talents as early as possible. Most importantly, her life's

DOI: 10.4018/979-8-3693-1074-8.ch001

Copyright © 2024, IGI Global. Copying or distributing in print or electronic forms without written permission of IGI Global is prohibited.

work exemplifies the significance of changing one's professional focus as needed then sharing one's gifts with the world.

The Making of Ms. Barbara Blackwell

Dr. Johnson's life began with her mother, Ms. Blackwell, who dreamt of a life filled with a good income, global travels, and accomplished children. Unfortunately, life's hardships diverted Ms. Blackwell onto a different path. She desired nothing more than a good life for her children – a life filled with educational achievements and successful careers, offering rich resources and unlimited possibilities.

Growing up in Shreveport, Louisiana in the 1940s amidst nine siblings and her maternal grandmother, Ms. Blackwell faced financial constraints due to low wages and a crowded household. Being the third oldest, she bore significant responsibility in raising her younger siblings, even sharing her meager meals. Despite these challenges, Ms. Blackwell harbored a profound desire for a better life for herself and her future children.

At 16, she met a young man in the neighborhood who shared her ambitions to escape poverty and the narrow-mindedness of the South. Determined, Ms. Blackwell left her family home, got married, and aimed to fulfill the dreams she had envisioned. However, her dreams faced a setback when she became pregnant, compelling her to drop out of high school to raise her son. Faced with the challenges of incomplete education and limited job opportunities, Ms. Blackwell, along with her husband and their first child, headed to California in pursuit of a life filled with dreams.

Adjusting to life in California presented unique challenges for Ms. Blackwell, as she had to overcome various psychological and socio-economic barriers. Over the years, two more sons added complexity to her quest to become the person she had always aspired to be. Despite the obstacles, Ms. Blackwell later reentered the educational system to earn her GED and an Associate's degree in Nursing. The 1960s presented challenges of racism and prejudices in the workplace, shaping Ms. Blackwell into a formidable force. These experiences fueled her determination to instill in her children the resilience to never quit until their dreams were realized. Harboring tenacity, resilience, and unwavering faith in herself and God, Ms. Blackwell played a crucial role in shaping Dr. Johnson into the person she is today.

An Absentee Father

In the 1970s, Ms. Blackwell separated from her husband, Mr. Blackwell, and later met Dr. Johnson's father, Mr. Jackson. Mr. Jackson, a Respiratory Therapist with multiple jobs, possessed a strong work ethic and believed in working hard to achieve the American Dream. He highly valued education and financial independence.

These values, combined with those Ms. Blackwell instilled in Dr. Johnson, played a crucial role in shaping her into the person she is today.

Mr. Jackson courted Ms. Blackwell, but unbeknownst to her, he was married with a daughter while she was pregnant with Dr. Johnson. This period was challenging for Ms. Blackwell as Mr. Jackson shied away from his responsibilities as a partner and father. Consequently, Ms. Blackwell had to rely on herself and the support of her three older sons to help raise Dr. Johnson. Dr. Johnson's father rarely visited and often made excuses for his absence. His visits were mainly driven by guilt, as Ms. Blackwell insisted that he should be a part of Dr. Johnson's life.

However, his visits were often disappointing, as he never addressed the reasons for his abandonment. Outings with her father were mere formalities, lacking any genuine effort to get to know her. On one occasion, her father took her to the race track to indulge in his gambling habit. He became so engrossed in gambling that he lost track of Dr. Johnson. This was a frightening experience for her, being lost in an unfamiliar setting and away from her mother who loved her dearly. Dr. Johnson, however, knew her home phone number and called her mother. While her father eventually found her, the incident left her traumatized.

This and many other incidents reinforced to Dr. Johnson that she was not a priority in Mr. Jackson's life. Many nights were spent in tears over the neglect, abandonment, and lack of regard she experienced from her father. Ms. Blackwell discovered her crying on one particular occasion and reassured Dr. Johnson that she was an amazing person. She emphasized that it would be to her father's dismay that he would never truly get to know how beautiful, hardworking, and tenacious she is.

Ms. Blackwell transformed that experience into an opportunity to strengthen her daughter. She encouraged Dr. Johnson to focus on the many blessings she already had in her life, including the support of a loving mother and three older brothers who made her a priority, keeping her safe and cared for. Their support became the foundation for her further development.

The Early Years

Dr. Johnson grew up with three older brothers, each over 14 years her senior. They took on the responsibility of raising her, particularly during the long 12-hour shifts their mother worked. However, being unfamiliar with caring for a girl, the brothers occasionally debated on tasks like changing her diaper. On one occasion, they all refused, resulting in Dr. Johnson getting a urine burn on her legs from being in her diaper and rubber pants all day. The incident left lasting scars, visible on her legs to this day. Fortunately, her brothers learned a crucial lesson in responsibility from this incident and never repeated such negligence.

Her brothers assumed roles more akin to pseudo-fathers than mere siblings, exposing her to various experiences, imparting valuable life lessons, and teaching her resilience. These outings were seen as adventures to be eagerly shared with her mother. They took her on bike rides, to the gym for basketball, to the park, and to their friends' houses.

Each brother contributed unique insights. The eldest brother, Willie, generously imparted his wealth of worldly knowledge to Dr. Johnson. Having traveled extensively and being well-read, he thrived on challenges and the exploration of new frontiers. Willie's eloquent expressions, showcased through his extensive vocabulary, never failed to amaze those who listened to him. He often demonstrated his linguistic prowess to those who underestimated his talents and skill set. Through Willie's example, Dr. Johnson learned the importance of being knowledgeable and possessing an extensive vocabulary in order to navigate the complexities of the world. The middle brother, Victor, shared profound sociological perspectives with Dr. Johnson. In his role as a social worker, he grappled with the challenging responsibility of removing children from their homes. Victor emphasized to Dr. Johnson the critical importance of a robust and supportive family system, along with the necessary resources to sustain it. Witnessing numerous breakdowns in different family structures, Victor observed firsthand the detrimental effects on children when families lacked essential financial, educational, and psychological resources. Unfortunately, these children often endured the negative consequences of a system that had failed them.

Despite finding the task of removing children from their homes distressing, Victor viewed it as a duty to protect the innocent in cases of abuse and neglect. He shared disheartening stories with Dr. Johnson, recounting instances where innocent children became victims of their parents' ignorance and neglect. One particularly poignant story involved a mother who left her toddler home alone at night, expecting the father to return soon, which never happened. The child cried all night until concerned neighbors eventually called the police for assistance.

These narratives deeply impacted Dr. Johnson, leading her to perceive her brother's job as that of a rescuer and protector for children who fell victim to circumstances beyond their control. This experience planted a seed in Dr. Johnson's mind, fostering her desire to pursue a path where she could actively contribute to helping others in challenging situations. The youngest sibling, Gregory, shared his insights into business administration. Notably, Dr. Johnson assumed the role of secretary in her brother's tow-truck business, handling tasks such as answering phones and keeping track of daily earnings. Counting her brother's money became an enjoyable activity, contributing to an improvement in Dr. Johnson's math skills in school. Her allowance, earned from assisting at her brother's business, often transformed into a playful store scenario. Dr. Johnson found delight in multiplication rather than subtraction during these imaginative exercises. This hands-on experience inspired her initial aspiration to become a cashier. However, Ms. Blackwell, Dr. Johnson's mother, had a different vision that aligned with broader goals. She envisioned her daughter as a lawyer, encouraging Dr. Johnson to pursue a path in law school to achieve a balance of extensive vocabulary, financial independence, and the ability to help others.

A Time of Exploration; High School

In high school, Dr. Johnson passionately pursued her interest in mathematics, aiming to enroll in the most advanced math classes available. While math generally came naturally to her, she faced a formidable challenge in geometry, particularly in mastering theorems—a different way of approaching math that she found unfamiliar. Despite this, Dr. Johnson's love for math prevailed, and she refused to let the challenges discourage her. On the other hand, English presented a different set of difficulties for her. The multitude of rules and regulations often led to her papers returning covered in red ink. Commas, word repetition, and run-on sentences seemed to be endless sources of correction. Despite her apprehension about writing, she decided to explore the possibility of becoming a lawyer, wanting to appease her mother's aspirations for her. However, Dr. Johnson soon discovered that lawyers are extensively involved in writing—legal memorandums, motions, contracts, discovery documents, and briefs. Writing became a task she struggled with, prompting her to seek tutoring during lunch to improve her skills. Learning from her family that hard work is essential for achieving one's goals, Dr. Johnson dedicated herself to honing her writing skills. Over time, she not only improved but also developed a positive relationship with her English teacher.

In her senior year, Dr. Johnson successfully convinced her mother to allow her to get a job. She started as a secretary at a tax agency, seeing it as an opportunity to leverage her secretarial experience and apply her math skills in tax preparation. The job provided an enjoyable and informative experience, teaching her about the significance of filing taxes and the relevant laws and regulations. Following this, Dr. Johnson took a job at a large retail company, fulfilling her dream of working as a cashier. However, the reality of earning $4.20 per hour as a cashier made it clear that this path would not lead to the financial independence she desired.

This realization prompted Dr. Johnson to embark on a journey of self-discovery to identify a fulfilling career. Rejecting the option of becoming a lawyer, she sought a profession aligned with her passion for helping others, knowledge acquisition, and financial stability. Through introspection and discussions with her mother, the idea of becoming a doctor emerged. Inspired by her mother's work in the medical field, Dr. Johnson explored various specialties and chose to become a pediatrician, drawn to the idea of working with babies. Her family welcomed this new direction with relief and hope for her future.

Human Agency

Fisk University or Bust

Dr. Johnson's decision to attend a Historically Black College stemmed from her belief that the African-American experience was more nuanced than portrayed in the news. During that period, the media was saturated with coverage of the Rodney King verdict, focusing on looting and negative depictions of African-Americans. Dr. Johnson's high school was affected by these stereotypes, with fellow students fearing African-American students based on these biased portrayals.

Unaware of this fear until a White American peer shared community concerns, Dr. Johnson felt isolated due to her ethnicity. Seeking an environment of acceptance, she applied to multiple Historically Black Colleges, ultimately choosing Fisk University for its partnership with Meharry Medical School, aligning with her dream of becoming a pediatrician. This decision marked a turning point, and Dr. Johnson cherished her time at Fisk.

At Fisk, Dr. Johnson delved into self-discovery, cultural understanding, and dispelling negative stereotypes about African-Americans. Noteworthy alumni like W.E.B. Du Bois, Ida B. Wells, John Lewis, and Nikki Giovanni inspired pride and excitement. Dr. Johnson found solace in an institution that produced individuals aspiring to be doctors, lawyers, ministers, educators, and politicians.

Despite the positive experiences at Historically Black Colleges, Dr. Johnson lamented the media's failure to showcase this positive side of African American culture. She emphasized the need for recognizing positive role models across cultures, advocating for media that inspires and uplifts rather than perpetuates negative stereotypes. Dr. Johnson believed that young people should find inspiration in the media, fostering a drive to surpass limitations and contribute to human agency.

Opting for Fisk University due to its collaboration with Meharry Medical School, Dr. Johnson felt she was moving in the right direction toward her aspiration of becoming a pediatrician. Her time at Fisk was transformative, challenging negative stereotypes and instilling pride in African-American culture. The university's distinguished alumni, including W.E.B. Du Bois, Ida B. Wells, John Lewis, and Nikki Giovanni, served as powerful inspirations for Dr. Johnson.

Her initial year in college was marked by academic excellence, earning her recognition in Who's Who in American and membership in the Mortar Board Society. However, when preparing for the Medical College Admissions Test (MCAT), Dr. Johnson confronted a significant challenge due to test anxiety. Despite her determined efforts, she couldn't attain the required score for medical school admission. This setback prompted her to explore alternative routes.

Upon discovering the Post-Baccalaureate program, Dr. Johnson interviewed at various universities but faced rejection. Undeterred, she recalled her high school counselor's advice to volunteer first. Embracing this guidance, Dr. Johnson enrolled as a volunteer at her mother's hospital, embracing a detour on her path to medical school.

Dreams of Medical School Unraveled

Dr. Johnson approached her volunteer work at her mother's hospital with enthusiasm, becoming a candy striper and proudly wearing her volunteer shirt as a stepping stone toward medical school. Opting to work in the emergency room for a more immersive experience, she found herself in a life-changing situation. Despite having taken a microbiology class at Fisk, emphasizing the careful handling of viruses and bacteria, Dr. Johnson was assigned the task of cleaning gurneys in the ER, where various patients with complex medical conditions were treated.

Encountering patients with head lesions, cancer, and HIV, Dr. Johnson felt a mixture of astonishment and fear. When faced with blood-soiled linens, she hesitated due to concerns about potential exposure to infectious diseases. Seeking guidance from an ER doctor, she learned that staff members occasionally faced needle pricks, and those exposed to HIV would undergo testing and treatment. Terrified by the stark reality, Dr. Johnson chose not to clean the gurney and spent the rest of the evening with the doctors.

This traumatic experience shattered her dream of becoming a medical doctor. Regretting not heeding her counselor's advice earlier, Dr. Johnson found herself at a crossroads, unsure of her next steps. The pressure mounted as her mother urged her to quickly figure out her career path and find a job. Struggling with uncertainty and a newfound fear of blood, Dr. Johnson grappled with the daunting task of redefining her aspirations and navigating an unknown future.

Self-Advocating 101

Dr. Johnson searched the classified ads in the newspaper, and found a job as a security guard. The thought was to get an easy job now to do until she figured out what the next step in her life would be. She got a job for a security guard company in Long Beach. All Dr. Johnson was assigned to do was observe and report any suspicious activity, which seemed easy enough. Dr. Johnson made sure she secured a security position that did not require the use of a firearm. She did not want to be viewed as an imminent threat to potential criminals. She thought carrying a flashlight should be nonthreatening enough to do the job. While on the job, Dr. Johnson became exposed to so many nefarious activities. This was the first time Dr. Johnson got a taste of the real world. First, Dr. Johnson witnessed her co-working doing drugs on the job. She witnessed another co-worker coming to work inebriated. Her co-worker was a true example of what it meant to be a functional alcoholic. Consequently,

Dr. Johnson became a victim to an unfortunate event. There was this one particular occasion, where Dr. Johnson was taking prescribed pain medication due to getting her wisdom teeth removed. It just so happened that during that time she was taking the medication, she was asked by her supervisor to participate in a random drug test. All employees were being instructed to partake in a random drug test. Each of us at different times had to go down to the health office for the drug test. The nurse asked Dr. Johnson did she use any drugs, and of course the answer was "no". Dr. Johnson did not think anything of her prescription medication, because she was thinking about illegal drugs. Dr. Johnson got a called from her employer a few days later, and was removed from her post. Her employer informed her that she failed her drug test. Dr. Johnson and her mother were shocked by the results. They went down to the corporate office, and demanded to speak with the supervisor about the test results. It was evident to Dr. Johnson and her mother that there was an error in the drug report. The supervisor insisted that Dr. Johnson failed the drug test because of cannabis usage. Dr. Johnson denied cannabis usage, but it fell on death ears. Therefore, Ms. Blackwell demanded to see the drug report. The company did not have the report at the time to show what drug it was. They needed more time to produce that report. A couple days later, the security company called Dr. Johnson and gave her a new security post. Dr. Johnson asked about the drug report, and they said that the drug that she tested positive for was Tylenol with codeine. The supervisor asked if she had a prescription for the medication, and for her to bring the proof to the office. Dr. Johnson brought the prescription in for proof, and she was handed another post. The supervisor asked why she did not tell the nurse about the medication, and Dr. Johnson replied, "I thought they were talking about illegal drugs not prescription drugs". Dr. Johnson learned a valuable lesson in the importance of advocating for yourself, and seeking justice. After that incident, Dr. Johnson knew that it was time to find her new passion in life, and to find it fast. Dr. Johnson knew that being a security officer was not a job to get comfortable in or the end goal.

A New Path Discovered Path: Graduate School

Dr. Johnson's passion for numbers led her to consider a career in finance, envisioning a role where she could leverage her expertise to assist others with their taxes and attain financial security. While patrolling a high-rise office building, she engaged with accountants and financial advisors, uncovering valuable insights into the demanding nature of the accounting profession and the path to higher salaries as Certified Public Accountants.

During her patrols, Dr. Johnson encountered an academic advisor from Pepperdine University, sparking her interest in exploring various career paths. As she perused brochures, she contemplated programs in Business Administration and Education.

The idea of becoming a teacher lost its appeal due to concerns about late hours and bureaucracy. However, a third program offering a Master's degree in Clinical Psychology with an emphasis in Marriage and Family Therapy caught her attention.

Reflecting on her role as a trusted advisor among friends, Dr. Johnson recognized the fulfillment she found in helping others enhance their happiness and contentment. This realization prompted her to enroll in Pepperdine's Clinical Psychology Program, delving into the study of psychological disorders and healing. The field proved captivating, and she developed a deep love for understanding human behavior and thought processes.

Completing two and a half years of schooling, Dr. Johnson earned her Master's degree. An unexpected suggestion from an academic advisor about enrolling in Pepperdine's School Psychology program led her to explore this previously unconsidered field. Discovering the benefits of School Psychology, including summers off, holidays, favorable work hours, and comprehensive benefits, Dr. Johnson enthusiastically enrolled in the program just three days after graduating from Pepperdine, marking the beginning of a new chapter in her academic and professional journey.

Reaching Higher: A School Psychologist

Dr. Johnson embarked on the School Psychology Credentialing Program at National University, delving into a fascinating branch of psychology. The focus of School Psychology on utilizing psychometrics to guide practice particularly intrigued her. Dr. Johnson immersed herself in the study of various assessment tools, understanding how they could be employed to collect data and determine the presence of learning disabilities, ultimately informing intervention strategies.

Throughout the program, Dr. Johnson excelled, demonstrating a keen understanding of the subject matter. However, she encountered challenges in the practical aspect of the program – finding willing participants for the comprehensive tests that could span 30 minutes or more. Undeterred, she resorted to creative measures, sometimes resorting to bribery with her nephews and cousins, offering money to incentivize their participation. In some cases, persuasion played a significant role in convincing them to take part.

After dedicating 11 months to the program, Dr. Johnson earned her credential as a School Psychologist. Armed with this qualification, she was now equipped to apply her knowledge of psychology to assist individuals dealing with mental disorders and learning disabilities. The ability to make a positive impact on others in this capacity became a rewarding aspect of Dr. Johnson's professional journey.

Living in Purpose on Purpose

Dr. Johnson initiated her career by working for an inner-city school district with Nonpublic Schools, an unfamiliar sector for her at the time. Nonpublic Schools catered to students requiring intensive intervention in a smaller, more specialized setting. In this initial position, Dr. Johnson faced challenges, including a lack of access to essential assessment tools. She had to seek external support to acquire the necessary resources for her role.

However, Dr. Johnson's perspective on a supportive work environment transformed when she transitioned to her second job. In the new school district, she experienced freedom in expressing herself, presenting ideas, and implementing creative and innovative practices. Crucially, she was provided with the correct tools to carry out her responsibilities effectively. This shift allowed Dr. Johnson to connect more deeply with students and their families, bridging the communication gap between home and school while advocating for the students and their families.

While engaged in her dream job, Dr. Johnson sensed a lingering fulfillment gap, a void that could only be filled by the title "doctor." Her longstanding aspiration, shared with her mother, was to achieve the status of a doctor. After exploring various doctoral programs, she discovered a suitable option at California Lutheran University, offering a program that integrated dissertation writing from the outset. This structure allowed students to work on their dissertations in the early stages, unlike many programs that reserve this aspect for the final year. Motivated by this opportunity, Dr. Johnson enrolled in California Lutheran University's Educational Leadership program to pursue her doctoral aspirations.

The Making of a Doctor

Dr. Johnson's decision to major in Educational Leadership was rooted in her realization that the field of education was where she belonged. Identifying as a lifelong learner, she embraced education as a continual journey. Through her experiences in the program, Dr. Johnson gained valuable insights into herself. She recognized that true passion should align with personal desires rather than external expectations.

Throughout the program, Dr. Johnson faced underestimation from her peers who doubted her resilience. Many expected her to drop out due to the program's challenges. Each semester, the surprise on their faces at her return spoke volumes. It wasn't until the final year that her peers acknowledged Dr. Johnson's unwavering commitment, realizing that she was there to stay. Support from remarkable professors played a pivotal role in Dr. Johnson's journey. These mentors not only supported her but also believed in her untapped potential. In navigating the challenges of the

Educational Leadership program, Dr. Johnson discovered not only her own strength but also the importance of staying true to her aspirations in the field of education.

CLU provided an exceptional program that granted students a remarkable opportunity to explore educational systems both abroad and within the United States. As part of the doctoral program, students could choose to study in London, England, Australia, or New Orleans, delving into diverse school organizations. Dr. Johnson, recognizing the potential for a life-changing experience, eagerly chose Australia for her academic exploration.

The school tours, conducted in Melbourne and Sydney, proved to be nothing short of amazing. Dr. Johnson's class had the privilege of visiting multiple school sites and engaging with administrators to gain insights into their curricula. Australia's emphasis on vocational training, offering students an alternative path to learning a trade instead of immediately pursuing college after high school, left a lasting impression on Dr. Johnson. This vocational approach harkened back to the 80s, reminiscent of the era when schools provided Woodshop classes, providing children with hands-on skills and alternative career options.

Dr. Johnson was also pleasantly surprised to discover that Australia mirrored California as a melting pot of diverse cultures. Witnessing people from various backgrounds living harmoniously in Australia was a captivating experience. The entire journey served as an eye-opener for Dr. Johnson, reinforcing the idea that mutual learning and cultural exchange are vital. It underscored the importance of building connections and networking, not only within local communities but on a global scale. The Australian adventure left a profound impact on Dr. Johnson's perspective, fostering a deep appreciation for the interconnectedness of the world and the richness that diverse experiences bring to education.

Dr. Johnson's transformative experience in Australia reinforced the belief that there is immense value in staying open to learning from one another. Embracing connections and fostering a culture of mutual learning contributes to the collective betterment of society. Dr. Johnson, who had never contemplated being an international student before, returned from her trip with a sense of disappointment that she had not explored such opportunities earlier.

This experience sparked a paradigm shift in Dr. Johnson's mindset, prompting her to reevaluate her perspectives on the education system and her role within the field of education. She began contemplating a more active role, one that went beyond merely encouraging students to pursue traditional paths like becoming a doctor or lawyer. Dr. Johnson envisioned her role as a guide in identifying students' strengths and assisting them in discovering careers aligned with those strengths.

Her newfound approach involved instituting an individualized method to help each student find their purpose in life. Recognizing that college might be the ideal path for some, Dr. Johnson acknowledged that for others, enrolling in a technical school or entering the workforce might be a more suitable choice. Regardless of the path chosen, her focus was on empowering students to become the best viable citizens in their chosen fields. This holistic perspective marked a significant departure from conventional career guidance, emphasizing personalized development and fostering a sense of purpose in each student's journey.

A True Inspiration to Others

Dr. Johnson aspires to be an inspiration for others, guiding them to achieve their life dreams and transform their aspirations into reality. Her philosophy emphasizes perseverance in the face of challenges and the enduring impact of education and psychology on individuals. Dr. Johnson acknowledges the unpredictability of the influence one may have on others, a realization often unveiled when former students revisit and share their experiences.

One recurring theme in the feedback from her students is the profound impact of her belief in them, the encouragement to strive for their best, and the insistence on never giving up. Her open-door policy and prioritization of their needs have been valued by those she has inspired. After dedicating eight years to motivating students to reach their full potential, Dr. Johnson transitioned to higher education, becoming an adjunct professor. Her goal is to share her knowledge and inspiration with future practitioners, urging them to become change agents in their respective fields.

Dr. Johnson believes that everyone, regardless of their role on a school campus or in a work setting, has the opportunity to utilize their skills to influence and help others. She emphasizes the daily decision individuals make on how to use their influence, encouraging students to recognize their duty to pay it forward. Dr. Johnson prompts students to reflect on the mentors and influencers in their own lives, urging them to be that source of support, encouragement, and empowerment for others.

In her teaching and psychological roles, Dr. Johnson imparts the knowledge she has gained from her experiences in psychology and education to future generations of change agents. Recognizing the importance of the support she received along her journey, she urges her students to extend a helping hand to others. Dr. Johnson advocates for a positive and intentional approach, hoping that the impact of their efforts reaches not only within their communities but also abroad. Her message is clear: be a force for positive change and support, for everyone needs help along their path to success.

Below are two letters that Dr. Johnson received from students from classes she taught. These are examples of the person that Dr. Johnson choose to model for her students so they too can be a positive role model for others. You would be amazed at the impact that one can have on another's life. Never take that for granted.

Human Agency

Letter #1

Hi Dr. Johnson,

Thank you for allowing me the opportunity to earn extra credit. I really appreciate it. I really wish that our courses were a bit longer simply because I feel that I could've given better effort in your course if I had more time. With that said, it was an honor being in your class. I feel that you are very understanding as a professor. I haven't come across too many that were in my lifetime.

I also feel that the knowledge I gained from your course has helped me in my current course. I will be able to apply a lot of the information towards future courses.

Also, I'm glad that you assigned group projects because the interactions with my fellow course mates proved to become a consistent group communication. We are all taking the same course this term and continuing to support each other. So once again I thank you for connecting us. I feel that it will prove to beneficial connections for our future if we all stay on the same educational path and complete our program together. I believe that it will help us all become mental health professionals by having colleagues to look to for advice once we receive our licensure. I hope that in the future, we all could have opportunities with many more professors such as yourself. You've been a great help to me, and I know that you will be to many others. Once again it was an honor to have taken your course.

Sincerely,

Your student

Letter #2

Hi Dr. Johnson,

Thank you so much!!

I've never done this before but I really wanted to say that I really enjoyed your class. It taught me a lot about myself and brought to my consciousness a lot of issues I have been dealing with. I wish it was a bit longer so I could dive deeper into everything. The way you conducted this class was VERY introspective and really helped me a lot. Something about the way you structured the class just made everything click inside of me on a very personal level. A couple of people have also seen the positive *changes I am trying to make now and have commented on it too!! Thank you so much!! You are such a great professor!!!*

Sincerely,

CONCLUSION

Dr. Johnson's life experiences have intricately shaped her understanding and embodiment of human agency, marked by intentionality, forethought, ownership, purpose, and self-efficacy. Her journey reflects a deliberate and purposeful approach to life, influenced by her desire to pursue her dreams and fulfill her potential. From her early exposure to negative stereotypes and biases, Dr. Johnson demonstrated intentionality in seeking environments that aligned with her values and aspirations. The decision to attend a Historical Black College was a deliberate choice to immerse herself in an atmosphere where acceptance and positive role models prevailed.

Forethought played a pivotal role as Dr. Johnson navigated the challenges of her academic and professional pursuits. Whether it was the shift from microbiology to psychology, transitioning from a security guard to a school psychologist, or pursuing a doctorate in Educational Leadership, each decision was carefully considered, reflecting her forward-thinking approach. Taking ownership of her educational and career paths, Dr. Johnson displayed resilience in the face of setbacks. The courage to redirect her trajectory from medicine to psychology showcased a profound sense of ownership over her life choices, steering them in alignment with her evolving passions.

Dr. Johnson's pursuit of education and continuous learning reflects a deep sense of purpose. The realization that being a doctor extended beyond the realm of medicine led her to embrace psychology as a means of making a significant impact on individuals' lives, underscoring her commitment to a purpose-driven life. Self-efficacy, the belief in one's ability to achieve goals, resonates throughout Dr. Johnson's narrative. Despite encountering obstacles, she persisted, demonstrating a strong belief in her capacity to overcome challenges and make a positive contribution to her community and beyond.

In essence, Dr. Johnson's life journey exemplifies how the components of human agency are not isolated concepts but are interwoven threads that collectively contribute to a narrative of purposeful living. Through intentionality, forethought, ownership, purpose, and self-efficacy, Dr. Johnson has become a beacon of inspiration, illustrating the transformative power of human agency in shaping a life of meaning and impact.

Chapter 2
Out of the Shadows:
An Unexpected College Journey

Venesta Poleon
Independent Researcher, USA

Musiki G. Glover
Independent Researcher, USA

ABSTRACT

This chapter presents an ethnography of the subject V. Poleon's journey and experiences towards gaining higher education. Utilizing story-telling methods including her private voice recordings telling and searching for memories of her schooling as well as one-on-one interviews, the authors delve through 40 years of life. Through the lens of addressing the low rates of minority enrollment in college, they examine Venesta's unique story and the barriers she faced including her undocumented status, denied access to financial resources, her impoverished upbringing, and the lack of educational empowerment within her home and community. Utilizing escapism, Ms. Poleon imagined routes to immigrate off the island and network survival to begin her steep mountain climb to success in the United States.

DOI: 10.4018/979-8-3693-1074-8.ch002

We ask you, the reader, to join us down a winding road of the learning experience - not the academics, but the societal challenges and endangerment.

Our Methods

V.P. and M.G.G. produced this body of work through a series of meetings. Storytelling methods included:

- V.P.'s private voice recordings
- In-person interviews and
- Virtual connections

Streams of Thought

M.G.G asked V.P. to reflect on her education from childhood to the present day. Examining over forty years of VP's life, this narrative seeks to provide insights into her struggles to gain access to the means of social and economic fulfillment.

We offer these personal accounts as a review of one individual's immigrant experience. The result for you is one framework to align your understanding of the gulf of the *minority education gap*.

We examine V.P. 's unique story - the barriers she faced including the hurdle of her undocumented status; along the way, we share records of denied access to financial resources and her impoverished upbringing. The lack of educational empowerment within her home and community is also explored as we weave her viewpoint within this chapter.

Utilizing escapism, V.P. imagined routes to immigrate from her roots on the island of St. Lucia. Her home life struggles to obtain daily food and water factored into her contemplations. And she wondered about all the possibilities that lay in other lands of plenty.

Over this chapter, you will read about her home life, school life, insecurities, anxieties, and triumphs. Her feelings of abandonment and responsibility play out through the scenes that follow. *And in the end,* you will witness - an interwoven pursuit of networks and the engagement of survival tactics; all eventually assembled, to assist V.P. in her steep mountain climb to success in the United States.

A Beginning Framework, Expressed by M.G.G.

was there a time when
knowledge was free?
And access was there for

Out of the Shadows

all to see?
when did we capture it
And lock it?
what was the purpose?
as we drain, as we contain
the pressure remains
Oh university, you call me
Oh university, you haul me
I come willingly
open your stores, open your doors!
what must I give, to live where you live?
to belong. to sing your songs.
thirsty, I am to find all
the words
the equations
the persuasions
the nations
the occasions
for knowledge to be mine,
for the divine,
for the grace and beauty of the equine
Time. give me time.
And call no crimes,
For he who shows
A desire to prose
Do not lock it away from me.
I'll dance the dance
And prance the prance
I burn, for you to let me learn.
I beg, for you to let me earn.
Do not lock it away
Who must I sway?
Come what may
That knowledge shall be mine
And whomever I can find
Must have it too

Are you scared of the dark? What if the sun never rose and there was no more moon? What about a black hole? Can you imagine, if you were to fall into it? And live? You're alive in the black abyss, a deep, bottomless pit. You're alive and must find your way along the streets - for food, for water, for shelter, for work, for medical care, for spaces to learn, spaces to play - figure it all out with no light as if your eyes were permanently closed. This is how V.P. and her family lived for twenty-two years...as shadow citizens.

I remember a film quote, *"Everybody alive is lucky, and were descended from the lucky. Our ancestors were all either fast, smart, or had really good immune systems. Luck, is why we're all here." (The Tender Bar, 2005).*

Under that premise, if you can accept it - then, V.P. 's presence in these United States and anyone else's presence, fair or foul, is of no heartache for 'the people that would hate, lock, and entrap' her back across the imaginary boundaries of the world. So, please sit back, relax, and let her take up as much space as she can.

V.P.'s Heart and Fears in America

With all this in focus, I'd like to share my journey and battle - the external and the innards - of arriving at my current destination as a senior at the great NYU - *GO* Bobcats!

I promptly entered the downtown Brooklyn building on the corner of Willoughby and Jay Street at 7:45 am. J.P. held my hand, her hair plaited in beautiful African Queen braids laced with bows. Her shoes were shiny, her stockings were bright white with a pattern of sunflowers, and her skirt and shirt were creased neatly. The whole ensemble was a tableau of perfection. She was the brightest and best dressed in the building. J.P. could play a viola solo to an audience of maestros. She could hold a conversation with a room full of philosophers contemplating the limits of man's free will. She was ready to dominate the third grade.

The attendance clerk took our names and found J.P.'s file. She was to be in classroom 3C. 3C? 3C!...I felt the horror in my own eyes, so I imagine the clerk must have seen the disdain upon her. I had an immediate reaction of rejection. Cold sweat dripped down my back and I felt a chill in my bones. NO! Who decided? Why? The waves of darkness begin to make themselves known again.

Down Memory Lane

As a little girl in St. Lucia, our abilities were tracked and classified - A Level - the highest quality of student: intelligent, inquisitive, (obedient), capable of challenge, from a *'good' family*. B Level - also capable of good work, needed further or more profound guidance - a very worthy student. C Level and below (D, E, F) - a waste of time; deficient, far below average, a range from the less serious students or perhaps from a family of poor reputation and socio-economic status. They didn't quite belong with us - the highest regarded students. Looking back, I now know that many factors place a child in C - F levels. Unaddressed learning disabilities and crippling poverty are often death sentences for children attending school. When death follows you, what hope is there in soaking up a lesson on idioms?

Despite our struggles, my family was lucky enough to be just above starvation. Also, lucky for me, was my natural affinity towards assimilating into the school system's structures. They always grouped with the A Levels. I relished in this with pride. I worked purposefully to earn and hold my position continuously. So why was my daughter, who was much like me, relegated to classroom 3C? I knew I needed to step back. I should ask questions and remember I was not in my homeland's the formerly French & British colonized state. I was in America! There would be an explanation for this injustice. Surely J.P.'s 3C placement was an error.

And still the sea of darkness would not let me see
Again trapped unable to breathe
Here sits my heart, eat it if you want
Here sits my bones, suck all the marrow
And as you have your fill, you crush my will
I've lost all my oxygen, I'm infected
And I'm bleeding out

A side note from M.GG.'s perspective - some ethnic immigrants who come to America (on occasion) seem not to grasp, forget (or forgive) the brutality of American colonization. As America is branded - Land of the Free and Full of Opportunity - often forgotten are the slaughtered natives of the land and the kidnapped African Americans who were captured and brought here. For those groups, this land's history is full of memories evoking a wasteland of vipers and excrement. These communities (survivors of genocide and enslavement) are expected to thrive here despite the well-documented evidence of trauma, brutality, and sanctioned disparity that continues to breathe as each new decade arrives. Freedom for one new generation of people is for another, a separate generation, a forced compliance of their domination.

Coming to Grips with Classroom Settings

Approaching the school administration to question my daughter's placement was difficult. I had to overcome my sense of inferiority. If I made too many demands would I look like a suspect? Would they investigate our records too closely? We survived by fading into the background. To capture *negative* attention was dangerous. But, I needed to know why they would do this to my child. She had proven herself in Kindergarten, First Grade, and Second. What right did they have and what wrong had she committed?

As it turned out, I did not approach the school leadership. Eventually, I did learn that the label C had always been the designation for what I now know is the Integrated Classroom of each grade level - KC (Kindergarten, as well as groups KA, KB), 1C (First Grade - along with classes 1A, 1B), 2C (Second Grade classes also 2A and 2B). The C label classes were a mix of Special Education kids with *NORMAL* students. The *right kind* of students. Thus, C classes had a variety:

1. Students with parents who cared and pushed the best out of their children (presumably) +
2. Students for whom the rules of the classroom setting were not a challenge +
3. Students who faced significant and glaring hardships in the traditional learning setting.

It was a small sigh of relief for me to discover this. Despite this new awareness, I would much rather my daughter had been selected for the 3A class - *a perfectly named classroom!*

My childhood classroom was a special place for me. In my classrooms, I visited new worlds. These worlds came to me via books. Each story took me on exciting detours far away from my life in St. Lucia. I would read everything available to me and then I would search desperately for something new to devour. Now, any time I walk past the many libraries of New York City or stop in the bookshops of the community, I still marvel at the abundance. So, much to read, so easily accessible.

In St. Lucia at that time, there was not an exploding library full of every book genre. We had to pay each year for our school books, our uniforms, and any supplies we needed. I have clear memories of learning to read. I felt special. My teacher and I enjoyed putting sounds to letters, letters to words, and words to sentences. School was a fascinating place because we gathered there, it seemed, to escape - to truly be children at play. Upon the dismissal of school, came the harsher realities of our lives.

Duty

We were a Black family of African ancestry. I was the oldest of three. And my responsibilities were extensive. Wash, clean, cook, prepare, care, work and repeat. Every morning. And then again the actual burden of running the home came every evening. My mother was far off working. And it was on me to maintain our home before my school day would start and after my school day's end.

As I reflect on this, I am gripped by these norms of our St. Lucian community. I resented it. I wanted so much to study, to read, to prepare my school work, to learn

Out of the Shadows

more, and to focus all my attention towards the highest scores possible. If you did a study of that period (and still possibly today), you would examine household after household - single-parented, typically no father, older children caring for the younger children; as older children cared for the younger ones, the mothers bore the sweat, tears, and heartache of leaving home twelve hours or more a day to earn a bit of money. *It seemed as if the slave plantations were still in full effect and operating effectively to tear families apart.*

By the time I had reached a high school level, my grades would suffer. And there were so many other distractions before me - boys, peer pressure, skipping school days for the surf and sand of the beach; and let us not forget the tubs and tubs of clothes to wash continually, dinners to scrape together, and little ones to discipline.

I wanted to leave the island. I felt if I left the island, I could do more. I applied to a college located in Florida. I wrote my request to attend by hand - no computer or typewriter to present myself as organized and intellectual. I had made a plea for an opportunity - an Oliver Twist moment - "Please sir I want some more" - not the bowl of porridge Oliver sought, but a higher learning experience - in my case. I was accepted. But, there was not a single fund for me to attend. Knowing that the finances were going to be an astronomical reach, I cannot remember why I dared to submit my application. Not to mention *who would be around to care for my siblings?* I was right back under a spell of murkiness - no way out to embrace the sun.

Go to the village. Go.
Just ten miles away.
Go to the village. Go.
For we must pay.
Your father is there
Somewhere.
Perhaps, he can give
A few coins.
Go to the village. Go.
A hill or two. A winding road.
You will get through.
Maybe, there, there is hope?
The fees must be paid.
So many fees.
Ask him. Ask him.
We are in need.
Go to the village. Go.
I don't want to. I don't want to.
There is nothing there.

I go hungry. I leave hungry.
There is nothing there.
But we must pay it.
Shall we borrow?
Shall we sorrow?
Say a prayer he says.
There is no coin here.
Say a prayer he says.
Does not look at my tears.
Go to the village. Go.
I don't want to go.
There?
There is no hope.
The teacher has said
Find a way,
She is so smart
Find a way,
A fire is in her heart
The teacher has said
She thinks, she writes
She grips the light
The teacher has said
Don't give up
The teacher has said
She has not enough
The teacher has said
Send your daughter to learn
The teacher has said
She sees the yearn
The teacher believes, the teacher believes,
She believes, she believes, she believes
In me

The Lack Deepens and I Drift Further Away From Shore

My father lived in a village some miles away. My mother would often make me visit him to see if he could lend us some financial support. He rarely did. I hated the walk I took each time for mere peanuts. I have no complete picture of the pressures he was under in his own life. However, his lack of care when it came to my childhood needs was something I had to overcome, *eventually*. I didn't want resentment to overwhelm me, but I would be remiss to say that I didn't at one time have a good bit of bitterness. Sitting in my living room now, in the present *(the Summer of 2023)*, we are having moments of reflection. He is here for a month traveling from St. Lucia for my graduation. He says he had hoped I'd aspire to be a nurse and asks if I remembered that he gave me some nursing books he'd found. I had. However, nursing held no interest for me. I remembered speaking with him about becoming a flight attendant. I wanted a 'ticket' out of the country and to move on to live and see other parts of the world. But, at the time these conversations were extreme fantasy. With him, I had no hint of support - only a long road back home with empty pockets.

My teachers believed in me and pushed for my continued education. I believed in myself. But the walls I had to climb from the lack of support from my dad, crushed me for quite a few years.

Still, I kept my head relatively level. There was so much I read that cautioned me and enlightened me about the world. The AIDS crisis, the statutory rape that was rampant in my community. I knew to recognize and ponder (and avoid) these issues as I grasped my hands upon encyclopedias and copies of National Geographic magazines. I felt certain of greatness and had an unquenchable thirst for more experiences.

And yet, I did not go to college upon graduation. My finals were a disappointment to me. My mother had made her way to England by then. She had joined my stepfather, working there to send home more funds. Such was the action and fate of many families with a connection or opportunity to seek work outside of the islands - the lure of a steady income and the promise of a bit of prosperity. My mother was off grasping at a better place for us in the world. Thus, I was alone serving as the single guardian of my two siblings by the time I was fifteen. Our lives were bare-knuckle survival - would there be a meal for the day, would we have fresh water to drink, would the funds arrive in time for my siblings and my books? These were the hourly concerns of our lives and the fantasy of walking the halls of the university was as tangible as the stars at night. An enchanting visual display. A misty apparition. In truth, another darkness to endure.

Just Won't Die: Hopes for My Own Family/ Hopes and Dreams for Myself

I had such a desire for a world-class education and I thus passed on these hopes to my children. I sought every possible advantage for them here in the United States. I did this while under almost constant fear and humiliation. In my head, I knew that my exploration of learning mattered. I had consumed information via books, documentaries, free lectures, and online research. I was smart. I was intelligent. I was

Out of the Shadows

shrewd. I could read people and situations, and I had a low tolerance for nonsense. But heavy on my heart was my reality.

I had no degree and no citizenship to back the confidence in myself. There were so many moments I wondered if my children suffered from my lack of status. Subtle tones of racism. Subtle tones of inferiority. Why was my daughter rejected during the interview process into a private school I had very much wanted her to attend? She had failed to show emotional maturity during an assessment of cooperative play and the admission officer told me she did not fit the student model they sought. I felt such a rage. I wanted to fight for her belonging there, but what tools did I have to challenge an institution that was under no legal or moral obligation to me; me, *an illegal nuisance to the true Americans*?

As an undocumented alien here in the United States, you never know who in a moment of rage, duty, or a sense of righteousness is going to report you. You work illegally hoping to never disappoint your bosses. You work whatever hours they demand of you. You accept minimal pay, no benefits, and forget about the concepts of a holiday or vacation. You are steps from drowning in inadequacy, debt, and lack. You barely have a moment to yourself. Your children must cope with the 'not quite enough' demarcation of your limited humanity. They cannot have your undivided attention. They cannot have your availability at school functions; you are busy taking your boss's daughter to and from school, then on to dance lessons, art therapy, and back to their home to prepare dinner. You hide from your employer that you have your own kids to nurture. Your employer wants all of your time - there is laundry to do, dry cleaning to pick up, grocery shopping, deep cleaning, and all manner of unexpected emergencies you must handle. Your undivided attention is needed so that their pursuit of wealth and success is not hindered by the distractions of a family life of your own.

As I toiled away in others' households, I dreamed. There was still a picture of higher learning in my mind. I wanted a college education! Round and round doubts swirled through me. Undocumented individuals faced obstacles in being accepted into higher education institutes. The costs of education seemed beyond reach as well. FAFSA was not available for us. I recall my sister, even as a new resident of the city, *was* charged international tuition rates. She eventually left New York for a state that offered better opportunities. But for me, still undocumented, another decade would roll around with seemingly no path. Where was my Golden Brick Road?

Eh? Listen, my friend.
Where are you? AMERICA!! You made it.
Eh? What is this you speak? College? Eh?
Go to work. Make the money. What I wouldn't give!
Make the money.

Out of the Shadows

You have a chance. You have something.
Make the money.
Eh? You want to study? Go to school? What? Fool.
Where are you? AMERICA!!
There is plenty.
Send a barrel home!
Send something back.
A pair of socks. Some soap. Lotion. Deodorant. Snacks.
Can you find me a pair of slacks?
Eh? You make money! You have food!
Can you send us some clothes? Can you send us shoes?
Can you send us some medicine? Some toys? Some beans? Some rice?
Ahhhhhh. You live nice.
Fancy house? Eh? Making some money, eh?
You are done with school. Send us back some tools.
A few books. A few knicks. A few knacks.
How about a drum for my birthday? A drum for the wedding?
A drum for the holiday.
Oh, it would mean so much.
You have the luck.
In America. In America. In America.

The focus of my life seemed to center on making money. That's what those in my community circles concentrated on; college aspirations were not on anyone's radar. The understandable priority of everyone's lives was surviving the high living costs in New York City. This we endured while balancing the expectations of our families back home in the Caribbean. The money and goods we sent back home were, in truth, life-saving resources for our loved ones. At the same time, we lived far below the poverty level in our day-to-day lives; we grappled with making rent, keeping the lights on, and having food in our pantries.

So, I worked and worked. From one job to the next. In childcare. In a salon. I took on any odd job I could to supplement our income. I had my first two of three children in my early 20s. First - M.P., then, A.P. M.P. had special learning challenges that took my life on another course far beyond anything I could imagine. As I navigated the minefield of his educational journey, I was juggling the demands of motherhood, marriage, and the challenges of being an undocumented immigrant.

However, I refused to give up on my dream. I decided to take the GED test to assess my academic ability within the American Education system. I wanted to have a window to college open to me. My GED scores could get me into college one day. I hoped I would find a way into a university. Somehow. Some way. Yet still, the clouds of doubt would shower rain:

1. an undocumented person cannot get into school, right?
2. how could I, a domestic, afford school? College was too pricey.
3. I needed my Green Card, yes?

A series of events began to transpire that helped me gain the courage I needed to cast aside my doubts about pursuing my college degree. I started to volunteer in my children's schools. The more I observed, the more I felt compelled to act. I began to advocate. I was offered a job in the school system. I learned a tremendous amount of information about special needs students. There was so much assistance available! You just needed to know how to navigate the offerings to improve the outcomes for your children. Being in these environments opened my eyes and helped me to support my own child (M.P.).

I took on leadership roles within Head Start. While in this role, I became more knowledgeable of pathways into higher education. Several informal mentors noted my engagement and informed me of educational opportunities. Without their guidance, I would have never known what programs to participate in; a lack of knowledge leaves so many of us in the dark. I count my blessings that I was surrounded by the generosity of others who helped me explore my potential.

Before I knew it, I had enrolled in a CDA (Child Development Associate) course through the City University of New York School of Professional Studies. Through this certificate program, I earned 12 college credits. This opportunity meant so much to me. I had CREDITS! I had received not just a document of participation, but earned college course hours that I could apply towards a degree! And these credits brought me confidence. Then, came the next big moment, I was informed that *all* my credits would transfer to BMCC - the Borough of Manhattan Community College. These fast-moving events left me in a daze. My passions and advocacy were aligning with my long-held dreams of hanging a plaque on my wall announcing my degree. The disbelief that had long followed me was fogging my brain at times, but I continued not knowing what lurked in the distance.

Mountains, on Top of Mountains, on Top of Mountains

It is important to note that the time I spent gaining new skills throughout my college course work, helped me build internal power to fight for my son's educational needs. Here was a young Black boy, from a family of immigrants, diagnosed with autism and other learning challenges. He was first diagnosed at the age of three and moved to many schools as we looked for the most appropriate setting. Through the years, I had to haul him and my eldest daughter, a toddler at the time, to numerous appointments for services - evaluations, counseling, attorneys' offices, hearings, specialists, a bout of homeschooling, and new school placements.

Living and navigating in what was once evaluated as the country's largest segregated school district - as the hidden - with a child who *struggled to blend in,* had us scaling mountains. The fears we faced and managed around our lack of citizenship nearly crippled us as we fought on my son's behalf (source 2014 The Civil Rights Project UCLA study, *New York State's Extreme School Segregation: inequality, inaction, and a damaged future*, Kucsera, Orfield).

When I tell you that the quality of education has a zip code, please picture and grasp that the wealthiest of our nation spend upwards of a combined $1.7 million per child in daycare, admission coaches, private schooling, college prep, and out-of-school enrichment *(*source 2017 Business Insider article, *It takes $1.7 million to get your kid into an elite college, according to rich people,* Abby Jackson*)*.

When you are not born with power, *AND* you do not live where power lives *AND* you have not yet gained any power, *AND* when your social status is at the bottom, *AND* your knowledge and understanding are limited, *AND* to top it off, you do not even have the right to make demands - you begin to drown in hopelessness.

Fortunately, I did not dwell for long in the despair of helplessness. I fought long and hard for my son to have an appropriate education. I faced the no's, the side eyes, the fees, the lies, the attempts to block our access and became his advocate; the shadows of my undocumented status in this country would not drown me. Every course, class, and professor I encountered opened my eyes to my purpose as an engaged inhabitant of the human race - yet a citizen of the United States. I was, I am, a whole person with worth and value; a whole person with desires and plans of my choosing. I would not stand limited by my status in the country. Period.

After several semesters of study, I earned an Associate's degree with honors in Early Childhood Education from BMCC. Initially, I only took one class a semester. This was all I could afford. I paid out of pocket not inquiring about government aid as I feared discovery and deportation. Eventually, my mother stepped in and paid for me to increase the amount of hours each semester. This allowed me to finish up the coursework a bit more expediently. The classrooms and the learning I received were so sacred to me; I wanted the highest scores for every test, paper, and assignment. Late into the night, and early in the mornings, I toiled away into Honor's lists, societies, and leadership associations.

Along this neck of my journey, one of my advisors in the BLA (BMCC Learning Academy) recommended me for the CCTOP program at New York University, NYU. CCTOP's (Community College Transfer Opportunity Program) scholarship and assistance program helps students in New York City's community colleges gain access to NYU. All my credits would transfer and I would qualify as a Junior. This came at me like a bolt of lightning.

Dare I? Reach?
Reach so HIGH and CLOSE to the Inferno of the SUN?
A Trial Has Begun.
The glories had decided. I'd abided.
I'd won. Battles. Skirmishes. Minor Wars.
I'd sought beyond the SOAR.
I didn't ignore the scores.
So much in my favor. Do I continue to savor?
I fought. I sought. And I caught. Dream after dream.
Paradise beside. Me. Don't hide. Me.
Wavering.
Is this desert heat? Will I thirst?
Do your worst. Fate. Destiny. I'm Flying Close.
And I'm bathing in the sun. Not quite done.
Reach. Dare I?

I reached. I signed up for a tour of the New York University campus. I was in awe of the library - the many floors of books. Thinking back on myself as a child, I felt a weight lifting. All that dreaming about and wishing for access to books…I was here in reality. Sitting among them and taking my time to absorb it all. I could if I wanted to, slowly devour, book after book.

I saw myself going there - New York University. The doubts were not gone. The same problems existed. Was I going to get enough of a scholarship? How much could I stretch my family's finances? And yes, I remained undocumented.

While at BMCC I also received an offer to attend the School of General Studies at Columbia University. This couldn't truly be happening! I was in awe. And under pressure. These offers were so alluring, drawing me into a wonderland. I applied to both programs. But, I sweated in anxiety up until the very last moments of the submission deadlines.

In many ways, I felt dread because how could I overcome all the obstacles? And with such hurdles to overcome, was I delusional? Still, just minutes before the deadlines, I submitted the applications. I did not want to live with thoughts of 'what if.' I had to try, to reach, to let hope linger longer. Memories of the Columbia campus were also flashing. One summer my daughter had performed in a program at Columbia's Teachers College. Walking those halls at the time, I had my daughter take pictures of me next to the signs and statues. I remember saying, "I will attend this university someday." And now years later, I was accepted not only to Columbia

Out of the Shadows

but also to NYU! I went to my room and cried once I had both those letters in my hands. These moments were not planned. They were imagined and teased. But, to hear you're wanted. You belong. Welcome. We are pleased to inform you. It's stunning. Overwhelming. And everything swirls in your head as your heart races.

The new struggle became, which school do I choose? I eventually ruled out Columbia because the program course offered did not match my preferred degree. Columbia's Teachers College is a grad program for which I was not yet eligible. Before accessing the Teacher Education coursework, I would have had to study an alternate degree program to finish my undergrad.

A defining moment for me was discovering I could begin my coursework at NYU without fingerprinting. As an undocumented individual, there are challenges in working in schools and proving you are not a safety risk to children.-

It's important to note that the fates aligned, and a year later, I obtained a work permit. Along with this came a social security number. Thus, I completed the fingerprinting process and began student teaching placements in NYC's Department of Education. It was a miracle 20+ years in the making. Landed right in my lap. Right on time.

And When You Land Where You Wanted

And thus, I arrived on campus. Wow. It was off to the races. Did I belong? So many young faces. I could have their mother. I was decades older than my classmates. The coursework hit me like a ton of bricks. I was also scraping funds to bridge the balance of the scholarship I had received. While it was a significant amount, there was still a gap in the full tuition payment.

I had to take out two loans. Throughout my junior year, though my husband was a rock of support in the house, (*with grocery shopping, preparing meals, cleaning the house, and in caring for our children*) - he was, however, out of a job. I had to support the family with part-time work while attending school. I wrestled with the decision to take out loans. Debt was something we tried never to allow to burden us. We had other fears to manage! However, I realized that I needed to take this risk. I was determined to create a legacy for my children, their future, and the generations of our family not yet realized. The gathered support of my husband and the patience and understanding of my children - made the achievement of my degrees a unified front; the success I achieved was truly a family affair.

I have to say a divine word about my mother. She once again contributed significant funds and helped me with the initial payments of my first semester's tuition at NYU. Time after time, her strong support - emotionally and financially - held me together. When it felt like the funds just wouldn't stretch to hold our family upright, my mother was a foundation; there for me to lean on.

the mother. she has hidden depths.
she walks along the long roads.
a strength unknown.
she finds a way when there is no light.
she stays up nights and manages her frights.
she has traveled afar, working on her stars.
behind the scenes of the universe,
she's been building.
A galaxy. just for you…

    I will graduate with my Bachelor's in May of 2023 at the age of forty-five. Twenty long, winding years past my youthful aims, I had finally achieved the education of my dreams. I am undoubtedly a product of the interwoven fabric of possibility. It hasn't been a straight shot to the moon, but the rocket has reached its destination. All systems go and I am off exploring new challenges.

    During my last year at NYU, my immigration status was finally resolved. I applied for FAFSA, which provided financial relief. I mustered the courage to speak directly with the NYU office of financial aid. I asked if they could increase my package; it made the final difference in my ability to focus the majority of my senior year on schoolwork and internship duties alone. Speak up. Share your needs. You never know who might understand. Depending on your explanation of need, the financial aid offices at universities may be willing to negotiate your offers and chip in additional scholarship funds.

    As I embark on this new journey, I see myself working in education policy to reform special education. I visualize starting a Non-profit, giving back to my home country, St. Lucia. I wish to support my mother in her retirement, buy groceries from stores, and never have to wait in pantry lines again. I want to set the bar for my children to complete their college educations. I dream of financial stability that allows our family to take vacations and see the world. As you can see, I am still reaching further and further. With a degree under my belt, life's options have broadened. Doors previously closed and labeled DO NOT ENTER, now have the locks removed. I can stand knocking and know there are no educational justifications for not letting me in.

    To you the reader I say - walk through open doors. Find windows to slide through if the doors are locked. Take second, third, and fourth chances on yourself. If you don't hit your marks the first time, keep shooting for your star. Obstacles are going to block your trail sometimes. Find your path around them - keep chipping away. Your life has so many options! And the surprises that are around the bend may startle you. Keep betting on yourself; speak and declare your hopes.

Out of the Shadows

It took me decades to realize my ambitions, and the doors that opened were nothing I anticipated. For those of you, living in the shadows with meager means to live, struggling to pay bills, or provide full meals to your family - it's hard. There is no getting around it. I don't have any easy answers. This is one woman's story of how she faced it all. I hope it can inspire, motivate, and bring you courage.

I still have moments where I forget that I am now a permanent resident. Legal! Coming out of the shadows. I still get anxious, look over my shoulder, and wait for disaster to strike. But the truth of the matter is I don't have to hide any longer. I can apply for real aid. I can apply for a legal job that will pay me a real salary and benefits. These are great new identities. But, don't you forget, I was someone before all that. Someone worth knowing, betting on, and fueling. And so are YOU!

Watch out world because I have a heart full of 'giveback' overflowing through me. What's in your heart? Let the floods begin.

We belong here! We have something to offer, we have a purpose. So hold onto that in your next endeavors. Remember from where you came and how you made it this far. Have continued faith and build your strength - the world needs You! I will leave you with this quote, one of my favorites, the words of Nelson Mandela, "Education is the most powerful weapon you can use to change the world."

In your arsenal are some powerful tools, your lived experiences, and the efforts you take to develop yourself. Use your weapons for the mass construction of your life, your family's life, and the communities you encounter.

Co-Arthur, M.G.G.'s Reflection

I advise every youth I encounter, every adult - old and young - to go to college. If it is just one class a year, go, learn, finish. I cannot speak across every nation, but if you are here in America - you should play the game. And a college education is part of that game. The game of the American Dream. As you participate in the college portion of The American Dream, you should also be learning every skill you can get your hands on. From plumbing to soil revitalization to NFTs, to planting trees, to designing wigs and hair braiding - never stop developing yourself. Learn to do every little piece of a thing that crosses your mind to do. You don't have to rush or be anywhere near perfection. Just move in a forward direction, piece by piece every day, year, or half-decade. Find iron to sharpen yourself. Mentors. Internships. Apprentice yourself within multiple disciplines.

If you can turn any of your passions, ideas, and hobbies into ethical ways to support yourself - do it…all of it! In your passions, I hope you are finding peace and purpose in waking up each day because your death is certainly around the corner - so WAKE UP with your dancing feet in great spirits and complete your waltzes and twerks.

"The beginning of the Declaration of Independence says that 'We the people' wrote the document. But the authors of the Declaration were really fifty-five privileged white men. They belonged to a class that wanted a strong central government to protect their interests. Right down to this day, government has been used to serve the needs of the wealthy and powerful. This fact is hidden by language that suggests that all of us - rich and poor and middle class - want the same thing." Zinn 2007, 2009.

For any reader of this chapter, for any educator, for anyone with interest, I ask that you not forget this history. This too is the REALITY of The American Dream. America is a science experiment. And you are both the elements in the petri dish and the scientists manipulating the formulas. *Please remember, however, that <u>there are owners and financiers of the laboratory space and tools</u> you are using and being used by.*

What must one do in life with all this knowledge? First, you **must** acquire it. It is a simple fact that without it, those who can will relegate you to the positions and limited opportunities they want you to have - some out of fear and the perceived threats to their standing. Some simply because that's the way it's done. They say, "This is how our system works; get on board or get left behind. When in Rome, do as the Romans do." I say, remember the destruction of the Roman empire.

> We must have knowledge of every perceivable thing to embrace our FREEDOM and refuse every form of ENSLAVEMENT that is imposed upon us from birth.
> We must have knowledge to tear down walls from the systems and individuals that stand in our way.
> We must have knowledge, decades of built upon bravery, and the resilience to carry on despite every mandated powerful force that comes against us.
> We must have knowledge to have the foresight to pass on the work, the passion, and the purpose of a life of freedom to our children, family, loved ones, and generations to come.

The ultimate evil is to acquire, lock, and seal it - leaving only those with economic means access. In fact, in my opinion - it's a borderline type of inhumane genocide.

We must find infinite ways to get knowledge in the hands of those who struggle and long suffer under unimaginable burdens so that America and her counterparts can thrive.

There are libraries, bookstores, museums, and plenty of spaces that may be easily accessible for some; we can send books, barrels of supplies, and shipping containers across the globe hoping to get pieces of knowledge into the hands of those *across the lands and seas* who go without.

Out of the Shadows

I have found nothing quite as magical as the University experience - leaving one's home base and the arrival into a whole new world ready to challenge, swallow, and possibly spit you out. The gathering of curious minds, opportunists, those desperate for a career, those seeking to test new ideas/new theories, those with inventions in their pockets and minds eager to create, or those seeking to change the world - the university is in part a Wizard of Oz gatekeeper as well as an audacious drawing room of frenzied minds seeking their own definitions of life.

ADDITIONAL READING

Kucsera, J., & Orfield, G. (2014). *New York State's extreme school segregation: inequality, inaction, and a damaged future.* The UCLA Civil Rights Project.

Moehringer, J. R. (2005). *The tender: A memoir.* Hyperion.

Stefoff, R., & Zinn, H. (2007a). *A young people's history of the United States.* Seven Stories Press.

Section 2
The Academic Trek

Chapter 3
Navigating Unfamiliar Terrain to J.D./Ph.D.

Christina S. Walker
https://orcid.org/0000-0002-2803-4849
University of Kentucky, USA

ABSTRACT

Nontraditional and underrepresented students face immense stressors in their pursuit of higher education. Their ability to fully realize their potential and capability to pursue higher education may be inhibited simply by the ways they've learned to perceive the world and themselves during childhood. These students' paths to attaining higher education are often more arduous as they counter unique and separate obstacles than their more privileged peers. Such challenges may include being the first in their families to pursue higher education or having little experience navigating higher education, being of lower socioeconomic status, balancing familial and work roles and obligations, and experiencing ostracism and invisibility. From poverty to military service, to stumbling blocks, to achieving undergraduate and graduate education, this chapter details a student's unconventional and arduous journey to attaining higher education and her successful pursuit of two doctoral degrees. The hope is that students experiencing similar struggles may be empowered.

ARDUOUS, BUT WORTH IT: NAVIGATING UNFAMILIAR TERRAIN TO DOCTOR OF LAW AND PH.D.

Nontraditional and underrepresented students face immense stressors in their pursuit of higher education (Allen & Alleman, 2019; Kundu, 2019; Van Rhijn et al., 2016). Their ability to fully realize their potential and capability to pursue higher education

DOI: 10.4018/979-8-3693-1074-8.ch003

Copyright © 2024, IGI Global. Copying or distributing in print or electronic forms without written permission of IGI Global is prohibited.

Navigating Unfamiliar Terrain to J.D./Ph.D.

may be inhibited simply by the ways they've learned to perceive the world and themselves during childhood. These students' paths to attaining higher education are often more arduous as they counter unique obstacles not often experienced by their more privileged peers. Such challenges may include being the first in their families to pursue higher education or having little experience navigating higher education, being of lower socioeconomic status, balancing familial and work roles and obligations, and experiencing ostracism and invisibility (Allen & Alleman, 2019; Kundu, 2019; Van Rhijn et al., 2016). Although these obstacles can seem insurmountable and have even detoured students from enrolling in college, they can be overcome. The author of this chapter provides her personal story as just one example that demonstrates this.

Growing up, life was not always easy for Christina Walker. She lacked the bare necessities like a bed, personal hygiene items, and even at times food, shelter, water, and electricity. Christina's walls were not filled with paintings or family photos; and her house was bare, empty, cold, and void of any furniture or indication that the physical structure that she resided in was actually someone's home. Additionally, there were even worse times when Christina and her family were homeless, sleeping in a car overnight; borrowing money or using government vouchers to stay in motels; or staying with distant relatives who were essentially strangers.

When times were better it was only because Christina and her family relied on food stamps and government assistance. Still, until this day, Christina recalls missing numerous and consecutive days of school because Christina and her sister had to travel from corner store to liquor store, using paper food stamps to purchase candy and treats often valued at a quarter or less, simply to get real change in return. When paper food stamps became less frequently used and Electronic Benefits Transfer (EBT) cards were introduced, Christina's parents again required that she convert food stamps to cash, forcing her to sell candy bars nearly every day at school while pretending like she was earning money for some beneficial school-related cause, all for the purpose of earning cash to bring home.

Likewise, although both of Christina's parents were in her life, they significantly lacked the ability to prioritize, leading them to sacrifice necessities of extreme importance. Medical visits went unscheduled; severe eye conditions went untreated; and essentially, Christina just had to adapt. Moreover, though Christina's parents were known disciplinarians, scolding her and her sister to attend grade school and turn in school work, beyond this, they provided no direction. Christina's parents did not discuss plans after high school, preparation for standardized testing, or attending college or trade school. Higher education was not a priority and graduate degree programs, especially professional and post-doctoral degree programs like law and medical school, were never even in Christina's dreams let alone thought of as realistic topics of discussion. Yet, Christina does not blame her parents, as they did the best they could with what they knew. Further, considering that their childhood experiences were both far more trying than Christina's experiences and at times even traumatic, she commends her parents for their ability to break generational cycles and generational trauma. Further, Christina commends them for the changes they've made and the vastly different life they've built for themselves today.

Sadly, Christina's childhood struggles were not vastly different from the struggles her peers of the same racial and ethnic backgrounds faced. In fact, some of her peers dealt with far harsher circumstances. However, somehow, she avoided being sucked into a life of crime, drugs, prostitution, or the other negativity associated with peer pressure in an environment rampant with poverty, depression and desperation, and void of motivation and hope. It was education that helped pave the way in Christina's life for something different.

Given her personal story, Christina aims to use this chapter to accomplish three objectives. First and second, to identify the obstacles she encountered on her journey to attain higher education, while equally identifying the strategies she employed to overcome such obstacles. Third, to highlight the milestones she accomplished while navigating her higher education journey. Christina vowed long ago that when she became able, she would give back. Now that Christina's education has enabled her to be in a better place, she desires to assist others in navigating their paths to educational success. When Christina started her journey it was scary and unfamiliar. In fact, she initially never saw herself enrolling in college and at certain moments during her journey she never envisioned herself succeeding, yet she persevered. Therefore, Christina's hope is that by writing this chapter, the experiences she encountered and strategies she employed might help to empower others to move beyond their fears of uncertainty to pursue higher education, thereby assisting in mitigating the college enrollment crisis. More specifically, Christina hopes to inspire and reach others from underrepresented and historically marginalized backgrounds who have previously or are currently experiencing similar barriers to education attainment. By reading this chapter, these individuals might come to understand that no matter how unfamiliar the college journey may seem and no matter how many obstacles they may face, there are strategies they can employ to overcome and be successful in attaining higher education.

EARLY ADULTHOOD: A CHANGE OF ENVIRONMENT

Christina remembers the feeling of needing to get away and needing to escape. "But, how?" she'd ask herself. The only plan she had was not in actuality a plan at all and was more of a fantasy with no action, no path forward, and no deliberate steps taken to prepare for success. Specifically, during Christina's final years of high school she narrowed down a list of three different plans for her future. Plan A, she would be a singer while modeling part-time. Plan B, she would attend the Fashion Institute of Design and Merchandising (or FIDM) in Los Angeles, California while modeling part-time. Upon graduating she would be a big-time fashion designer. Plan C, she would attend one of the many make-up artists training programs in Los Angeles, California. Upon graduating, she would become a world-renowned make-up artist known for working with famous celebrities and doing special effects make-up for theatre and movie productions.

The problem with plan A was that the likelihood of becoming a famous celebrity such as a rapper, singer, or social media influencer is highly improbable. Beyond talent, achieving the status of a famous celebrity requires being part of certain networks or social circles to gain exposure and build relationships, and more importantly, it requires luck (Currid-Halkett, 2010; Zanatta, 2017). Moreover, during Christina's time attending and transitioning from high school, social media platforms like YouTube, Facebook, Twitter, and others that could increase one's chances of gaining notoriety through independent means were just beginning or non-existent (Soukup, 2014; Van Dijck, 2013). Another issue with plan A was that regardless of Christina's level of talent, this plan nor any of her other plans included any mention of education as a back-up on which she could rely in case her aspirations of fame did not go as planned.

As for plans B and C, though seemingly less improbable to outsiders with no context of Christina's situation and circumstances, there were several problems with these plans. First, although Christina lived in California and was originally from southern California, during her final years of high school she lived in northern California, nearly seven hours away from Los Angeles. Christina had no housing arrangements in Los Angeles where she could live while attending school. What's more, by the end of her senior year in high school and even upon graduating, she had not taken any college entrance exams and she knew little to nothing about the Free Application for Federal Student Aid (FAFSA), scholarships or other funding. Further, Christina had not applied to any schools including those she "planned" to attend and had no experience with make-up artistry and a less than amateur level experience with designing clothing.

It is well-known that the cost of living in Los Angeles is ridiculously expensive and unaffordable. In fact, since the 1960s, "the average California home cost about three times the average household's income" (Tobias et al., 2022, paragraph 5). This cost has only continued to rise, with average home prices reaching as high as seven times the average California household income as of 2022, and "nearly 2.5 times higher than the median national home" as of 2019 (Tobias et al., 2022, paragraph 6). Los Angeles is listed among the top cities in California that have contributed to this issue (Tobias et al., 2022). Further, FIDM's fashion design programs are highly competitive with only thirty-eight percent of applicants being accepted (College Gazette, 2022). Similarly, the make-up artistry programs Christina was interested in had equally grueling requirements and expectations. Thus, with the unaffordable cost of living in Los Angeles, tuition prices and school expenses, Christina's then nonexistent room and board, and lack of proper skill and experience to enable her to even be eligible to compete for admission to the schools and programs she desired, her dreams were far from reality. Christina communicated these plans to her parents several times, and as an adult looking back on this today, she often wonders what possessed her parents to never question her plans or to intervene.

Upon graduating high school, reality hit Christina hard. She remembers the rush of reality while at a graduation party with her best friend and her best friend's sister. They talked about the college acceptance letters they had received and how they would be going off to attend college together in the upcoming Fall semester. During that moment, Christina was lost and besides her job working in the mall, she did not have any plans for the future.

Yet, this all changed one day after Christina unexpectedly began entertaining the thought of joining the military. After going back and forth to the recruitment office and exploring career options simply out of curiosity, Christina realized that this surprising and unanticipated path provided a viable option to leave her environment and pursue not only independence and financial freedom, but to contribute to a cause where she had purpose and where she would fulfill a mission much bigger than herself and much bigger than she had ever envisioned.

Military Life

In September 2007, Christina shipped out to basic training to take her place as a soldier in the United States Army. She was scared and extremely out of her comfort zone in this unfamiliar setting, but Christina knew she had made a very difficult, yet necessary decision. It took some time to get adjusted to the new military life and admittedly the transition was not always easy. There were times when Christina wondered if she made a mistake and even times when she simply regretted joining and wanted to give up. Still, outside those moments, when Christina reflects on her military service and even as she looks back on her journey since finishing her time serving in the Army, Christina would never change her decision. Without her military experience, Christina would not be where she is today.

Christina has never forgotten the impact the U.S. Army has had on her life. It was as a result of her experience in the military that she broadened her perspective and outlook on life and realized her potential and the importance of education. Particularly, in the military Christina was exposed to different types of people, places, and cultures while learning leadership and other core values. It was in the military that Christina met her husband. Finally, it was in the military where Christina earned funding to assist her with paying for her college education.

As it relates to Christina's journey to attaining higher education, the military enabled her to develop maturity and discipline. The traditional path of attending college directly after high school is a well sought after goal and achieving it should be celebrated and highly respected. Still, this is not always the best or possible route for everyone. Many students need time to mature, to learn more about themselves and what goals they seek to pursue, and to take time to break away in order to prevent burnout (Guidi, 2018; Haigler & Nelson, 2005; Kundu, 2019).

In fact, students who attend college directly after high school without taking a break may experience higher levels of stress and other harmful mental health consequences (Kundu, 2019). This is especially true for racial and ethnic minority students, students from lower socioeconomic status (SES) backgrounds, and first-generation students. This is because these students may feel more pressure to meet certain expectations, may need to balance competing obligations and responsibilities to meet basic life needs, and may also lack belonging and support while in college in comparison to their peers (Kundu, 2019). Likewise, failing to take a break between high school and college can mean prolonging one's college stay and increasing the subsequent costs as a result of being unsure about college majors and career plans and lacking the maturity and discipline required to take full advantage of the college experience. For instance, a lack of maturity and discipline can lead to students making mistakes that can have severe consequences such as repeatedly missing classes, not taking time to study, or not turning in coursework (Guidi, 2018; Haigler & Nelson, 2005). Thus, for Christina, as a result of going into the military after high school she had time to build her character while developing habits and qualities that were essential to her academic success and motivation and appreciation to learn.

An even more impactful benefit of Christina's military service was the resulting educational funding. Upon honorably completing her terms of service, she was awarded funding to pursue higher education. The Post-9/11 GI Bill refers to educational benefits given to military members (or their families) based on meeting certain eligibility requirements (U.S. Department of Veterans Affairs, 2023a; U.S. Department of Veterans Affairs, 2023b). The benefits can be used to pay for traditional and vocational post-secondary education, such as undergraduate, graduate, and professional degrees; apprenticeships; and trade school. In addition to funding paid directly to an institution to cover the direct costs of education, The Post-9/11 GI Bill includes a housing stipend (or allowance), and, in many cases, an allowance for books and supplies (U.S. Department of Veterans Affairs, 2023a; U.S. Department of Veterans Affairs, 2023b). The total amount that a military member or their family member is eligible for varies and is dependent on different factors such as time in service, type of institution or educational program, whether enrollment is full or part-time or online or in-person, and average cost of living (for housing stipend calculations). However, typically, benefits are paid out for up to three years (U.S. Department of Veterans Affairs, 2023a). Thus, obtaining The Post-9/11 GI Bill assisted Christina by not only providing her with access to tuition dollars, but it also contributed to her living expenses and other school-related costs.

UNDERGRADUATE EDUCATIONAL JOURNEY

Post-Military Stumbling Blocks: Hard Lessons About Accreditation

As Christina transitioned from the military and was awarded the Post 9/11 GI Bill, she was at the point in her life in which she possessed the motivation to attend college and the maturity to realize the instrumentality of such decision. For this reason, Christina began seeking out educational programs shortly after exiting the military. Nonetheless, she was naïve regarding navigating higher education generally. This was because her childhood experiences had left her underprepared for college. Christina had no knowledgeable mentors, and even as an adult she had never enrolled in college before. Because of this, though Christina believed she was at the beginning stages of her higher education journey, she would find out that this was not necessarily the case. Instead, Christina attended an institution that, due to issues of accreditation, only prolonged her higher education attainment while adding to the costs and chipping away at her Post 9/11 GI Bill funding and time remaining to be eligible to continue receiving this military benefit. This section details Christina's personal experience dealing with this stumbling block.

Upon exiting the military, Christina and her husband both had the goal of attaining higher education in order to better ourselves and increase the chances of entering into a rewarding and sustainable career field. Particularly, they were both interested in pursuing business related majors. Therefore, they conducted some preliminary research, looking for programs that would cater to adult learners and that would also not take a long period of time. Christina and her husband also researched important information such as information about accreditation and degree recognition. After investigating, Christina located an institution, whose name will be withheld, that seemed to be a great fit. Christina had multiple conversations with the admissions representatives who emphasized the small, yet welcoming and supportive environment that was geared toward adult learners and working professionals. Further, the admissions office communicated that the institution was accredited, and that the degrees and educational credentials were widely recognized. Additionally, the office sold up the fact that once a student obtained their credential, it could not be denied or taken from them and that all institutions would have no choice but to acknowledge it in the event that the student desired to later pursue further education elsewhere.

Based on those conversations with admissions and individual research findings, Christina and her husband decided to attend the institution. While attending, some occurrences and ways in which the institution operated became standard and expected. However, Christina realized later that what she thought were standard operating procedures were actually not standard at all, but only became normalized and tolerated within the institution because many students enrolled (including Christina) had no other educational experience to compare and contrast the institution to. For instance, on most occasions any excess funding from grant money or financial aid was paid out toward the end of the semester. Also, in some instances, books were given out at an unreasonable period after the start of the semester, even though the military stipend for books was made directly to the institution (Dickson, n.d.).

One primary purpose of tuition funding including grants and financial aid is to assist students with cost of living and other related expenses after tuition has been paid. This can help to alleviate barriers to enrolling in higher education, especially for historically underrepresented and marginalized populations such as non-traditional students, minority students, and students from lower SES backgrounds who usually experience financial challenges in accessing higher education (Dick et al., 2003; Haynes, 2008). Considering this, it would be contradictory and unjust to make a habit of continually waiting until the end of the semester to disburse such excess funding, as in the interim, many students are at a standstill as they are unable to meet daily school expenses. Resultantly, these students may experience difficulties and hardships such as food insecurity, lack of transportation, and lack of access to other resources which may complicate their higher education journey and can even lead to drop-out (Bahrainwala, 2020).

Another thing worth noting that did not necessarily line up with the information the admissions office initially communicated was that the course schedule was not so much more conducive to adult learning than a traditional university or college setting, as promised. One class was generally four hours long and either students attended in the mornings to early afternoon or in the evening. Hence, in addition to the fact that there were only a few class options each semester, there was not much flexibility in terms of scheduling. Thus, arguably, for a working professional or adult with children or other obligations these limited scheduling options might not provide much flexibility.

Last and worst of all, after attending the institution for a year and getting ready to enroll for another semester, Christina and her husband first decided to explore other options. Upon having conversations with admission representatives at the local universities and community colleges, they realized that none of the courses they had taken could be transferred toward another degree program. In fact, though the institution they attended was accredited, not all its programs were accredited by a recognized accreditor. Specifically, many of the non-medical programs were accredited by a private accreditor rather than being regionally accredited. Regional accreditation refers to a type of accreditation held by institutions or programs accredited by one of six "regional accrediting agencies . . . recognized by both the United States Department of Education (USDE) and the Council for Higher Education Accreditation (CHEA)" (McFarlane, 2010, p.120). Moreover, "regional accreditation is the most commonly accepted form of accreditation" both in the U.S. and internationally (McFarlane, p.12, 2010). Recognition by USDE and CHEA means the institution and its programs adhere to a certain level of academic rigor and meet certain quality standards (McFarlane, 2010).

Christina attended a for-profit institution which lacked accreditation and failed to adequately disclose the consequences of accreditation, such as the difficulties associated with transferring coursework. Not all for profit institutions have these shortcomings, thus, it is not Christina's goal to condemn all for-profit institutions, but rather to inform readers of her personal encounter with a specific for-profit institution. Due to ignorance of the higher education environment, many students lack basic knowledge about accreditation such as understanding what accreditation is; how one type of accreditation differs from others; and most significantly, the practical importance that accreditation has on degree recognition and recognition of professional qualifications, continuing and advanced education, and career prospects (Glastris & Sweetland, 2015). For instance, some students may have a dream of entering a certain career field without realizing that such a career requires a professional license or certification and not fully realizing the steps required to obtain that license or certification (Bardon, 2013; O'Herrin, 2017). In addition, some students pursue career fields requiring these credentials, yet enroll in programs that do not have the right form of accreditation which would allow them to qualify to take the examinations necessary to obtain professional license or certification (Apgar, 2022; Bardon, 2013; O'Herrin, 2017). Alternatively, students might enroll in programs that do not adequately prepare them to pass such examinations as evidenced by the history of pass and fail rates of the students who attended the particular institution (Apgar, 2022). Further, the institution could be known for habitually misleading its students regarding matters of accreditation or professional licensure or engaging in this unethical behavior without its actions ever becoming known (*Sweet v. Cardona*, 2023).

In Christina's case, the institution she attended was one amongst many other for-profit institutions that was later found by the Department of Education to have defrauded its students. (Federal Student Aid, n.d.a.; *Sweet v. Cardona*, 2023; The Project on Predatory Student Lending, 2023). Unfortunately, students who often fall prey to institutional misconduct, misleading, and illegal behaviors include vulnerable populations which lack the knowledge required to successfully negotiate the higher education environment. This includes veteran students; black, indigenous, and people of color (BIPOC); lower SES students, and others from non-traditional backgrounds (Pusser & Ericson, 2018). This is because these students, many of whom may be first-generation college students, often have less familiarity with navigating higher education in comparison to their peers. Thus, this lack of experience and guidance can make these students especially susceptible to being subjected to such illicit practices (Pusser & Ericson, 2018).

Starting from Scratch: Attainment of The Bachelor's Degree

In the aftermath of attending the for-profit institution, Christina was left with the task of picking up the pieces and recovering from her encounter. More than ever, she realized that, despite what she was sold and told, upon completion of an educational credential (e.g., an associate degree or technical certificate), a student cannot simply transfer such credential and apply it toward a bachelor's degree, if the course or program completed to obtain the credential was not properly accredited (Appel & Taylor, 2015). Now knowing this and living with it, Christina realized just how injurious the consequences of attending the for-profit institution had been and the additional barriers she would be subjected to as a result. She was, essentially, starting her higher education journey all over, from scratch. It was like she had nothing and every credit she worked hard to earn up to that point was a complete waste of time, money, and effort. Despite this, Christina began attending the University of Kentucky.

Upon attending the University of Kentucky, one barrier Christina faced while pursuing her bachelor's degree was learning to navigate an unfamiliar educational setting historically conducive to traditional students. For instance, Christina began to understand why the for-profit institution advertised its adult learner environment. It was true that the for-profit institution did not have class times, class options, or other scheduling flexibilities that were conducive to adults and working professionals. Also, it was true that there were also no childcare options or other resources and support for parents, and no resources and support networks or organizations for veterans or other non-traditional student populations, which are offered at the University of Kentucky (UK Human Resources, n.d.a; UK Student Success, n.d.; UK Veterans Resource Center, n.d.). However, admittedly attending a traditional four year university and working in an environment with primarily traditional students was tasking and presented difficulties. For example, many of the courses Christina took early in her undergraduate college career involved some form of group work. It was typical for Christina to be one of the few Black students or minorities in a general education classroom and the only Black student in a class tailored toward her undergraduate major. Furthermore, she did not see much variation in the ages of students. Consequently, the students she became grouped with were generally white traditional college students and many of these students lived on or near campus. Given this, it was typical for group members to schedule meetings or social gatherings with little or no notice.

Regarding group work and assignments, it was typical for group members to focus on topics primarily impacting white and traditional student populations. Therefore, in group settings in which Christina was already a cultural outsider, she became even more isolated when she would have to explain that she couldn't attend last minute meetings or social gatherings because she lived off campus and did not have immediate access to transportation, or because she was working in a non-campus job and therefore did not have the flexibility to change shifts due to competing academic responsibilities. Likewise, when Christina offered to meet with group members via a conference or video call rather than in person because she was with her bonus daughter (or step-daughter) and her husband was working, the group didn't understand and seemingly, Christina appeared troublesome and difficult to some group members.

Christina's work ethic and individual contributions to group assignments enabled her to earn outstanding grades for group assignments. This included group assignment grades that were, in part, calculated based on ratings given by fellow group members. Nonetheless, her relationships suffered. It wasn't that her relationships with group members were tumultuous or involved conflict. Instead, it was just that they were stagnated. Christina strongly believes the cultural and social differences between herself and group members made it challenging to connect, as this didn't appear to be the case between other group members who seemed to easily form friendships despite the fact that they were initially strangers. It also didn't help that Christina couldn't attend social gatherings on most occasions, which might have helped her formulate friendships and may have appeared to her group that she was making more of an effort to do so.

Christina's experience is similar to those of many non-traditional students in higher education including veterans, first-generation students, lower SES students, minority students, adult learners, and others. Such students have reported finding it difficult to connect with both peers and professors alike, while adult learners with competing obligations have reported the challenges inherent in balancing parenthood, marriage, and employment with school responsibilities. Moreover, they've experienced isolation and a lack of support in this regard (Exposito & Bernheimer, 2012; Rausch & Buning, 2022; Van Rhijn et al., 2016).

A sense of belonging within higher education can be the difference between succeeding academically or sinking (Allen, & Alleman, 2019). Incontestably, students residing on and near campus feel more connected to the campus community and feel immersed in the college experience in comparison to students living off campus (Bahrainwala, 2020). Also, students who tend to fit less neatly within the identity constructs of traditional students and instead possess more intersectional and historically marginalized identifiers such as lower SES, minority, working adult, parent, and first-generation generally experience more life stressors and barriers during their higher education journey that may make formulating connections less of a priority, resulting in detachment and feelings of ostracism (Allen & Alleman, 2019; Van Rhijn et al., 2016). Consequently, students who experience a sense of belonging have greater rates of academic success and retention than their peers who lack belonging. They also build greater networks, while gaining relationships instrumental to future career and advanced higher education endeavors (Litzler & Samuelson, 2013). For example, building mentor-mentee relationships with faculty who can later be relied on for recommendation letters. Unfortunately, and all too commonly, it is the non-traditional, first-generation, lower SES and minority students, and similar others who often feel disconnected and thereby are at heightened risk of suffering adverse consequences (Allen & Alleman, 2019; Bahrainwala, 2020; Litzler & Samuelson, 2013; Van Rhijn et al., 2016).

An even larger barrier that Christina faced and which she felt the pressure and significance of from the onset of attending University of Kentucky was that she only had two years remaining of the Post 9/11 GI Bill. Bachelor's degrees are generally designed to be completed in four years, though many students complete their degrees in four to five years and some even take six years (Rhoden, 2015). Thus, Christina wondered and asked herself, how would she ever finish a bachelor's degree meant to be completed in four years in half the time? Or, at the very least how would she cover a four-year program with two years of funding?

It was unrealistic for Christina to achieve her bachelor's degree in two years, especially given the fact that she changed majors multiple times, which is common amongst many students (Guidi, 2018; Haigler & Nelson, 2005). Nonetheless, and even with major changes, Christina was able to finish her undergraduate degree in exactly four years. She spent most semesters completing fifteen credit hours and in some semesters, she would even take seventeen or eighteen credit hours. Christina was very organized and focused and as she became more familiar with the college environment she mapped out her curriculum multiple times and in consideration of multiple degree pathway changes. As a result of curriculum mapping, she learned that it was not likely that many students, even those that stuck with one major, could finish an undergraduate degree in four years when only taking the minimum number of courses all semesters (Rhoden, 2015). What's more, the ability to complete an undergraduate degree within a four-year time frame diminishes as students must overcome more obstacles to successfully complete coursework requirements. For example, when students are required to complete prerequisite courses, meaning they must take certain courses first before being eligible to take more advanced courses that are needed for completion of their bachelor's degree (Thompson, 2021). When prerequisite courses are taken one semester after another and do not interfere with scheduling, these pose no problem. On the other hand, prerequisite courses may prolong a student's higher education journey in certain circumstances (Dechter, 2009). A case in point is when students must take on even more coursework before they are eligible to enroll in a prerequisite course (Thompson, 2021). For instance, students who completed lower-level math courses in high school may first be required to take an introductory college math course before being able to enroll in the math course that is needed as the prerequisite for an introductory chemistry course. Upon successful completion of all three classes, then and only then would these students be able to enroll in a required advanced chemistry course. In this case, the introductory college math course might not be counted toward the credit hours required for completion of a student's major. Because minority, first-generation, and lower SES students are historically more likely to be enrolled in less advanced math, science and foreign language courses throughout high school, this type of scenario is likely to have the greatest impact on these types of students (Thompson, 2021). In addition, when such courses aren't offered each semester, this poses other scheduling issues that prolong students' higher education journeys even further (Dechter, 2009).

Still, despite navigating similar scheduling challenges, Christina ultimately decided to pursue a bachelor's in business and organizational communication. In nearly all of her courses she earned an A. In Christina's opinion, this wasn't because she was so smart but because she dedicated so much time and effort to earn such grades. As a result, Christina was able to earn scholarship and fellowship funding. Along with grant money and additional financial aid, this helped her cover the costs of higher education for the two-year period in which her post 9/11 GI Bill was exhausted. Christina graduated summa cum laude.

PREPARING FOR LIFE AFTER A BACHELOR'S AND POST GRADUATION

The Doctor of Law: Law School and the Bar While Working Multiple Jobs

Up to the final year of Christina's undergraduate degree program, she was undecided about what she wanted to do after graduating. Christina applied for jobs and contemplated continuing to pursue further higher education. She thought about law school and additional graduate programs based on the conversations she had with her husband. Christina was just getting used to the fact that she would be the first in her family to graduate from a university and that this was actually going to be a reality, her reality. This was overwhelming given that attending college had never been part of the conversations in Christina's household nor even in the memories she held in her childhood dreams. Yet, Christina's husband pushed her to see her potential beyond this and even when Christina was still fearful that everything might suddenly fall apart at the last moment, her husband saw something greater in her than she saw in herself and encouraged her to apply for law school and ivy league institutions. Christina battled with herself and created excuses as to why she should not apply or why she might not be accepted. However, right before the application deadlines, Christina completed the Law School Admission Test (LSAT) and applied for law school at the University of Kentucky and two ivy league graduate programs at Columbia University and Dartmouth College. She was accepted into each of the programs. Ultimately, Christina selected law school due to the accompanying fellowship offer she received. She was one of two students to receive such fellowship across all programs across the University of Kentucky campus.

The Law School Journey

Law school was the most challenging experience Christina ever encountered in her higher education journey. In particular, Christina felt like an outsider. She felt unheard and overlooked by students and professors alike. She also worked multiple part-time jobs and balanced familial roles and responsibilities which made attending law school more demanding. One of the memories salient in Christina's mind when attending law school was her law school orientation. One orientation session involved cultural sensitivity related training and students were encouraged to engage in open dialogue. A white male student explained that less students from minority groups should be accepted into the law school because the more minority students who were accepted the more diminished the law school's reputation would become. Some of the other students verbally agreed. Christina and the facilitator, respectfully, yet assertively addressed the student's assertion while educating him why this wasn't the case and the value and contribution of diverse students and diversity of thought. This was just one example of the climate Christina experienced.

On another occasion, Christina was acting as the prosecution with a group of students in a case involving a Black teen who had physically injured someone. She was the only Black student in the class. After she recommended an alternative sentence due to the teen's non-existent criminal record and otherwise honorable past, Christina and the other students were told point blank by a professor that the teen's race should be considered in the sentencing and therefore the sentencing recommendation was too lenient. In the same class, besides the times when Christina was cold called to answer questions, she always felt as if she was ignored. She would raise her hand on many occasions to weigh in on issues predominately impacting people like herself, minorities, and particularly Black individuals of lower SES backgrounds. Yet, Christina can't remember one time that she was able to openly articulate her thoughts. She remembers hearing many students making many assertions based on stereotypes. Given the things they said when she was in the room, Christina would always wonder what they'd say if she was a fly on the wall.

In some of Christina's other classes, she similarly felt ignored by professors. Additionally, she felt isolated, as if she was invisible amongst many students. When Christina entered law school, there were only about ten to twelve Black students across all three graduating classes, and she was informed that her class was one of the largest classes within the law school's history. Christina was glad that there were some students she shared a cultural connection with, and she also connected with some of the veteran students as well. Still, she didn't quite feel a sense of belonging and at times the stress, frustration, and sadness she experienced because of it was overwhelming. Although Christina could connect with many of the Black students culturally, many came from very different backgrounds than her. They were raised in well-established families, were not first-generation college students, and had parents or other close family members who were attorneys. Thus, their backgrounds aligned with much of the diversity represented in the legal profession which includes many minority attorneys who have not experienced living in impoverished conditions (Sander, 2010). Hence, Christina was doubly disadvantaged, entering an unfamiliar space and profession in which she was not only racially and culturally underrepresented but in which she was even underrepresented amongst those whom she shared the same racial and cultural identities with (Jack, 2019; Sander, 2010).

Despite the difficulties, not all students or professors in law school engaged in biased behavior or caused Christina's experience to be more challenging. Many were friendly and welcoming. Christina found her torts, evidence, and legal writing professors to be particularly welcoming and invested in her success. Most impactfully, they believed in her and believed she was just as capable as her peers. Another professor was also instrumental in helping Christina prepare for the bar examination. Ultimately, though difficult, Christina successfully graduated from law school. Overcoming her obstacles was well worth the reward.

The Bar: Preparation and Completion

Like many law students, one of the fears Christina had as her time in law school progressed was that after investing so much work into studying, learning law, passing each class, and finally graduating, she would fail the bar examination which would prevent her from earning a law license to engage in the practice of law (Nussbaumer & Johnson, 2011). For Christina, this fear was elevated because she knew she would not be able to participate in a traditional bar preparation study program. While it is standard procedure for law school graduates to purchase study materials and training courses for thousands of dollars and study full-time on months end, Christina was not as privileged to have been in this situation (Jackson & Cochran, 2021; Nussbaumer & Johnson, 2011). Enrolling in such a study program would not only require her to pay the high costs for tuition and course materials, but it would equally require that she'd spend that time eating, sleeping, and breathing the bar exam. This meant two things. First, that Christina would need to commit to studying about ten to twelve hours per day. Second, that she would need to choose between working full-time or studying full-time. Christina couldn't do both (Jackson & Cochran, 2021; Nussbaumer & Johnson, 2011). She was not in the financial situation to make such a sacrifice, given that she had already done so for the past three years, and more significantly, given that making such a sacrifice also included paying out more money. It was time for Christina to focus on contributing more to her family.

With these considerations in mind, when entering the final year of law school, Christina developed a plan to begin studying for the bar exam nearly one year before it was scheduled. She understood that she would immediately need to gain full-time employment upon graduating from law school. Therefore, this was a way to mitigate and make up for the lack of time she would have to dedicate to studying. Christina's plan was augmented by the tools and strategies she learned from attending courses taught by her professor, Jane Grisé. Christina attended Professor Grisé's non-credit course that occurred during lunch hours for the last year of law school. During this course, Christina was taught effective study techniques tailored toward the bar examination, time management for multiple choice questions, how to plan, the importance of study breaks, how to analyze essay questions, and other strategies. Christina also learned about free and less costly bar preparation materials and resources. Throughout the spring semester of her final year, Christina spent two times during the week studying for about an hour to an hour and half, while dedicating about three hours of study time during the weekend. During the fall of Christina's final semester, she increased her bar preparation time, studying three times a week for about an hour and a half, while dedicating about six hours of study time during the weekend.

One of the considerations Christina contemplated when applying for jobs was whether the climate and responsibilities of the job would be flexible enough to allow her to dedicate an adequate number of hours to studying. Simply put, she needed a position that did not have such a great learning curve and that wasn't so demanding that she'd feel obligated to take work home or spend time outside of normal working hours to master the skills of the job. Christina was able to find such a position in the same institution, the University of Kentucky. After graduation, she immediately began working and studying for the bar exam for several months. Except for application software Christina used for multiple choice practice and less than one week of access to materials of a bar preparation program, she relied primarily on free resources, her own study plan and materials, and stuck to a very strict study schedule. She'd study each weekday for four hours, while studying twelve to sixteen hours each weekend. Christina passed the bar exam on her first attempt.

Pursuing the Doctor of Philosophy and Beginning the Dissertation

Christina has always desired to pursue further studies in higher education, academia, and research. This was one of the reasons she initially applied to the Ivy League graduate programs in addition to law school. During her time in law school, she became even more passionate about this endeavor and even more determined to pursue it. Consequently, when seeking out post-law school employment opportunities, achieving this goal was a paramount factor in addition to considerations related to bar preparation. Accordingly, although Christina applied to multiple jobs and received multiple offers, another major reason why she accepted the position at the University of Kentucky was that doing so would enable her to pursue a Doctor of Philosophy (or Ph.D.), and such costs would be covered by employee benefits (UK Human Resources, n.d.b).

Employer-sponsored education or other forms of employer educational assistance are employee benefits that are not only extremely beneficial in recruiting and retaining prospective and current employees, but they provide invaluable resources to employees who might not otherwise be able to fund education (Faulk & Wang, 2014; UK Human Resources, n.d.b). Particularly, adult learners, non-traditional students, and first-generation students are most likely to take advantage of such benefits, enabling them to progress to new heights in their careers by attending college while still being able to balance work and earn income (Faulk & Wang, 2014). Alternatively, employees who are parents or spouses might be able to pass all or a portion of such benefits to their dependents such as their children or partners, who may be the first in their families to attend college and who may have been unable to do so otherwise without incurring additional and often unaffordable costs (Faulk & Wang, 2014; UK Human Resources, n.d.b). Thus, Christina's decision to take on employment at the University of Kentucky was a deliberate strategy to not only enable her to study for the bar exam while being employed in a full-time capacity, but moreover, to allow her to pursue a Ph.D. at her employer's expense. The relationship would be mutually beneficial. Christina would give to her employer, dedicating her time, expertise, knowledge, commitment, and service, while getting something invaluable back at the same time.

Upon beginning work at the University of Kentucky, Christina promptly began taking classes thereafter. Everything lined up perfectly. She graduated from law school, began working and studying for the bar a couple of months before summer, took the bar exam at the end of summer, and began taking Ph.D. courses in the fall. Christina's Ph.D. program was in Communication. Broadly, her research explores pertinent issues intersecting areas of law/social justice, communication, and culture. Christina equally explores issues of communication and culture separately without a legal approach. Christina has had some scheduling hurdles that have increased her number of semesters and prolonged her course enrollment. Nevertheless, she's pleased to say that she is entering the final stages of her Ph.D., which consist of beginning her dissertation.

CONCLUSION AND KEY TAKEAWAYS

What Christina Walker hope readers take away from this chapter is not her personal successes or accomplishments, as one's successes or accomplishments may look different from the desires, goals, passions, and pathways of others. Although Christina experienced challenges and obstacles, she does not assert to be the poster child of oppression who can speak for or on behalf of all others. Each student (current and prospective) will experience their own difficulties in their journey to pursue higher education. This remains true even when students share experiences and encounter common struggles such as those associated with identifying as a first-generation, underrepresented, or non-traditional student, or being from a lower SES background.

Instead, Christina hopes those reading this chapter will walk away with useful lessons and strategies. For current and prospective students reading this chapter, they should understand that their journeys may be different from their peers. A student does not need to fit a traditional identity or take a traditional pathway to be successful. Although some students may embark upon the college journey while learning to navigate the terrain as they go, understand that it is possible. More importantly, students should to learn to understand themselves, their needs, and the obstacles they face, which will help them when selecting and enrolling in a college that will be conducive to their personal success. Also, students should make an attempt to find their people or social circles. In other words, prospective or current college students should find other students who may be of their same background or who may have experienced similar struggles. This will allow them to feel less alone, more understood, and more connected. Further, when in college students should find mentors who can help them feel supported. A sense of belonging can be the difference between enrolling in college or not, and when enrolled, can determine continued enrollment and academic success (Allen & Alleman, 2019; Van Rhijn et al., 2016).

For educators and administrators reading this chapter, please take the lessons from Christina's experience to understand some of the challenges non-traditional students endure. Further, use these lessons to make college spaces more inclusive, welcoming, and considerate of the needs of all students rather than solely prioritizing the large majority. Moreover, use mentors and college students as peers to reach prospective non-traditional students early as they are contemplating college enrollment. This exposure can help familiarize students with the college journey and thereby lessen their uncertainties and reduce their fears (Allen & Alleman, 2019; Bahrainwala, 2020; Litzler & Samuelson, 2013; Van Rhijn et al., 2016).

REFERENCES

Allen, C. C., & Alleman, N. F. (2019). A private struggle at a private institution: Effects of student hunger on social and academic experiences. *Journal of College Student Development*, *60*(1), 52–69. doi:10.1353/csd.2019.0003

Apgar, D. (2022). Linking social work licensure examination pass rates to accreditation: The merits, challenges, and implications for social work education. *Journal of Teaching in Social Work*, *42*(4), 335–353. doi:10.1080/08841233.2022.2112809

Appel, H., & Taylor, A. (2015). Education with a debt sentence: For-Profit colleges as American dream crushers and factories of debt. *New Labor Forum*, *24*(1), 31–36. doi:10.1177/1095796014562860

Bahrainwala, L. (2020). Precarity, citizenship, and the "traditional" student. *Communication Education*, *69*(2), 250–260. doi:10.1080/03634523.2020.1723805

Bardon, E. (2013). *Career goals and decisions: An intersectionality approach* (Publication No. AAT 1570888) [Master's thesis, University of Toronto]. The SAO/NASA Astrophysics Data System.

College Gazette. (2022, March 24). *The 10 best fashion design schools in the us*. https://collegegazette.com/best-fashion-design-schools-in-the-us/#:~:text=With%20such%20high%20accolades%2C%20it%20is%20not%20surprising,the%20list%2C%20with%20an%20acceptance%20rate%20of%2038%25

Currid-Halkett, E. (2010). *Starstruck: The business of celebrity*. Farrar, Straus and Giroux.

Dechter, A. (2009). Facilitating timely completion of a college degree with optimization technology. *AACE Review*, *17*(3), 215–299.

Dick, A. W., Edlin, A. S., & Emch, E. R. (2003). The savings impact of college financial aid. *Contributions to Economic Analysis & Policy*, *2*(1), 1–29. doi:10.2202/1538-0645.1044

Dickinson. (n.d.). *Yellow ribbon program*. Dickson College. https://www.dickinson.edu/info/20046/tuition_and_aid/3312/yellow_ribbon_program#:~:text=While%20the%20VA%20pays%20the%20tuition%20and%20fee,allowance%20stipend%20is%20paid%20monthly%20to%20the%20student

Exposito, S., & Bernheimer, S. (2012). Nontraditional students and institutions of higher education: A conceptual framework. *Journal of Early Childhood Teacher Education*, *33*(2), 178–189. doi:10.1080/10901027.2012.675942

Faulk, D. G., & Wang, Z. (2014). Undergraduates with employer-sponsored aid: Comparing group differences. *Journal of Student Financial Aid*, *43*(3), 3. https://ir.library.louisville.edu/jsfa/vol43/iss3/3. doi:10.55504/0884-9153.1043

Federal Student Aid. (n.d.-a). *Apply for borrower defense loan discharge*. https://studentaid.gov/borrower-defense/

Federal Student Aid. (n.d.-b). *Sweet v. Cardona settlement*. https://studentaid.gov/announcements-events/sweet-settlement

Federal Student Aid. (n.d.-c). *Who is included in the group of people (the "class") represented by Sweet v. Cardona (formerly Sweet v. Devos)?* https://studentaid.gov/help-center/answers/article/borrower-defense-sweet-v-devos-class

Glastris, P., & Sweetland, J. (2015). *The Other College Guide: A Roadmap to the Right School for You*. The New Press.

Guidi, C. (2018). *Experiencing a gap year: Perceptions from students in the united states* (Publication No. 2047) [Doctoral dissertation, Northeastern University]. Northeastern University Library.

Haigler, K., & Nelson, R. (2005). *The gap-year advantage: Helping your child benefit from time off before or during college*. Macmillan.

Haynes, R. M. (2008). The impact of financial aid on postsecondary persistence: A review of the literature. *Journal of Student Financial Aid*, *37*(3), 3. doi:10.55504/0884-9153.1047

Jack (2019). *The privileged poor: how elite colleges are failing disadvantaged students*. Harvard University Press.

Jackson, J., & Cochran, T. (2021). Approaching the bar: An analysis of post-graduation bar exam study habits. *University of Massachusetts Law Review*, 6(1).

Kundu, A. (2019). Understanding college "burnout" from a social perspective: Reigniting the agency of low-income racial minority strivers towards achievement. *The Urban Review*, *51*(5), 677–698. doi:10.1007/s11256-019-00501-w

Litzler & Samuelson, C. (2013). How underrepresented minority engineering students derive a sense of belonging from engineering. *Association for Engineering Education - Engineering Library Division Papers*, 23.674.1

McFarlane, D. (2010). Accreditation discrimination: Impact on school choice, costs, and professional prospects in academia. *Academic Leadership: The Online Journal*, *8*(4), 7. https://scholars.fhsu.edu/alj/vol8/iss4/7

Nussbaumer, J., & Johnson, C. (2011). The door to law school. *University of Massachusetts Roundtable Symposium Law Journal*, 6, 1.

O'Herrin, K. T. (2017). *Urban forestry at a crossroads: Development of an emerging profession* (Publication No. 16514) [Doctoral dissertation, Virginia Tech]. VTechWorks.

Pusser, B., & Ericson, M. (2018). *The impact of the PROSPER act on underrepresented students in for-profit colleges.* https://escholarship.org/uc/item/1k76g8rz

Rausch, & Buning, M. M. (2022). Student veterans' perspectives of higher education contexts: Beyond the non-traditional student. *College Teaching,* 1–11. doi:10.1080/87567555.2022.2106469

Rhoden, B. J. (2015). *Understanding the impact of academic entry characteristics, remediation requirements, and semester course hour load in the first year on the academic performance and persistence to graduation for Latino students* (Publication No. 2031) [Doctoral dissertation, University of Houston]. University of Houston Libraries.

Sander, R. H. (2010). Class in American legal education. *Denver University Law Review*, *88*(4), 631.

Soukup. (2014). Looking at, with, and through YouTube. *Communication Research Trends, 33*(3), 3.

Sweet v. Cardona, 2023 U.S. Dist. LEXIS 31518, 2023 WL 2213610 (United States District Court for the Northern District of California, February 24, 2023, Filed). https://advance-lexis-com.ezproxy.uky.edu/api/document?collection=cases&id=urn:contentItem:67N4-VK01-FGCG-S0D0-00000-00&context=1516831

The Project on Predatory Student Lending. (2023, April 13). *Sweet v. cardona.* PPSL. https://www.ppsl.org/cases/sweet-v-cardona

Thompson. (2021). Grade Expectations: The role of first-year grades in predicting the pursuit of STEM majors for first- and continuing-generation students. *The Journal of Higher Education (Columbus), 92*(6), 961–985. doi:10.1080/00221546.2021.1907169

Tobias, M., Levin, M., & Christopher, B. (2022, March 3). Californians: Here's why your housing costs are so high. *Cal Matters.* https://calmatters.org/explainers/housing-costs-high-california/

UK Human Resources. (n.d.-a). *Child care resources.* https://hr.uky.edu/work-life-and-well-being/working-parents/child-care-resources

UK Human Resources. (n.d.-b). *Employee education program – frequently asked questions.* University of Kentucky. https://hr.uky.edu/more-great-benefits/employee-education-program-frequently-asked-questions

UK Student Success. (n.d.). *Get help.* https://studentsuccess.uky.edu/get-help

UK Veterans Resource Center. (n.d.). *Resources.* University of Kentucky. https://studentsuccess.uky.edu/veterans-resource-center/resources

United States Department of Veterans Affairs. (2023a, March 21). *Post-9/11 gi bill (chapter 33).* https://www.va.gov/education/about-gi-bill-benefits/post-9-11/

United States Department of Veterans Affairs. (2023b, March 21). *Post-9/11 gi bill (chapter 33) rates.* https://www.va.gov/education/benefit-rates/post-9-11-gi-bill-rates/

Van Dijck. (2013). The culture of connectivity: A critical history of social media. Academic Press.

Van Rhijn, T. M., Lero, D. S., Bridge, K., & Fritz, V. A. (2016). Unmet needs: Challenges to success from the perspectives of mature university students. *Canadian Journal for the Study of Adult Education, 28*(1), 29–47.

Zanatta, J. A. (2017). *Understanding YouTube culture and how it affects today's media* (Publication No. 83) [Senor Thesis, Dominican University of California]. Dominican Scholar. https://doi.org/doi:10.33015/dominican.edu/2017.CMS.ST.03

Chapter 4
Empowering Persistence:
Autoethnography Unveiling the Path of Non-Traditional Doctoral Attainment

Kia A. Glimps-Smith
https://orcid.org/0000-0002-2494-8926
The University of Virgin Islands, US Virgin Islands

ABSTRACT

Autoethnography melds autobiography and ethnography, dissecting personal experiences for cultural insight. It challenges conventional research methods, emphasizing political and social justice. This research delves into transformative learning for non-traditional Black women in doctoral programs, amplifying their narratives amid often overlooked voices. Emphasizing determination and resilience, the research aims to offer critical insights, enhance academic support, create a successful environment, and improve graduation rates. It contributes to discussions on adult education, highlighting transformative learning's impact on inclusion, reflective thinking, and emotional flexibility. The research, which is dedicated to Dr. Blanche Jackson Glimps, helps shape policies, improve support systems, and direct the development of curriculum.

INTRODUCTION

Embarking on this reflective endeavor, I do so with profound gratitude and admiration for my late mother, Dr. Blanche Eloise Jackson Glimps, who not only instilled in me the values of resilience and persistence but also served as a guiding light throughout my academic journey. This autoethnography stands as a dedicated tribute to my

DOI: 10.4018/979-8-3693-1074-8.ch004

Copyright © 2024, IGI Global. Copying or distributing in print or electronic forms without written permission of IGI Global is prohibited.

mother's unwavering confidence in the transformative power of academic pursuits and the strength of determination. She was a woman who earned four college degrees.

Children are significantly impacted by their parents' pursuit of continued education, demonstration of highly effective learning practices, and practice of self-discipline. This reinforces the importance of academic accomplishments (Boysen, 2016). As I sit down to write this, I cannot help but reflect on my journey as a first-year non-traditional doctoral student and single mother of two daughters. I have learned from personal experience how profoundly academic development can transform one's life and how crucial it is to persevere. At the commencement of my doctoral program, I found myself facing numerous obstacles. During the initial phase of my doctoral studies, I encountered a diverse range of trials that marked this intellectually transformative journey. These trials included navigating through demanding coursework, deciphering unfamiliar academic expectations, and establishing a coherent research direction. The demands of doctoral-level courses proved intellectually challenging, requiring heightened engagement and comprehension. Simultaneously, adapting to unfamiliar academic expectations demanded swift adjustment to the rigorous standards and scholarly discourse at the doctoral level.

Furthermore, delineating and refining a research direction added complexity to my academic journey, necessitating a strategic approach to align my pursuits with a meaningful and cohesive research agenda. Beyond academic challenges, the personal adjustments needed to balance the program's demands with my responsibilities as a single mother introduced additional layers of complexity. This balancing act underscored the significance of flexibility and efficient time management in maintaining a delicate equilibrium. Forming meaningful connections within the academic community presented yet another layer of complexity as I sought to establish relationships with peers, faculty, and mentors. These challenges collectively served as unique tests, demanding resilience, adaptability, and an unwavering commitment to academic growth. The commencement of my doctoral program marked not only the beginning of rigorous intellectual exploration but also a transformative phase in which resilience and adaptability became essential companions on the path to academic achievement.

The transition into this academic journey brought about a series of hurdles that required my attention and resilience. These obstacles encompassed a spectrum of academic, personal, and navigational difficulties that were part of the initial phases of my doctoral pursuit. As I embarked on this scholarly expedition, each challenge presented a unique test, necessitating adaptation, learning, and perseverance. Navigating through the intricate landscape of doctoral studies, I confronted the complexities of rigorous coursework, unfamiliar academic expectations, and the imperative to establish a cohesive research direction. Additionally, the personal adjustments required to meet the program's demands, along with the intricacies of forming meaningful academic connections, added further layers to this multifaceted journey. The commencement of my doctoral program marked not only the initiation of rigorous intellectual exploration but also a transformative phase in which resilience and adaptability became indispensable companions on the path to academic achievement.

In my research, I will employ a combination of persistence theory and transformative learning theory as overarching frameworks, complemented by the methodology of autoethnography. This approach will be applied to investigate the experiences of non-traditional doctoral students, including my own journey, providing a comprehensive and nuanced exploration of the challenges, growth, and transformative learning within this academic context. It continues to motivate me to overcome the demanding schedule and obstacles associated with being a working professional and single mother. Despite an already overloaded agenda, the pursuit of a higher degree remains a driving force in my life, propelling me to navigate and conquer the challenges that come with balancing multiple roles and responsibilities. The potential outcomes of such a transformation are what ignite my passion to keep moving forward. It has not been easy, and there have been countless late nights and moments of exhaustion. Nevertheless, I am resolute in my determination to not only advance my education but also my career.

As a full-time special education teacher, I can attest to the tangible benefits of transformative learning theories in shaping both my teaching practices and the outcomes of my students. The dynamic nature of transformative learning, with its emphasis on self-reflection, reevaluating beliefs, and challenging assumptions, aligns seamlessly with the intricacies of special education. This framework provides a robust foundation for fostering a vibrant connection with diverse student needs, driving meaningful and positive transformations in the learning experiences I facilitate. Through the lens of transformative learning theory, the potential for growth and evolution in both educators and students becomes not only apparent but actively harnessed, making it the most compelling and suitable framework for this study.

As a non-traditional first-year doctoral candidate, one cannot undertake this endeavor in isolation. The support of my family, friends, and cohort members has been instrumental in my success thus far. Without their encouragement and unwavering support, I would not be where I am today. I am grateful for their understanding and willingness to lend a hand when needed. An increasing number of students in their late twenties are emerging as a significant cohort within the realm of non-traditional students. This shift is attributed to a range of factors, including the postponement of college enrollment, extended degree completion timelines, challenges in securing employment, a rising preference for online learning alternatives, and enrollment deferrals due to the ongoing pandemic (Battiste & Battiste, 2022). In response to these evolving dynamics, older students are actively considering higher education career paths or revisiting the pursuit of degrees they initiated but did not complete in their younger years (Battiste & Battiste, 2022). To frame this discussion, Bean and Metzner's (1985) definition of "non-traditional students" is particularly pertinent, encompassing individuals aged at least 25, enrolled part-time, and typically not residing on campus. In contrast to traditional college students, whose motivations often intertwine social and academic aspects, academic considerations take precedence for non-traditional students. This demographic, often navigating the complexities of married life with dependents, carries additional financial obligations such as mortgages and engages in work to supplement their income.

Considering the observations of Davidson and Wilson (2013), the integration of students into a larger collective identity serves as the bedrock of a cohesive group dynamic. If this contextual identity proves to be the foremost determinant of retention, the significance of individual characteristics diminishes, emphasizing the pivotal role of the cohort model in supporting the academic journey of non-traditional students.

In my current academic journey, I am an active cohort member within the close-knit community of the University of the Virgin Islands' doctoral degree program. Our cohort, though physically dispersed, has fostered a familial bond that extends beyond the typical academic association. Introduced two years ago at the commencement of our doctoral journey, we have become a virtual family, maintaining daily communication through text messaging. The demonstration of our mutual assistance transcends geographical boundaries and embodies our collective dedication. Whether assisting in class registration, deciphering complex assignments, or providing emotional support, our interactions exemplify the essence of the cohort model. This unique connection, orchestrated by a higher force, underscores the pivotal role of collective support in navigating the challenges of our doctoral pursuit.

The inception of this research effort arises from the convergence of my own journey as a non-traditional doctoral student and the broader domain of higher education. As a working professional and a single mother, my pursuit of a doctorate in education has been characterized by distinct obstacles. This journey involves managing the intricate balance between career obligations, family duties, and academic endeavors. As I navigate through the complex network of responsibilities, I have observed a lack of in-depth research that specifically examines the experiences, successes, and challenges of non-traditional doctorate students, especially those in circumstances like mine.

This autoethnography is not merely a reflection of my individual academic odyssey; rather, it aspires to contribute to the existing body of knowledge surrounding the success and challenges encountered by non-traditional doctoral students. By delving into the transformative learning experiences of a non-traditional Black woman in her inaugural year of postgraduate studies, this research seeks to unveil the nuances of the doctoral journey often overlooked in traditional academic narratives. Through an autoethnographic lens, the study transcends statistical data, offering an intimate exploration of the personal, emotional, and academic dimensions that shape the educational pursuits of non-traditional doctoral scholars.

WEAVING A NARRATIVE: A PERSONAL AND SCHOLARLY JOURNEY THROUGH NON-TRADITIONAL DOCTORAL TRANSFORMATION

This section of this autoethnography goes beyond my personal story, serving as a roadmap for those considering a similar path. It involves balancing multiple responsibilities while challenging conventional doctoral expectations. My research aims to empower future non-traditional doctoral candidates by shedding light on the obstacles they may face and the strategies they can employ to enhance their academic experiences. Additionally, the findings have the potential to influence institutional policies and support systems, creating a more accommodating environment for non-traditional doctoral scholars.

This autoethnography embodies the principles of openness and fairness in higher education. It offers guidance and support to anyone pursuing a non-traditional path to a doctoral degree and invites all stakeholders to participate in shaping a more inclusive and supportive educational landscape. At this stage of the study, "perseverance" refers to the ability to overcome obstacles, navigate challenges, capitalize on professional growth opportunities, and maintain unwavering dedication to continuous learning. My role in this study involves dual perspectives: as an immersed participant and as a researcher observing the proceedings. These dual perspectives bring both strengths and limitations that influence the study's trajectory.

My intimate familiarity with the subject allows for a high level of engagement and insight into the experiences under investigation, capturing the phenomenon's complexities and enriching the study's findings. However, my personal involvement introduces the potential for research bias, as my subjective experiences and perspectives may inadvertently influence data collection, interpretation, and analysis. To address this concern, I will provide a brief account of my own experiences in the program, acknowledging my biases and their potential impact on the research. This reflexive practice aims to maintain the study's integrity and enhance the credibility of its findings, ensuring scholarly rigor in exploring the phenomenon.

A spark of achievement motivation ignited within me during a volatile period of social unrest and adversity. The calls for justice and equality in the wake of the tragic deaths of George Floyd and Breonna Taylor profoundly impacted me, intertwining my personal journey with the broader societal narrative. This tumultuous confluence fueled my motivation to effect meaningful change through academic endeavors, recognizing the potential for transformative outcomes. As a non-traditional doctoral student navigating the rigors of academia, these events underscored the significance of my educational pursuit.

I made the decision to return to college for a doctoral degree after a 10-year hiatus. I applied to a nearby university in Southwest Florida and was accepted. In August, I began my doctoral classes with anticipation and commitment. However, in September 2020, I received a heart-wrenching call from my mother in another state, revealing her recent ovarian cancer diagnosis, mere days before my birthday. In that heartbreaking moment, the weight of emotions overwhelmed me. Waves of anger and sorrow clashed within me, nearly overcoming me. Tears streamed down my face as I collapsed to the floor. In that moment, I reached out to a steadfast friend, an incredible assistant principal, a pillar of wisdom, and she reminded me of the unyielding power of my faith. Guiding me to Deuteronomy 31:8 in the Bible, she left me with a verse that ignited a spark within me: "God himself will lead the way and stay by your side the entire way. Do not be afraid; do not be discouraged" (Deuteronomy 31:8, New International Version). In that sacred moment, my motivation surged back to life, and I found myself fervently praying for my mother, myself, and my loved ones, channeling my strength into the battle against ovarian cancer that we were united to face. This crisis reshaped my priorities, leading me to take a considerable leave of absence from my job to tend to my parents' needs and join the fight alongside my mom.

My educational experience became a complex web of obligations and goals. The three months I spent taking care of my parents allowed me to repay the selfless care they had given me. However, beneath the upbeat tone, a complex web of responsibilities played out as I juggled my full-time teaching position, my role as a single mother to two recent high school graduates, and my pursuit of a doctorate degree. Despite the challenges, these experiences contributed to my personal growth and determination.

My first year as a doctoral student was extremely demanding, pushing me to tap into reserves of strength and persistence I had not realized I possessed. With guidance from my therapist, I embarked on a life-altering process that shifted my perspective on handling life's challenges. Due to the emotional demands of being a first-year doctoral student, such as adjusting to a new academic environment and balancing work-life and family responsibilities, I had to draw on strengths of character like perseverance and resilience that I had hidden within. With guidance from my therapist, I embarked on a life-altering process that shifted my perspective on handling life's challenges. This introspection prompted me to prioritize my mental health and seek improvement. I began to seek out doctoral support groups on social media and attended workshops and seminars on stress management and self-care specifically tailored for doctoral students. These resources provided me with a sense of community and a safe space to share my experiences and learn from others who were going through similar struggles. Additionally, I started incorporating mindfulness practices into my daily routine, which helped me cultivate a greater sense of self-awareness and allowed me to better manage my emotions during times of stress.

In a profound conversation with my therapist, a fellow Black woman, I delved into the deeper meaning behind my pursuit of a doctorate. I realized that my goals extended beyond personal fulfillment. I aspired to make a difference in my community and inspire other Black women to follow in my footsteps, echoing my mother's lifelong commitment to learning, which culminated in her earning a doctorate in education more than four decades ago. My decision to pursue this goal became a mission to advance professionally, acquire knowledge, and contribute positively to my community. The more I advanced in my education, the more I felt that I was paying tribute to my mother's tenacity and lighting a path for the next generation. Family history and the desire to effect positive change in both personal and societal contexts propelled this journey, born out of adversity and nurtured by resilience.

In August 2022, I continued my education by enrolling in an online doctoral program at a Historically Black College or University (HBCU) located in the U.S. Virgin Islands while simultaneously caring for my aging parents and helping my youngest daughter transition to post-college life. The faculty and staff's dedication to a well-rounded education emphasizing cultural awareness and social responsibility had a profound impact on my life. This experience transformed me into a doctoral student with a strong sense of purpose, eager to contribute to society through research and teaching.

Throughout this journey, which involved caregiving and academic pursuits, I developed a strong work ethic and a commitment to making meaningful contributions to society through my education and experiences. In essence, my steadfast determination and life's challenges shaped this transformation. I also sought guidance from mentors and sought out resources that could help me navigate the difficulties I was facing. These experiences taught me the importance of seeking support and building a strong network of individuals who can offer guidance and encouragement. Overall, my transformation was a result of both internal reflection and external support, allowing me to grow into a resilient individual ready to face any obstacles that come my way.

In summary, while the reasons mentioned above hold validity, I, as the researcher, wanted to provide an additional, more personal perspective for examining this experience through an autoethnographic lens. As a non-traditional college student, myself, I believe that this research will not only contribute to existing literature but also provide me with a deeper understanding of my own experiences and their relevance to others in similar situations.

STITCHING SUCCESS: A QUILTED CHRONICLE OF MY NON-TRADITIONAL DOCTORAL JOURNEY

In the stillness of the morning, the sun's radiance of revelation sways over my spirit like a long-awaited tune. It was a normal morning, but it would forever change my life. An ivory-colored letter, the herald of whispered hopes, waited in the mailbox among the bills and boring mailings. My shaking hands traced the letters that may change my life forever: "admission to a doctoral program." Disbelief, thankfulness, and the heady excitement of the unknown flooded through me like a symphony. I take this moment of clarity and reflection, knowing I am one step closer to achieving my dreams.

My life as a Black single mother has been interwoven with grit and determination, but this was a chapter I could never have imagined. I stood at the crossroads of potential, a light of hope for my children and a witness to the fortitude that pours through my veins. It was not only a confirmation of acceptance; it was the cosmos nodding in recognition of my efforts so far and hinting that this chapter in my life's narrative was only the beginning.

Fifty years have passed with ease, a mosaic of events decorating the canvas of my spirit. While my daughters were asleep in the quiet of the night, I fantasized about academics' uncharted territories. Now, such hopes may be realized through classroom instruction and academic debate. Even though I may not be able to control every event that happens in my life, I do have the choice not to let it define me (Angelou, 2008), as Maya Angelou's work from 2008 echoes in my ears and soul. Those words serve as a constant reminder that despite the challenges and setbacks I may face, I have the power to rise above them and continue pursuing my academic aspirations. With each passing day, I am filled with a renewed sense of determination and excitement for the future that lies ahead.

Right now, I am starting a journey that will take me well beyond my current situation. It is not only a quest to obtain a doctorate; it is a testimonial to the tenacious spirit that pulls me onward. As I make my way through the academic world, I bear the expectations of future generations on my shoulders, paving the way and sowing seeds of hope for those who refuse to let age, situation, or social standards limit the boldness of their dreams. This admission is written in more than just ink; it is inscribed in the pages of my story, a tale of victory over adversity, a song of possibilities that echoes through the pages of my future.

As I write this autoethnography to share my narrative, I cannot help but reflect on my journey as a non-traditional doctoral student and a single mother of two daughters. In my personal experience, I have realized the transformative power of persistence and academic growth through autoethnography. The first couple of months of my graduate program were difficult for me. I was overwhelmed by the work I had to do and struggled to balance my responsibilities as a mother, teacher, and doctoral student. For instance, to get everything done before heading off to work as a teacher, I had to set my alarm for two hours earlier than usual so that I could continue reading and researching. Despite feeling overwhelmed, I kept progressing in my doctoral program. I realized I needed to transform my academic thinking and meet the program's demands. To do this, I adopted a growth mindset and implemented various strategies, such as reading research articles for an hour each day. I also broke down large assignments into manageable tasks. My worries calmed down after using these strategies, and I stayed focused. I found that I could progress if I kept my end goal in mind and was mindful of my capabilities. I also made sure to take breaks between tasks and celebrate the small successes along the way. This experience taught me the importance of perseverance, resilience, and the power of diligent work and dedication. In my research, I will use persistence theory, transformative learning theory, and autoethnography methodology to study non-traditional doctoral students like me.

My firm belief in the effectiveness of transformative learning theory led me to choose it as the guiding framework for studying the experiences of non-traditional doctoral students, including myself, in this autoethnography examination. The challenge, rather than discouraging me, became a motivator, inspiring a renewed commitment to academic pursuits amid a hectic and demanding lifestyle. The potential outcomes of such a transformation fuel my passion to keep striving. It has been challenging, with countless late nights and exhausting moments. However, I am determined to further my education and career. As a special education teacher who teaches full-time, I have seen firsthand how transformative learning theories can significantly impact my teaching practices and my students' outcomes. My strong belief in the effectiveness of transformative learning theory led me to choose it as the guiding framework for studying the experiences of non-traditional doctoral students, including myself, in this autoethnographic study.

The transformative learning theory reveals a symphony of deep and lasting enlightenment. The abilities of self-reflection, reevaluating beliefs, and challenging presumptions are what give transformative learning theory its melody. It mirrors my journey as a special education teacher, painting a vibrant canvas of the potential for growth and evolution. Witnessing the impact of achievement, motivation, and persistence firsthand, I have harnessed these tools to shape my classroom dynamics, breathing vitality into my students' academic journeys. Transformative learning is the pause amid chaos that allows clarity—a moment to untangle emotions and regain mastery. The intricate threads that weave together my doctoral journey become more visible through the lens of transformative learning. With reflection as my comfort quilted blanket, I can embrace change and adapt to new situations with ease. My understanding of autoethnography continues to grow as an independent thinker and scholar. I am excited to see how my journey in autoethnography will shape me into a better researcher and writer.

Transformative learning theory breathes life into the learner's journey, encouraging the infusion of new knowledge into their existing understanding. This dynamic process fosters a vibrant connection with the world, a vital aspect for a devoted special education teacher addressing diverse student needs. Its impact resonates deeply, illuminating the path through my doctoral voyage. With a focus on critical introspection, meaningful discourse, and daring to challenge assumptions, this theory has been my guiding light. Thus, this autoethnographic exploration finds its anchor in transformative learning theory. For individuals like me, unconventional doctoral seekers, this framework becomes a precious lens through which our transformative stories come to life. Its resonance with my journey as a special education teacher and echoes loudly as it shapes my personal and professional evolution through the mirrors of reflection. A symphony of growth unfolds as it uncovers a ceaseless passion for education, forever evolving and radiating its brilliance.

My non-traditional doctoral student's journey unfolds with the same care and artistry as the quilt my mother sews. Just as each intricate patch of fabric comes together, my journey is woven with threads of collaborative harmony. During shared dreams, the support from my loved ones and a steadfast cohort act like a harmonious symphony, guiding me to overcome challenges. Their encouragement and unwavering presence bind the chapters of my academic venture, infusing strength into every seam. The objective of this writing is to engage in an autoethnographic exploration of my non-traditional doctoral journey, drawing a metaphorical connection between the intricate process of my academic pursuit and the meticulous artistry involved in my mother's quilt-making. Through this narrative lens, I aim to showcase the collaborative harmony within my support network, emphasizing the role of loved ones and a steadfast cohort as a harmonious symphony guiding me through challenges. The article seeks to transform these challenges into a colorful quilt of success, providing insights into the unique experiences of non-traditional doctoral scholars and contributing to a nuanced understanding of their academic journey. As a non-traditional doctoral scholar and devoted single mother, my commitment is to self-actualize and command professional success.

PURPOSE OF RESEARCH

Attrition Rates Do Not Scare Me!

Higher education's high doctoral student attrition rates are alarming; 40–60% of doctoral students drop out, and this trend is rising for online doctoral programs.

Despite these troubling statistics, doctoral institutions have not yet identified the root causes (Hurt et al., 2022). This alarming statistic motivates me to persist and succeed in my doctoral journey. I am nevertheless persistent in my pursuit to transcend attrition rates and successfully earn my doctoral degree. Non-traditional doctoral students often face limited access to resources, a lack of mentorship opportunities, and the challenge of balancing work and personal commitments. By establishing support networks, providing access to resources, and promoting personal growth and development, we can address these challenges by promoting openness and fairness in higher education. The difficulties associated with high attrition rates can be daunting. Attrition rates do not intimidate me; instead, they serve as motivation to work harder and smarter, transforming me into a "lifelong scholar."

A study by the Council of Graduate Schools found that 56.6% of doctoral students finish within ten years (Moran, 2021). Young, William R. VanWye, et al. (2018) discovered that, depending on the field of study, the proportion of students who withdraw from doctoral programs in the United States varies from 36% to 51%. This includes the humanities, engineering, biological sciences, social sciences, mathematics, and physical sciences. The number of students enrolled in master's and doctoral programs increased by 8% between 2009 and 2019, and it was anticipated to increase by an additional 2% between 2019 and 2020 (Irwin et al., 2022). As someone who is determined to complete their doctoral program, these statistics are concerning. Universities and policymakers should be aware of these high attrition rates and strive to provide doctoral students with adequate support to increase their chances of success.

Interesting to me as a non-traditional doctoral student is the breakdown of doctoral student demographics. According to the U.S. Department of Education and Institute of Education Sciences, 2022 Report (2022), in the Fall semester of 2019, 75% of full-time doctoral students at public degree-granting institutions were under the age of 30, compared to 71% at private for-profit institutions (33% ages 30 to 39, and 37% ages 40 and over), while part-time doctoral students at private for-profit higher education institutions were 79% over the age of 30 (compared to 63% at private and 60% at public institutions). Students who are between the ages of 20 and 26 have a higher completion rate than students who are older, between the ages of 27 and 75 (Wollast et al., 2018). Although previous research has suggested that age may not be a significant factor in degree completion, there is a noticeable age gap among doctoral students that may require support for non-traditional students like me. Further investigation is required to determine the factors which influence the completion and retention rates of non-traditional doctoral students.

In conclusion, this research endeavor is not merely a personal quest for academic achievement but a call to action against the prevailing challenges of high attrition rates in doctoral programs, particularly for non-traditional students. In addition to the strong desire to earn my doctorate, I am motivated to make meaningful contributions to this academic journey in the hopes of laying the groundwork for a more welcoming and inclusive atmosphere in universities. By acknowledging the alarming statistics and demographics surrounding doctoral student attrition, this study seeks to prompt universities and policymakers to recognize the urgency of comprehensive support systems. Through this research, I aspire to foster a transformative impact on the doctoral education landscape, advocating for resilience, persistence, and equitable resources for students of all backgrounds and ages pursuing advanced degrees.

Autoethnographic Approach

As a researcher, I have been interested in using autoethnography to better understand the experiences of adult learners at risk of dropping out of school. Through my own experiences and those of my colleagues, I have grown to understand the significance of utilizing this method to gain a deeper understanding of the obstacles encountered by non-traditional students. My research has focused on the persistence of first-year non-traditional doctoral students. I have used data from a group class project in which I participated to comprehend the phenomenon of attrition in my research. By utilizing an autoethnographic approach methodology, I was able to identify the personal and group characteristics that helped individuals adhere to the cohort model and complete their doctoral degree programs. Through asking inquiries and learning from one another's experiences, we were able to establish a culture of personal support that fostered transformation and persistence.

I have noticed a growing number of students pursuing their doctoral degrees in unconventional ways. Non-traditional graduate students, who are normally over 24 years old, frequently hold down full- or part-time jobs in addition to their academic studies. As a result of the fact that these students frequently confront one-of-a-kind obstacles and demands on their time, it is essential for educational institutions to establish support systems that are both adaptable and inclusive. As a result of the fact that these students frequently confront one-of-a-kind obstacles and demands on their time, it is essential for educational institutions to establish support systems that are both adaptable and inclusive. Mitchell et al. (2019) state that deep state cuts in higher education funding over the last decade have contributed to rapid, significant tuition increases and shifted more of the costs of college to students, making it more difficult for them to enroll and graduate. Non-traditional students often must juggle multiple responsibilities, such as work, family obligations, and financial constraints. To support themselves and their families, for instance, many of these sorts of doctorate students may be required to have part-time or full-time jobs, which might reduce the time they have available for researching as well as attending lectures. Furthermore, it may be more difficult for non-traditional students

Empowering Persistence

to manage childcare obligations in addition to their academic pursuits, hence further complicating the process of scheduling time for courses and assignments.

There are others who contend that allocating supplementary resources to non-traditional students is an inequitable treatment towards traditional students. However, it is important to recognize that non-traditional students often face unique challenges and barriers that can impede their academic success. By providing equitable support systems, universities are not only leveling the playing field for non-traditional students but also creating a more inclusive and supportive environment for all students. By addressing the specific needs of non-traditional students, universities can ensure that all students have an equal opportunity to succeed academically. This can be achieved through initiatives such as mentorship programs, academic support services, and flexible scheduling options. These resources can help non-traditional students navigate the challenges of balancing work, family, and school responsibilities. Ultimately, investing in the success of non-traditional students benefits the entire university community by fostering a diverse and inclusive learning environment.

Additionally, the benefits of these resources extend beyond the individual non-traditional students, as their diverse perspectives and life experiences enrich the learning environment for all students. By advocating for equitable resources, such as financial aid, childcare options, and mentorship programs, universities can empower all students pursuing advanced degrees to succeed, regardless of their background or age. "Lifelong scholars," as these are non-traditional students who bring a wealth of real-world experience and diverse perspectives to the academic community. Their unique life experiences can enhance classroom discussions and contribute to a more vibrant and well-rounded learning environment. By recognizing the value of these lifelong learners and providing the necessary support, universities can foster an inclusive and enriching educational experience for all students, regardless of their age or unconventional paths to academic success.

Transformative learning is a captivating concept that has deeply resonated with me throughout my research journey, particularly as I identify myself as a "lifelong scholar." This term, "lifelong scholar," is intentionally chosen to provide a nuanced and comprehensive perspective on a diverse and dedicated group of students, moving beyond the conventional label of "non-traditional doctoral students." I want to convey the idea that these people's pursuit of a doctoral degree is just one aspect of a larger educational journey they are taking, a journey that mirrors mine, by using the term "lifelong scholar." As a lifelong scholar, I recognize that the pursuit of knowledge extends far beyond the confines of a classroom or a specific degree program. It encompasses a continuous thirst for learning, personal growth, and intellectual exploration. This term acknowledges that these individuals are not defined solely by their current academic endeavors but rather by their unwavering commitment to expanding their understanding and making meaningful contributions to their fields of interest. By embracing the concept of lifelong scholarship, we can celebrate the diverse paths and motivations that lead individuals to pursue higher education, ultimately fostering a community of lifelong learners who are united in their passion for knowledge.

Delving into transformative learning, I find Mezirow's (1978) framework particularly illuminating. According to Mezirow, the transformative learning process unfolds across ten distinct stages, each contributing to a profound evolution of one's perspectives and understanding. These phases include (a) encountering a disorienting dilemma; (b) engaging in self-examination of assumptions; (c) critically reflecting on assumptions; (d) recognizing dissatisfaction; (e) exploring alternative perspectives; (f) formulating a plan for action; (g) acquiring new knowledge; (h) experimenting with new roles; (i) building competence; and (j) integrating new perspectives into one's life (Mezirow, 1991). Each of these stages represents a crucial step in the transformative learning journey, shaping the educational experiences of lifelong scholars as they navigate the complexities of doctoral studies.

This multifaceted exploration aligns with my conviction that understanding the dynamics of transformative learning is key to comprehending the intricate paths of lifelong scholars within the realm of doctoral education. It underscores the importance of recognizing the diverse phases and challenges that contribute to the continuous growth and development of these individuals throughout their educational endeavors. By recognizing the diverse phases and challenges that "lifelong scholars" face, we can better support their continuous growth and development throughout their educational endeavors. This understanding allows us to provide tailored guidance and resources to help them navigate the complexities of doctoral studies. Ultimately, by acknowledging the importance of transformative learning in the realm of doctoral education, we can ensure that lifelong scholars have the necessary tools and support to succeed in their academic pursuits.

Transformative learning has the propensity to be a very useful tool. This method uses Mezirow's (1978) four stages of transformative learning. The four steps are: (a) having a learning experience that changes you; (b) making assumptions; (c) challenging viewpoints; and (d) challenging perspectives. The choice of the transformative learning framework for this autoethnographic research of non-traditional doctoral students is deliberate and strategic. Mezirow's conceptualization of transformative learning theory offers a solid framework for comprehending and interpreting the significant changes and growth that people go through as they pursue their doctorates. This framework resonates with the nuanced narratives of non-traditional doctoral students, capturing the multifaceted nature of their experiences. The ten stages outlined by Mezirow offer a comprehensive lens through which to examine the challenges, reflections, and transformative moments that shape the academic and personal trajectories of these students.

Moreover, transformative learning theory aligns with the overarching theme of personal and academic growth inherent in the autoethnographic approach. It allows for an in-depth exploration of the internal processes and external factors influencing the development of lifelong scholars within the doctoral education landscape. Using transformative learning theory, this autoethnography tries to get to the bottom of the complicated doctoral experience for non-traditional students by giving more than just surface-level observations. The framework's focus on critical reflection, exploring alternatives, and incorporating new perspectives is in line with the goals of autoethnography. It helps people get a deeper understanding of the unique challenges and successes that non-traditional doctoral scholars face in their academic pursuits.

In conclusion, this section unveils the intricate layers of the transformative learning journey undertaken by "lifelong scholars" within the realm of doctoral education. By embracing the term "lifelong scholar," the narrative expands beyond the traditional label of "non-traditional doctoral students," emphasizing the holistic educational journey that extends beyond the pursuit of a doctoral degree. Mezirow's transformative learning framework, delineated across ten distinct stages, serves as a guiding light in understanding the profound shifts and growth experienced by individuals navigating the complexities of doctoral studies. This multifaceted exploration aligns with a fundamental conviction: that a nuanced comprehension of transformative learning dynamics is pivotal in unraveling the intricate paths of lifelong scholars. The framework not only captures the diverse phases and challenges contributing to continuous growth but also serves as a cornerstone for the autoethnographic approach. Transformative learning theory, which stresses critical reflection, exploring alternatives, and incorporating new perspectives, fits well with the goals of autoethnography. It helps us deeply understand the unique challenges and successes that non-traditional doctoral scholars face in their academic pursuits. As we transition to the next section, the research problem statement and the insights gained from this exploration lay the foundation for a deeper examination of the challenges faced by non-traditional doctoral students. The transformative learning lens, coupled with the autoethnographic approach, promises to illuminate the nuances of my experiences, and contribute to the broader discourse on doctoral education.

An Autoethnographic Approach to Understanding Non-Traditional Doctoral Students

As a researcher, I am drawn to autoethnography to gain deeper insights into the experiences of adult learners at risk of dropping out of school. This method allows me to tap into my personal experiences and those of my colleagues, shedding light on the unique challenges faced by non-traditional students. My autoethnography research focuses on me as a non-traditional doctoral student's persistence, resilience, and strategies for success. By examining my own journey and the experiences of others, I hope to uncover valuable insights that can inform support programs and interventions for non-traditional doctoral students. Additionally, this approach allows me to challenge traditional notions of what it means to be a successful student and instead recognize the diverse strengths and capabilities that non-traditional students bring to academia. Through my research, I learned that non-traditional doctoral students face unique challenges such as balancing multiple roles and responsibilities, navigating institutional barriers, and feeling a sense of isolation. These findings highlight the importance of creating tailored support systems that address the specific needs of non-traditional students, promote inclusivity, and foster a sense of belonging within academia. Furthermore, my research also revealed the significance of mentorship and peer support networks in enhancing the success and well-being of non-traditional doctoral students, emphasizing the need for collaborative approaches in higher education.

The increasing number of doctoral students taking unconventional paths, often while juggling work and family responsibilities, underscores the need for adaptable and inclusive support systems in educational institutions. Mitchell et al. (2019) attribute these shifts to reductions in higher education funding, leading to higher tuition costs and making it challenging for students to enroll and graduate. Non-traditional students often must balance multiple commitments, such as work and family obligations, which can limit their time for research and coursework. As a result, universities and colleges need to address these challenges by offering flexible academic programs, online courses, and part-time options. Additionally, providing financial aid and scholarships specifically tailored to non-traditional students can help ease the burden of high tuition costs. Moreover, implementing mentorship programs and support networks that cater to the unique needs of non-traditional students can facilitate their academic success and alleviate some of the pressure associated with their multiple responsibilities. Overall, by recognizing and accommodating the diverse circumstances and demands faced by doctoral students, institutions can foster an inclusive and supportive higher education environment.

Additionally, managing childcare responsibilities alongside academic pursuits further complicates their schedules. It is important to recognize that providing additional resources to non-traditional students is not inequitable but rather a means to level the playing field and create a more supportive environment for all students. Universities can achieve this through mentorship programs, academic support services, and flexible scheduling options tailored to the unique needs of non-traditional students. This investment benefits the entire university community by promoting diversity and inclusion. By offering mentorship programs, non-traditional students can receive guidance and support from experienced individuals who understand the challenges they may face. Academic support services, such as tutoring or counseling, can help these students navigate their coursework and develop effective study strategies. Moreover, flexible scheduling options can allow non-traditional students to balance their responsibilities and commitments more easily, ensuring they have the time and energy to succeed academically. Ultimately, by investing in the success of non-traditional students, universities can create a more inclusive and diverse community that benefits all members. Furthermore, it leads to an increase in the percentage of kids who graduate from high school as well as an improvement in academic proficiency.

Secondly, tools that are geared toward non-traditional students improve the learning environment for all students by embracing a variety of viewpoints and experiences from life. By advocating for equitable resources, such as financial aid, childcare options, and mentorship programs, universities empower all students to succeed, regardless of their background or age. These "lifelong scholars" bring real-world experience and diverse viewpoints, enriching classroom discussions and fostering a vibrant academic community. Embracing the concept of lifelong scholarship emphasizes that their pursuit of a doctoral degree is part of a broader educational journey characterized by continuous learning and personal growth. In this way, universities not only provide opportunities for personal and professional development but also contribute to the overall enrichment of society. Lifelong scholars serve as role models for future generations, proving that it is never too late to pursue education and make valuable contributions to academia. By prioritizing the needs and experiences of all students, universities can create a more inclusive and diverse academic environment that benefits everyone involved. Given the importance of lifelong scholarship in cultivating an inquisitive, driven, and intellectually curious spirit, it is imperative that non-traditional doctoral graduates continue to work toward significant and consequential objectives even after they receive their degree.

In exploring transformative learning, Mezirow's (1978) framework, consisting of ten stages, provides a comprehensive understanding of the profound shifts and growth experienced by lifelong scholars throughout their doctoral studies. This framework aligns with the autoethnographic approach's goals, emphasizing critical reflection, alternative exploration, and new perspective integration. It allows for a deeper exploration of the challenges and successes that non-traditional doctoral scholars encounter during their academic journeys. Understanding transformative learning within doctoral education is pivotal to offering tailored guidance and resources to support lifelong scholars' growth and development. By examining the profound shifts and growth experienced by lifelong scholars, we can gain valuable insights into the transformative learning process within doctoral education. This understanding can help educators and institutions develop personalized guidance and resources that address the specific challenges and successes encountered by non-traditional doctoral scholars. Ultimately, this approach fosters a supportive environment that nurtures lifelong scholars' growth and development, enabling them to reach their full potential and make significant contributions to their respective fields.

The autoethnographic approach offers valuable insights into the challenges and successes of first-year non-traditional doctoral students. By acknowledging the diverse experiences and perspectives of lifelong scholars, universities can create a more inclusive and supportive environment. The transformative learning lens, combined with the autoethnographic approach, promises to illuminate the nuances of these experiences, and contribute to the broader discourse on doctoral education. This approach allows for a deeper understanding of the unique struggles faced by non-traditional doctoral students, such as balancing work and family responsibilities while pursuing their studies. Additionally, it sheds light on the successes and strategies employed by these lifelong scholars, providing valuable lessons for universities to better support and empower them. Ultimately, by embracing the autoethnographic approach and transformative learning lens, universities can foster a more inclusive and enriching environment for all doctoral students, regardless of their background or circumstances.

According to C. Ellis et al. (2010), autoethnography is the systematic analysis of cultural experiences using personal experiences as a starting point. As a first-year non-traditional doctoral student, I persist in my studies, and this experience has led to transformative learning as I enter my second academic year. This process has underscored the value of research in understanding and analyzing cultural experiences. Saxena (2022) highlights the significant impact of non-traditional college students on society, emphasizing their role in voting, volunteering, and community involvement. These students are vital to higher education and the economy, representing a substantial portion of the population. Furthermore, as a non-traditional student, I have come to appreciate the unique perspectives and insights that this diverse group brings to the classroom. Interacting with my fellow classmates, who come from a variety of backgrounds and life experiences, has broadened my understanding of the world, and enriched my learning. This has reinforced my belief in the power of diversity and inclusivity in education, and the importance of creating an environment where everyone's voices are heard and valued. Overall, my journey as a non-traditional doctoral student has not only furthered my academic pursuits but has also highlighted the invaluable contributions that non-traditional students make to society.

It is essential to acknowledge that autoethnography provides a subjective perspective and may not encompass broader cultural trends. While diverse perspectives are crucial, solely relying on autoethnography may limit the scope and validity of conclusions. It is important to recognize that multiple factors, including socioeconomic status, can be barriers to higher education (Rowlands, 2010). Low-income and socially disadvantaged students, single parents, and high school dropouts may experience difficulties in obtaining doctorates. To address these problems, institutions should investigate mandatory reporting of attrition and retention rates, as Lively (2022) suggests. This data can help institutions overcome obstacles and support non-traditional students effectively. By understanding the reasons behind attrition and retention rates, institutions can implement targeted interventions and strategies to better support non-traditional students.

In conclusion, the autoethnographic approach provides valuable insights into the experiences of non-traditional doctoral students. Recognizing the unique challenges faced by these students and advocating for equitable support systems can lead to a more inclusive and enriching educational environments for all. By implementing mandatory reporting of attrition and retention rates, universities will have a clearer understanding of the specific obstacles that non-traditional doctoral students face. This data can then be used to develop targeted support programs and initiatives that address the unique needs of these students. By making these adjustments, universities can create a more inclusive and supportive educational environment for non-traditional students and increase their chances of successfully completing their doctoral degrees.

Research Problem Statement

As a current doctoral candidate pursuing a degree in creative leadership at a Historically Black College or University (HBCU), I have first-hand experience with the pressing need for higher education institutions to address the increasing dropout rates in doctoral programs. Gittings et al. (2018) suggest that postgraduate students require specific opportunities and resources to ensure program completion. Doctoral candidates, often highly educated individuals with a proven academic track record, embark on a demanding and lengthy journey. While it is encouraging to note the rising number of doctorates awarded in the United States, as highlighted by Nietzel (2021), this growth has coincided with a rise in attrition rates among doctoral students.

The path to obtaining a doctorate is filled with challenges, necessitating comprehensive support to help students overcome obstacles. To effectively address this issue, universities and policymakers must allocate resources and provide positive assistance to all doctoral candidates, ensuring their academic success. Factors influencing doctoral persistence, such as the extent and quality of student-supervisor contact, socialization abilities, and the utilization of vicarious learning, should be considered (Graham & Massyn, 2019). Achieving a doctorate is both demanding and time-consuming, requiring comprehensive support to navigate potential obstacles. Therefore, it is imperative for universities and policymakers to collaborate in offering the necessary resources and guidance.

Nonetheless, traditional doctoral programs often favor privileged males, marginalizing non-traditional students. Regrettably, the literature on doctoral attrition does not differentiate between traditional and non-traditional students, except for part-time completions (Graham & Massyn, 2019). This lack of distinction perpetuates the marginalization of non-traditional students and fails to address the unique challenges they face. Non-traditional students often juggle multiple responsibilities outside academia, such as family or full-time jobs, hindering their progress in a traditional doctoral program. Universities and policymakers must acknowledge and address these barriers by providing flexible scheduling options, financial support, and mentorship programs tailored to the needs of non-traditional students. By doing so, they can create a more inclusive and supportive environment that promotes doctoral persistence for all students, regardless of their background.

As a doctoral student, I am keenly aware of the imperative for higher education institutions to address high dropout rates among doctoral students. Earning a doctorate can open doors professionally and personally, offering benefits such as higher salaries, improved job prospects, and contributions to society (Litalien, 2020). However, attrition rates remain high in North America. To ensure students' success in the program, Gittings et al. (2018) suggest that they require specific opportunities and resources, including manageable course demands, strong student-faculty relationships, inspirational academic experiences, a supportive atmosphere, and a caring college environment (Caruth, 2018).

McClelland's achievement motivation theory, initially focused on optimism, fear of failure, and fear of success in the 1950s, has evolved over time to incorporate additional factors such as power and affiliation. According to McClelland, these drives are learned and arranged in a hierarchy, with high-achievement incentive at the top, potentially taking precedence over other motivations, even influencing behaviors related to basic needs like hunger (McClelland, 2005). Achievement motivation is crucial for students to succeed academically, as emphasized by Steinmayr et al. (2019). Few studies have examined motivational constructs as predictors of students' academic achievement beyond cognitive abilities and previous performance. A person's ability, motivation, and value of their own work can be more influential than setting goals and being motivated by achieving them. Edgar et al. (2019) highlights the critical role of self-motivation in student success during university transitions. To improve success, psychosocial well-being, and retention rates, higher education institutions should address students with low self-esteem and align the curriculum with motivational factors. Undoubtedly, achievement motivation plays a pivotal role in determining success and retention in higher education, offering insights into student engagement and the connections between self-motivation and performance.

In 2019, U.S. colleges and universities awarded 55,614 doctoral degrees, indicating a 1.0% change from the preceding year. Moving to 2020, there were 55,283 recipients of doctoral degrees, marking a decrease of 0.6% from the previous year (Kang & National Center for Science and Engineering Statistics (NCSES), 2020). According to Nietzel (2021), the recent increase in U.S. doctorates is a positive trend. However, this surge in doctoral students also brings forth the challenge of addressing growing attrition rates. Over the years, the count of doctorates awarded in the United States surged from 41,369 in 2000 to 55,283 in 2020, reflecting a substantial 33% increase, with 14 of the past 20 years witnessing year-over-year growth (Nietzel, 2021).

Embarking on the journey of attaining a doctoral degree reveals a path that is both lengthy and demanding, with numerous obstacles along the way. As I, along with other non-traditional doctoral students, continue down this transformative road, we are reminded that achievement is a collective effort, not merely an individual pursuit. It is crucial for institutions of higher learning and policymakers to collaborate in providing us with the means for success. With access to helpful tools and a supportive learning environment, we can conquer classroom challenges with perseverance and motivation, weaving the fabric of our academic achievements from the threads of assistance and optimism.

Research Questions

My first year in the doctoral program as a non-traditional student was not merely an academic endeavor; rather, it was a profoundly transformative journey. The turning point in my life was when I went from being a traditional undergraduate student to a non-traditional doctoral student. From that experience, I learned how important it is to be persistent. The transformative learning theory guided me through challenging situations and assisted me in determining the experiences that were the most formative for me during my first year. My overall research questions are:

1. How does the combination of persistence and transformational learning affect my view of the most meaningful events I experienced in my first year as a non-traditional doctoral student?
2. What individual steps did I take as a first-year non-traditional doctoral student to successfully complete the significant lived experiences of my first year?
3. How did my lived experiences as a first-year non-traditional doctoral student contribute to my understanding of the benefits of collaboration and resource utilization in achieving personal and academic goals?

In summary, my progression from a conventional undergraduate to a non-traditional doctoral candidate has been a profoundly transformative experience, illustratively illustrating the significance of perseverance and informed by transformative learning theory. As I progress in my investigation, my fundamental inquiries will direct me to examine the ways in which the convergence of perseverance and transformative learning has influenced my understanding of the most significant occurrences throughout my freshman year. Furthermore, an examination will be conducted into the precise measures I implemented to effectively manage the obstacles encountered during my first year as an unconventional doctoral candidate. These experiences will also serve to underscore the significance of resource allocation and collaboration in the pursuit of individual and scholarly objectives. By means of this investigation, my objective is to illuminate the complex intricacies of my doctoral trajectory and provide perspectives that might strike a chord with other non-conventional scholars embarking on their own transformative trajectories in academia.

Definitions of Key Terms

To ensure a comprehensive understanding of the concepts discussed in this chapter, I will define several key terms central to my research. These terms have been carefully selected to align with my research question and shed light on the subject matter. By presenting these definitions at the outset, readers will have a solid foundation for following my understanding and gaining insight into the topics under discussion.

1. *Non-traditional Doctoral Students*: These individuals are adults who pursue higher education degrees on a part-time basis while working full-time or return to full-time education after a significant break, such as starting a family, changing careers, or military service, all while juggling employment, family responsibilities, and other adult obligations (University of Nebraska-Lincoln, 2022).
2. *Doctoral Students*: These are college students who hold master's degrees and are engaged in advanced coursework and research as part of their doctoral degree programs. They are self-directed learners who must meet high standards in professional content knowledge, critical thinking, and problem-solving (U.S. Department of State, 2015).
3. *Persistence Theory*: Originating from Tinto's (1975) work, this theory explores the phenomenon of dropouts from higher education through various perspectives. According to Tinto's model, students must successfully integrate into both academic and social systems, including peer-group interactions, academic performance, faculty/staff interactions, and extracurricular activities, in order to persist.
4. *Transformative Learning Theory*: Transformative learning is a dynamic process that challenges and transforms individuals' fixed assumptions and frames of reference in learning. It fosters inclusivity, discrimination, and emotional responsiveness (Mezirow, 2003). This theory encourages individuals to reevaluate and transform their pre-existing perspectives, ultimately leading to more meaningful and authentic beliefs.

5. ***Perseverance:*** Perseverance is the quality of persisting in a course of action or achieving a goal despite facing obstacles, setbacks, or opposition ("Perseverance," 2022).
6. ***"Doctorateness":*** A term introduced by Yazdani and Shokooh (2018) to describe a common feature shared by all doctoral degrees.
7. ***Autoethnography:*** Autoethnography is a form of academic autobiography that draws from the author's life experiences to gain insights into self-identity, cultural resources, communication strategies, traditions, values, and broader social, cultural, and political issues (Poulos, 2021).
8. ***Persistence:*** Persistence is the quality of possessing the attribute or state of persevering in a path of activity or accomplishment in the face of obstacles or difficulty (APA Dictionary of Psychology, 2023).
9. ***Retention:*** Student retention in higher education refers to a student's continued enrollment from the first year to the second year or from year two until graduation. It is often equated with persistence (Burke, 2019).
10. ***Self-Motivation:*** Based on Abraham Maslow's Theory of Human Motivation, self-motivation implies seeking ongoing improvement beyond necessities. It refers to individuals who aspire to personal growth and development (Akrani & J. Trivedi, 2019).
11. ***Cohort Model:*** An educational approach increasingly adopted by institutions to create a sense of community among students as they progress through coursework and, in some cases, live together (Burke, 2019).
12. ***First-Year:*** Pertaining to the initial year of attending a university or college, a first-year student is in the first year of university or college courses. It also relates to the first year of a university or college course ("First Year Definition and Meaning: Collins English Dictionary," 2023).
13. ***Achievement Motivation:*** Steinmayr et al. (2019) suggest that achievement motivation encompasses various factors, including ability self-concepts, task values, goals, and achievement motives. It is a predictor of academic success beyond intelligence and previous achievement.
14. ***Lifelong Scholar:*** The term "lifelong scholar," as introduced by Glimps-Smith (2023), effectively characterizes non-traditional doctorate students who are dedicated to an ongoing intellectual endeavor; it describes them as people who are dedicated to learning throughout their lives and for whom earning a Doctorate is just one part of their larger educational trajectory.es a component of this more extensive educational trajectory.
15. ***Attrition:*** The progressive decrease in the number of participants over time is referred to as attrition. It may compromise the validity of research and may arise due to a multitude of factors. Longitudinal research dropouts may contain

distinctive characteristics pertinent to the research subject, hence introducing a possible bias into the sample (American Psychological Association, 2023).

In conclusion, my journey into the doctoral program began with feelings of isolation and the formidable challenge of meeting academic and social expectations as a non-traditional student. My success, however, was forged through reliance on my cohort, the unwavering support of my family, and the vast resources available online. As Gittings et al. (2018) have highlighted, non-traditional doctoral students often face attrition risk factors, including family responsibilities, age, part-time enrollment, geographical distance from campus, limited socialization opportunities, and demanding employment commitments. In recognition of these challenges, this article strives to provide valuable support to non-traditional doctoral students who encounter similar obstacles, while also encouraging educational institutions to enhance their efforts in addressing attrition.

To the first-year non-traditional doctoral students who engage with this research, I hope you come to recognize how closely you embody the principles of persistence theory and transformative learning theory. Your remarkable levels of self-motivation and unwavering perseverance in the pursuit of "doctorateness" are evident, as exemplified by your adept use of autoethnography to explore the intricate relationship between retention and persistence within your academic journeys. May this knowledge empower you to navigate the challenges ahead with confidence and resilience, ultimately contributing to your continued success in the pursuit of your doctoral dreams.

A QUILT OF THEORETICAL FRAMEWORKS

A theoretical framework is the basis upon which academic research is conducted; it is the "blueprint" for the study (Grant & Osanloo, 2014). Researchers use theoretical frameworks to investigate a phenomenon or problem. It guides people through a complicated issue like a map. As a researcher, I recognize theoretical frameworks as blueprints or designs showing how everything fits together before beginning a research study. These frameworks provide a structure for organizing and interpreting data, allowing researchers to draw meaningful conclusions and make recommendations for future action. The theoretical framework organizes and relates ideas and concepts like a blueprint.

This study's theoretical assumptions are postpositivist in nature. This study is grounded in the idea that knowledge is gained through observation and experience and that reality exists independently of our perceptions. This viewpoint highlights the significance of objective measurement and empirical evidence in the research process. In my autoethnography, I utilized a postpositivist theoretical framework to analyze the literature. When I first started my doctoral program as a non-traditional student, I had preconceived notions about what it meant to be a successful doctoral student. However, through my research and analysis, I could objectively examine the empirical evidence and challenge my own perceptions. Post positivism is based on theories that are known ahead of time and is reductionist, logical, empirical, cause-and-effect-oriented, and certain (Creswell & Poth, 2018, p. 23). The postpositivist approach allowed me to grow both as a researcher and as an individual, as I learned to question my assumptions and embrace new perspectives. It allowed me, as the researcher, to recognize the influence of personal perspectives in research while prioritizing rigorous methodology and systematic observation of my own view.

As a theory, postpositivist researchers view the research process as a logically interconnected set of steps that must be followed to reach a conclusion. When it comes to dealing with the significant problem of academic attrition that non-traditional doctoral students face when they return to graduate school after a long absence, it is of the utmost importance to implement this theory. My return to graduate school after a break from obtaining my master's degree years ago was met with academic difficulties and uncertainty. Without a structured approach to tackling my coursework, I felt disjointed by my attempts to understand and engage with the research materials. The absence of a systematic problem-solving method left me feeling frustrated and questioning my decision to pursue a doctoral degree. This lack of structure made it challenging to navigate complex issues, contributing to a sense of overwhelm and casting doubt on the feasibility of my academic journey. While researching different problem-solving methods for my quantitative research methods course, I came across the concept of post positivism. It appealed to me to approach problems systematically, and I decided to apply this approach to my academic challenges. Through persistence and determination, I began breaking down my problems into manageable steps and identifying logical connections between them. Slowly but steadily, I noticed a shift in my problem-solving abilities. I began to navigate my coursework with more confidence, leveraging my newfound approach to tackling assignments and complex topics. The narrative of my journey illustrates how adopting a postpositivist perspective transformed my academic experience, empowering me to overcome challenges and thrive in my class.

When faced with challenges, it is important to approach them with a postpositivist mindset. This approach explains how strategic thinking and logical reasoning overcome obstacles. By viewing the research process as a systematic progression of interconnected steps, individuals can gain a deeper understanding of complex issues and effectively tackle them. This approach is especially useful for researchers and students who want to fully comprehend the intricacies of a problem and address it in the most effective way possible.

The difficulty of picking up academic writing again awaited me when I returned to academia after a significant break. Although I had developed my journalistic writing skills during my undergraduate studies, I quickly realized that academic writing required a completely different structure and set of requirements. The prospect of writing scholarly papers and assignments felt increasingly intimidating due to my unfamiliarity with this style. This growing worry that I wouldn't be able to meet the high academic standards was impeding my production and progress. But I understood to succeed, I would have to change how I looked at things and take a fresh approach to my writing projects.

I adopted a growth mindset because I realized that I needed to change and that my skills and abilities could be improved with effort and practice. I began to see writing as a skill that could be developed over time rather than as an innate talent that I either possessed or lacked. With this perspective, I started to see the difficulties of academic writing as chances for growth and learning.

I started by thoroughly researching and outlining the writing process before breaking it down into smaller steps. I knew my first drafts might not have been perfect, but they were still important steps in the right direction. I welcomed criticism as a useful tool for improving my work and actively sought out chances to absorb other people's perspectives. I continued to write, and I reminded myself that each sentence, paragraph, and paper was a chance to enhance my writing skills. I celebrated every milestone, whether it was crafting a clear thesis statement, organizing ideas coherently, or mastering the art of citing sources accurately. With each assignment, I felt a growing sense of accomplishment and a stronger belief in my ability to succeed.

In adopting a growth mindset and tackling obstacles head-on, I was able to not only overcome the difficulties of re-entering the world of academic writing but also rediscover a hidden passion for putting my ideas and insights into words. This change in perspective has not only helped me become a better writer but has also reignited my enthusiasm for learning and sharing what I've learned with others. Adopting a postpositivist perspective in my studies has been instrumental in rekindling my love of writing after a long dormancy. As I made my way through the maze of academic writing, I realized that breaking it down into manageable chunks helped me overcome the fears and doubts that had previously stood in my way. Every word I write and every thought I share echoes the postpositivist belief that a methodical and rational approach can spur both individual development and a cultural revival.

Employing an autoethnographic lens, this study intricately explores the experiential journey of an adult graduate student within the distinctive setting of a medium-sized Historically Black College and University (HBCU) situated in the culturally rich landscape of the United States Virgin Islands. This method, called autoethnography, lets you look deeply into your own experiences, giving you a more nuanced view that connects your personal stories to the bigger picture of college life at HBCU. Through this lens, the study aims to provide valuable insights into the unique challenges, triumphs, and transformative moments encountered by adult graduate students within the specific cultural and educational context of the US Virgin Islands. As the researcher, my story unfolds, shedding light on the critical role that perseverance played in shaping my success trajectory.

This research goes beyond a simple recounting of personal experiences; it strives to weave the nuanced essence of perseverance into the fabric of the narrative, ensuring its interpretative resonance with the reader. It acknowledges that, while persistence can emerge as a powerful tool for some people, its effectiveness may be nuanced and contextually variable. Drawing on my own graduate experience, I personally used persistence to propel my journey toward success. Nonetheless, academic success is a complex tapestry woven from various threads, and what works unwaveringly for one may require adaptation for another. As my story demonstrates, the transformative impact of persistence has made pursuing higher education an enlightening odyssey. While my journey emphasizes the transformative power of perseverance, it also acknowledges the presence of various equally effective strategies and techniques capable of producing the same results.

In conclusion, a theoretical framework serves as the blueprint for guiding researchers through the complex landscape of a study, providing a foundation for academic research. The theoretical assumptions of this study align with a postpositivist perspective, emphasizing the importance of objective measurement and empirical evidence in understanding complex phenomena. This approach allows for systematic problem-solving, particularly crucial for non-traditional doctoral students facing challenges like academic attrition. By adopting a postpositivist mindset, individuals can navigate complex issues systematically, fostering a deeper understanding and effective problem resolution.

Returning to academic writing after a significant hiatus presented challenges, requiring a shift in mindset. Embracing a growth mindset, I viewed writing as a skill to be developed over time, turning obstacles into opportunities for learning and improvement. Breaking down the writing process into manageable steps, seeking feedback, and celebrating milestones proved instrumental in overcoming initial fears and doubts. This transformative shift not only enhanced my writing skills but also reignited my passion for learning and sharing knowledge.

The autoethnographic exploration of an adult graduate student's journey in an HBCU setting revealed the nuanced role of perseverance in shaping success. Beyond a recounting of personal experiences, this study aims to intricately weave the essence of perseverance into the narrative, recognizing its contextual variability. While my journey highlights the transformative power of persistence, it acknowledges the presence of diverse strategies contributing to academic success. The transformative impact of perseverance, as illustrated in my story, underscores the enlightening odyssey of pursuing higher education.

Navigating the Academic Odyssey: Embracing Lifelong Learning as a Non-Traditional Doctoral Student

In the pursuit of becoming a "Lifelong Scholar," the journey of lifelong learning takes center stage. Lifelong learning, characterized by the continuous acquisition of skills and knowledge, stands as a pillar for social inclusion, active citizenship, personal development, competitiveness, and employability (Laal & Salamati, 2012). Lifelong learning assists people in achieving other goals, such as participating actively in community life, living a more sustainable lifestyle, and enhancing their health and well-being. It also benefits society by lowering crime and increasing communal activities (Dunn, E., 2003). As a first-year non-traditional doctoral student, this odyssey back to academia after a substantial hiatus is a profound and enriching experience. Through persistence and an unwavering motivation to learn, I navigate the challenges inherent in pursuing a doctoral degree with gratitude for the supportive community and personalized resources that aid me on this academic venture.

People who learn for life have a beneficial effect on the economy because it helps them understand, analyze, and integrate the knowledge they acquire. Ongoing education helps people become more adaptive to the dynamics of the job while also supporting the economy by allowing them to achieve greater incomes, better quality of life, and involvement in the system (Laal & Salamati, 2012). I am confident that this journey will lead to personal and professional growth. By immersing myself in this academic pursuit, I am not only gaining knowledge and expertise in my field of study but also honing essential skills that are highly sought after in the job market. The emphasis on active citizenship and inclusion has made me more aware of the social issues and challenges faced by our society, motivating me to actively engage in community service and make a positive impact. This comprehensive approach to education has not only made me a more competitive candidate in the job market but has also fostered personal development, empowering me to become a well-rounded individual capable of tackling any professional challenge that comes my way. This is demonstrated by the creative leadership courses I have completed at my current Historically Black College or University (HBCU), where I am learning how to use divergent and convergent thinking to produce unique solutions to complicated situations. This skill has proven invaluable in my current role as a special education teacher, where I am constantly faced with unique challenges that require creative problem-solving. Additionally, my HBCU's emphasis on inclusivity and diversity has equipped me with the tools to create an inclusive and supportive learning environment for my students, regardless of their abilities or backgrounds. This has not only helped me excel in my role as a special education teacher but has also allowed me to make a lasting impact on the lives of my students and their families.

In conclusion, as a "lifelong scholar," I am committed to continuously learning and growing as an educator to continue to inspire and support my students to reach their full potential. Education is the key to meaningful social transformation and the ability to access new opportunities. Through the cultivation of an enthusiasm for knowledge and the promotion of analytical reasoning, my objective is to enable my pupils to develop into engaged and initiative-taking members of society who can make positive contributions to their respective communities. It is my strong conviction that each student is entitled to an equitable opportunity for achievement, and that social equality can be advanced by dismantling obstacles via education.

The Benefits and Challenges of Lifelong Scholars

In this analysis, we will explore the benefits and challenges of being a lifelong scholar. Specifically, we will delve into the emotional terrain of persisting through graduate school and discuss the importance of prioritizing emotional well-being and providing specialized support for students who do not fit the standard student profile. By addressing these needs, we can create a more inclusive and supportive academic environment. Previous research has highlighted the emotional challenges faced by doctoral students. For example, Yazdani and Shokooh (2018) define "doctorateness" as the transformative apprenticeship process that doctoral students go through, which can lead to feelings of overwhelm, inadequacy, and uncertainty. Other studies have shown that emotional well-being plays a crucial role in academic success, with students who receive specialized support for their emotional needs demonstrating higher rates of completion and satisfaction. The definition mirrors the aspirations of a doctoral student, emphasizing the creation of original contributions and the management of the discipline. As a "lifelong scholar" and non-traditional student, I understand firsthand the challenges that come with not fitting the standard student profile. Many non-traditional students have responsibilities outside of their studies, such as work or family obligations, which can add additional stress and time constraints. They may also have different learning styles or educational backgrounds that require tailored support. By acknowledging and addressing the unique needs of non-traditional students, we can create a more inclusive and supportive academic environment for all.

This analysis is based on autoethnography, which involves reflecting on firsthand experiences and using them to understand broader social and cultural phenomena.

To address the emotional needs of doctoral students and create a supportive environment, institutions should consider implementing mentorship programs, providing access to counseling services, and offering workshops or training on stress management and self-care. Additionally, raising awareness about the challenges faced by non-traditional students and advocating for policies that support their unique needs can contribute to the overall improvement of mental health support systems within academia.

Qualitative Research and Autoethnography in Investigating Doctoral Experiences

Qualitative research serves as a powerful means to comprehend and elucidate the significance of participants' experiences, aligning with my research objectives centered around exploring my journey as a first-year non-traditional doctoral student. As Creswell (1994, 2007, 2013) posits, qualitative research offers versatile approaches to delve into various social and human issues. Its unique capacity to capture individuals' lived experiences, allowing them to narrate their stories, makes it an ideal avenue to gain profound insights into human encounters. Furthermore, I firmly believe that qualitative research, particularly within the context of cohort-based doctoral education, fosters a sense of community by facilitating the exchange of experiences and perspectives among participants. This collaborative environment can lead to a more profound comprehension of the research subject and yield richer insights.

Autoethnography, an established qualitative methodology employed in educational research, finds its expression through diverse mediums such as books, book chapters, dissertations, blind peer-reviewed journal articles, and professional development courses, as noted by Hughes (2020). Advocates of autoethnography emphasize its role in prompting individuals to critically examine their leadership, teaching, and learning experiences, thereby providing a valuable lens for self-reflection. As a researcher, autoethnography empowers me to delve into my own experiences and emotions, thereby offering a unique and insightful perspective on the research topic. Moreover, it serves as a tool for personal growth and self-reflection, enabling me to confront my preconceptions and evolving ideas.

In my research endeavor, I explore the influence of the cohort model, self-motivation, and persistence in overcoming challenges during my first year as a non-traditional doctoral student, encompassing both a medium-sized university in Southwest Florida and the U.S. Virgin Islands. By framing my investigation through the lens of autoethnography and guided by my research questions, I seek to compare my experiences with those of the participants, thereby gaining deeper insights into the challenges and opportunities encountered. Autoethnography provides a platform for self-reflection, enabling me to interpret and understand my own experiences in shaping my comprehension of the research topic, resulting in a nuanced perspective on the acquired knowledge. Furthermore, this approach facilitates an exploration of potential biases or assumptions that might have influenced the interpretation of research findings.

In essence, while the reasons underscore the validity of employing autoethnography, I am personally driven by the prospect of gaining a deeper and more intimate understanding of my doctoral journey. Through my research questions, I aim to draw meaningful comparisons between the experiences of participants and my own, shedding light on the challenges and opportunities that lie therein. By harnessing the power of autoethnography, I embark on a reflective journey, allowing my own experiences to mold and enrich my grasp of the research topic, ultimately contributing to a more nuanced interpretation of the collected knowledge. This introspective approach also equips me to scrutinize any potential biases or preconceptions that may have influenced my interpretation of research findings.

Theoretical Framework: Stitching Together Post-Positivism

Researchers employ theoretical frameworks as guiding maps to navigate complex phenomena. These frameworks, akin to blueprints, offer a structural foundation to arrange and interpret data, facilitating the derivation of meaningful conclusions and recommendations. Just as a blueprint organizes and links ideas, post positivism serves as the theoretical cornerstone of this study, grounding it in the belief that knowledge is acquired through observation and experience, independent of subjective perceptions. This perspective accentuates the importance of empirical evidence and objective measurement in the research process. This perspective accentuates the importance of empirical evidence and objective measurement in the research process, ultimately leading to reliable and valid conclusions.

In the realm of autoethnography, I've adopted a postpositivist framework, allowing me to scrutinize the literature with an objective lens. For instance, at the outset of my doctoral journey as a non-traditional student, I held preconceived notions about success in doctoral studies. However, my research and analysis compelled me to objectively assess empirical evidence and challenge my own perceptions. Post positivism, characterized by its reductionism, logicality, empiricism, causality, and a priori theories (Creswell & Poth, 2018), facilitated my growth as a researcher and individual. It encouraged me to question assumptions while prioritizing rigorous methodology and systematic observation. By embracing post positivism, I learned to approach my research with a critical mindset and to consider alternative explanations for my findings. This allowed me to develop a more nuanced understanding of the complexities within my field and to contribute to the existing body of knowledge in a meaningful way. Additionally, post positivism helped me recognize the importance of collaboration and seeking diverse perspectives, as it emphasized the value of multiple viewpoints in generating reliable and valid conclusions.

Much like my mother's quilt artfully weaves disparate pieces into a unified whole, post positivism stitches together logical steps and systematic approaches in research, creating a cohesive problem-solving framework. The choice of post positivism as the foundation for this research emanates from its emphasis on a systematic, methodical approach. Unlike hasty problem-solving, post positivism advocates a persistent and logically structured path, treating the research process as a series of interconnected steps contributing to comprehensive problem understanding. This approach ensures that all relevant factors are considered and accounted for, leading to more accurate and reliable conclusions. Additionally, post positivism promotes objectivity in research by encouraging researchers to acknowledge their biases and strive for impartiality in data collection and analysis. By adhering to a systematic and logical framework, researchers can minimize the influence of personal beliefs or preconceived notions on their findings, enhancing the credibility and validity of their research outcomes.

This perspective requires the researcher (in this case, me) to elucidate the logical reasoning and strategies employed to tackle the core issue addressed in this study: the high risk of academic attrition among first-year doctoral students returning to graduate school. It is crucial to recognize the theoretical underpinning of persistence in meeting the unique needs of graduate students pursuing advanced degrees. To effectively support these students and promote their success, it is important to understand the factors that contribute to academic attrition and develop targeted interventions. By identifying the specific challenges faced by first-year doctoral students, such as feelings of isolation or a lack of mentorship, institutions can implement programs and resources that address these issues. What is more, fostering a sense of community among graduate students can create a supportive environment where they can thrive academically and persist in their studies. This can be achieved through organizing social events, workshops, and seminars that encourage networking and collaboration among non-traditional doctoral degree students. Furthermore, offering prospects for mentorship and consultation with seasoned faculty members can significantly augment the scholarly process of their dissertation. By investing in these interventions, institutions can help ensure that first-year doctoral students are equipped with the necessary support and resources to overcome challenges, stay motivated, and ultimately complete their advanced degrees.

From a theoretical standpoint, this research delves deep into the concept of persistence and its pivotal role in the academic journey of graduate students pursuing advanced degrees. However, it is vital to acknowledge that while persistence may be a potent tool for some individuals, it may not universally apply. Different students may necessitate alternative strategies to attain similar levels of success. Understanding the diverse needs of doctoral students is crucial for providing effective support. Factors such as personal strengths, learning styles, and outside commitments can greatly impact an individual's ability to persist through challenges. Therefore, it is important for institutions to offer a range of resources, such as individualized mentorship programs, mental health counseling services, and tailored academic support, to cater to the unique requirements of each student. By recognizing and addressing these individual differences, universities can ensure that all doctoral students are equipped to reach their goals and complete their degrees successfully.

As a theoretical framework, post positivism provides a structured approach to research, emphasizing logical steps in problem-solving. When addressing the significant problem of academic attrition that non-traditional doctoral students who return to graduate school face, this viewpoint becomes essential. My personal experience of returning to academia after an extended break highlighted the challenges posed by the absence of a systematic problem-solving approach. Without such a framework, I felt overwhelmed and uncertain about pursuing a doctoral degree. However, discovering the concept of post positivism introduced a transformative change in my academic journey. I realized that there was a structured and rigorous way to approach problem-solving, ultimately giving me the confidence and direction needed to successfully pursue a doctoral degree.

By breaking down problems into manageable steps and establishing logical connections, I gained confidence in navigating coursework and tackling complex subjects. My journey exemplifies how adopting a postpositivist perspective can empower individuals to overcome obstacles and thrive in their academic pursuits. In essence, when faced with challenges, embracing a postpositivist mindset proves valuable, emphasizing strategic thinking and logical reasoning as effective tools for overcoming obstacles. This approach fosters a deeper understanding of complex issues and enhances problem-solving abilities.

My return to academia after a significant hiatus presented the daunting task of reacquainting myself with academic writing. The transition from journalistic writing to scholarly writing was formidable, and the fear of not meeting academic standards hindered my progress. However, adopting a growth mindset allowed me to view writing as a skill that could be developed over time. I began breaking down the writing process into manageable steps, actively sought feedback, and celebrated small victories. This shift in mindset ultimately led to significant improvement in my writing abilities. For example, when I started writing my first academic paper, I felt overwhelmed by the extensive research required and the need to adhere to strict formatting guidelines. However, by breaking down the task into smaller chunks, such as outlining, researching one topic at a time, and drafting sections separately, I was able to tackle each step with more confidence.

Furthermore, upon obtaining feedback from various sources, which included my mother, Dr. Blanche Jackson Glimps, peers, and professors, I received valuable input that enabled me to pinpoint areas requiring enhancement that would improve the quality of my discourse. As an outcome, my writing progressively improved and became more in line with the standards of scholarly writing. Absorbing their comments was sometimes as reassuring as wrapping myself in a completed quilt while they provided insightful commentary, and other times as sharp as my mother's needle, which she used to add details to her quilts. Their insights not only enhanced the clarity and coherence of my writing but also instilled a sense of comfort and reassurance, much like the warmth and security provided by a well-crafted quilt. With their guidance, I was able to transform my initial drafts into polished pieces that met the rigorous demands of scholarly writing. I also made it a point to read extensively in my field, which not only expanded my knowledge but also exposed me to different writing styles and techniques. By incorporating these strategies into my writing process, I was able to develop a stronger command of language and effectively communicate my ideas.

This transformative shift not only improved my writing skills but also reignited my passion for learning and knowledge sharing. In the context of autoethnographic exploration, my journey as an adult higher education student in an HBCU setting emphasized the pivotal role of persistence in shaping academic and personal success. This study goes beyond personal narratives to intricately weave the essence of persistence into the narrative, recognizing its contextual variability. By delving into my own experiences and reflecting on the challenges I faced, I was able to gain a deeper understanding of the importance of persistence in overcoming obstacles. This study acknowledges that persistence looks different for everyone, considering individual circumstances and societal factors that may impact one's journey towards success.

While my journey highlights the transformative power of persistence, it also recognizes the presence of diverse strategies contributing to academic success. The transformative impact of perseverance, as illustrated in my story, underscores the enlightening odyssey of pursuing higher education. For instance, when I commenced my doctoral journey, I initially struggled to navigate the complexities of academic research. In the beginning, my approach to research was characterized by uncertainty and confusion. I felt overwhelmed by the sheer volume of literature and the intricacies of scholarly discourse. However, as time progressed, I underwent a significant transformation. I honed my research skills through continuous learning and dedicated effort. I transitioned from a novice researcher grappling with the basics to a confident scholar capable of critically analyzing and contributing to academic discussions. Furthermore, my journey also saw a profound transformation in my self-perception. Initially, I harbored doubts about my abilities and questioned whether I belonged in the realm of doctoral studies. Yet, as I persevered through challenges, my self-confidence grew. I began to view myself as a capable and competent researcher, capable of making meaningful contributions to my field.

In addition, my journey led to a shift in my perspective on collaboration. Initially, I was inclined to work in isolation, believing that academic success was solely an individual endeavor. However, as I engaged with my peers and mentors, I recognized the immense value of collaborative learning. I discovered that by pooling our knowledge and experiences, we could collectively achieve more than we could as individuals. This shift in mindset transformed my academic journey from a solitary pursuit into a collaborative and enriching experience. Transformational learning theory provides the foundation for this study. Mezirow argues that "development is at the heart of transformational learning" (p. 60). Transformation is a critical component of development in adulthood. Accordingly, learners can adjust their thinking, becoming "more inclusive, discriminating, open, emotionally capable of change, and reflective" (p. 61) based on new information. The goal of transformational learning is independent thinking. Merriam argues that engaging in transformative learning requires a certain level of cognitive development. Mezirow found that critical reflection and critical review could lead to a transformation of understanding. Transformation does not occur without reflection. Premise reflection, a key type of reflection, involves "examining long-held, socially constructed assumptions, beliefs, and values" (p. 62) about the experience. Rational discourse, critical review, and discussion result in a new perspective on the experience. Transformational learning can occur in a variety of settings, including formal education, personal experiences, and interactions with others. The process of transformational learning is not always easy and can be uncomfortable as it challenges individuals to question their beliefs and values.

In conclusion, my academic journey as a non-traditional doctoral student is characterized by transformative moments that encompass skill development, enhanced self-confidence, and a shift towards collaboration. These transformations have not only enriched my scholarly experience but have also underscored the profound impact of persistence and adaptability in the pursuit of higher education. A theoretical framework serves as the foundation for academic research, guiding researchers through complex studies to achieve academic success. Post positivism has stitched together in my mind the importance of combining persistence, transformational learning, and a theoretical framework in academic research. By recognizing the value of both perseverance and a solid theoretical foundation, researchers can navigate the complexities of their studies and ultimately achieve academic success. This holistic approach not only enhances the quality of research but also contributes to the advancement of knowledge in various fields. The postpositivist perspective emphasizes the use of objective measurement and empirical evidence to understand complex phenomena. This approach facilitates systematic problem-solving, which is particularly valuable for non-traditional doctoral students facing challenges like academic attrition. Embracing a postpositivist mindset allows individuals to systematically navigate intricate issues. This fosters deeper understanding and effective problem resolution.

Transformative Learning and Research Methodology: A Journey of Personal and Scholarly Growth

Mezirow (1997) defines transformative learning as the process of changing our beliefs about experiences and expectations. Life frames, according to Mezirow, are the perspectives and beliefs that shape our actions and decisions. Transformative students possess qualities such as inclusiveness, discernment, self-reflection, and integration. This means that they are open to different perspectives, able to make thoughtful judgments, reflect on their own experiences, and integrate new knowledge into their existing understanding. As a non-traditional doctoral student in the field of psychology, my academic journey has been an odyssey characterized by transformative moments. These moments underscore the profound influence of persistence and adaptability in the pursuit of higher education. Coming from a non-traditional background, I initially grappled with the complexities of academic research. I felt overwhelmed by the rigorous demands of the doctoral program. As a student who had been out of the academic setting for several years, I had to navigate unfamiliar territory and learn new skills. One transformative moment came when I realized that my life experiences and unique perspective could be valuable assets in my research. Embracing this mindset, I began to approach my studies with a fresh perspective, allowing me to make meaningful connections between theory and real-world applications. This increased self-assurance helped me succeed academically and stoked my desire to advance psychology research. This experience not only enhanced my research skills but also boosted my confidence in my ability to contribute to academic discussions. Throughout my academic journey, I have realized the immense value of collaboration. Working with peers and mentors not only expanded my knowledge base but also provided me with valuable insights and perspectives. For example, during group discussions, I gained a deeper understanding of different research methodologies and their strengths and limitations. This collaborative mindset also helped me develop stronger communication and teamwork skills, as I learned to effectively articulate my thoughts and actively listen to others' ideas. These transformations have not only enriched my academic journey but have also highlighted the significant impact of perseverance and flexibility.

The transformative learning theory, according to Mezirow (2003), contends that learning entails more than just acquiring knowledge and skills. It emphasizes the importance of critical reflection and cognitive dissonance in challenging and reshaping existing meaning systems. According to this theory, individuals undergo a transformative process of change where they critically examine their assumptions, beliefs, and values, leading to a shift in their worldview and higher-order thinking skills. Critical reflection, a fundamental aspect of transformative learning, involves deeply questioning and examining one's assumptions, beliefs, and values. It provides individuals with the opportunity to challenge the status quo and consider alternative perspectives. Through critical reflection, individuals can construct their own reality by critically analyzing information, evaluating its relevance and appropriateness, and making informed judgments. This process of critical reflection is rooted in constructivism, where learners actively engage in constructing their knowledge and meaning. The transformative framework of learning is considered essential, especially in contexts where traditional educational structures may fail to address the needs of marginalized individuals or groups. Transformative learning theory provides a platform for marginalized individuals to critically reflect on their experiences, challenge oppressive systems, and empower themselves. One example of critical reflection is when individuals deeply question and examine their assumptions, beliefs, and values. This process allows them to challenge the status quo and consider alternative perspectives. Through critical reflection, individuals can construct their own reality by critically analyzing information, evaluating its relevance and appropriateness, and making informed judgments. By engaging in critical reflection and reshaping their meaning systems, marginalized individuals can develop a deeper understanding of their own agency and actively work towards social change and justice.

Furthermore, transformative learning is a process that prompts individuals to reconsider their understanding of themselves, their societal roles, and the potential for change. It necessitates an epistemological shift, driving changes not only in behavior but also in an individual's thoughts and perceptions. Transformative learning theory is considered essential, especially in contexts where traditional educational structures may fail to address the needs of marginalized individuals or groups. It provides a platform for marginalized individuals to critically reflect on their experiences, challenge oppressive systems, and empower themselves. By engaging in critical reflection and reshaping their meaning systems, marginalized individuals can develop a deeper understanding of their own agency and actively work towards social change and justice. By being conscious of their epistemological position and challenging existing understandings, students embark on a profound transformation within their academic journey. This transformation empowers them to critically analyze information, question assumptions, and seek new knowledge. For example, Gray et al. (2019) conducted a study on incarcerated individuals participating in a transformative learning program. They found that the participants' worldview changed because of their engagement in the program. Additionally, discussing specific prison-university education collaborations in the UK and their goals of prison education and community reintegration would provide further evidence of the transformative impact of education in marginalized communities.

Incorporating the transformative learning theory into research methodology, it becomes evident that qualitative methodologies are well-suited for exploring uncharted domains. Transformative learning theory, rooted in the belief in an individual's capacity to reach a new state of consciousness, emphasizes critical learning dimensions and the reassessment of assumptions and expectations. It acknowledges value conflicts and constraints and underscores the long-term and interactive nature of transformative learning. In reflecting upon their experiences, first-year doctoral students can harness transformative learning theory to enhance their sense of persistence, take charge of their learning experiences, seek feedback, connect with peers, and shape their career perspectives.

In conclusion, as discussed in this section, my academic journey demonstrates the profound impact of transformative learning and its integration into research methodology. It highlights the importance of persistence, adaptability, and critical reflection in the pursuit of higher education and personal growth. Additionally, transformative learning theory serves as a valuable framework for understanding the epistemological shifts and transformations that students undergo during their academic journeys. Transformative learning prompts individuals to reconsider their understanding of themselves, their societal roles, and the potential for change. It necessitates an epistemological shift, driving changes not only in behavior but also in an individual's thoughts and perceptions. By being conscious of their epistemological position and challenging existing understandings, students embark on a profound transformation within their academic journey. This transformation empowers them to critically analyze information, question assumptions, and seek new knowledge.

RESEARCHER POSITIONALITY

This autoethnography research explores the concept of research positionality, focusing on the experiences and motivations of a Black woman who is a first-year non-traditional doctoral student. It discusses the impact of personal challenges, such as racial oppression and a family medical crisis, on the writer's academic journey. A review of existing literature on research positionality reveals that scholars have long recognized the importance of personal experiences and identities in shaping the research process. Bourke (2014) shows how researchers, along with participants, shape a shared space. Our impressions of people and expectations of them shape our identities. Positionality is reflexivity if self-analysis is ongoing. The researcher's subjectivity will have an impact on their research and reporting. Qualitative research examines a problem through the lives of people and their details. Trinidad's 2024 research explores the positionality of education reformers, focusing on their strategies and constraints. It provides conceptual categories for understanding reformers, highlighting the importance of understanding their primary strategy and focus. By understanding the positionality of education reformers, Trinidad's research aims to shed light on the underlying motivations and biases that influence their decision-making processes. This analysis can help inform future reform efforts by recognizing the potential constraints and limitations faced by these individuals. Additionally, it emphasizes the need for a nuanced understanding of their primary strategies and areas of focus to address educational challenges effectively. By situating my own research positionality within this scholarly conversation, I aim to contribute to the ongoing dialogue on non-traditional doctorate scholars and their unique perspectives in the field of education. Furthermore, by examining the experiences and perspectives of non-traditional doctorate scholars, my research can provide valuable insights into how their contributions can be maximized and their voices amplified in academia. This understanding is crucial for fostering inclusivity and diversity within educational institutions and ensuring that all scholars have equal opportunities for success.

The year 2020 will forever be etched in our collective memory as a time of unprecedented challenges and reckoning with social injustices. As the world grappled with the devastating impact of the COVID-19 pandemic, the brutal killings of George Floyd and Breonna Taylor sent shockwaves through the nation, exposing the harsh realities of racial oppression and systemic racism. In August 2020, their names became a rallying cry for a movement determined to advocate for fairness, justice, and dignity for all. It was at this precise moment, amidst a global pandemic and a nationwide awakening to the pervasive issue of racial injustice, that a spark of motivation ignited within me. The tragic and unjust deaths of George Floyd and Breonna Taylor served as a catalyst for profound personal reflection. I was compelled to act, to contribute meaningfully to the ongoing struggle for equality and justice. In that transformative instant, I made a resolute decision – I would return to college to pursue a doctoral degree, after a ten-year hiatus from formal education.

With unwavering determination, I embarked on this new academic journey. I applied to a nearby university in Southwest Florida and, to my delight, received the news of my acceptance. However, the challenges that lay ahead were not confined to academia alone. In September, just days before my birthday, my mother called me from another state with heart-wrenching news – she had been diagnosed with ovarian cancer.

I comforted my mother over the phone, as she was distraught and terrified by the news. When I finally finished talking to her, I felt a rush of conflicting emotions. Both anger and sadness were washing over me. I cried out and collapsed to the floor. As I was crying, I called my prayer warrior friend and confidante to tell her that my mother was sick and that I was considering dropping out of college. My friend told me to stop crying and get up from the floor immediately. My incredible assistant principal friend helped me remember that my faith in God is more powerful than any illness, diagnosis, or academic challenge I may face. Right away, she had me turn to Deuteronomy 31:8 in the Bible, and we hung up. I spoke the verse aloud to myself, God himself will lead the way and stay by your side the entire way. Do not be afraid; do not be discouraged. A renewed burst of motivation led me to pray for my mom, myself, and my loved ones. I was now prepared to fight the battle against ovarian cancer alongside my mom. As a result of a medical crisis in the family, I took a significant amount of time off from my job to attend to my parents' needs.

The confluence of these pivotal events, the awakening to racial injustice and the profound impact of my mother's diagnosis, created a unique and deeply motivating moment. It became clear to me that pursuing a doctoral degree was not merely a personal aspiration; it was a means to effect positive change, to honor my mother's legacy of resilience and educational achievement, and to inspire future generations. This precise moment, characterized by anguish and determination, became the driving force behind my decision to navigate the challenging path of a non-traditional doctoral student. It symbolized my commitment to confronting adversity head-on and striving for academic excellence as a Black woman, dedicated to making a difference in a world in need of transformation and justice.

The juggling act I had to perform was extremely challenging, and the ongoing effort to find a healthy balance between these obligations constantly pushed me to my limits. Occasionally, the excessive stress and strain became too much for me to handle, prompting me to seek shelter in my closet, where I would find relief thanks to emotional episodes of sobbing. Amidst these instances, as tears commingled with the flavor of french fries, I pondered the notion of forsaking my doctorate studies. The burden of my responsibilities weighed heavily on me, leading me to adopt unhealthy coping strategies to deal with the constant strain.

However, over time, I came to realize that these strategies for dealing with stress were really making things worse, intensifying rather than reducing my stress and mental distress. The occurrence served as a pivotal moment that motivated me to pursue healthier choices for maintaining my overall well-being. I went on a quest to explore and understand myself better, choosing exercise to relieve stress and finding comfort in discussions with a therapist. This period of turmoil and personal exploration served as evidence of my unwavering resolve and taught me a valuable lesson about the significance of comprehensive wellness and adaptability. The experience highlighted my unwavering determination as I strive to obtain a doctoral degree as a Black woman non-traditional student, while remaining dedicated to both my family and academic goals.

The challenges of my first year in my doctoral program were highly specific and often felt like a relentless balancing act. One vivid example that encapsulates the struggles I faced was the rigorous coursework combined with my responsibilities as a middle school special education teacher. Imagine a situation where I found myself preparing for a crucial class presentation while simultaneously handling the intricacies of Individualized Education Programs (IEPs) for my students, each with their unique needs and learning plans.

The pressure was immense, and as my therapist guided me through this tumultuous journey, I realized that my usual coping mechanisms were inadequate and, in fact, detrimental to my well-being. This stark realization served as a catalyst for change, prompting me to prioritize my mental health. In one of our conversations, my therapist, a fellow Black woman, posed a poignant question: Why was I pursuing my doctorate?

Heeding her advice, I commenced a deep introspection of my motivations. It became clear that my pursuit was motivated not only by personal ambition but also by a strong desire to bring about positive change in my community. The recollection of my mother's resolute commitment to her academic pursuits, culminating in her attainment of a doctoral degree in the field of education more than forty years ago, rekindled my resolve to emulate her path. My determination to persist in the face of challenges went beyond my individual goals. I desired to serve as a role model for my family, particularly my girls, and showcase the significance of perseverance and resolve in the quest for advanced education. In addition, my objective was to enhance my knowledge and skills to progress in my professional life and, consequently, create a significant and beneficial influence in my community.

In August 2022, I decided to further my education by enrolling in an online doctoral program at a Historically Black College and University (HBCU) located in the U.S. Virgin Islands (UVI). This undertaking occurred while taking care of my elderly parents, helping my youngest daughter adjust to life after finishing college, and helping my oldest daughter manage her independence. Choosing to enroll in an HBCU for my doctoral program was a deliberate decision rooted in my commitment to supporting and uplifting historically marginalized communities. HBCUs have a long-standing tradition of providing high-quality education to Black students and have been instrumental in producing leaders in various fields. By enrolling in an HBCU, I am not only furthering my own education but also contributing to the legacy and impact of these institutions. Furthermore, I believe that being immersed in an environment that celebrates and prioritizes Black excellence will enhance my academic experience and allow me to connect with like-minded individuals who share my passion for social justice and equality. Additionally, by choosing an HBCU, I am actively supporting the mission of these institutions to empower and uplift people of color communities, which aligns with my personal values and aspirations for creating positive change in society.

All of this had a profound impact on my life. I had transformed into a doctoral student with a powerful sense of purpose, eager to contribute to society through research and teaching, and motivated by the desire to leave a lasting impact on the world. All that has transpired in my life has shaped me into someone different. During the day, I helped my parents, and in the evenings, I prepared for my two doctoral courses and authored papers. I am motivated to use my education and experiences to make a positive difference in the world, whether through research or teaching. My upbringing has transformed me into someone with a strong work ethic and the persistence to succeed, which I hope to channel into meaningful contributions to society.

In summary, even though the reasons stated above are valid ones, as the researcher, I wanted to provide an additional, more personal one for looking at this experience from an autoethnographic point of view. With the help of research questions, I will be able to compare the experiences of the participants to my own and learn more about the challenges and opportunities that non-traditional college students face. As a non-traditional college student, myself, I believe that this research will not only contribute to the existing literature but also provide me with a deeper understanding of my own experiences and how they relate to others in similar situations. The role in this study was that of a participant or researcher. As a participant in this study, I am enrolled at the University of the Virgin Islands as a first-year doctoral student. My interest in conducting my research arose from being a first-year non-traditional doctoral student facing challenges in life while pursuing a doctorate degree and learning how to be persistent in pursuing a goal while balancing personal responsibilities. This is an autoethnography of my personal journey as a transformative learning theory researcher, where I played a unique role and had a unique perspective.

NAVIGATING THE JOURNEY OF A NON-TRADITIONAL DOCTORAL STUDENT: CHALLENGES, TRANSFORMATIONS, AND THE POWER OF LIFELONG LEARNING

In this section, I reflect on my transformative journey as a non-traditional doctoral student. I emphasize the significance of lifelong learning and the crucial role that social-emotional skills play in achieving academic success. Additionally, I acknowledge the unique challenges faced by non-traditional students and advocate for the creation of a supportive and inclusive academic environment.

Here I am, back as a student. That was my precise idea on the first day of the first year of my doctoral program. On the first night of class, I thought, "This will be simple; all I have to do is stay up late and read papers on Saturday," because my professor had assigned ten lengthy peer-reviewed articles to read in a week. Was I ever mistaken? As the days went by, I noticed that each piece was full of difficult concepts and theories that I needed to read many times to properly comprehend. It took more time and effort on my side to make the necessary changes to balance my career, personal life, and academic schedule. I was finding who I was as a student and adopting new study habits to help me thrive academically. However, the struggle helped me mature and become a more confident and accomplished student.

Jenkins (2007) asserts that self-discovery is an essential component of the educational process. Therefore, going through the challenge of discovering who I was as a learner was not only necessary but also beneficial for my overall academic and personal growth. It allowed me to understand my strengths and weaknesses, which helped me transform effective study habits that have continued to serve me well in my academic pursuits. Is it possible for a student's own learning to be transformed through the process of self-discovery? In 1975, Mezirow introduced adult educators to transformative learning theory. Later, Habermas and Freire's work influenced Mezirow's theory. Adult education uses Mezirow's ideas (Wang et al., 2020). An example of my self-discovery through transformative learning would be when, as a working professional, I returned to school to pursue a doctoral degree. First-year non-traditional doctoral students are forced to adjust their routines and develop new study habits to balance work, personal life, and academic requirements. Through this process, the individual discovers who they are as learners and becomes a more confident and capable student.

Lifelong Learning: A Pathway to Personal Growth

Learning should become a routine for the individual to fulfill their purpose (Mercado & Shin, 2022). As a result of sustainable development, nations can build resilience and prepare for future challenges. Through lifelong learning, interdisciplinary discourse and research reveal brain development, degeneration, and plasticity. This interactive, life-wide space empowers learners from diverse backgrounds and societies to contribute to a learning planet through inclusive and participatory knowledge production and sharing (Goodwill & Chen, 2021). Found that better social-emotional skills were associated with better outcomes in all of these domains. This suggests that social-emotional skills are essential for student success and well-being.

Moore et al. (2010) explain that McClelland's accomplishment motivation theory, often known as the acquired needs hypothesis, states that people want connection, authority, and success. This concept argues that these expectations are learned throughout life and developed from his 1940s work. The premise that most people have a combination of these three goals emphasizes how important it is to understand human motivation to predict behavior and output. As a dedicated lifelong learner, I embrace my role as a first-year non-traditional doctoral student with the crown of "lifelong scholar." To be on a "lifelong scholar" path is to reap great benefits, and it has been and will continue to be a constant source of achievement motivation for me. I am resuming this path after a significant break because of my unwavering persistence and insatiable curiosity. The unwavering support of a nurturing community and specific resources, both of which illuminate the path through the complexities of pursuing a doctorate, strengthen the pillars of my journey.

After a long absence, I have returned to the academic world because I am determined to always be learning and improving. The symbolic crown adorning my head, bearing the title "lifelong scholar," stands as a testament to my unwavering dedication to intellectual ascent and the unending pursuit of knowledge. It is a constant reminder that education is not limited to a specific time or place but rather a lifelong journey, which fuels my passion for understanding the world around me.

Embracing the distinct paths traversed by non-traditional students pursuing doctoral studies, I wholeheartedly recognize the importance of delving into their exceptional challenges and diverse backgrounds. Working, taking care of family, and pursuing academic pursuits require an understanding of this delicate dance and specific resources. Through addressing these numerous challenges and fostering an inclusive and supportive academic environment, universities can significantly increase the success and satisfaction of their non-traditional doctoral scholars. Research, based on empathy and adaptability, could lead to a transformative and enriching academic journey for everyone.

As a result of my exploration, I am intimately aware of the emotional toll that graduate school can impose. At various points, I was confronted with overwhelming feelings, a sense of inadequacy, and a cloud of uncertainty regarding my own abilities. I frequently wondered if my struggles were isolated or if my fellow students had experienced similar difficulties. I found that other researchers had identified similar themes, reassuring me that my experiences were not unique.

Furthermore, identifying specific skills such as self-control, trust, optimism, and energy allows for targeted interventions and support to enhance academic achievement and overall well-being among students. I experienced this firsthand as a non-traditional doctoral student who struggled with time management and self-discipline. I enhanced my focus and achievement motivation through the development of social-emotional skills, which resulted in increased research productivity and academic victory. This personal experience reinforces the importance of integrating social-emotional learning into educational settings to support students' holistic growth and success.

Learning is not bound by time or place; it is a lifelong journey that continuously fuels my passion for understanding the world. As a dedicated lifelong learner, I proudly wear the crown of a "lifelong scholar." This symbolic crown on my head serves as a constant reminder that education knows no limits. It inspires me to pursue knowledge tirelessly, regardless of age or circumstance. Returning to academia after a significant hiatus, I am driven by an unwavering commitment to intellectual ascent and the unending pursuit of knowledge.

Non-traditional doctoral students, like me, embark on unique journeys marked by challenges and triumphs. Balancing a full-time job, caring for my family, and pursuing a rigorous academic program is no small feat. The delicate dance between these responsibilities requires specific resources and a deep understanding of the nuances involved. To enhance the success and satisfaction of non-traditional doctoral scholars, universities must address these challenges and foster an inclusive and supportive academic environment. During my journey, I have keenly felt the emotional toll that graduate school can impose. Moments of overwhelming doubt and inadequacy were not uncommon. I often wondered if my struggles were isolated or shared by fellow students. Discovering that other researchers had encountered similar themes provided reassurance that I was not alone in my experiences.

The Power of Social-Emotional Skills: A Personal Transformation

Identifying specific social-emotional skills, such as self-control, trust, optimism, and energy, has allowed for targeted interventions to enhance both academic achievement and overall well-being. As a non-traditional doctoral student who initially grappled with time management and self-discipline, I experienced firsthand the transformative impact of developing these skills. The result was increased research productivity and academic success. This personal journey reinforces the importance of integrating social-emotional learning into educational settings to support holistic growth and achievement among students.

In my pursuit of a doctorate, I am motivated not only by personal achievement but also by the desire to create a positive impact in my community and inspire other Black women to pursue higher education. My mother's dedication to her own education, culminating in a doctorate more than four decades ago, serves as a powerful example. My persistence is a testament to my family, especially my daughters, and a commitment to expanding my knowledge and skills to contribute meaningfully to my community.

Evolving Landscape: The Unique Challenges and Resilience of Non-Traditional Students

As the world grapples with an unprecedented global health crisis, the landscape of non-traditional students is evolving. One big change is that there are more college students in their late twenties than ever before. This is because people are delaying going to college, taking longer to finish their degrees, having trouble finding work, and using online learning options (Battiste & Battiste, 2022). Non-traditional students are a diverse and complicated group. They are often defined by their age (especially those over 24), race, gender, living off-campus, full-time jobs, and enrollment in occupational programs that do not lead to a degree. These individuals, typically juggling family, work, and financial responsibilities, navigate educational pursuits amidst a unique set of challenges. In contrast to their traditional counterparts, who attend college for social and academic reasons, non-traditional students prioritize academic considerations. Often married with dependents and burdened by financial obligations like mortgages, these students work to supplement their income, reflecting the multifaceted nature of their academic journey.

I have faced my fair share of obstacles as a non-traditional doctoral student, such as balancing my academic responsibilities with my family and work commitments. Being a non-traditional student means that I often must navigate through a different set of challenges compared to my traditional counterparts, such as managing my time effectively and finding resources that cater to my specific needs. These challenges can include juggling multiple roles and responsibilities, adapting to new learning environments, and seeking support systems that understand the unique demands of non-traditional students. However, despite these obstacles, being a non-traditional student has also provided me with valuable life experiences and a strong sense of determination to succeed in my academic pursuits. Both successes and difficulties have influenced the decisions I have made at every academic crossroad I have come to, but they have all strengthened my resolve. I am inspired to help other non-traditional students overcome their own hurdles and create their own unique narratives.

Using an autoethnographic lens, I am equipped to gain a deeper understanding of the unique experiences of non-traditional students. With this knowledge, I can provide guidance to universities to facilitate the necessary transformation. By advocating for the implementation of more inclusive policies and support systems, I hope to create a more welcoming and accessible environment for non-traditional students. Additionally, I aim to raise awareness about the valuable contributions that these students can make to the academic community, fostering a culture of appreciation and respect for their diverse perspectives.

Building on Davidson and Wilson's (2013) perspective, the concept of collective identity is identified as the cornerstone of student integration within a larger group. They argue that a student's perception of themselves within this broader context forms the foundation of their collective identity. In this framework, the significance of the larger identity within the given situation takes precedence over individual traits. Consequently, if the collective identity holds the utmost importance in determining retention, individual characteristics diminish in significance, highlighting the increasing relevance of the cohort model in fostering a sense of community and supporting academic persistence.

Unlike their traditional counterparts, non-traditional students are motivated primarily by academic considerations, prioritizing educational objectives over social aspects. This cohort is frequently composed of married individuals with dependents, who contend with additional financial obligations such as mortgages. To meet these financial demands, non-traditional students often engage in employment to supplement their income. Qualitative research seeks to uncover the meanings individuals ascribe to their experiences (Van Manen, 1990; Morrow & Smith, 1995; Creswell, 2013). According to Creswell (1994, 2007, 2013), this method delves into human issues, enabling authentic storytelling and offering the most effective avenue to comprehend human experiences. Cultivating a sense of community through shared personal narratives enriches understanding in qualitative research and cohort-based doctoral education, leading to profound insights. This research approach not only stimulates creativity and collaboration but also allows researchers to delve more deeply into complex topics with thorough exploration.

Finally, in the field of educational research, Adkins and Hughes (2020) underline the varied formats in which autoethnography is presented, including books, book chapters, dissertations, blind peer-reviewed journal articles and professional development courses. Hughes (2020) underscores its effectiveness in prompting users to critically examine their leadership, teaching, and learning experiences. Employing autoethnography as a qualitative methodology in this study has allowed me, as the researcher, to delve into my own experiences and emotions related to the research topic, providing a distinctive and valuable perspective. Furthermore, autoethnography has served as a tool for personal growth and reflection, compelling me to confront and reassess my own perspectives and ideas.

TRANSFORMATIONAL LEARNING THEORY

students' academic journeys cannot be overstated. It serves as a powerful tool that can catalyze personal growth, enhance decision-making skills, and empower individuals to navigate the intricate landscapes of higher education. The benefits of transformative learning extend beyond the individual, positively impacting institutions and society as a whole. Transformative learning can lead to a more educated and empowered population, fostering innovation and progress in various fields.

Research by Chang et al. (2011) sheds light on the transformative potential of graduate education programs, emphasizing their role in creating a more supportive and effective model for doctoral students. Their findings indicate a notable increase in the number of doctoral degrees awarded, particularly among underrepresented minority students, in institutions that implement transformative graduate programs. This highlights the transformative power of education programs designed to foster critical reflection and holistic growth. These programs not only provide students with the necessary skills and knowledge in their respective fields but also encourage them to think critically, challenge existing norms, and push the boundaries of innovation. By creating a supportive and inclusive environment, transformative graduate education programs empower students to become agents of change and contribute to societal progress in meaningful ways.

Due to global rivalry, Chang et al. (2011) report a growing need for highly qualified workers in science, technology, engineering, and mathematics. If graduate education trends change, the US may lose its dominance in scientific and technical disciplines. The lack of doctorate advancement threatens faculty recruitment and could start a downward spiral. This could have detrimental effects on innovation and economic growth in the long run.

Furthermore, according to Chang et al.'s (2011) research, the influence of transformative graduate programs extends to diverse student populations, including transgender and gender non-conforming individuals. Their presence contributes positively to the overall completion rates of doctoral degrees, emphasizing the inclusivity and equity that transformative approaches can bring to higher education. However, it is crucial to acknowledge that the impact of these programs may vary depending on institutional settings, especially concerning the experiences of women and minority students. It is important to recognize that while transformative graduate programs have been shown to have a positive impact on completion rates for doctoral degrees, there are still challenges that need to be addressed. For example, women and minority students may face additional barriers and inequalities that can hinder their success in these programs. It is essential for institutions to actively work towards creating a more inclusive and supportive environment for all students, regardless of their gender or minority status, to ensure equitable outcomes in graduate education.

In conclusion, the integration of transformative learning theory in the educational journey of non-traditional doctoral students not only enhances their individual growth but also promotes inclusivity, diversity, and higher academic attainment. As educators and learners alike prioritize reflection and critical review, they pave the way for a more equitable and transformative educational landscape that benefits all members of the academic community. By actively incorporating transformative learning theory into graduate education, institutions can create a supportive environment that acknowledges and embraces the diverse experiences and perspectives of students. This approach encourages students to critically examine their own assumptions and biases, fostering a culture of respect and understanding. Ultimately, the integration of transformative learning theory empowers non-traditional doctoral students to reach their full potential while contributing to a more inclusive and equitable academic community.

Ortiz et al. (2021) conducted a comprehensive study exploring the transformative impact of the COVID-19 pandemic on higher education. The study revealed a rich tapestry of 14 higher education trends, thoughtfully classified into themes of online, blended, and lifelong learning. The result of this seminal effort was the compilation of an inventory consisting of thirty-four novel pedagogical approaches, which made a substantial contribution to a more nuanced comprehension of the evolving educational environment. Researchers used a detailed thematic analysis to find and look into 30 chosen institutional initiatives. This led to the discovery of 12 main themes in pedagogy. This exploration resulted in the emergence of the IDEAS framework as a guiding beacon for the transformation of next-generation pedagogy. The study tells an interesting story of how collaborative and flexible innovations in education have led to smart and distributed teaching methods that make learning fun, flexible, and situated.

In their academic work, Ortiz et al. (2021) gave a deep look at how quickly college classes moved online after the pandemic, pointing out important differences in quality, acceptance, completion, and learning. Their research included a close look at new teaching methods and methods, which led to the discovery of 14 distinct trends in online, blended, and lifelong learning. This in-depth exploration ultimately led to the recognition of 34 pioneering teaching approaches within the evolving educational landscape.

The findings of Ortiz et al. (2021) are in perfect accord with Mezirow's (1991) formulation of transformational learning theory, despite the unprecedented difficulties brought about by the global pandemic. The study supports the theory's main ideas by focusing on flexible and learner-centered approaches. It challenges traditional ways of teaching to make learning more interesting and dynamic. It also emphasizes the importance of personalized and tailored learning experiences. The study also demonstrates that transformational learning can be effectively implemented despite the obstacles posed by the pandemic.

Ortiz et al.'s (2021) emphasis on higher education institutions breaking away from rigid structures and embracing flexibility resonates with Mezirow's (1991) vision of transformative learning. The study suggests changing the way schools work to meet the needs of all kinds of students, which is similar to how transformative learning needs to break away from old ways of thinking. Transformative learning requires learners to be open to new ideas and ways of thinking. It also requires them to reflect on their own beliefs and values and to challenge existing assumptions. Finally, it requires them to act and apply new knowledge and skills to their own lives.

In addition to being an empirical study, Ortiz et al.'s (2021) study plays a key role as an empowering guide, which is perfectly in line with the transformative learning framework's main goal of promoting empowerment and agency. The results help educators, policymakers, and other interested parties move toward a future where education changes to meet the needs of students and society. This is a strong reflection of the empowering nature of transformative learning and this shift in education has the potential to create a brighter future for lifelong scholars globally. It is an important reminder that education can be a powerful tool for positive change.

The study's resonance with transformational learning theory underscores its significance as a catalyst for positive change within higher education. Echoing Mezirow's (1991) vision, the research leaves an indelible imprint, serving as an ode to education's intrinsic ability to transcend conventional boundaries and propel future generations toward an enlightened and empowered future. Therefore, it is important to ensure that students have access to adequate support and community to help them stay achievement-motivated and engaged. Furthermore, educational institutions should provide the necessary resources and guidance to help students stay on track and achieve their goals.

After 45 years, the concept of transformative learning, with all its accompanying theories and approaches, is now a "mature," broadly, and sometimes vaguely defined area of research and practice (Hoggan & Finnegan, 2023). For example, a student who enters a transformative graduate program may be challenged to rethink their assumptions about education and their role as a scholar. Through reflection and critical review, they may develop new perspectives and approaches to research that leads to breakthroughs in their field of study. This type of transformational learning can have a ripple effect, impacting not only the individual student but also their colleagues, mentors, and future students or collaborators.

The study of transformative learning theory has allowed me to reflect extensively on my identity as a non-traditional doctoral student in my first year. This transformative learning understanding has helped me to approach my studies with a growth mindset and to seek out opportunities for mentorship and collaboration with my peers. I believe that incorporating transformative learning principles into doctoral programs can benefit all students, regardless of their background or academic discipline. By forcing me to reflect on my own perspective and biases, this method has helped me gain a deeper appreciation for the varied life experiences of my peers and cohort members. By embracing the transformative learning theory, I have been able to develop a more open-minded and empathetic way of doing my schoolwork and talking to people in my personal life. For example, I now look at problems with a "growth mindset" and see mistakes as chances to learn.

As a doctoral candidate, I must conclude that prior to developing an understanding of transformational learning theory, I often experienced discouragement and abandoned endeavors when confronted with difficult tasks or setbacks. That experience has transformed me by leading me to discover the term "doctorateness" and the importance of persistence in the pursuit of academic and professional goals. Through transformative learning theory, I have learned to embrace challenges as opportunities for growth and development. My first year as a non-traditional doctoral student has shown me the importance of perseverance and the idea of "doctorateness" in the pursuit of academic and professional success. As non-traditional first-year doctoral students, we should see challenges as opportunities to grow and learn as seen in our contributions to expanding the body of knowledge and producing useful information. By persistently pushing through obstacles and setbacks, we not only enhance our own knowledge and skills, but also contribute to the broader academic and professional community. Our unique perspectives and experiences as non-traditional students can bring valuable insights and innovations to the table. Therefore, it is crucial for us to maintain a mindset of resilience and determination, continuously seeking out new challenges and opportunities to further our academic and professional goals. With persistence, we can overcome any hurdle and make meaningful contributions to our chosen fields.

PERSISTENCE THEORY

Persistence is the ability to persevere in the pursuit of a goal even when obstacles exist. It is characterized as an active kind of motivation and is based on the belief that a student must persevere and expend significant effort to increase student retention (Tinto, 2017). To guarantee academic achievement, Tinto's idea of student retention emphasizes the significance of intellectual, social, and emotional integration (Massyn, 2021). According to Nicoletti (2019), Tinto's persistence theory is the key variable that creates an interplay between a student's academic involvement and the achievement of an educational goal. Persistence is the fuel that drives learners to achievement, and retention is how this outcome can be attained. I believe that by fostering a culture of persistence and providing support systems for students, educational institutions can greatly enhance student success rates. Additionally, understanding the factors that contribute to persistence, such as motivation and self-efficacy, can help educators develop targeted interventions to promote student engagement and ultimately improve outcomes.

Elliott (according to Tinto's "Model of Institutional Departure," students must be integrated into formal (academic performance) and informal (faculty/staff interactions) academic systems, as well as formal (extracurricular activities) and informal (peer-group interactions) social systems, to persist. The first semester of college was a struggle for me academically and mentally, but I found a supportive community among my cohort members who were teachers, and we became close friends who helped me navigate the academic and social systems of the university, providing an example of the persistence theory in action. As a Black woman and non-traditional doctoral student in my inaugural year, I grappled with challenges that echoed the experiences of many on similar academic journeys. Balancing off-campus work during the day created a distinct hurdle, particularly in establishing connections with professors and participating in on-campus activities, predominantly tailored for undergraduates. As a teacher, for instance, I was able to make the most of my short lunch breaks by participating in online writing labs and research workshops that fit into my workweek. Struggling to harmonize these responsibilities persisted throughout my doctoral studies. In moments where I could not virtually attend research workshops during my workday, my cohort members emerged as vital allies. They played a pivotal role by ensuring I did not miss crucial information, diligently taking notes and sharing resources. Additionally, a supportive teacher friend at work proved indispensable, graciously covering my class during lunch to acknowledge the dedication I poured into my research paper until my class returned. These collaborative efforts became keystones in surmounting the challenges of managing both academic and professional responsibilities. Despite the obstacles, the unwavering support from fellow non-traditional doctoral students, especially within our cohort of teachers and working professionals, illustrated the theory of persistence in vivid, empowering detail. The hurdles underscored that perseverance propels students to success, with a supportive community serving as the vehicle through which this success is achieved.

Boulton et al. (2019) describe the concept of persistence as the significance of attrition in American doctoral programs, which was developed in the works of Holmes et al. (2016) and Santicola (2013). The previous studies of Boulton et al. (2019) reveal the personal qualities needed to complete a doctoral degree in the face of typical challenges. These qualities are crucial for providing intrinsic motivation and assisting doctoral students in achieving their goals. With a high level of requirements, many doctoral students doubt their abilities and consider quitting when they believe they lack the necessary skills to succeed as researchers (Van der Linden et al., 2018, p. 100). In the literature on persistence, is defined as "a characteristic in which an individual displays a voluntary, enduring commitment to a goal or course of action despite obstacles and/or opposition" (Cohen, 2011, p. 65). Facing the demanding nature of doctoral programs, many students begin to question their abilities and contemplate quitting. (Van der Linden et al., 2018). Doctoral students who felt less isolated and were more engaged in their studies were more likely to be persistent (Van Rooij et al., 2019).

Because earning a doctorate degree in teaching is a rigorous multiple year endeavor that demands students' undivided attention, persistence is of the utmost importance for achievement (Boulton, 2019). The support and community provided by cohort members and friends can help individuals overcome obstacles and remain committed to their goals (Westbrooks et al., 2020). Boone et al. (2020) assert that personal qualities such as self-motivation and active engagement in studies are essential for maintaining persistence and achieving success. To strive for excellence, one must commit to lifelong learning, a commitment that demands both persistence and commitment (Boysen, 2016).

Self-Motivation Theory: The Key to Success for Non-Traditional Doctoral Students

Bandura (1991), the founding father of motivation theory, explains that the self-motivating function is an important factor in goal attainment because it encourages people to pay close attention to their performances and set progressive improvement goals for themselves. Variations in motivation are reflected in motivation diversity, and those who do not set goals for themselves experience no change in effort. Bandura (1991) adds that attributes, self-monitoring type and nature, and temporal proximity to change-worthy behavior can all affect the likelihood of self-reflective influences from observing behavior. Regular self-regulation works better.

As a non-traditional doctoral student who has learned to be self-motivated, I set specific goals for myself, such as completing a certain amount of research each week or practicing academic writing through my assignments on a weekly basis. I make it a point now to monitor my progress regularly and consistently work towards my academic goals. This helps me stay motivated and persistent in achieving success. Keeping a journal and scheduling regular "me time" has also been instrumental in helping me push past setbacks and remain persistent and motivated in my own and my academic pursuits.

According to Bandura (1991), people cannot effectively influence their own motivation and actions if they do not pay attention to their own performances, the conditions under which they occur, and the immediate and distal effects they produce. As a result, the fidelity, consistency, and temporal proximity of self-monitoring play a role in self-regulation success (1991). Through my experiences, I have gained knowledge and an understanding that self-monitoring involves paying attention to one's own performance, the circumstances surrounding it, and the outcomes it produces. By doing so, first-year non-traditional doctoral students can effectively influence their own motivation and actions, leading to greater success in self-motivation.

Students quit universities for the following three primary reasons, according to Vincent Tinto (1993): academic difficulties, incapacity to achieve educational and professional objectives, and incapability to engage in or stay a part of the intellectual and social life of the institution. Individuals possess the capacity to regulate their thoughts, emotions, drive, and behaviors by utilizing their self-reflective and self-reactive capabilities. A pertinent illustration pertaining to the insight would be when I encountered scholastic challenges but perseveres by establishing precise objectives and consistently assessing my advancement, hence maintaining motivation and persistence in pursuit of academic achievement. An individual's perspective is altered when they confront life-altering obstacles. Success and accomplishments in conquering obstacles are sparked by divine intervention (Boysen, 2016). By practicing this form of self-regulation, students can enhance their probability of achieving success and reduce the potential of dropping out of the program.

Therefore, it is important for educational institutions to provide resources and support to help students overcome academic difficulties and achieve their goals, as well as create a welcoming and inclusive environment that fosters intellectual and social engagement. Additionally, promoting the development of self-reflective and self-reactive abilities can empower students to take control of their own success and stay committed to their educational journey. I believe that providing students with resources such as academic advising, tutoring services, and mentorship programs can help them overcome academic difficulties and achieve their educational goals. Additionally, creating a welcoming and inclusive campus environment that fosters social connections and community involvement can help students feel more connected to higher education organizations and reduce the likelihood of departure.

Academic establishments are crucial in facilitating the progress of non-traditional learners. Considering the parallel between my personal experience and Tinto's integration framework, it is imperative that academic institutions take the initiative to furnish students with the necessary help and resources to surmount academic challenges and attain their desired educational goals. Student integration is promoted by participation in information networks, according to study by Mechur Karp et al. (2008). These interconnected systems empower learners to effectively traverse the campus setting, get college-related information, foster a sense of social inclusion, and ultimately, recognize the concern of others for their scholastic well-being. Academic advising, mentorship programs, and supportive campus communities are among strategies that academic institutions may employ to enable non-traditional students to flourish in their scholarly endeavors.

In the grand tapestry of academic success, it is evident that self-motivation, while undeniably pivotal, does not operate in isolation. Just as Bandura's theory accentuates the value of self-motivation, Deci and Ryan's (2000), self-determination theory provides a complementary perspective on the role of external motivation. The harmony between these forms of motivation becomes apparent as I navigate my academic path. By embracing both intrinsic and extrinsic sources of motivation, I am in a much more positive frame of mind than I was. I have learned to prioritize self-care and set realistic expectations for myself. By taking breaks when needed and celebrating small successes along the way, I am able to maintain a positive outlook and stay committed to my academic pursuits.

EXPLORING DOCTORATENESS: DEFINITION, CHARACTERISTICS, AND IMPLICATIONS

Doctorateness is a term developed in the 1990s in discourses about threshold academic standards for degrees. It is more commonly used than "doctoralness" as it relates to "graduateness," a term used in UK education discourses, where "graduateness" is employed (Feast, 2022). In 2013, researcher Wellington (2013) first used the term "doctorateness." The word "doctorateness" is frequently characterized by the work done, such as generating new information, pushing the boundaries of what is known, contributing new or "original" knowledge, establishing a new research stance, or developing knowledge that may be "transferred" to industry or propagated. Wellington believed that the "doctorateness" debate should be revisited regularly and proposed five principles to address the question, creating a framework for future use. To what extent do students who have completed or are still engaged in a professional doctoral program consider that the product of their doctorate, or the process of doing it, has "impacted" their professional practice and development?

Bitzer (2015) says that "doctorateness" is a level of knowledge, skills, and attitudes that goes beyond fields of study, institutions, and doctoral procedures. Blitzer also says that it is expected to be shown in doctoral dissertations, which involve intellectualizing, conceptualizing, and adding to existing knowledge, skills, and attitudes (2015). Trafford and Leshem (2008) explain that "Doctorateness" is a term for behaviors that are common in academic settings, especially the university. It is a diagnostic tool for describing and explaining doctoral students' unique characteristics. Shokooh and Yazdani (2018) state that the term 'doctorateness' does not appear in dictionaries but can be found in almost all dictionaries with the meaning of the highest degree awarded by the university. No straight answer can be found in the doctoral education literature, and earlier authors have highlighted the difficulty of giving a definition.

Doctoral students are expected to make an "original contribution to knowledge," according to Trafford and Leshem (2009), and examiners determine whether or not this has been accomplished. Examiners form their opinions after reading the doctoral candidate's dissertation and discussing it with them during an oral examination. The path to a doctorate is intellectually rigorous for all candidates, and supervisors are active in guiding them (Trafford & Leshem, 2009).

Shokooh and Yazdani (2018) looked into what it means to have a doctorate and defined the term. "Doctorateness" is a term for behaviors that come up in different academic settings, especially among college students. Walker and Avant (2005) utilized a systematic eight-step method to evaluate "doctorateness" Shokooh and Yazdani (2018) explain that this evaluation method includes identifying the concept, determining the aims of the analysis, identifying relevant contexts, defining attributes and antecedents, specifying consequences and related concepts, validating the definition, and developing a model case. Their findings found that doctorateness is not just about academic achievement but also encompasses a set of behaviors and attitudes that are essential for success in academia. Students will use their resources as graduate students to see if it is possible for them to work with and/or manipulate an implicit or explicit concept. The doctorateness model addresses all the required characteristics from a variety of perspectives. It emphasizes the doctoral graduate's unique development. Having a clear understanding of the concept of "doctorateness" helps first-year non-traditional doctoral students and professors in their field of study because it expands their intellectual abilities and gives them a clear picture of their work, which makes it easier for them to remember their academic purpose.

When I initially became a doctoral student, I did not understand the idea of "doctorateness" and how it could benefit me in my academic pursuits. I started off thinking and acting like an "advanced undergraduate student," procrastinating and focusing on short-term goals. As I got further into my studies, I realized how important it was to make long-term plans and build a scholarly identity. I had to learn that "doctorateness" is more than just finishing classes and passing comprehensive exams. It also requires a commitment to research, critical thinking, and giving back to the academic community.

Understanding the value of "doctorateness" is an ongoing process that can help non-traditional first-year doctoral students become more knowledgeable and well-rounded scholars because it allows them to see the bigger picture of what it means to hold a doctoral degree and how they can make a meaningful impact in their field of study. Accepting the principles of doctorateness can also help non-traditional first-year doctoral students get better at managing their time, working with others, and communicating effectively. Now that I have changed the way I think, I realize how important it is to understand the concept of "doctorateness" and how it can help me improve my research skills and make important contributions to my field through original research. A comprehension of the concept of "doctorateness" and the development of research perseverance can significantly impact the motivation and capabilities of doctoral students, ultimately resulting in substantial contributions to their respective professional domains.

THE EDUCATIONAL COHORT MODEL: A POWERFUL STRATEGY FOR ENHANCING PERSISTENCE

As a student who entered and pursued a program of study with a group of purposefully selected peers, I experienced the benefits and drawbacks of the cohort approach. Like academic cohort models, these co-curricular program areas provide students with opportunities to interact with like-minded peers and have been shown to improve students' satisfaction with the institution (Bowman and Culver 2018; Reader 2018; Soria and Taylor 2016). Similar co-curricular programming can be more impactful in terms of the retention of students from historically underrepresented groups (Bowman and Culver 2018, Grier-Reed et al. 2016, Mosholder et al. 2016). My personal journey within this framework reaffirmed the transformative impact of this approach. By progressing as a collective, we developed a shared understanding that surpassed individual concerns, fostering a resilient spirit that bolstered our academic endeavors.

According to Pemberton and Akkary (2005), educational cohort models are groups of students who enter and go through a program of study together. They are characterized by social and cultural processes, increasingly utilized in both undergraduate and graduate programs as a response to evolving student demographics, aiming to enhance retention and overall program completion rates. Characterized by shared experiences and interactions, group, collaborative efforts, a sense of community, and a sense of belonging to a group. Researchcollective commitment to educational goals, group admissions and lock-step curricular development define the cohort approach (Pemberton & Akkary, 2005). According to research conducted by Lake et al. (2016) found that the cohort model helped students graduate and study, proving instrumental in fostering student graduation and mitigating the phenomenon of doctoral isolation. This data shows that the cohort model is more effective than traditional approaches. Students in a cohort model may receive more academic support than traditional students who do not remain with their cohort. Research by Lake et al. (2016), also found that the cohort model positively influenced student persistence to graduation and studied the reasons that contributed to doctoral isolation. When all of this information is looked at together, it shows that the cohort model is more likely to help students succeed than traditional methods. This means that students in a cohort model might find that they receive more support in their courses than traditional students who do not move along with their cohort through their curriculum.

Cohort models, in which students move through their courses in groups, can lessen the amount of anxiety that can arise from having new instructors every semester as they move through the course material. It gives them the tenacity they require to persevere and achieve academic success. Persistence as a doctoral student within this cohort model leads to eventually being awarded a doctoral degree. Transforming into "doctorateness" takes patience and persistence, which in turn promote well-being and future success. The most successful approach to being a doctoral student within this cohort model is to persistently work hard with the support of family and friends.

Anxiety brought on by frequently changing classes and professors can be lessened with the aid of cohort models.(Opacich, 2019). It can support first-year non-traditional students to develop persistence and succeed academically. This cohort model can help doctoral students earn their degrees. Within the cohort model, I learned the importance of collaboration and community-building, which not only helped me succeed academically but also provided a sense of belonging and support throughout my doctoral program in my first year. Reflecting on my personal journey through the educational cohort model, I've come to a profound realization that transcends mere academic insight. The ultimate key to not just surviving but thriving as a doctoral student within this nurturing framework is rooted in unwavering dedication. This dedication, however, is not a solitary endeavor but one that draws strength from the unwavering support of my cherished family and friends who steadfastly walked beside me every step of the way. Their encouragement, belief in my potential, and willingness to lend a helping hand, whether through late-night discussions or words of encouragement during challenging times, have been the bedrock upon which my academic journey within the cohort model has been built. Their presence has transformed mere dedication into a resilient force, propelling me forward with an unshakable resolve to overcome obstacles and achieve my aspirations.

Martinez-Vogt (2021) states that informal knowledge factors supporting doctoral student transition include program communication, point of concept onsite or remotely, academic program plan, cohort model, and online resources. Students should be informed of the cohort model, online resources, and program plan several weeks before the first fall semester. As a first-year non-traditional doctoral student, I know many of us struggle with the academic transition. Sharing experiences and communicating academic program requirements and resources can foster community and support in the cohort model. This can foster persistence and ultimately lead to the successful completion of the doctoral degree program. Martinez-Vogt (2021) adds that several factors can help doctoral students succeed, including good academic standing in the first semester and continued enrollment in the following semester (Martinez-Vogt, 2021). I have learned through experience that while the cohort model may be beneficial for some students, it may not work for everyone as individual learning styles and needs vary. Additionally, success in the first semester and continued enrollment are not solely dependent on the cohort model but also on various other factors, such as personal motivation, persistence with academic and career goals, and time management skills.

Anxiety and despair can cause doctoral students to fall behind on homework. Recognizing these pressures is essential for academic performance. By strengthening collegiate relationships with classmates and staff, the cohort approach can reduce turnover and ease feelings of negativity (Boysen, 2016). Educational cohort models are a powerful strategy for enhancing persistence and academic success, but they are not a guarantee of success on their own. In a few years, the mind is being molded in preparation for the completion and defense of a dissertation on a significant subject matter. This process is being guided by research, cohort models, and self-motivation (Boysen, 2016). Therefore, it is important for students to also develop and maintain good study habits and a strong work ethic to ensure continued success throughout their academic journey.

NEW AVENUES FOR FIRST-YEAR NON-TRADITIONAL DOCTORAL SCHOLARS

As a non-traditional doctoral student, I stand at the intersection of multiple identities, each shaping my academic journey in unique ways. The pursuit of knowledge at the doctoral level brings forth a plethora of factors that impact student well-being. Previous research on student well-being in doctoral programs has explored various factors that influence student success and retention. For example, Sverdlik et al. (2018) conducted a study that examined the impact of supervision, socialization, and motivational factors on doctoral students' well-being. In this autoethnography study, I contributed to the existing body of research by examining the role of cultural identity and its influence on doctoral students' well-being. By delving into my own experiences as a doctoral student from a diverse background, I shed light on the unique challenges and opportunities that arise when multiple identities intersect in academia. Through this study, I hope to contribute to a more comprehensive understanding of the factors that impact student well-being in doctoral programs and inform strategies for supporting the success and retention of diverse doctoral students. However, there is still a need for further research to fully understand the complex landscape of doctoral education and the factors that contribute to student well-being. By conducting more research, we can gain a deeper understanding of the specific barriers and resources that affect diverse doctoral students. This knowledge can then be used to develop targeted interventions and support systems that address their unique needs and promote their overall well-being throughout their academic journey. Additionally, exploring the experiences of diverse doctoral students can also help uncover any systemic issues within academia that may hinder their success and retention, leading to more inclusive and equitable doctoral programs.

In the intricate tapestry of my academic journey as a non-traditional doctoral student, my experiences are woven together much like the vibrant patches of my mother's colorful quilt. Just as every thread in that quilt carries a unique story and purpose, I, too, bring a diverse set of experiences and aspirations to the academic world. The rich diversity of non-traditional, first-generation, and part-time students is one that universities have the chance to embrace and celebrate, according to B. Holmes (2019). This acknowledgment, much like the selection of different fabrics for a quilt, is a crucial step in recognizing and valuing the unique backgrounds and needs of each doctoral student.

In this intricate pattern of support, institutions should place a heightened emphasis on providing a comprehensive array of services, including but not limited to career development opportunities and mental health resources. Just as a well-crafted quilt requires various materials, we, as doctoral candidates, require a robust support structure to flourish academically and personally. Much like the comforting warmth of a quilt on a cold night, mentoring programs and peer support groups play a vital role in nurturing the academic and psychological growth of non-traditional doctoral candidates in their first year of study, particularly within a cohort model setting. These programs create a sense of community and belonging, akin to the sense of togetherness one feels while working collectively on a shared project, such as quilting.

Throughout this academic quilt-making process, these initiatives not only provide invaluable guidance but also offer constructive criticism and feedback, much like fellow quilters discussing the placement of patches and the intricacies of design. In essence, my journey as a non-traditional doctoral student is like creating a beautiful and meaningful quilt, with each experience, challenge, and support system contributing to the intricate and colorful design. Just as my mother's quilt represents warmth, comfort, and a sense of home, I aim to create an academic journey that is inclusive, supportive, and ultimately enriching for myself and my fellow doctoral candidates.

The educational landscape is rife with structural constraints that contribute to significant disparities in educational attainment, perpetuating cycles of economic inequality and limiting social mobility. Addressing these disparities is a critical imperative, as it is vital to promote equitable outcomes and ensure that more individuals can attain qualifications beyond high school (Lumina Foundation, 2023). To bridge these gaps and provide equal opportunities, investments in educational programs targeting underserved communities are paramount. I experienced the hardships of financial barriers firsthand as a non-traditional doctoral student who is a single mother struggling to afford the cost of higher education. Without access to scholarships and financial aid, I would not have been able to pursue my own educational goals. Therefore, it is crucial that we prioritize initiatives that increase access to affordable higher education for all doctoral students, regardless of their socioeconomic background. However, it must be noted that simply providing scholarships and financial aid does not guarantee equal opportunities for all underserved communities. For instance, even with financial support, certain communities may still face systemic barriers such as a lack of quality educational resources, inadequate representation and support from faculty, or discriminatory admissions practices. These factors can hinder the ability of students from underserved backgrounds to fully benefit from and succeed in higher education, highlighting the need for comprehensive reforms that address these structural inequalities.

Empowering Persistence

Increasing the representation of minority graduate faculty members, particularly Black individuals, holds the key to fostering a more inclusive academic environment. By expanding opportunities for Black students, as well as women of all races, to engage and excel at the doctoral level, we not only enhance economic growth but also contribute to societal well-being (Ellis, 2001). When life for me became challenging, I sought support from mentors and advisors who understood the unique struggles I faced as a student from an underserved background. Their guidance and encouragement helped me navigate the obstacles and persevere in my educational journey. With their advice, I was able to transfer to the HBCU online postdoctoral program, where I was able to take care of my sick mother and my wheelchair-bound father without having to drop out of school. Their understanding and support allowed me to excel academically and fulfill my responsibilities as a caregiver. Through the online program, I was able to balance my studies with the demands of my personal life, ensuring that both my education and my family received the attention they needed. This experience not only strengthened my determination to succeed but also reinforced my belief in the power of education to transform lives. I am now more committed than ever to using my knowledge and skills to make a positive impact on society, particularly in underserved communities like the one I come from.

Additionally, I discovered the importance of building a strong network of peers who shared similar experiences, as we could provide each other with emotional support and share resources to overcome barriers together. This network of peers became like a second family to me, and we pushed each other to excel academically and professionally. Now, as a "lifelong scholar," I continue to seek out opportunities for growth and learning. I actively participate in conferences, workshops, and webinars to stay updated on the latest research and advancements in my field. This commitment to lifelong learning has not only expanded my knowledge but has also allowed me to contribute to the academic community by presenting my own research findings and insights. I am grateful for the support and guidance I have received throughout my educational journey, and I am excited to continue making meaningful contributions in my field of education.

To achieve these goals, a concerted effort is needed from higher education institutions. They must recognize the diversity within their student populations and celebrate it. Prioritizing comprehensive support services, including career development opportunities and mental health resources, is crucial to ensuring that every doctoral student has the tools needed to thrive academically and personally. Mentoring programs and peer support groups, particularly within a cohort model setting, can play a pivotal role in nurturing academic and psychological growth during the first year of doctoral study. However, a detailed counterexample to this approach can be seen in situations where higher education institutions fail to address the unique needs of their diverse student populations. For example, if a university does not provide adequate resources for career development or mental health support, it can hinder the academic and personal growth of doctoral students. Additionally, if mentoring programs or peer support groups are not inclusive or accessible to all students, it may further isolate certain individuals and limit their opportunities for growth during their first year of doctoral study.

In conclusion, there is an urgent need for more research on this subject, specifically with the experiences of non-traditional doctoral applicants, whom I affectionately refer to as "lifelong scholars." These individuals grapple with unique challenges, including the delicate balancing act of work and family responsibilities, which can significantly impact their academic journey. By gaining deeper insights into the triumphs and tribulations of these students, universities can tailor their resources and guidance to bolster their success, ultimately leading to higher retention rates. My hope for future first-year non-traditional doctoral students, particularly Black women like me, is that they do not feel defeated by the hurdles they encounter. By sharing our experiences, we can inspire and uplift others who face similar challenges. It is incumbent upon universities to create an environment that not only supports but also celebrates diversity, providing equitable opportunities for all students to thrive and succeed in their academic pursuits. Together, we can build a more inclusive and equitable future for all doctoral degree scholars.

SUMMARY OF NON-TRADITIONAL DOCTORAL STUDENT LITERATURE

This ethnography talks about the theories of transformational learning, persistence, motivation, and the postpositivist approach in terms of higher education and the motivation, persistence, and transformational learning of first-year non-traditional doctoral students who are working toward a doctorate degree. The reviewed literature related to the research questions in the literature review section and discussed how the research approaches are applied to transform graduate students' learning behaviors. It also defined "doctorateness" as the desired outcome, offered the concept of transformed graduate students and applied literature, and discussed the research approaches in relation to doctorateness. The ethnography further explored the factors influencing graduate students' learning behaviors, such as their prior educational experiences, personal motivations, and institutional support systems. Additionally, the literature review section identified various theoretical frameworks and models that have been used to understand and analyze graduate students' learning behaviors. These frameworks include transformative learning theory, self-motivation theory, and persistence theory. These frameworks provide a comprehensive understanding of the complex dynamics involved in graduate students' learning behaviors.

Transformative learning theory emphasizes the importance of critical reflection and personal growth in the learning process, while self-motivation theory focuses on intrinsic factors that drive individuals to engage in learning activities. Persistence theory, on the other hand, explores the factors that contribute to students' ability to persist and overcome challenges in their academic journey. By considering these theoretical frameworks, researchers can gain valuable insights into the multifaceted nature of graduate students' learning behaviors and develop effective strategies to support their educational development.

The ethnography further explored the practical implications of these theoretical frameworks in the context of graduate education. It delved into the ways in which transformational learning theory can be applied to foster growth and development in graduate students, highlighting the importance of self-reflection and critical thinking. Additionally, the ethnography examined the role of persistence theory in understanding the factors that contribute to graduate students' ability to persevere and succeed in their doctoral programs. It shed light on the significance of motivation and goal-setting in this process, emphasizing the need for intrinsic motivation and a clear sense of purpose. Furthermore, the postpositivist approach was critically examined, discussing its potential to provide a comprehensive understanding of the complex nature of graduate education and the diverse experiences of doctoral students. The ethnography aimed to integrate these various theoretical frameworks and research approaches to offer a holistic understanding of the concept of "doctorateness" and its impact on graduate students' learning behaviors.

In summary, the study highlighted the importance of understanding the unique challenges faced by doctoral students and the necessity of tailoring support and resources to meet their specific needs. It emphasized the significance of fostering a positive and supportive learning environment that promotes collaboration, self-reflection, and personal growth. Ultimately, the findings of this ethnographic study contribute to the ongoing conversation about how to best support doctoral students in their journey towards becoming successful scholars and professionals in their respective fields. I believe that creating a supportive and inclusive environment is crucial for fostering collaboration, self-reflection, and personal growth.

DISCUSSION

In this discussion, I will reflect on how persistence and transformational learning influenced my perception of the most significant events that occurred in my first year as a non-traditional doctoral student. "Lifelong scholars" who pursue their academic interests can benefit from personal growth and development, as well as contribute to the advancement of knowledge in various disciplines. They can also build a sense of community and receive valuable support throughout the research process, resulting in positive outcomes for themselves and society. Lifelong scholars gain a wealth of information and abilities that may be applied to improving their personal and professional lives through consistent intellectual engagement. Transformational learning adds to this process by enabling them to question their existing beliefs and perspectives, leading to a deeper understanding of themselves and the world around them.

The individual steps I took to successfully complete the most significant events that I experienced in my first year as a non-traditional doctoral student. These steps included finding a mentor, creating a strong support system, and managing my time effectively. These steps helped me overcome the difficulties of juggling coursework, research, and personal obligations while staying on track with my academic goals. I will also explain how my experiences as a non-traditional doctoral student enhanced my appreciation of the benefits of collaboration and resource utilization in achieving personal and academic goals. The assistance I need to accomplish my learning goals came from my university cohort family, friends and family for emotional support, and the ability to utilize accessible resources such writing centers, academic advisers, and research mentors. Furthermore, my research and coursework have been enhanced by the fresh perspectives and insights I have gained through collaboration.

In this autoethnography, I discussed how my first year as a non-traditional doctoral student taught me the value of seeking out encouragement from my cohort friends, mental support from family and friends, and the ability to make use of available resources like academic advisors, writing centers, and research mentors. My lived experiences have shown me that collaboration is not only beneficial for academic success, but also for personal growth and development. Through working with others, I have learned to value diverse perspectives and the importance of teamwork in achieving common goals. Utilizing resources has also helped me to stay on track and make the most of my time as a doctoral student. By taking advantage of available resources, I have been able to improve my writing skills, receive feedback on my research, and stay up-to-date on academic opportunities. Overall, my lived experiences have reinforced the importance of collaboration and resource utilization in achieving personal goals.

Furthermore, my experiences have shown me that collaboration is beneficial not only for academic success but also for personal growth and development. Through working with others, I have learned to value diverse perspectives and the importance of teamwork in achieving common goals. Utilizing resources has also helped me stay on track and make the most of my time as a doctoral student. By taking advantage of available resources, I have been able to improve my writing skills, receive feedback on my research, and stay up to date on academic opportunities. Overall, my lived experiences have reinforced the importance of collaboration and resource utilization in achieving personal goals.

In conclusion, research is limited on the topic of first-year non-traditional doctoral student retention due to the complexity and diversity of this population, but it is crucial for universities to prioritize their success to promote diversity and inclusivity in academia. Overall, utilizing resources and collaboration are keys to success as a doctoral student. Cohort models and mentorship programs can also be effective strategies for supporting doctoral students from diverse backgrounds, as they provide a sense of community and guidance throughout the academic journey. Additionally, universities should also prioritize funding and resources for research that addresses the unique challenges faced by underrepresented doctoral students.

CONCLUSION: ILLUMINATING THE TAPESTRY OF NON-TRADITIONAL DOCTORAL STUDENTS

As a result of this in-depth research of first-year non-traditional doctoral students, there is a need for more resources and support for these lifelong scholars. Mentoring programs and peer support groups can play a crucial role in their academic and personal development, providing a sense of community and valuable guidance throughout the research process. Additionally, further research is necessary to better understand the experiences of these "lifelong scholars" and the positive outcomes that can result from supporting their continued learning and intellectual pursuits. This ethnography starts with the fascinating journey of non-traditional doctoral scholars in higher education. It unfolds like a colorful tapestry, connecting the main themes of motivation, persistence, and learning that change lives. Using transformational achievement motivation theory, learning theory, persistence theory, and self-motivation theory, these narrative paints a comprehensive picture of the challenges and triumphs faced by a Black woman in her first year as a non-traditional doctoral student. This exploration, like the delicate patches of a soul-comforting handcrafted quilt, knits together theoretical insights and personal experience to build a dynamic tapestry that illustrates the nuanced topography of first-year doctoral literature.

As transformational approaches, ultimately, doctoral students can profit significantly by embracing the utilization of existing resources and seeking mentoring in order to attain their academic and personal objectives by capitalizing on the ample resources at their disposal. It is important for universities to recognize and address the unique needs of first-year non-traditional doctoral students in order to promote their success and retention in doctoral programs. Retention rates should motivate higher education institutions to provide adequate resources and support for non-traditional doctoral students, such as cohort model programs, mentorship programs, academic advising, and financial assistance, to ensure their academic and personal success. First-year non-traditional students are the hope for the future of higher education, and it is crucial to invest in their success to increase diversity, innovation, and excellence in academia. By providing the necessary resources and support, institutions can create a more inclusive and equitable environment for all students pursuing doctoral degrees.

Keep telling yourself, "I am capable of achieving my academic and personal goals, and there are resources and support available to help me succeed." Seek out mentorship opportunities and peer support groups in person and/or online, and don't be afraid to ask for help when needed. Remember that as a non-traditional doctoral student, your unique experiences and perspectives can bring valuable contributions to the academic community. Allow the echo of this empowering affirmation to resonate in your journey: "I possess the inherent power to manifest both my academic and personal aspirations. The path ahead is illuminated by the collective brilliance of my unique experiences, the steadfast support of my loved ones, and a wealth of accessible resources that will pave the way for my success in this transformative doctoral journey." Remember, as I did, doctoral candidates, that you will find your bearings by actively seeking out mentorship and making connections within peer networks, whether those networks exist in the real world or online. Helping yourself is a sign of strength, not weakness, so don't be afraid to ask for help when you need it. Keep in mind that your unconventional background is a treasure trove of insights that will transform the academic landscape and help to draw the map for tomorrow's educational adventure.

In the pursuit of my doctorate through non-traditional means, I am acutely aware of the myriad obstacles one must overcome. The distressingly high rates of attrition among doctoral students in higher education, particularly in online programs, are particularly concerning. The mysterious causes of this trend fuel my determination to defy the odds and achieve my academic goals. Despite alarming dropout rates, I have not allowed them to deter me; instead, they have served to fortify my resolve to succeed and attain the distinguished title of "lifelong scholar." Earning a doctorate degree demands unwavering tenacity.

This autoethnographic approach aims to delve into the nuances of doctoral student attrition rates, encompassing both on-campus and online options. The research aims to shed light on the main reasons why people drop out of programs and also on the good things that help people stay in and finish because the researchers really want to understand and solve the problem. Doctoral programs attract students from diverse backgrounds, necessitating an analysis of demographic data to develop interventions that speak to a wide range of individuals. Grounded in first-hand accounts, this study aspires to reform higher education by providing institutions with the data needed to create efficient support networks for their students. Inspired by my experience as a non-traditional doctoral student, the application of autoethnographic principles reveals crucial insights, paving the way for ongoing academic success.

My goal is to offer readers a nuanced picture of student attrition rates by illuminating the specific challenges faced by non-traditional doctoral candidates, especially those related to age. Intending to contribute to the broader discussion of doctoral programs through the lens of autoethnography, this initiative seeks to create a setting where students can thrive through perseverance and engagement. Studying completion rates across disciplines encourages me to maintain an attitude of "I can, and I will" continuously.

As a non-traditional student, I faced a lot of challenges when I began my doctoral studies, including feelings of isolation and the overwhelming pressure to perform well academically and socially. I overcame them with the help of my friends, family, and the internet. According to the findings, non-traditional doctoral students face higher rates of dropout due to factors such as family responsibilities, age, part-time enrollment, geographic distance from campus, and work-related demands. My goal in conducting this research is to help both other non-traditional students and their educational institutions reduce dropout rates. My goal is to inspire non-traditional doctoral students to persist in their studies by highlighting how they embody persistence theory and transformative learning. Non-traditional first-year doctoral students can gain confidence in their ability to shape their own educational experience by reading this study, which provides an inside look at the qualities of persistence and transformative learning exemplified by these students.

Beginning my doctoral studies as a non-traditional student presented me with a few difficulties, including feelings of isolation and intense pressure to succeed in both my academic and social pursuits. Overcoming them with the support of friends, family, and the internet, I discovered that non-traditional doctoral students face higher dropout rates due to factors such as family responsibilities, age, part-time enrollment, geographic distance from campus, and work-related demands. Conducting this research aims to assist both non-traditional students and their educational institutions in reducing dropout rates. The study seeks to inspire non-traditional doctoral students to persist in their studies by highlighting how they embody persistence theory and transformative learning. By offering an inside look at the qualities of persistence and transformative learning exemplified by these students, the study instills confidence in non-traditional first-year doctoral students to shape their educational experience.

As you navigate the intricate tapestry of your doctoral journey, envision yourself succeeding as a non-traditional student, fortified by abundant resources and unwavering support. Your path, strengthened by encouraging mentors and fellow travelers, stands as a testament to your enduring determination. The vibrant colors of your experiences, akin to the diverse patches in my mother's quilt, artfully paint the academic landscape. As a non-traditional doctoral scholar, wear the pride earned through your perseverance as you navigate this expansive canvas of knowledge, leaving behind a legacy that illuminates the way for future scholars. In every step, remember that your journey is not just a personal triumph but a contribution to the ever-evolving narrative of academia, where your unique story enriches the broader tapestry of scholarly pursuits.

REFERENCES

Adkins, S. D. H., & Hughes, S. (2020). Back to the future of autoethnography. *Journal of Autoethnography*, *1*(3), 297–303. doi:10.1525/joae.2020.1.3.297

Akrani, G., & Trivedi, J. A. (2019). Maslow's hierarchy of needs - theory of human motivation. *International Journal of Research in All Subjects in Multi Languages*, *7*(6). https://kalyan-city.blogspot.com/2010/06/maslow-hierarchy-of-needs-theory-of.html?

American Psychological Association. (2019). APA dictionary of psychology-persistence. *APA Dictionary of Psychology*. https://dictionary.apa.org/persistence

American Psychological Association. (2023). *Attrition*. APA Dictionary of Psychology. https://dictionary.apa.org/attrition

Ames, C., Berman, R., & Casteel, A. (2018). A preliminary examination of doctoral student retention factors in private online workspaces. *International Journal of Doctoral Studies, 13*, 79–107. doi:10.28945/3958

Ampaw, F. D., & Jaeger, A. J. (2011). Completing the Three Stages of Doctoral Education: An Event History Analysis. *Research in Higher Education*, *53*(6), 640–660. doi:10.1007/s11162-011-9250-3

Angelou, M. (2008). *Letter to my daughter*. Random House.

Arbelo-Marrero, F., & Milacci, F. (2015). A Phenomenological Investigation of the Academic Persistence of Undergraduate Hispanic Nontraditional Students at Hispanic Serving Institutions. *Journal of Hispanic Higher Education*, *15*(1), 22–40. doi:10.1177/1538192715584192

Bandura, A. (1991). Social cognitive theory of self-regulation. *Organizational Behavior and Human Decision Processes*, *50*(2), 248–287. doi:10.1016/0749-5978(91)90022-L

Battiste, K., & Battiste, K. (2022). *Who Are Today's Nontraditional Students?* AMG Higher Education Marketing. https://www.amghighered.com/who-are-todays-non-traditional-students/

Bernery, C., Lusardi, L., Marino, C., Philippe-Lesaffre, M., Angulo, E., Bonnaud, E., Guéry, L., Manfrini, E., Turbelin, A., Albert, C., Arbieu, U., & Courchamp, F. (2022). Highlighting the positive aspects of being a PhD student. *eLife*, *11*, e81075. Advance online publication. doi:10.7554/eLife.81075 PMID:35880403

Bitzer, E. (2015). Language of the doctorate: Doctorateness as a threshold concept in doctoral literacy. *Per Linguam*, *30*(3). Advance online publication. doi:10.5785/30-3-585

Boone, S. C., De Charon, L., Hill, M. J., Preiss, A., Ritter-Williams, D., & Young, E. (2020). Doctoral student persistence and progression: A program assessment. *Journal of Applied Research in Higher Education*, *12*(4), 753–765. doi:10.1108/JARHE-07-2019-0192

Börgeson, E., Soták, M., Kraft, J., Bagunu, G., Biörserud, C., & Lange, S. (2021). Challenges in PhD education due to COVID-19 - disrupted supervision or business as usual: A cross-sectional survey of Swedish biomedical sciences graduate students. *BMC Medical Education*, *21*(1), 294. Advance online publication. doi:10.1186/s12909-021-02727-3 PMID:34022871

Boström, M., Andersson, E., Berg, M., Gustafsson, K., Gustavsson, E., Hysing, E., Lidskog, R., Löfmarck, E., Ojala, M., Olsson, J., Singleton, B., Svenberg, S., Uggla, Y., & Öhman, J. (2018). Conditions for transformative learning for sustainable development: A theoretical review and approach. *Sustainability (Basel)*, *10*(12), 4479. Advance online publication. doi:10.3390/su10124479

Boulton, A. B. (2019). Personal motivation for professional identity: Persistence in the education doctorate. In *Doctoral student perspectives on motivation and persistence: Eye-opening insights into the ideas and thoughts that today's doctoral students have about finishing the doctoral degree* (1st ed., pp. 11–20). Education Doctorate Books. https://openriver.winona.edu/educationeddbooks

Boulton, A. B., Durnen, A. K., Boysen, B., Perry, C. L., Bailey, D., Mollner, J., Del La Fosse, K., Sinning, M. W., Guillaume, N. M., Breuninger, R., Jones, S., & Webber, S. (2019). *Doctoral Student Perspectives on Motivation and Persistence*. Academic Press.

Boysen, B. (2016). Realizing imperative motivation: A doctoral student's reflection. In *Doctoral student perspectives on motivation and persistence: Eye-opening insights into the ideas and thoughts that today's doctoral students have about finishing the doctoral degree* (1st ed., pp. 21–26). Education Doctorate Books. https://openriver.winona.edu/educationeddbooks

Bringle, R. G., Hatcher, J. A., & Muthiah, R. (2010). The Role of Service-Learning on the Retention of First-Year Students to Second Year. *Michigan Journal of Community Service Learning*, *16*(2), 38–49.

Brown-Rice, K., & Furr, S. (2019). Am I My Peers' Keeper? Problems of Professional Competency in Doctoral Students. *Teaching and Supervision in Counseling*, *1*(1). Advance online publication. doi:10.7290/tsc010104

Burke, A. (2019). Student Retention Models in Higher Education: A Literature Review. *College and University*, *94*(2), 12–21. https://eric.ed.gov/?id=EJ1216871

Carrington, L. G. (2016). *A Qualitative Phenomenological Study of Employee Perceptions of the Impact of Layoffs | Semantic Scholar*. Retrieved September 6, 2022, from https://www.semanticscholar.org/paper/A-Qualitative-Phenomenological-Study-of-Employee-of-Carrington/7804b43498bfb5624a1163ff1634614694f5129d

Caruth, G. D. (2018). Student Engagement, Retention, and Motivation: Assessing Academic success in Today's college students. *Participatory Educational Research*, *5*(1), 17–30. doi:10.17275/per.18.4.5.1

Chang, M., Kniola, D., & Olsen, D. (2011). Transformative graduate education programs: An analysis of impact on STEM and non-STEM Ph.D. completion. *Higher Education*, *63*(4), 473–495. doi:10.1007/s10734-011-9453-8

Chen, J. C. (2017). Nontraditional adult learners. *SAGE Open*, *7*(1), 215824401769716. doi:10.1177/2158244017697161

Clark, A. M. (1998). The qualitative-quantitative debate: Moving from positivism and confrontation to post-positivism and reconciliation. *Journal of Advanced Nursing*, *27*(6), 1242–1249. doi:10.1046/j.1365-2648.1998.00651.x PMID:9663876

Cohen, S. M. (2011). Doctoral persistence and doctoral program completion among nurses. *Nursing Forum*, *46*(2), 64–70. doi:10.1111/j.1744-6198.2011.00212.x PMID:21517879

Creswell, J. W. (1994). *Research Design: Qualitative, quantitative, and mixed methods approaches*. http://www.revistacomunicacion.org/pdf/n3/resenas/research_design_qualitative_quantitative_and_mixed_methods_approaches.pdf

Creswell, J. W. (2001). *Educational Research: Planning*. Conducting, and Evaluating Quantitative and Qualitative Research.

Creswell, J. W. (2007). *Qualitative inquiry and research design*. SAGE Publications.

Creswell, J. W. (2013). *Qualitative inquiry and research design: Choosing among five approaches*. SAGE Publications.

Creswell, J. W., & Poth, C. (2017). *Qualitative inquiry and research design: Choosing among five approaches* (4th ed.). SAGE Publications. https://us.sagepub.com/en-us/nam/qualitative-inquiry-and-research-design/book246896

Creswell, J. W., & Poth, C. N. (2018). *Qualitative inquiry and research design: Choosing among five approaches* (4th ed.). SAGE Publications, Inc.

Crumb, L., Haskins, N., Dean, L., & Avent Harris, J. (2020). Illuminating social-class identity: The persistence of working-class African American women doctoral students. *Journal of Diversity in Higher Education, 13*(3), 215–227. doi:10.1037/dhe0000109

Davidson, C., & Wilson, K. (2013). Reassessing Tinto's concepts of social and academic integration in student retention. Journal of College Student Retention: Research, Theory &Amp. *Journal of College Student Retention, 15*(3), 329–346. doi:10.2190/CS.15.3.b

Dictionary, C. (2022). *Doctoral meaning*. Retrieved October 9, 2022, from https://dictionary.cambridge.org/us/dictionary/english/doctoral

Edgar, S., Carr, S., Connaughton, J., & Celenza, A. (2019). Student motivation to learn: Is self-belief the key to transition and first year performance in an undergraduate health professions program? *BMC Medical Education, 19*(1), 111. Advance online publication. doi:10.1186/s12909-019-1539-5 PMID:30999916

Edwards, C. W. (2019). Overcoming imposter syndrome and stereotype threat: Reconceptualizing the definition of a scholar. Taboo. *Communications on Stochastic Analysis, 18*(1). Advance online publication. doi:10.31390/taboo.18.1.03

Elliott, K. E. (2022). *Academic achievement and degree attainment among college students with children* [PhD Dissertation]. University of Louisville.

Ellis, C., Adams, T. E., & Bochner, A. P. (2010). Autoethnography: An overview. *DOAJ (DOAJ: Directory of Open Access Journals)*. https://doaj.org/article/be64f48522e74cadba03b10a6794cb90

Ellis, E. M. (2001). The Impact of Race and Gender on Graduate School Socialization, Satisfaction with Doctoral Study, and Commitment to Degree Completion. *The Western Journal of Black Studies*, 25(1), 30–45. https://eric.ed.gov/?id=EJ646531

Feast, L. (2022). Down the brain drain: Searching for doctorateness in all the wrong places. She Ji. *The Journal of Design, Economics, and Innovation*, 8(1), 147–170. doi:10.1016/j.sheji.2021.11.001

Feenstra, S., Begeny, C. T., Ryan, M. K., Rink, F. A., Stoker, J. I., & Jordan, J. (2020). Contextualizing the impostor "Syndrome." *Frontiers in Psychology*, 11, 1–6. doi:10.3389/fpsyg.2020.575024 PMID:33312149

First year definition and meaning: Collins English dictionary. (2023). In *Collins Dictionaries*. https://www.collinsdictionary.com/us/dictionary/english/first-year

Frechette, J., Bitzas, V., Aubry, M., Kilpatrick, K., & Lavoie-Tremblay, M. (2020). Capturing Lived Experience: Methodological Considerations for Interpretive Phenomenological Inquiry. *International Journal of Qualitative Methods*, 19, 160940692090725. doi:10.1177/1609406920907254

Gibbs, K. D. Jr, & Griffin, K. A. (2013). What Do I Want to Be with My PhD? The Roles of Personal Values and Structural Dynamics in Shaping the Career Interests of Recent Biomedical Science PhD Graduates. *CBE Life Sciences Education*, 12(4), 711–723. doi:10.1187/cbe.13-02-0021 PMID:24297297

Gill, P. (2008, March 22). Methods of data collection in qualitative research: Interviews and focus groups. *Nature*. https://www.nature.com/articles/bdj.2008.192?error=cookies_not_supported&code=96b76f2d-0608-4b0f-8598-c28c87684671

Gittings, G. L., Bergman, M., Shuck, B., & Rose, K. C. (2018). The Impact of Student Attributes and Program Characteristics on Doctoral Degree Completion. *New Horizons in Adult Education and Human Resource Development*, 30(3), 3–22. doi:10.1002/nha3.20220

GoodwillA. G.ChenS. A. (2021). Embracing a culture of lifelong learning: The science of lifelong learning. *UNESCO Institute for Lifelong Learning UIL*, 1–11. https://doi.org/ doi:10.31234/osf.io/juefx

Grant, C., & Osanloo, A. (2014). Understanding, selecting, and integrating a theoretical framework in dissertation research: Creating the blueprint for your "House." *Administrative Issues Journal Education Practice and Research*, 4(2). doi:10.5929/2014.4.2.9

Grimes, D. A., & Schulz, K. F. (2002). Cohort studies: Marching towards outcomes. *Lancet*, *359*(9303), 341–345. doi:10.1016/S0140-6736(02)07500-1 PMID:11830217

Guo, J., Tang, X., Marsh, H. W., Parker, P. D., Basarkod, G., Sahdra, B. K., Ranta, M., & Salmela-Aro, K. (2023). The roles of social–emotional skills in students' academic and life success: A multi-informant and multicohort perspective. *Journal of Personality and Social Psychology*, *124*(5), 1079–1110. doi:10.1037/pspp0000426 PMID:35666915

Herrera, L., Trinh, E., & De Jesús Gómez Portillo, M. (2021). Cultivating calm and stillness at the doctoral level: A Collaborative Autoethnography. *Educational Studies (Ames)*, *58*(2), 121–140. doi:10.1080/00131946.2021.1947817

Hoggan, C., & Finnegan, F. (2023). Transformative learning theory: Where we are after 45 years. *New Directions for Adult and Continuing Education*, *2023*(177), 5–11. doi:10.1002/ace.20474

Holmes, B. (2016). *Decoding the persistence and engagement patterns of doctoral students who finish*. OpenRiver. https://openriver.winona.edu/educationeddfacultyworks/11

Holmes, B. (2019). *Doctoral student perspectives on motivation and persistence: Eye-Opening insights into the ideas and thoughts that today's doctoral students have about finishing the doctoral degree*. OpenRiver. https://openriver.winona.edu/educationeddbooks/1?utm_source=openriver.winona.edu%2Feducationeddbooks%2F1&utm_medium=PDF&utm_campaign=PDFCoverPages

Holmes, B. D., Birds, K., Seay, A. D., Smith, D. B., & Wilson, K. N. (2010). Cohort learning for graduate students at the dissertation stage. *Journal of College Teaching & Learning (TLC)*, *7*(1), 5–12. doi:10.19030/tlc.v7i1.73

Hurt, S., Woods Ways, E., & Holmes, B. (2022). Wait! Don't quit! Stay with your doctoral program during the global pandemic: Lessons learned from program completers global pandemic: Lessons learned from program completers. *The Journal of Advancing Education Practice*, *3*(1), 2. https://openriver.winona.edu/jaep/vol3/iss1/2

Hyde, B. (2021). Critical discourse and critical reflection in Mezirow's theory of transformative learning: A dialectic between ontology and epistemology (and a subtext of reflexivity mirroring my own Onto-Epistemological movement). *Adult Education Quarterly*, *71*(4), 373–388. doi:10.1177/07417136211003612

Irwin, V. I., De La Rosa, J., Wang, K. W., Hein, S. H., Zhang, J. Z., Burr, R. B., & Roberts, A. R. (2022). Report on the condition of education 2022. In *National Center for Educational Statistics* (NCES 2022-144). U.S. Department of Education. https://nces.ed.gov/pubsearch/ pubsinfo.asp?pubid=2022144

Janse, B. (2022, August 26). *Transformative Learning Theory (Mezirow).* Toolshero. Retrieved October 9, 2022, from https://www.toolshero.com/personal-development/transformative-learning-theory/

Kang, K. & National Center for Science and Engineering Statistics (NCSES). (2020). *Doctorate recipients from U.S. universities: 2020 NSF - National Science Foundation. Survey of Earned Doctorates.* https://ncses.nsf.gov/pubs/nsf22300/data-tables

Kuk, L., & Banning, J. H. (2014). A higher education leadership distance Ph.D. program: An assessment using blocher's ecological learning theory. *Creative Education, 05*(09), 701–712. doi:10.4236/ce.2014.59082

Lake, E. D., Koper, J., Balayan, A., & Lynch, L. (2016). Cohorts and connections. Journal of College Student Retention: Research, Theory &Amp. *Journal of College Student Retention, 20*(2), 197–214. doi:10.1177/1521025116656386

Litalien, D. (2020). *Improving PhD completion rates: Where should we start?* doi:10.1016/j.cedpsych.2015.03.004

Lively, C. (2021). The emerging scholars issue: Insights on teaching and leading through reshaping policy and practice: Reporting of doctoral student attrition: A policy brief. *Journal of Multicultural Affairs, 7*(3). https://scholarworks.sfasu.edu/jma/vol7/iss3

Martinez-Vogt, E. (2021). Students transitioning to a non-traditional doctoral program: Identifying success factors promoting Doctoral-level Academic Success. *Academia Letters.* Advance online publication. doi:10.20935/AL2285

Maslow, A. H. (1943). A theory of human motivation. *Psychological Review, 50*(4), 370–396. doi:10.1037/h0054346

Massyn, L. (2021). Persistence in doctoral education: A Part-Time research student perspective in a developing context. Journal of College Student Retention: Research, Theory &Amp. *Practice,* 1–19. doi:10.1177/15210251211007110

Maxfield, R. J. (2017). Epistemology and ontology: The lived experience of Non-Traditional adult students in online and Study-Abroad learning environments. *Journal of Organizational Psychology, 17*(6). Advance online publication. doi:10.33423/jop.v17i6.1513

McClelland, D. M. (2005). Achievement motivational theory. In *Organizational Behavior*. M.E. Sharpe. https://books.google.com/books?hl=en&lr=&id=kUO5N WwaySYC&oi=fnd&pg=PA46&dq=mcclelland+achievement+motivation+theor y&ots=UHcHDcKqEN&sig=luRy4GRDzJMEd_khRWysxm_o-v0

Mechur Karp, M., Hughes, K. L., & O'Gara, L. (2008). *An exploration of Tinto's integration framework for community college students* [PhD Dissertation]. Columbia University.

Mercado, F. M. S., & Shin, S. (2022). Teacher professional development in the 21st century. In IGI Global eBooks (pp. 227–254). doi:10.4018/978-1-6684-5316-2.ch012

Merriam, S. B. (2004). The Role of Cognitive Development in Mezirow's Transformational Learning Theory. *Adult Education Quarterly*, *55*(1), 60–68. doi:10.1177/0741713604268891

Metz, G. W. (2002). Challenges and changes to Tinto's persistence theory. *Annual Meeting of the Mid Western Educational Research Association*, 28. https://eric.ed.gov/?id=ED471529

Mezirow, J. (1978). Perspective transformation. *Adult Education*, *28*(2), 100–110. doi:10.1177/074171367802800202

Mezirow, J. (1991). *Transformative dimensions of adult learning* (1st ed.). The Jossey-Bass. https://www.umsl.edu/~henschkej/henschke/fostering_transformative_ adult_learning

Mezirow, J. (1994). Understanding Transformation Theory. *Adult Education Quarterly*, *44*(4), 222–232. doi:10.1177/074171369404400403

Mezirow, J. (1997). Transformative Learning: Theory to Practice. *New Directions for Adult and Continuing Education*, *1997*(74), 5–12. doi:10.1002/ace.7401

Mezirow, J. (2008). An overview on transformative learning. *Lifelong Learning*, 40–54. https://doi.org/ doi:10.4324/9780203936207-12

Mihalache, G. (2019). Heuristic inquiry: Differentiated from descriptive phenomenology and aligned with transpersonal research methods. *The Humanistic Psychologist*, *47*(2), 136–157. doi:10.1037/hum0000125

Miller, K. (2018). *Persistence*. Routledge Encyclopedia of Philosophy. doi:10.4324/0123456789-N126-1

Moran, M. (2021). *Almost 50% of all Doctoral Students Don't Graduate*. Statistics Solutions. https://www.statisticssolutions.com/almost-50-of-all-doctoral-students-dont-graduate/#:~:text=The%20Council%20of%20Graduate%20 Schools,program%20remains%20low%20at%2056.6%25

National Center for Education Statistics (NCES). (n.d.). *Nontraditional undergraduates-definitions and data. Who Is Nontraditional?* Retrieved August 21, 2023, from https://nces.ed.gov/pubs/web/97578e.asp

Nerstrom, N. (2014). An emerging model for transformative learning. *Adult Education Research Conference*, 325–330.

Neto, M. (2015). Educational motivation meets Maslow: Self- actualisation as contextual driver. *Journal of Student Engagement: Education Matters*, 5(1), 18–27.

Neubauer, B. E., Witkop, C. T., & Varpio, L. (2019). How phenomenology can help us learn from the experiences of others. *Perspectives on Medical Education*, 8(2), 90–97. doi:10.1007/S40037-019-0509-2 PMID:30953335

Nicoletti, M. D. C. (2019). Revisiting the Tinto's theoretical dropout model. *Higher Education Studies*, 9(3), 52. doi:10.5539/hes.v9n3p52

Nietzel, M. T. (2021, October 13). Ten ways U.S. doctoral degrees have changed in the past 20 years. *Forbes*. https://www.forbes.com/sites/michaeltnietzel/2021/10/13/ten-ways-us-doctoral-degrees-have-changed-in-the-past-20-years/?sh=3533ed5a2a71

Nimer, M. (2009). The doctoral cohort model: Increasing opportunities for success. *College Student Journal*, 43(4), 1373–1379. https://go.gale.com/ps/i.do?id=GALE %7CA217511799&sid=googleScholar&v=2.1&it=r&linkaccess=abs&issn=0146 3934&p=AONE&sw=w&userGroupName=tel_oweb#:~:text=The%20cohort%20 model%20consists%20of,a%20masters%20or%20doctoral%20degree

Northcentral University. (2016, December 9). *What is a doctorate degree*. Northcentral University. https://www.ncu.edu/student-experience/online-education-guide/doctoral-education/what-is-a-doctorate-degree#gref

Opacich, K. J. (2019). A cohort model and high impact practices in undergraduate public health education. *Frontiers in Public Health*, 7, 132. Advance online publication. doi:10.3389/fpubh.2019.00132 PMID:31192184

Ortiz, L. G., Clougher, D., Anderson, T., & Maina, M. F. (2021). IDEAS for Transforming Higher Education: An Overview of Ongoing Trends and challenges. *International Review of Research in Open and Distance Learning*, 22(2), 166–184. doi:10.19173/irrodl.v22i2.5206

Paprock, K. E. (1992). Mezirow, Jack. (1991) Transformative dimensions of adult learning. San Francisco: Jossey-Bass, 247 pages. $29.95. *Adult Education Quarterly*, *42*(3), 195–197. doi:10.1177/074171369204200309

Pemberton, C. L. A., & Akkary, R. K. (2005). A cohort, is a cohort, is a cohort. . .or is it? *Journal of Research on Leadership Education*, *5*(5), 179–208. doi:10.1177/194277511000500501

Perrine, R. (1998). Stress and college persistence as a function of attachment style. *Journal of the First-Year Experience & Students in Transition*, *1*(14), 25–38. https://www.ingentaconnect.com/content/fyesit/fyesit/1998/00000011/00000001/art00002

Perseverance. (2022). In *The Merriam-Webster.com Dictionary*. https://www.merriam-webster.com/dictionary/perseverance

PHD Researcher Demographics and Statistics [2022]: Number of PHD Researchers in The US. (2022, September 9). https://www.zippia.com/phd-researcher-jobs/demographics/

Phenomenology (Stanford Encyclopedia of Philosophy). (2013, December 16). https://plato.stanford.edu/entries/phenomenology/

Poock, M. C. (1999). Students of Color and Doctoral Programs: Factors Influencing the Application Decision in Higher Education Administration. *College and University*, *74*(3), 2–7. https://eric.ed.gov/?id=EJ588129

Poole, B. D. (2015). The rather elusive concept of 'doctorateness': A reaction to Wellington. *Studies in Higher Education*, *40*(9), 1507–1522. doi:10.1080/03075079.2013.873026

Poulos, C. N. (2021). Essentials of autoethnography. In American Psychological Association eBooks. doi:10.1037/0000222-000

Rigler, K. L., Jr., Bowlin, L. K., Sweat, K., Watts, S., & Throne, R. (2017). *Agency, socialization, and support: A critical review of doctoral student attrition.* Paper Presented at the 3rd International Conference on Doctoral Education, ED580853. https://www.google.com/url?sa=t&rct=j&q=&esrc=s&source=web&cd=&cad=rja&uact=8&ved=2ahUKEwjF8s2HrNn7AhUymmoFHR2LDGMQFnoECBMQAQ&url=https%3A%2F%2Ffiles.eric.ed.gov%2Ffulltext%2FED580853.pdf&usg=AOvVaw3hwtObTyWn9Mi7ht7QmbLk

Rogers-Shaw, C. A., & Carr-Chellman, D. (2018). Developing care and socio-emotional learning in first year doctoral students: Building capacity for success. *International Journal of Doctoral Studies*, *13*, 233–253. doi:10.28945/4064

Rowlands, S. L. R. (2010). *Nontraditional students: The impact of role strain on their identity* [PhD Dissertation]. Southern Illinois University Carbondale.

Ruud, C. M., Saclarides, E. S., George-Jackson, C. E., & Lubienski, S. T. (2016). Tipping Points. Journal of College Student Retention: Research, Theory &Amp. *Journal of College Student Retention, 20*(3), 286–307. doi:10.1177/1521025116666082

Ryan, R. M., & Deci, E. L. (2000). Self-determination theory and the facilitation of intrinsic motivation, social development, and well-being. *The American Psychologist, 55*(1), 68–78. doi:10.1037/0003-066X.55.1.68 PMID:11392867

Santicola, L. (2013). Pressing On: Persistence Through A Doctoral Cohort Program In Education. *Contemporary Issues in Education Research, 6*(2), 253. doi:10.19030/cier.v6i2.7736

Saxena, L. (2022, November 15). *Higher education fails to support non-traditional students – The Statesman*. The Statesman. https://www.sbstatesman.com/2022/11/13/higher-education-fails-to-support-non-traditional-students/

Schaffner, A. K. (2020). Perseverance in psychology: Meaning, importance & books. *PositivePsychology.com*. https://positivepsychology.com/perseverance/#google_vignette

Schiller, C. J. (2018). Teaching concept analysis to graduate nursing students. *Nursing Forum, 53*(2), 248–254. doi:10.1111/nuf.12233 PMID:29327788

Seniuk Cicek, J., Ingram, S., Friesen, M., & Ruth, D. (2017). Action research: A methodology for transformative learning for a professor and his students in an engineering classroom. *European Journal of Engineering Education, 44*(1–2), 49–70. doi:10.1080/03043797.2017.1405242

Sheehan, S. (2014). A Conceptual Framework for Understanding Transcendental phenomenology through the lived experiences of biblical leaders. *Emerging Leadership Journeys*, 7. https://www.regent.edu/journal/emerging-leadership-journeys/understanding-transcendental-phenomenology/#:~:text=Transcendental%20phenomenology%20(TPh)%2C%20largely,experience%20(Moustakas%2C%201994)

Shokooh, F., & Yazdani, S. (2018). Defining doctorateness: A concept analysis. *International Journal of Doctoral Studies, 13*, 31–48. doi:10.28945/3939

Sonia, VanWye, Schafer, Robertson, & Poore. (2018). Factors Affecting PhD Student Success. *International Journal of Exercise Science, 12*(1), 34–45. PMID:30761191

Steinmayr, R., Weidinger, A. F., Schwinger, M., & Spinath, B. (2019). The importance of students' motivation for their academic achievement – replicating and extending previous findings. *Frontiers in Psychology*, *10*, 1730. Advance online publication. doi:10.3389/fpsyg.2019.01730 PMID:31417459

Stringer, H. (2022). *The nontraditional student*. American Psychological Association. https://www.apa.org/gradpsych/2015/04/nontraditional-student

Sverdlik, A., Hall, N. C., McAlpine, L., & Hubbard, K. (2018). The PhD Experience: A Review of the Factors Influencing Doctoral Students' Completion, Achievement, and Well-Being. *International Journal of Doctoral Studies*, *13*, 361–388. doi:10.28945/4113

The Stanford Encyclopedia of Philosophy. (2013, December 16). Phenomenology. *Stanford Encyclopedia of Philosophy*. https://plato.stanford.edu/entries/phenomenology/

Tinto, V. (1993). *Leaving college: Rethinking the causes and cures of student attrition*. University of Chicago Press. https://eric.ed.gov/?id=ED371658

Tinto, V. (2017). Reflections on student persistence. *Student Success*, *8*(2), 1–8. doi:10.5204/ssj.v8i2.376

Trafford, V. (2008). Conceptual Frameworks as a Threshold Concept in Doctorateness. *BRILL eBooks*, 273–288. doi:10.1163/9789460911477_021

Trafford, V., & Leshem, S. (2009). Doctorateness as a threshold concept. *Innovations in Education and Teaching International*, *46*(3), 305–316. doi:10.1080/14703290903069027

Trinidad, J. E. (2024). Positionality in the politics of education: Mapping the strategies and constraints of education reformers. *Educational Policy*, 08959048231220038. Advance online publication. doi:10.1177/08959048231220038

University of Nebraska-Lincoln Office of Gr. (2022). *Non-Traditional students graduate connections Nebraska*. Graduate Connections. Retrieved October 9, 2022, from https://graduate.unl.edu/connections/non-traditional-students

U.S. Department of Education & Institute of Education Sciences. (2022). *Characteristics of postsecondary students: Postbaccalaureate enrollment*. Condition of Education. Retrieved March 19, 2023, from https://nces.ed.gov/programs/coe/indicator/csb

U.S. Department of State. (2015, December). *What is a Graduate Student?* EducationUSA. Retrieved October 9, 2022, from https://educationusa.state.gov/your-5-steps-us-study/research-your-options/graduate/what-graduate-student

Van Der Linden, N., Devos, C., Boudrenghien, G., Frenay, M., Azzi, A., Klein, O., & Galand, B. (2018). Gaining insight into doctoral persistence: Development and validation of doctorate-related need support and need satisfaction short scales. *Learning and Individual Differences, 65*, 100–111. doi:10.1016/j.lindif.2018.03.008

Van Rooij, E., Fokkens-Bruinsma, M., & Jansen, E. (2019). Factors that influence PhD candidates' success: The importance of PhD project characteristics. *Studies in Continuing Education, 43*(1), 48–67. doi:10.1080/0158037X.2019.1652158

Wall, S. (2008). Easier Said than Done: Writing an Autoethnography. *International Journal of Qualitative Methods, 7*(1), 38–53. doi:10.1177/160940690800700103

Wang, V., Torrisi-Steele, G., & Reinsfield, E. (2020). Transformative learning, epistemology and technology in adult education. *Journal of Adult and Continuing Education, 27*(2), 324–340. doi:10.1177/1477971420918602

Wellington, J. (2013). Searching for 'doctorateness.'. *Studies in Higher Education, 38*(10), 1490–1503. doi:10.1080/03075079.2011.634901

Westbrooks, D., Guillaume, N., Jones, S. M., & De La Fosse, K. (2020). Academic residency: Effective engagement and mentorship of doctoral students. *Journal of College Teaching and Learning, 17*(1).

Willis, B., & Carmichael, K. (2014). The Lived Experience of Late-Stage Doctoral Student Attrition in Counselor Education. *The Qualitative Report*. Advance online publication. doi:10.46743/2160-3715/2011.1046

Wollast, R., Boudrenghien, G., Van Der Linden, N., Galand, B., Roland, N., Devos, C., De Clercq, M., Klein, O., Azzi, A. E., & Frenay, M. (2018). Who Are the Doctoral Students Who Drop Out? Factors Associated with the Rate of Doctoral Degree Completion in Universities. *International Journal of Higher Education, 7*(4), 143. doi:10.5430/ijhe.v7n4p143

Yazdani, S., & Shokooh, F. (2018). Defining Doctorateness: A Concept Analysis. *International Journal of Doctoral Studies, 13*, 31–48. doi:10.28945/3939

Young, S. N., & William, R. (2018). Factors affecting PhD student success. *International Journal of Exercise Science, 12*(1), 34–45. https://www.ncbi.nlm.nih.gov/pmc/articles/PMC6355122/

Zhou, E. (2022). Graduate Enrollment and Degrees: 2011 to 2021. In *Graduate Enrollment and Degrees*. Council of Graduate Schools. https://cgsnet.org/wp-content/uploads/2022/11/CGS_GED21_Report_v1-1.pdf

Zhou, E., & Okahana, H. (2016). The role of department supports on doctoral completion and time-to-degree. Journal of College Student Retention: Research, Theory &Amp. *Journal of College Student Retention*, *20*(4), 511–529. doi:10.1177/1521025116682036

Znamenak, K., Lieberth, M., Murphy, J. L., & Sheaffer, A. (2022). Experiences and viewpoints of PhD students completing their dissertations during crises. *New Directions for Adult and Continuing Education*, *2022*(173–174), 33–43. doi:10.1002/ace.20450

Chapter 5
Schooled in Black Hair

Melony Smith
Arkansas State University, USA

ABSTRACT

This chapter narrates the journey of three women through their early education into the unfamiliar realm of college, while fitting together their educational and professional pursuits within the context of their hairstyle choices. The telling of these women's stories is layered in deeply rooted connections to the socio-cultural history and experiences of Black people in American society. Each segment of the chapter begins with an overview of the history of a Black hair style and then moves on to chronicle pivotal common episodes and experiences across all three women's lives. Within the chapter, the women explore: how they felt about education early on, when and why they realized college was the next step, their college experiences, their pursuit of advanced degrees, and finally their professional lives. This exploration is narrowly focused on commonalities across the women's experiences allowing for an account of the inequities, microaggression, and racism that complicated their journey and making their triumphs all the richer.

INTRODUCTION

For women, the obsession with hair forced on them as a standard of beauty and acceptance transcends differences in color, culture, demographics, and religion. Women labor to create and sustain their crowning glory for the world's approval. However, Black women's relationship with hair goes much deeper. Research has illustrated how Black hair permeates all realms of experiences, particularly for black women, from hair used to orchestrate ostracizing or removing them altogether in academic spaces to Black women being told that their hairstyle underscores

DOI: 10.4018/979-8-3693-1074-8.ch005

whether they are given their just due in professional spaces. Dr. Wellington has chosen to tell the story of two other Black women's experiences in higher education leading into their professional lives because she intimately understands that Black hair can be used to chronicle Black women's journey into the discovery of how to successfully navigate new spaces. She sees this autoethnographic narrative study as her responsibility, "for to whom much is given, much is required." This work stems from her desire to share a roadmap so that other generations of women might learn to recognize the doubt and self-loathing, particularly in academic and professional spaces, often fed by microaggression, discrimination, prejudice, and racism that keep Black women from excelling and achieving their aspirations. These women share their story maneuvering through their formative years, college, advanced degrees, and the professional world while intimately revealing their evolution through doubt, discovery, and dominance told through black hair.

BACKGROUND

According to Poulos (2021), an autoethnography is an autobiography shaped from the author's analysis, interpretation, and connection of personal lived experiences into a formulated self-identify. Jones et al. (2016) affirm

That autoethnography is a qualitative research method that: 1) uses a researcher's personal experience to describe and critique cultural beliefs, practices, and experiences; 2) acknowledges and values a researcher's relationships with others; 3) uses deep and careful self-reflection—typically referred to as "reflexivity"—to name and interrogate the intersections between self and society, the particular and the general, the personal and the political; 4) Shows people in the process of figuring out what to do, how to live, and the meaning of their struggles; 5) balances intellectual and methodological rigor, emotion, and creativity; and 6) strives for social justice and to make life better. (p. 2)

The purpose of this chapter is to share the lived experiences of two women during their pursuit of higher degrees and careers amid the complex emotional and social issues they faced.

It has been nearly 50 years since Pierce's (1970) seminal study where he coined phrase "microaggression" defined as "subtle stunning, often automatic, and 'non-verbal' exchanges which are 'put downs' of blacks" (Pierce et al., 1978, p. 66). Sue et al. (2007), later redefined the term as "brief and commonplace daily verbal, behavioral, or environmental indignities, whether intentional or unintentional, that communicates hostile, derogatory, or negative racial slights and insults towards people of color" (p. 271). Several studies have confirmed and expounded on the nature, experiences, and consequences of microaggressions (Pierce, 1970; Sue et al., 2007; Dittman, 2002) as well as the discriminatory and racist encounters Blacks experience on college campuses (Kim, 2016; Lewis et al., 2012; Dittman, 2012). Moreover, according to Dittman (2012), the result can be a taxing effect on Black students' sense of belonging and emotional stability. Additionally, Black students usually do not directly combat microaggression when they find themselves a target for discrimination, microaggression, and racism. Many develop low self-esteem and can become so distracted by microaggression that their academic performance and grades suffer. Given the harm of microaggression and the impact on the likelihood of Black students' attaining advanced degrees, we must understand the experiences Black students encounter in college and later in the workplace if we are to create environments that support their success.

For women of color, this microaggression calls in to question their worthiness to be in certain spaces as much as it is an attack on their skin color and appearance. The intersection of race and hair for Black women in higher institutions and the workplace often isolates them all the while assaulting them with messages of inferiority and unworthiness. This is where this book chapter attempts to situate itself: two women of color, one having pursued her doctorate and the other her masters, at the intersection of race and black hair.

The Press and Curl

For many black women, the press and curl achieved with a hot comb marks a rite of passage. This being leaving behind infancy and moving towards burgeoning adolescence, signaling young adulthood directly ahead. Like many other young Black girls, Alexis longed for the gleaming bouncy European-like coils the hot comb created. She deeply coveted the power of the hot comb even if she did have to endure the pain of a burn on her ear or the nape of her neck. For Alexis and many other Black women, straight hair meant "good hair," pretty hair that made one accepted, liked, and even envied. It meant hair that was equated to beautiful, smart, powerful women. Yet, for Alexis, the hot comb created a love-hate relationship, reminding her of all that her hair was not nor would ever be able to achieve with her kinky coils. By this time, Alexis had realized what every Black girl eventually comes to know, described Dr. Lukate (2019) as an innate awareness, that Black women are judged by physical attributes over which they have no control but are born to that being skin color and hair texture. This mental and emotional angst was mirrored in her early educational experiences.

Even before clear memories and recollections of days in school, Alexis was aware that her kindergarten teacher and principal had persuaded her mother to have

Schooled in Black Hair

her repeat kindergarten. This would remain a great source of embarrassment and shame for her spawning her feelings of inadequacy. Alexis says her experiences early with school admittedly began with feelings of negativity. At home, the school was a place where "you better not be showing out and embarrassing me, having folks think you ain't got no sense," that was her mother's non-negotiable. Alexis' father was a very quiet man and the epitome of a provider. He mostly left parenting up to her mother. Alexis would heed her mother's warning by avoiding attention. She was quiet, respectful, and compliant, believing this would keep her out of trouble. One of her earliest memories is having to defend herself from an attack by my third-grade teacher. Even today, Alexis says, "The memory of my teacher standing at my desk, finger pointing in my face, hand on her hip, her face bright red yelling at me for not doing my classroom work is as clear as if it just happened yesterday. The memory has always stayed with me. The teacher began yelling when Alexis explained that she had completed the assignment. The more she tried to explain, the louder the teacher became, eventually screaming and shouting accusations of dishonesty and thievery at her. Looking back, Alexis now wonders if her teacher was angered by her audacity to talk back as a challenge to her white authority. Afterward, it was discovered that Alexis had written her name on the back of her paper. Her teacher's response was to line all the other students up at her desk, one at a time; she asked them whether Alexis had somehow snuck to the stack of papers and written her name on a stolen sheet after asking for the work. It ended with none of the other students corroborating the teacher's explanation that Alexis had stolen a fellow student's work. Alexis still got a zero and was lectured about how she had caused herself to get into trouble by not following instructions. If that were not enough, Alexis was also sent to the principal's office, where she remained for the rest of the day. Alexis says she was made to feel that she had caused the teacher to punish her with a zero. What all of that demonstrated to Alexi is something she continues to try to unwrap and understand even today. However, she says that she knew then what she knows now school was not the same for her and other children. A hostile, treacherous place for Alexis that required careful navigation and negotiation if I would stay out of trouble.

Jheri Curl

The Jheri curl was a popular hairstyle of the 1980s achieved by applying a chemical to straighten the hair, tightly rodding the hair, and then drying it under a hooded dryer. For many women, it was a partial answer to their hair woes. The Jheri curl added a little length while giving more bounce and wave to tresses and created a texture closer to the "good hair" many Black women are convinced they should covet.

By middle school, Alexis had been to experience more academic success. Her parents feared that she might fail again and had gotten her tutoring, giving Alexis more confidence, skills, and strategies, all of which were advantages over her peers. Alexis had nurtured a love for books, and the reading and the tutoring together had begun to pay off. Academics had become something Alexis was now good at doing. What her academic excellence earned her in school was further isolation. She was placed in classes where she was the only African American female. Popular television shows like It is A Different World and the movie School Daze gave her a vision of college that she knew she wanted, though she did not yet see college as an opportunity for a better future. Her parents said she was headed to college, and family members and friends were impressed. The reality was that no one in her family understood the college admissions process, and she would be the first to graduate. By high school, her feelings of isolation had only worsened. When Alexis told her counselor of her aspirations to attend college at a prestigious midwestern PWI, he told her it would be very expensive and that she should consider a state school. What Alexi heard was that she was not worthy of such a place. Looking back, Alexis wonders why her school counselor was not working to help find scholarships if that was his concern. The female black counselor at the school told Alexis that according to her transcripts, she did not seem to be enrolled in classes that would adequately prepare her for college and that it might hurt her chances for admission. The counselor worked with Alexis to change classes, and she found scholarships to assist Alexis with college tuition. Alexis also recalled a similar incident in high school with a teacher where she felt attacked again because of her ethnicity. In a Social Studies class, the teacher had an activity where he would assign students to debate "for" and "against" sides of an issue. He had decided Alexis would debate with one of her white male classmates on the topic of welfare. The teacher decided Alexis would be "for" welfare and her classmate would be "against" it. Alexis says she strategized for the debate, reasoning that her classmate would lean into the depiction of Ronald Reagan's Black welfare queen because that was how the teacher had chosen to introduce the topic in the form of an article about Black women's abuse of the welfare system. Alexis spent the next week preparing her debate. She researched the history of welfare and its beginnings in President Franklin D. Roosevelt's administration. She felt strongly that swaying the teacher and her classmates to her side meant presenting undeniable facts regarding the system's merit. What Alexis recalls about the day of the debate is that when her turn came, her classmate, the one she had been debating, started heckling her. She says, "He blurted out comments that had the other students snickering. When he was not addressed or corrected, he became louder and more aggressive, eventually yelling. However, he got up, crossed the room, and stood in my face yelling. I looked at the teacher for him to interfere, help me, and regain control of the class. He did nothing. He just sat at his desk, leaning back in his chair, his hands behind his head,

Schooled in Black Hair

watching what was happening. I was speechless. I was humiliated, but I was also very angry." Once again, she was reminded that school was not where others thought she belonged. For her, the school was hostile and treacherous.

Perm

Perms are a chemical relaxing of African American hair's tightly coiled shaft. For black hair, perming is one-way women can achieve straight hair; straighter hair is more desirable and attractive for some. Celebrities like Nia Long, Halle Berry, Jada Pinkett, Monica, and Toni Braxton had popularized the pixie cut, making it fashionable and causing the style to be associated with decidedly beautiful sexy Black women. It has recently been discovered that perms, while the product does provide straight hair, it is not necessarily healthy. In addition to the long-term damage to hair follicles, hair shafts, and the scalp recently, research has suggested that perms could be linked to cancer. Most adolescent girls do not receive perms until their late teens unless their hair is unruly or coarse.

Alexis can now see the similarity between the perm and PWI she attended. On the surface, the institution was a great opportunity. Alexis says it is undeniable that the rigor of instruction prepared her for her Master of Arts and Teaching program and opened many other opportunities. Still, pursuing her bachelor's left her financially burdened, and it failed to support her in ways that would undergird her growth as a Black woman. Even still, there were things that the college got right and did very well. Alexis had chosen the PWI after a weekend college visit. In her mind, there were just two colleges she desired to attend, and another institution had declined to extend her an acceptance letter. It looked good, but there is a downside and even more happening beneath the surface at the college.

Alexis strode onto campus with her newly permed pixie cut and blond highlights full of confidence and excitement to there on campus in the fall of 1995. In the first semester, it became apparent that not only was she woefully academically unprepared, but she was also in real danger of not being able to meet the cost of attendance. At one point, she worked the night shift in the hospital cafeteria and a work-study job. Alexis understood that some would say this was building character and simply pulling herself up by the bootstraps. However, Alexis says people should understand that she did not have the luxury of being a student and only focused on grades. She was already stressed from financial pressure, and academics were also weighing on her, but then adding race issues seemed like adding more than she should have to handle.

Alexis says she felt that high school had not prepared her for what she would face in college, so she struggled to keep up her grades. She remembers feeling like her peers seemed to know more and were able to add a great deal to class discussions. More than that, Alexis says the only time she felt like her input was sought or acknowledged was when it seemed there was a need to put a voice to something considered "black." Alexis recalls an experience in marketing and advertising class where she "suggested black images and culture had been appropriated and commodified rather than respected. My classmates became angry and defensive when I said it. I was accused of reverse racism. I was told the problem was that Black people were always ready to play the race card. All this was said with murmurings in the background that I was probably there on a racing scholarship. I wish that were the case. All I could do that day was excuse myself from the remainder of class and go down to the courtyard. I was so upset that I began humming and singing Kirk Franklin's gospel song, *Why We Sing*. Later one of my classmates came to me and expressed how bad she felt. She told me she could hear in my voice how upset the exchange had made me and that it was not right. At the time, Alexis says she did not know how to explain their behavior, and looking back on it, defining was not what was important. It was important that these women did not feel they belonged there and had no problem expressing how they felt. There were other occasions for Alexis, including a very uncomfortable discussion in her multicultural studies led by the professor who told the class that the description of a black woman sharing crack with her child to be, for its savagery, was the most difficult text she had ever attempted to read. While Alexis acknowledges that it being a difficult text for the professor may have been the professor's truth, what Alexis felt and heard was condemnation and accusation. She felt that the professor completely missed the opportunity to challenge these affluent white students to consider the disparities and institutionalized racism that black and brown people face that had led to the prevalent usage and presence of drugs in their communities. Alexis saw that the bigger problem was that for these white students, their knowledge and understanding of African Americans and our experiences had been provided by the images they saw on television. Their knowledge and experience of minorities consisted of viewing the perfect Huxtable family sitcom with their perfect upper-middle-class lives and problems that could be solved in a half hour, the Fresh Prince of Bel-Air, disproportionate black crime television news reports, as well as the highly sexualized or violent lyrics and music video images. The college was doing little to confront these constructions of minorities; thus, Alexis was an oddity, a rarity. Her enunciation, articulation, and command of standard English made her an unwilling black ambassador of all Black culture-related. It left Alexis questioning whether she was meant to be there. Alexis says that the confidence she had come there with was beginning to fade. Outside of class, there were other hurdles. She was one of seven African American women attending the college; there were only three African American women on staff, and one was an adjunct faculty member. Alexis says she did not realize how much that mattered at the time. She did not understand that the lack of professional black women stifled her growth opportunities. She said she felt the impact of the lack of successful Black women in that setting because none could serve as role models to help her to navigate college and the decisions she was making. She says it also left her with no narrative of the possibilities of what she could achieve in higher education. Thus, navigating the terrain of college, particularly at a PWI, was especially challenging with no one to mentor her. Alexis recalls that there were faculty members who attempted to fill in these spaces an anonymous donor who provided her with books one semester, a professor who recognized she was struggling and quickly directed her to the writing lab on campus, and a professor that took her aside and explained some studying strategies that he wanted her to utilize. Searching for a degree major, Alexis settled on Mass Communication, emphasizing Advertising and Public Relations. She reasoned it would allow her to capitalize on what she was best at in school, writing and speaking.

In the end, Alexis says a couple of factors made all the difference in her turning around her grades, staying at the college, and earning her degree. She says it was "the community of three women that provided support. Now I realize that we were unfairly burdened with supporting one another and figuring things out while still trying to fulfill all our other roles and responsibilities. They told me I was worthy even when I believed I was not. They made college life not just bearable but memorable. There was one that naturally took on the role of big sister and protector, but we all in on each other. Together they celebrated their triumphs and survived their worst moment. Alexis says that during her junior year of college, she began focusing on a career and determining what she would do after college. She had met her future husband, and his career aspirations centered around returning to Memphis, Tennessee, where he would coach and teach. Alexis says that for her husband, his coaches had been instrumental in keeping him from the trouble of the streets and him going on to play football at Notre Dame. When the couple graduated, they moved to Memphis Alexis began to substitute teaching.

Weave and Wigs

Weaves and wigs changed the range of styling for black women drastically; not only could Black hair be straight, but it could also be very long (Tate, 2007; Thompson, 2009). Hair weaving involves sewing synthetic or human hair into naked cornrows, cornrows covered by weave caps, or, a third way, tracks bonded with glue to hair roots. For me, hair weaves and wigs meant "looking the part," as wigs allow what many Black women consider more professionally appropriate styles.

Alexis explains that pursuing education as a career was a logical move because teaching meant returning to something familiar and something she was good at doing. She had become a good student; surely would be a good teacher. Initially, obtaining her master's in arts and teaching was necessary as she did not have a teaching certification or a Bachelor's in education. Right away, Alexis says she witnessed first-hand the disparities and disenfranchisement her students faced in their communities. She says it was like society had turned its back on her students, who were struggling to understand their circumstances. All she felt she had to offer her students was English Language Arts. She started telling stories of her childhood, building relationships and connections with her students. However, Alexis remembers feeling like it was not enough, and she says she was desperate to give them more and wanted to be better at what she was doing. Alexis states, "Yes, there were students who were grade levels behind, and they deserved the best chance they could be given to have meaningful comfortable adult lives. Then some bright students deserved to be pushed and exposed to more rigor. When my husband and I bought a home and began our family, we felt the financial strain. It became clear that my best choice was getting my Ed.S and Doctorate. Not only would I be better equipped for my students, but I could then move up the career ladder, which meant more money for my family."

Natural Hair and Braids

For many women, going natural often entails a "big chop" and transitioning from years of straightening the hair or chemical treatments that necessitate removing over-processed or burned dead hair. Natural hair can be manipulated into styles ranging from wash and goes, afros, braid and twist outs, braided twists, and blowouts. While there is a myriad of style versatility, caring for Black hair in its natural state requires the careful handling of hair that is far more delicate than most realize.

Alexis says, "At this point, I was starting to sense a feeling of unfulfillment on the job. I wanted to do more and felt I should be doing more." She felt she needed to fall back in love with teaching and that she could love it again if she found a way to approach the work differently. She made a smooth transition into instructional coaching. Deciding to return to school for an Ed.S, she reasoned that she did not have much time. Having put off returning to school till her late forties, she chose an online program at a nearby university. The university offered an Ed.S. in fewer than two years. She earned it in 18 months and entered a three-year Doctoral program in Curriculum and Instruction.

Alexis is convinced that her doctoral program was pivotal because what had been missing for her was a mentor, and she met Dr. Timberly Baker in her program. Alexis says that for the first time, she was fully aware of having an example of what her degree offered and the potential for what she could become. Alexis explains, "As part of my dissertation committee, Dr. Baker provided feedback and direction on my work, but she went beyond her duties as a part of my committee, providing me additional access to her despite her busy schedule. She offered additional online office hours and would drive out of town and come to Memphis to meet up with me to discuss my dissertation. Dr. Baker repeatedly assured me of my ability and my grit. She encouraged me to work beyond my dissertation to attend conferences to present and publish additional work. She discussed with me, at length, higher ed and what it would look like and entail if I were to work in this sphere of my field. I knew that I wanted to work with teachers, but now I know where I am meant to do this work. She did not just galvanize me; she also showed me how to get there.

Alexis says that before Dr. Baker, she had no real sense of what to do or how to plan for the next stages of her career aspirations. Now Alexis says she knows, "I am working my way towards a tenured professorship in the college of education. I do not know where I will eventually be, but I am excited that it could mean going anywhere in the U.S. Before, the thought of leaving Memphis and what I know was terrifying, but not anymore. I am searching now for the right opportunity in the right place because I know I am meant to support women like me. However, I want all students to feel supported toward their goals and aspirations, and I want to build equitable opportunities for all students in higher ed."

Michelle: The Hot Comb

Michelle grew up despising the hot comb; every encounter with this instrument resulted in pain, a stinging burn on the nape of her neck or behind her ear that throbbed for days. It also represented hours invested in a process that often began the night before with washing the hair and plaiting it in braids to dry. The next day more hours of combing through the hair and sitting for hours while my hair was straightened. Michelle pointed out a scar she still has on her arm from a burn from the hot comb slipping from her mother's hand. Looking back, Michelle is sure that the worse part was everything she could not do once her hair had been curled and coiled. She could not go outside because she might sweat out her curls or destroy her hairstyle. She had to keep up and maintain her hairstyle. This would become the central premise of her life, keeping up appearances and maintaining all that each news space entailed. Michelle felt that for her mother, hair reflected status. Because her mother felt that your appearance dictated your experience of the world around you, she went to great lengths to ensure that her little girl's hair was perfectly styled and adorned. Her mother even had her hairbows custom-made. In other words, people treated you according to how you looked. Michelle would have a similar sense of having to "keep up" and "maintain" an appearance regarding her schooling.

Michelle descended from a family of educators. Her maternal grandparents were well-known educators, and her grandfather was a principal most of his career at a Mississippi high school. Her grandmother was a teacher, and her mother's sister was a kindergarten teacher. She fondly recalls growing up; she spent her days running in and out of classrooms at her grandfather's high school. She sat in lessons and instruction far beyond her primary grades. She would climb into a desk and sit absorbed in the lessons and learning in Algebra, French, and Science classes, being allowed to participate with the high schoolers. She seemingly was doted on by the faculty and staff and treated like the school mascot by the older students. She loved school from the start, convinced that she could learn anything. Her family felt education was a status symbol marking all that they had overcome and accomplished. Michelle's grandfather began as a sharecropper working hard to leave the fields to go high school, earn a diploma, and then work through college. He eventually went on to earn Principal licensure and became the principal of a large high school in the south, elevating himself and his family to middle-class comfortability. Her schooling was a personal point of pride for Michelle's grandfather. As early as elementary school, she had begun these intellectual debates with him and would sit for hours in his office across the desk from him, immersed in discussing the Bible. He encouraged her comprehension of the text and congratulated her for her interpretation. At other times he challenged her thoughts. With her family's guidance and support, academia gave her comfort and confidence early on in her life.

Michelle's mother was a single parent, and Michelle says now, when she thinks about it, the school was a carefully negotiated contract between her self and her single-parent mother, who was busy elevating the status of the family and also working towards a Master that would allow her to climb the corporate ladder of a Fortunate 500 company to hold a position very few Black women would achieve. Michelle's mother would often tell her that school and earning "good" grades were Michelle's only jobs, and she felt her mother and she were partners. A bright child, intellectually and emotionally advanced for her age, Michelle always felt she was expected to keep up her end of the contract by excelling at school, being reliable enough to take care of herself, and staying out of trouble while her mother was at school or work. This is exactly what Michelle did; she went to school, excelled, and stayed out of trouble, which she felt was easy because she loved school and was good at it, and family dynamics had made her an ardent people pleaser. As an only child, Michelle knew herself to be an important extension of all her family had earned. She knew the stories of her great-grandparents, who were enslaved people, and her grandparents, who had fought their way out of sharecropping. They both went to college, got degrees, became school teachers, and worked towards the American dream. Most importantly, she knew she was expected to do the same, so she felt obligated to do well in school. She did excel despite moments in her secondary education, albeit fleeting ones, where she felt she had the weight of representing her family and all that Black people could accomplish on her shoulders.

Schooled in Black Hair

Weaves

By the end of her middle school years, Michelle's mother's hard work toward her degree and advancing her career had paid off. Her mother was managing her department, had married a department manager at a successful Fortune 500 company, and the family had moved to an affluent neighborhood. Michelle attended a private school and credited her desire to earn high grades with what she saw as a partnership with her mother. Michelle earning good grades and staying out of trouble made life easier for her hardworking mother. In high school, Michelle was finding herself. She was already conscious of being different from her immediate and extended family. She describes herself as artsy and most interested in things that other Black kids her age were. In high school, she found freedom in accepting that she did not meet society's beauty norms and says she had rectified her mind that she was "weird" and "quirky." Michelle felt accepted by her eclectic mix of white friends and ostracized for being what she reasoned was "black enough" by the black kids in school. Michelle felt liberation through accepting who she was and did not feel the pressure of fitting in because she had already accepted that she did not fit in with the people around her. However, she still felt the pressure to have her hair professionally styled. Her mother's words often echoed, "How people treat you is based on your appearance." She recalls the idea of appearance concerned her mother so much that she remembers being at the beauty shop all of the time, almost every week, getting her hair styled, and it was always a straight weave. Due to a bad perm, Michelle experienced devastating hair loss and a blow to her self-confidence. Until then, Michelle had thought, if nothing else, if she was not going to be the standard of beauty, at least her hair was cute, and with her hair gone, she felt she might as well embrace being different. Early on in college, Michelle's confidence in security in being herself would be challenged at best and diminished and ignored at worst.

Michelle felt that college was never a choice. It was always her mother's expectation that she would go to attend and graduate college. She would eventually choose a PWI in the south, forfeiting her dream to attend Emory, a choice she says she would gladly make again. She has never regretted her choice of undergraduate schools. However, she never questioned the challenges she might face at a PWI because those were spaces where she felt there would at least be some familiarity, having attended a mostly white high school. She had discovered an interest in politics and was swept up in campaigning and the excitement of Obama's first run for office. This catapulted them into the world of politics, and Michelle says she felt catapulted into the world of politics. This was largely due to her belief that a liberal arts education would afford her the life she had begun to dream about. Michelle envisioned herself as a smart, quirky, politically active Black woman, which helped solidify her college choice. It certainly had helped that the institution had actively recruited her, and she felt wanted and welcomed.

However, at her PWI, Michelle says she felt challenged by her blackness. Looking back, she explains that her undergrad experience made her consciously make the daily choice and effort to embrace her blackness.

Wigs, Weaves, and Everything in Between

Michelle clearly remembers realizing what she describes as making the conscious decision to embrace her Blackness. She credits her undergrad with connecting her to her Black culture, even if it was out of fear and caution of not surrendering to or accommodating the microaggression that she felt was challenging her integrity and identity as a Black woman. Michelle felt she came to a point where she realized that her white counterparts saw her as a Black girl who lacked the intellectual capacity to deserve a place alongside them in their classes and at the institution altogether. By this time, there had been occurrences of outright racism on the campus. A fraternity had been ousted on social media for making racial slurs and chants. One of the advisors, an African American male, had shared that he had experienced the baseball team yelling racist remarks and calling him names. For the first time, Michelle found herself directly experiencing racism, and what she now understands was microaggression. Her white roommate openly used the word "nigger" in everyday conversation. Michelle recalls feeling caught between her black friends wanting her to confront the girl and demanding she stop or confront her with physical violence. However, it was likely what Feagin et al. (2014) describe as a fear of being faulted for the occurrence rather than the blame resting on the perpetrator.

Meanwhile, she notes she had begun to question whether she had the aptitude and the intellect to be at the institution. Michelle explains that imposter syndrome had squarely smacked her in the face. She notes having begun a downward spiral. She struggled to maintain her grades and experienced a crushing sense of defeat when she fell behind in her favorite courses and what she initially thought would be her career field. She had been an academic superstar in high school and was completely unprepared for the academic rigor and social pressures she was now facing. She aspired to work in psychology and eventually perhaps become a sex therapist; however, now she found herself in danger of failing her Psychology 101 course—some of the blame she lays, in part, on her secondary education. In high school, her AP psychology teacher had been the gym teacher assigned the additional psychology course due to staffing shortages, and he had put up slides every day and flipped through them, directing the students to take notes. She had failed her advanced placement test in psychology because she was not properly prepared, and it was also now showing in class. Her college professor had an altogether different approach. He told his students to sit through his lecture and listen and formulate ideas, questions, and responses to the information that was being presented. His style of lecture was a big shift for Michelle. She was struggling with how to make it work, unable to retain information, unsure of the ideas and connections she was making, and was also performing poorly on his assessments. She had no idea what to do.

Furthermore, their academic struggles were worsened by the notion that she must be an example for her race and all they could accomplish. She understands now that she is suffering from depression. She fought to get out of bed and even to go to classes. With imposter syndrome hitting hard, Michelle felt her struggles indicated she was not meant to be at the university. Eventually, knowing no other course of action, Michelle went to the professor's office in what she describes as a "hot mess," crying and imploring him to tell her what to do. What Michelle feels stands out the most from this experience is not the utter defeat and hopelessness she felt but his reaction to her coming to his office. She felt crushed when he told her that he had recognized early on that she was struggling and falling further behind and that he was worried that she might not make it. However, what stung was that he said he had just been waiting for her to ask him for help. Years later, she still wonders why he did not offer his assistance earlier. Michelle's view of school and her place in it had undergone a rapid transformation. The transformation had started the moment she stepped onto the campus of her PWI school. For Michelle, attending college was no longer working hard or earning passing grades. Now the school was about earning that space and proving she was meant to be there. The experience left her questioning whether she was smart and how she would maintain the persona of a smart black girl. Michelle had already felt pressure from her mother and maternal grandparents to select a sensible major. Added to that was the pressures of living up to their expectation. Now she was also contending with proving to her white counterparts her worth. More than ever before, she felt that she had to be the perfect student. There was no space for testing life or experimenting to find what she would enjoy. Her family and all of their hard work and sacrifices had given an appearance of success, and now she had to keep up those appearances. Education had afforded her the status of a better life. However, to keep this life and maintain it, Michelle felt she knew without a doubt that there was a clear road that she had to travel. She would have to make sacrifices and do what was necessary, including working ten times as hard to maintain the level of safety and financial comfort her family had acquired. Now there could never be space to be mediocre. She felt the responsibilities of an adult responsible for caring for herself and continuing the family's trajectory. Though Michelle had desired to pursue a career in psychology and was considering sex therapy, she knew corporate was the expectation and that it would afford a life of financial security. However, it also meant that her appearance would be controlled and dictated.

Wigs, Weaves, and Everything in Between

Having exited college with a liberal arts degree, Michelle felt pressured by her commitment to continuing her family's upward mobility to go on to obtain a Master's degree that would make her more employable. All around her, she felt everyone else had answers and was putting their adult lives together, and she felt left behind. She was now in a corporate job, and to climb the corporate ladder, a Master's would be a necessary step. The Master's would afford her the credentials she needed to be taken seriously in the workplace and to be considered for upward promotion. Moreover, a carefully chosen Master's program meant gaining access to a network of colleagues and potential career advancements. However, Michelle also recognized that as a woman, particularly a Black woman, the choice to continue school and to focus on growing her career meant that there were other things that she would sacrifice. Michelle says she sees chances for a serious relationship and a family dwindling and envisions a life of singlehood. She has grown to accept singlehood and even welcomes it at times. She says the more difficult aspect for her to accept is feeling like she has been held back from pursuing and ultimately realizing her personal goals and aspirations. She says she gave all this up to do the "right" things expected of her. She wistfully dreams of her practice as a successful therapist and believes there may still be a point at which she can change directions and do something she desires. For now, it is Corporate America; she must maintain appearances in this space. She no longer questions why in college, she felt enraged enough and entitled to the equity she demanded that she was willing to challenge the voice around her and fight for her place. Now in Corporate America, with her survival and livelihood at stake, she feels silenced and begrudgingly accepting of her struggle to fit into white corporate America's expectations. Michelle had once gone to work with a red fire engine wig and felt uncomfortable all day. Her white co-workers did little to hide their surprise and condemnation, and she was certain her Black counterparts were equally disapproving. The experience with the wig had been more harrowing than the day her company announced it would be speaking to employees individually about layoffs. These days, she sticks to safe hair—wig styles that closely resemble more European looks not to give her supervisors any reason to doubt her capability, preparedness, and worth for promotion. She saves her more authentic self for the weekends and time away from work. She meticulously dresses in professional work attire and strictly avoids anything too urban or Afrocentric. It is clear to Michelle that her hair has become part of the extension of her pursuit to climb the corporate ladder and a necessary evil.

Lessons Learned

In conclusion, institutions must understand the experiences of Black female students at predominantly white institutions. Microaggression is not just about whether Black females matriculate or whether they have enjoyable campus experiences. It is about the physiological complications and the detrimental impact on these women's physical and mental health and whether the institutions that admit them also seek to empower these women to navigate and obtain advanced degrees successfully. The experiences of these two women affirm many of the issues documented by research on the racism and microaggression Black students face on college campuses across the United States (Caplan & Ford, 2014; Bennett et al., 2017; Harwood et al., 2012; Sue et al., 2007). Both women spoke of how the microaggression that they encountered hurt their self-esteem. Ditman (2002) contends that these encounters leave Black students questioning their reactions to these encounters rather than confronting their assailants. Black students fall silent and avoid interactions on campus, and the resulting isolation and the attacks they suffer potentially erode their mental health. Furthermore, many students develop low self-esteem or become so distracted with readying themselves to deal with such incidents that they lose focus on course performance, their grades suffer, and they face academic failure (Ditman, 2002). Student affairs practitioners must understand the nature of these assaults on their students in all spaces, including but not limited to classrooms, dormitories, and around the campus, to alleviate the impact of these occurrences and eventually remove them altogether. First, institutions must provide their students with a safe space where they can report incidents of microaggression, discrimination, racism, and prejudice without fear of retaliation. For example, an anonymous reporting system would go a long way in allowing students to bring their concerns to the attention of campus officials without fear that they will face the consequences, thereby allowing the campus to carry out efforts to make their schools equitable spaces for all students. Another avenue that all colleges should undertake is mandatory diversity and inclusion training for all faculty, staff, and administrators. It is equally important that diversity and inclusion training address the culture and climate on campus. This means that the campus needs to spend time collecting data that accurately depicts race relations, multiculturalism, and equity on campus. If training is going to be accurate and impactful, it needs to occur from a place of informed understanding of what is occurring in all campus spaces. Eliminating microaggression means faculty and staff must learn to identify these tendencies in themselves, their colleagues, and students. Faculty and staff must be equipped to resolve these occurrences in a way that validates and acknowledges the victim and corrects the situation. Diversity initiatives will mean not only training faculty and staff but affirming the rewards and benefits of a diverse campus by hiring diverse faculty and providing students with mentors to help guide and support students.

REFERENCES

Dittman, M. (2002). *The study says Self-esteem based on external sources has mental health consequences.* Retrieved from http://www.apa.org/monitor/dec02/selfesteem.aspx

Feagin, J. R., Vera, H., & Imani, N. (2014). *The agony of education: Black students at a White University.* Routledge.

Jones, S. H., Adams, T. E., & Ellis, C. (2016). *Handbook of autoethnography.* Routledge.

Kim, P. Y. (2016). Religious support mediates the racial microaggression-mental health relation among Christian ethnic minority students. *Psychology of Religion and Spirituality.* Advance online publication. 10.1037/rel0000076

Lewis, J. A., Mendenhall, R., Harwood, S. A., & Browne Huntt, M. (2013). Coping with Gendered Racial Microaggressions among Black Women College Students. *Journal of African American Studies, 17*(1), 51–73. doi:10.1007/s12111-012-9219-0

Lukate, J. M. (2022). Space, race and identity: An ethnographic study of the Black hair care and beauty landscape and Black women's racial identity constructions in England. *The Journal of Social Issues, 78*(1), 107–125. doi:10.1111/josi.12433

Pierce, C. (1 970). Offensive mechanisms. In F. Barbour (Ed.), *The Black seventies* (pp. 265–282). Porter Sargent.

Pierce, C. (1989). Unity in diversity: Thirty-three years of stress. In G. Berry & J. Asamen (Eds.), Black students: Psychosocial issues in academic achievement (pp. 298-3 1 2). Newbury, CA: Sage Publications Inc.

Poulos, C. N. (2021). *Essentials of autoethnography.* doi:10.1037/0000222-000

Sue, D. W., Capodilupo, C. M., Torino, G. C., Bucceri, J. M., Holder, A., Nadal, K. L., & Esquilin, M. (2007). Racial microaggressions in everyday life: Implications for clinical practice. *The American Psychologist, 62*(4), 271–286. doi:10.1037/0003-066X.62.4.271 PMID:17516773

Chapter 6
Life Begins at 40:
An Investigation Into the Educational Journey of Selected Undergraduate Students in the Caribbean

Ruth Baker-Gardner
University of the West Indies, Jamaica

Suzette S. Brown
University of the West Indies, Jamaica

Nicoleen Saunders-Grant
HEART Trust, Jamaica

ABSTRACT

Colleges have traditionally recruited from among high school graduates to meet their enrolment targets, ignoring the possibility of exploiting the interest of older working adults who desire to enter tertiary institutions. This chapter details the experiences of 10 undergraduate students 40 and over who are currently enrolled in undergraduate programs. It explores the reasons for their late entry into tertiary education, their motivations for choosing to continue their education, the challenges they experienced, and how they overcame these challenges. This sample was chosen using purposive sampling, and data was collected using the interview method. The findings indicate that participants were unable to continue their education earlier due to financial constraints but enrolled in tertiary studies for several reasons including financial gains to be achieved and self-actualization. They experienced significant challenges while pursuing their degrees, chief among which was the difficulty of balancing school, work, and family obligations.

DOI: 10.4018/979-8-3693-1074-8.ch006

INTRODUCTION

According to United Nations Educational, Scientific and Cultural Organization (UNESCO), global higher education enrolment rates surged from 19% to 38% between 2000 and 2018 (Vieira et al., 2020). UNESCO further reports that the "number of students in Europe and Northern America increased by 24% between 2000 and 2020 (UNESCO, 2022, p. 9). However, falling enrolment rates has been listed as one of the eight biggest challenges facing higher education ("The Biggest Challenges Facing Higher Education in 2022/2023", 2022; "Number of Students Enrolling in Tertiary Institutions Declines", 2016; Nietzel, 2022). Institutions in both the United States and Canada have been affected with enrollment rates falling in the former by 13% in the last decade, with community colleges feeling the brunt of this decline ("The Biggest Challenges Facing Higher Education in 2022/2023", 2022). Binkley and the Associated Press (2023) citing the National Student Clearinghourse Research Center further verify this decline. They stated "Nationwide, undergraduate college enrolment dropped 8% from 2019 to 2022, with declines even after returning to in-person classes". Brinkley and the Associated Press further noted, "The slide in the college-going rate since 2018 is the steepest on record, according to the U.S. Bureau of Labor Statistics" (2023).

Roman believed that much of this decrease can be attributed to the pandemic (2022). He also cited the National Student Clearinghouse Research Center report that showed enrollment falling by 4.1% at United States public and private colleges for the spring 2022 term (2022). Furthermore, he purported that changes in population demographics, a contracting job market, along with new upskilling avenues have also contributed to the decline. Prior to the pandemic, enrollment shortfalls in American and Canadian universities were met by recruiting international students from the Caribbean (Worldwide Colleges Tour, 2018; Cross, 2017), China, India, Germany and France (International Students, 2024).

Higher education institutions (HEIs) are "producing limited numbers of graduates with aging expertise" as they remain focused on recruiting from the shrinking pool of high schoolers (Dauenhauer et al., 2016, p. 483) . On the contrary, Bellare et al. (2021) noted that the number of adult and non-traditional learners enrolling in colleges to pursue a degree in the United States has steadily increased. In discussing the experiences of non-traditional students in Canada, Panacci (2015) noted that the cohort of adult learners has steadily increased. The researcher identified several strategies cited by that institutions have been using to assist adult learners to further their education. These strategies included continuing education; online learning; pathway, preparatory, and upgrading programs; advising and learning support services; credit for life and work experience; academic orientation; financial aid and on-campus childcare. It is therefore possible for universities to successfully graduate cohorts of adult learners 40 years and older. This can be achieved by giving due consideration to their life situations and implementing strategies to decrease the negative effect of these on their educational pursuits.

Across the globe, there are demographic trends that are creating the need for more focused attention on education for mature students. Dauenhauer et al., 2016 (quoting the United States Census Bureau), reported that the American population has age. This resulted in the adult population of approximately 40 million people being 15% of the entire population. (p. 483). Additionally, a study in Jamaica by Perue indicated a shift in the Jamaican population with the majority of persons being in what he called the "prime working age" range of 25 years to 54 years (2023). An aging population is likely to result in an increased demand for entry into tertiary education at a later period in life, and so this should be given due consideration. In a bid to tap into this market of adult learners, the Irish government redefined adult learners as persons over 23 years old. This enabled the government to implement a national strategy aimed at increasing the number of adult learners in higher education (Brunton & Buckley, 2021, p. 2696). Higher education institutions (HEIs) internationally which are experiencing a decline in enrollment would do well to learn from the strategies adopted by Canada and Ireland.

In an effort to understand the educational journey of non-traditional students in Jamaica, this study is guided by four objectives. It

1. investigates the factors which hindered them from completing their education earlier;
2. discusses the motivators for them to enroll in an undergraduate degree at this age;
3. examines the challenges encountered and how these were overcome; and
4. and explores their expectations of the benefits to be gained from acquiring degrees.

Based on the findings from this small-scale study, the researchers made recommendations as to how local institutions can meet their enrolment targets while simultaneously providing non-traditional students with a chance of obtaining their degrees.

This study is important as it focuses attention on a demography not often given attention in the literature in the Caribbean culture, as evidence by the absence of empirical studies on the topic. It has relevance for various groups within the higher education sector. For policy makers, it points to the importance of having policies aimed at recruiting and retaining non-traditional students. For administrators, it provides them with strategies for recruitment, engagement and retention of non-traditional students. It also provides administrators with information about the challenges faced by these students so they can implement mitigation strategies. It provides researchers with information regarding gaps in the literature that need to be filled.

This study adds to the literature on tertiary education in the Caribbean and internationally. At a time when Caribbean institutions are implementing strategies to combat decreasing enrollment in tertiary education (The University of the West Indies Mona Campus, n.d.; Campus Office of Planning and Institutional Research, n.d.), it provides recommendations which address – the challenge of declining enrolment. One significant limitation is the small sample utilised for this study, as a larger sample might have provided more valuable data. However given the few students in this cohort it was difficult to find others who had the time to do the interview and were willing to participate.

The chapter is organised in four main sections. The background provides a historical overview of higher education in the Caribbean and examines the differences between traditional and non-traditional students. It then discusses enrolment trends for non-traditional students in the Caribbean and looks at challenges to providing and accessing higher education in the region. The literature review provides a summary of important studies on the topic. It looks at factors that delayed entry of participants into higher education and their motivation for enrollment in an undergraduate program. It then considers challenges experienced by non-traditional students and how they overcame these. This section closes with a discussion of the benefits participants expect to derive from obtaining a degree. The methodology section provides information on the data collection methods and procedures. The data is presented and analysed in the final section, and from the findings, the researchers present their conclusions.

BACKGROUND

The Anglophone Caribbean comprises nineteen territories which were formerly colonised by Britain and where English is the official language. It is home to about six million people (Caribbean English, 2021). Due to the shared history of the islands, the Caribbean education system is highly linked through its two regional educational institutions: Caribbean Examination Council (CXC) and The University of the West Indies with four landed campus located in different territories and a global (online) campus. A brief overview of the education system in the Caribbean is important to a discussion of why recruiting mature entrants into degree programs is worth considering.

Historical Overview of Higher Education in the Caribbean: The majority of the Caribbean people are descendants of ex-slaves who were brought to the region to work on sugar plantations (Miller, 2008, p. 15). The education system of the Caribbean is modelled after that of the British, the former colonial masters (Ellis, et al., 2007). According to Coates (2012) the establishment of formal education in the English-speaking Caribbean Community (CARICOM) countries dates back to 1743 when the Codrington Grammar School in Barbados was established (p. 347). Firstly, Coates noted that during the post-emancipation era religious groups led the charge to establish schools with the financial assistance of governments and grants. Coates further explains this move "drove and shaped the development of education at all levels" (p. 347). As a result, a four-tiered education system emerged that reflects what obtains internationally. This included early childhood, primary/elementary, secondary and tertiary level institutions (pp. 348-349).

"Caribbean governments and people place a high value on education and on the acquisition of academic qualifications" (Ellis et al., 2007, 13). Education became a route of upward social mobility for the peasant class, although this was more beneficial to females than males (Miller, 2008, p. 15). As noted by the World Bank there is improvement in the the number of persons from the lower socio-economic groups in Latin America and the Caribbean who are enrolling in higher education. It notes, "On average, the poorest 50 percent of the population only represented 16 percent of higher education students in 2000 but that rose to about 25 percent in 2013" (2017). There were also significant disadvantages to those who did not choose this route as lack of higher education significantly impacted one's fortunes in life. In the United States persons who chose to forgo college usually end up with lifetime earnings of 75% less when compared with those who attained bachelor's degrees (Binkley and the Associated Press, 2023). This finding suggests that the view of Caribbean people that having a degree results in upward mobility is justified. The increased demand for higher education in the region is being met by the "emergence of new universities, multi-disciplinary colleges and specialized non-university tertiary institutions" (Coates, 2012, p. 350).

Characteristics of Non-Traditional Learners

There are varying ways to define and characterise non-traditional students. On its admissions page, the Rutgers University defines non-traditional students as undergraduate students enrolled in a degree-granting school who has "personal and professional demands on their lives that make it challenging to meet their academic goals" (Defining Non-Traditional, 2024). Rutgers further outlines that for a student to be classified as non-traditional, he or she has to meet at least one of the following criteria:

- has been out of high school for 4+ years at the time of first undergraduate registration;
- has had at least a 2-year interruption in their undergraduate education;
- is a veteran or active-duty military service member;
- is enrolled in an off-campus or on-line bachelor's degree completion program;
- is pursuing post-baccalaureate studies, primarily in undergraduate courses;
- is a parent/caregiver and/or
- must take less than 12 credits due to significant non-academic commitments. (such as work or family responsibilities).

Whereas the "active-duty military service" criteria is not applicable in the Caribbean context, all the others are. It must also be noted, that some institutions categorize students from minority groups as non-traditional. Conversely, the National Center for Education Statistics categorise students from single parent families and students without high school diplomas as non-traditional (Coursera Staff, 2023). Single parent families is a historical feature of Caribbean households as more than half of Jamaica's population live in single parent households headed by women (Duncan-Price, 2021). In addition, the high school diploma criterion is not applicable to the Caribbean context, where matriculation to higher education is usually dependent on passes in Caribbean Secondary Education Certificate (CSEC) subjects.

Compared to non-traditional students, traditional students "typically includes full-time students who enroll immediately after high school, are between 18 and 22 years old, and who do not have other major responsibilities and roles that compete with their studies" (Panacci, 2015, n.p.). Based on data from the United States, non-traditional students outnumber traditional students (Coursera Staff, 2023). The descriptors for non-traditional students used elsewhere do not readily apply to the Caribbean context, however, they can serve as a guide in this discussion until the Caribbean articulates such.

Enrolment in Higher Education in the Caribbean: There was continuous growth in higher education enrollment in Latin America and the Caribbean from 11.5% of the population in 2000 to 28.9%% in 2020. However, the pace of growth slowed considerably, and for the last four years of this period the recorded growth was less than 1% (Education in Latin America and the Caribbean at the Crossroads, 2022). The average rate of participation in higher education in 10 territories to be 27.4%. This ranged from a low of 7% in Dominica to a high of 65% for both Barbados and Trinidad and Tobago (Thompson 2023). The government of Trinidad and Tobago implemented a tuition free higher education programme called Government Assistance for Tuition Expenses (GATE) in 2006 (Steele, 2016). Higher education is also provided free in Barbados, but students are required to do community service (Give Back Policy, 2024). In Jamaica, primary and secondary education are free, but

Life Begins at 40

higher education students are required to pay a significant portion of their tuition, while the government subsidizes a portion. This financial requirement becomes a barrier to access as is discussed later in this paper.

One characteristic of traditional students is that they proceed from high school to university. The age for traditional students is below 24 years (PostSecondary National Policy Institute, 2023), and entry to universities in the Caribbean is comprised primarily of students in this age cohort (Chisholm & Kennedy, 2014). At t The UWI Mona Campus in Jamaica, admissions data for the 2021-2022 academic year shows that figures for first degree entrants in the age group 35 – 54 was approximately 3.1% of 3,168 undergraduate students (The University of the West Indies Mona Campus, n.d., pp 95 and 99). The enrollment figure for the 35 and above age group for the St. Augustine campus in Trinidad and Tobago was also low (Campus Office of Planning and Institutional Research, n.d.). Of the 11,296 undergraduates enrolled, 6.5% were 35 years old and older (Campus Office of Planning and Institutional Research, n.d.).

In keeping with international trends, entry into higher education in the Caribbean seems to favor traditional students. Figure 1 illustrates the number of students registered in first degree programmes during a five-year period at The UWI, Mona Campus in Jamaica.

Figure 1. Enrolment in undergraduate degree programmes at The UWI, Mona Campus for the period 2018 – 2023.

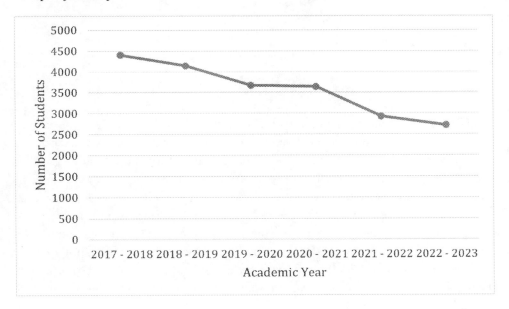

Overall, registration of new students in undergraduate degrees during this period decreased significantly from a high of 4,405 students in 2017 – 2018, to a low of 2,715 in 2022 – 2023, a 38.3% decrease. The decline in enrolment began in the pre-pandemic period and worsened during and after the pandemic. A closer look at registration data by age cohort shows significant disparity between age cohorts during this period as is shown on figure 2.

Figure 2. Enrolment trends for The University of the West Indies, Mona campus for the period 2018 – 2023

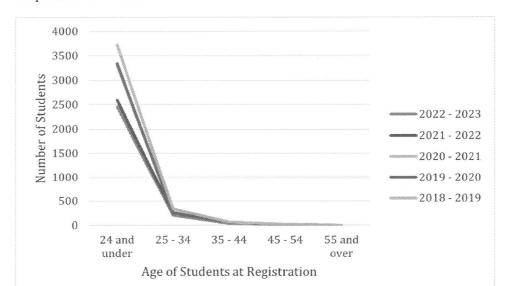

The largest group of incoming students registered on the campus for each of the five academic years displayed on the chart is traditional students based on their age. In the five academic years, this cohort accounted for more than 85% of the total registration. The remaining were non-traditional students who were 25 years old and over. It must be noted that the numbers of students in each group decreased as the age increased. In terms of the cohort which is of interest in this study, the number of students over 35 years old consistently remained less than a hundred for the period. The University of the West Indies does not publish completion rates by age; therefore it was difficult to compare the rates of completion with the enrolment. Data (although dated) for Latin America and the Caribbean point to low completion rates. It was reported that

One of the major problems affecting the region is that a high percentage of students entering HEI courses do not graduate, with vulnerable students being the worst affected. In the mid-2010s, a regional average of one third of students completed their courses on time, and among people between 25 and 29 years of age who had enrolled in a HEI programme at some point, only 46% had graduated, 22% had dropped out and 32% were still studying. (Venezuela & Yanez, 2022)

The World Bank concurs, adding that only half of the students in Latin American and the Caribbean completed their program in the prescribed time so "there's still a lot to do in terms of efficiency and quality" (2017). Although access to higher education in Latin America and the Caribbean has improved significantly, there is a huge disparity between enrolment and completion.

Higher Education Challenges in the Caribbean: In the Caribbean, there are many challenges to both providing and accessing higher education. As is the case with institutions in the United States, there has been a decline in enrolment in some tertiary institutions. In Jamaica however, in some cases this decline predates the pandemic. The 2015 Economic and Social Survey Jamaica records a sharp decline of 36% in the 2014 – 2015 academic year at Northern Caribbean University which is located in Mandeville in Manchester, in the centre of the island. Additionally, the Kingston based University of Technology had a marginal decrease of 0.4%. In the face of these less-than-optimal developments, The University of the West Indies had a marginal 1.8% increase in enrollment. However, as a result of the pandemic, Wilks reported that enrolment at the Mona Campus of the University of the West Indies had fallen by 6% for the 2020 – 2021 academic year (2023). Dale Webber, the principal of The UWI, Mona spoke about changes to the recruitment strategies to make greater use of technology in a bid to increase enrolment (Wilks, 2023). None of the strategies focused specifically on mature students.

Policies are critical to the efficient delivery of education at all levels (HR Management DTI, 2023) and this is also true of the Caribbean. However, "there were few explicit policy statements or documents in which governments clearly articulated policies on adult education" (Ellis, Ramsay & Small, 2007, 22). Jamaica was in the final stages of developing draft policies for higher education (Spence, 2023). The absence of policy means that there is no explicit focus on providing higher education to niche populations such as the non-traditional students.

Thompson (2023) identifies four cultural barrier to higher education in the Caribbean. These are:

- cultural mindset – acceptance of low quality of life;
- short-term thinking with preoccupation on financial liquidity in the immediate term versus a willingness to defer gratification, particularly among males;

- concepts of quality of life which are focused in survival and getting by rather than generating wealth and long-term savings
- loss of interest in having a degree given that so many people with degrees struggle financially. (p. 31).

Thompson (2023) also identifies another set of barriers which he categorised as financial barriers. These include lack of emphasis on tertiary which results in parents ending financial output on secondary schooling and absence of a political philosophy which supports higher education. Another barrier which manifests itself in an almost 3:1 enrolment ratio of females to males is the negative view of higher education and the willingness of the parents and non-governmental organisations to support girls.

Other challenges to the delivery of higher education in the Caribbean included of lack of student connectivity (Caribbean consultation held on adult education.., 2021). which might have implications for students who want to pursue online programmes. It will also affect students who need to complete assignments and learning tasks involving the use of technology. There is also lack of financial, infrastructure, and human resources. Additionally, there are concerns pertaining to student dropout rates and mental health and wellbeing which need to be given attention. (Caribbean consultation held on adult education, 2021).

UNESCO noted a gap between completion rates at the secondary level and enrolment into tertiary education (2022, p. 9), a trend also evident within the Caribbean (Caribbean Examination Council, 2023; Radio Jamaica News, 2016). Based on Thompson's (2023) conclusions, this could be a result of parents' commitment to fund secondary and not higher education for their children. One can therefore conclude that there is an out-of-school population that might be qualified to enter tertiary education but has delayed this process for several reasons. This could represent a pool of possible entrants from which local institutions could draw. But what hinders them from entering tertiary education? How can HEIs tap into this population in a more significant way? The aim of this research is to investigate the experiences of ten undergraduate students who were enrolled at a university in the Caribbean to see if we can find answers.

Higher education in the Caribbean region is impacted by various cultural, historical social and economic factors. This has implications for all students who desire to enter higher education institutions and those who administrate and provide higher education. One of the current challenges facing higher education in the region is the declining enrollment rates, which can be attributed to factors other than the pandemic. Non-traditional students, one cohort within higher education institutions, represent a very small segment of the higher education market currently. As such, their issues and concerns have largely been overlooked in the literature of the Caribbean. A better understanding of this cohort could help institutions to develop strategies for recruitment and retention of this cohort, and possible halt sliding enrolment trends.

Literature Review

There is very little focus on non-traditional students in the literature of the Caribbean, a fact that could be due to the size of this cohort. Therefore, a snapshot of trends within other geographic location is important to bring context to the respective study. This review draws mainly from studies in developed countries such as Ireland, the United States of America and the United Kingdom. It also has smatterings from other locations such as The Bahamas, Scotland, Spain and Ghana. The studies are current, ranging from 2013 to 2022.

CHARACTERISTICS OF NONTRADITIONAL STUDENT COHORTS

A demographic profile of non-traditional students enrolled in higher education might offer an enhanced understanding of the cohort sampled in this study. This population's interaction and engagement differ from the traditional learner. Older students are usually classified as non-traditional students (Hunter-Johnson & Smith, n.d., 70; Baharundin, Murad, and Mat, 2013, p. 773). They are more mature than traditional learners and are usually more aware of what and why they need to study (Kara et al., 2019, p. 5). The literature has shown that older learners tend to enroll in part-time degree programs rather than full-time options likely due to other commitments such as employment and family responsibilities (Merrill, 2015, 1860; Cummins et al., 2018, p. 25; Bellare et al., 2021, p. 35; Sayago et al., 2013, p. 532).

There are various reasons adult learners enroll in HEI. They generally opt for programs that potentially lead to a career change (Bellare et al., 2021, p. 31). They also seek for programs which are industry related and can heighten career opportunities or expose them to new pools of jobs. Others students enroll to finish a degree they started in their younger adulthood (Bellare et al., 2021, pp. 30-34). The research also indicates when selecting colleges or universities older learners are usually influenced by three major factors: the cost of the program; the degree options offered and the flexibility of the class schedules (Bellare et al., 2021, p. 32). These factors correspond to their financial status and responsibilities.

Factors that delayed entry to HEIs: The traditional student is usually enrolled in higher education at approximately 20 years old (Hunter-Johnson & Smith, n.d., 70; Baharundin, Murad, and Mat, 2013, p. 773). Conversely, a variety of factors influence individuals to delay their educational journey until a more suitable time.

It was found at the age of forty individuals still hold on to aspirations of completing their degree (Merrill, 2015, p. 1865). Hunter-Johnson and Smith (n. d.) found that fear of failure, instability (p. 70) and family responsibilities have been identified as factors that delayed early entry into tertiary education (p. 75).

A major reason for delayed entry into higher education was a lack of financial resources (Delayed Entry into Higher Education, 2016; Merrill, 2015, p. 1860). This resulted in students entering the workforce to strengthen their financial positions. Consequently, when they returned to school, they have work experience while being in a better position to pay their way (Delayed entry into higher education, 2016). Unbeknown to them, such delays predisposed them to experience greater financial difficulties than other students who decided to attend college earlier. (Delayed entry into higher education, 2016). Tattersfield (2022) noted that 89% of non traditional students experienced financial challenges (The issue of lack of financial resources is critical in the Caribbean as it is internationally, as "the poorest population continues to lag behind" (Vieira, Mutize & Chinchilla, 2020). In addition, there is the difference in access between developed and developing countries which sees the latter "with 10% access to higher education in 2018 compared to 77% of the higher income sector in the same year" (Vieira et al., 2020). Students who come from households where parents lack higher education are likely to delay entering tertiary institutions (Delayed entry into higher education, 2016). This could also be a manifestation of the financial challenges as these parents are likely to be among low-income earners who find it challenging to meet expenses associated with their children's education (Delayed entry into higher education, 2016).

MOTIVATORS TO ATTAIN HIGHER EDUCATION AS A NONTRADITIONAL STUDENT

Owusu-Agyman (2016) categorized the motivating factors into several related groupings, namely: individual, socio-political and industry. For example, the factors that fall under the individual category may include: building career or specialization; getting better pay; economic investment; increased productivity and contribution to work group (pp. 8-10). Bellare et al. (2021) concur with these findings as their research showed that older learners' enrollment in higher education was influenced by factors that differ from those of their younger counterparts (pp. 34-35). The research showed that "older people orientation and motivation for learning is always life-centered" and they participated in learning activities of mutual interest or benefit to themselves (Sayago et al., 2021, p. 540; Dauenhauer et al., 2016, p. 484). Driven by their real-life needs, older adults decide to start studying because they wanted to change some aspect of their lives (Sayago et al., 2021, p. 534).

Another significant motivator for entry into higher education was professional advancement or promotional opportunity which can lead to increased remuneration (Bellare et al., 2021, 30-31; Oneill & Thomson, 2013, p. 170; Hunter-Johnson & Smith, n. d., p. 71). Many adult learners pursue higher education to enable them to move from their current position within their organization to a higher position that requires advanced qualifications. This is necessary as constant changes in the industry-driven workplace require new skills and reorientation "(Bellare et al., 2021, p. 35; Oneill & Thomson, 2013, p. 162). Thus, enrolling in higher education and achieving the necessary qualifications is seen as the only way to avoid being made redundant (Bellare et al., 2021, p. 31). They are able to remain in their jobs because the new knowledge and skills acquired help the employees to remain relevant (Shift Disruptive eLearning, 2021).

Aljohani and Alajlan identified social contact, family togetherness, social stimulation, cognitive interest, and religious stimulation as additional motivational factors (2018, p. 38). Trust and exploration are also identified as motivational factors for adult learners, and these are critical considering the characteristics of this demographic (Aljohani & Alajlan, 2018, p.38). Enrolling in tertiary education can also result from internal forces such as the desire for self-actualization (Owusu-Agyeman, 2016, p. 5). Additionally, these learners can be said to have an individualized demand for knowledge acquisition which fuels the desire for advanced learning (Owusu-Agyeman, 2016, p. 5). Given these factors, institutions should create an environment that is reliable and facilitate creative learning (Breaking the code: What motivates adult learners, 2021).

STRATEGIES EMPLOYED TO OVERCOME CHALLENGES

Most nontraditional students experience various difficulties which make their academic journey challenging (Sayago et al., 2013, p. 534; Bellare et al., 2021, pp. 31-32; Brunton & Buckley, 2021, pp. 2696-2698). Due to their life stage, these are likely to be unique to this demography (Baharundin, Murad, and Mat, 2013, p. 773). Merrill (2015) stated that "working-class adult students may experience setbacks and struggles relating to academic study, the institutional culture and/or their personal lives" (p. 1859). These can negatively impact academic satisfaction, which may lead to lower job satisfaction, increased turnover rate and burnout (Bellare et al., 2021, p. 32; Oneill & Thomson, 2013, p. 163). Many of the challenges are interrelated. For example, the rigid expectation to attend classes at specific times (Sayago et al., 2013, p. 534) may be overwhelming because of an adult learner's need to balance school work, full time employment and manage a household (Bellare et al., 2021, p. 30; Baharundin, Murad, and Mat, 2013, p. 773; Kara et al., 2019, p. 5; Bok, 2021, p. 26).

Another difficulty for these non-traditional learners is transitioning from the identity of family members to the identity of adult learners (Carpenter 2022, p. 79). This identity-forming and/or changing process influences whether adult learners successfully complete their programs. This was reiterated by Brunton and Buckley (2021) as they explained that transitioning from family member to adult learner can be seen as an identity-forming process, and managing this process may affect the rate of completion of these adult learners (p. 2698). Additionally, adult learners often try to "treat university as if it were a work context" where they manage learning tasks and responsibilities the same they would a work assignment. This can lead to a conflict between their new learner role and their previous roles (p. 2698).

One way of overcoming the challenges of transitioning into tertiary education is by establishing relationships with peers in the learning environment. This is advantageous as it facilitates the building of social networks and fosters a sense of belonging, which will ease the difficulty of the transition into their adult learner identity (Brunton & Buckley, 2021, p. 2699). Building peer networks enables adult learners to deal with situations that can be overwhelming if dealt with alone, as it provides the support students need to complete their programs (Carpenter, 2022, p. 75). Carpenter also posits that understanding the transition necessary for adult learners can "provide colleges with the tools and strategies needed" when planning and conducting learning activities with instructional precision that is geared towards adult learners" (Carpenter, 2022, p. 79). These strategies are seen as ways in which universities can play their part in making acquiring a degree easier for the adult learner. Challenges can also be mitigated if employers create career development opportunities that support employee growth and education, for example, tuition reimbursement (Bellare et al., 2021, p. 34).

Sayago et al. (2013) provided several strategies which could be used to assist non-traditional students overcome some of the challenges they are likely to encounter during their tenure in a degree programme. One such strategy was collaborative learning. Collaborative learning could be structured as coffee breaks accompanied by informal conversations. These conversations could include activities which involve sharing or comparing knowledge gained during a previous class (Sayago et al., 2013, p. 534). Sayago et al. went on to explain that linking learning to real life by turning daily activities into learning activities (2013, p. 531) is advantageous. It allows adult learners to put their memory to work by capitalizing on their life experiences in the teaching and learning context (Sayago et al., 2013, p. 531).

BENEFITS OF ATTAINING A DEGREE

Many opportunities can be gained from obtaining a college degree. Higher education is a bridge to better job opportunities, higher pay rates, more promotional opportunities, and an increase in the person's knowledge base (Bellare et al., 2021, p. 30; Oneill & Thomson, 2013, 166). University graduates experienced an approximate increase of 17% in earnings compared to those who graduated from both primary and secondary school (Higher Education, 2021). In Latin America and the Caribbean, the degree is also valuable as on average "a student with a higher education degree will earn more than twice as much as a student with a high school diploma" (2017),

It should be noted that adult learners will select majors where the knowledge and skills connect to their career advancement plans (Bellare et al., 2021, p. 31). This can lead to advancing their goal of upward mobility, as they are seeking a competitive edge with the aim of pursuing increased responsibility in their career (Bellare et al., 2021, p. 31). In turn, these students tend to lean towards university programs designed with industry-recognized credentials which could can broaden their career options. This will increase their skillsets for current jobs. In addition, acquiring new knowledge and skills, helps to make the employee more effective and efficient and thereby decreases the need to outsource job functions . It also lessens the possibility of being laid off due to the "demand by industries for highly skilled" personal (Owusu-Agyeman, 2016, p. 6). Non-traditional students will enroll in courses that will equip them to "respond to both social and job demands" (Owusu-Agyeman, 2016, p. 5).

The literature revealed that older persons are interested in and willing to engage in higher education. Even though there are barriers to attaining a degree, there are strategies that can be employed by the learners, employers and colleges to ensure adult learners complete their programs. These strategies should mitigate barriers or challenges in attending college while helping the learners successfully complete their programs. Thus, ensuring self-actualization through the attainment of personal and professional goals (Bellare et al., 2021, p. 30; Owusu-Agyeman, 2016, p. 9).

METHODOLOGY

This qualitative research uses an ethnographic approach in that it examines the lived experiences of the participants. Fraenkel and Wallen found that the ethnographic study focuses on "documenting or portraying the everyday experiences of individuals by observing and interviewing them" (2000, p. 12). In this study, a semi structured interview was used as a data-gathering tool. Purposive sampling was used to select ten undergraduate students from the population of 8,780 undergraduate students located on the Mona Campus of The UWI, located in Kingston Jamaica (Student Statistics 2021 – 2022, n.d. p. 107).

Criterion based sampling; a type of purposive sampling was used to select the participants. The criteria for selection were as follows. Each participant had to be: forty years or older; currently registered in an undergraduate programme, and completed at least the first year of the programme. Purposive sampling is best used when investigators need specific information, so they use their knowledge of the population to select the required sample (Fraenkel and Warren, 2000, p. 112). In terms of sample size, InterQ Research LLC advises the ideal sample size for interviews is 30 participants (2023). However, this group concedes that a sample size of 10 can yield "extremely fruitful and applicable results" in the case where there is adequate recruiting (InterQ Research, 2023). The researchers ensured that they recruited the most ideal participants for this study, by applying the criteria for selection.

Data was collected using a semi-structured interview schedule which was divided into five sections. Fraenkel and Wallen noted that the strength of using an interview guide approach is that it "increases the comprehensiveness of the data and makes data collection somewhat systematic for each respondent." Additionally, through probing, gaps in the data can be closed and these interviews can be conversational and situational (2000, p. 511). Section 1 of the questionnaire consisted of items aimed at collecting demographic data. The remaining four sections contained items designed to collect data for each research objective. Interviews lasting for approximately forty-five minutes were conducted with each participant at the place of work.

The data were analyzed using Creswell and Poth's (2018) five steps for analysis of qualitative data. These steps were: managing and organizing data; reading and memoing emerging ideas; describing and classifying codes into themes; developing and assessing interpretation; and representing and visualising the data. Where necessary, charts and graphs were used to provide a visual representation of the data. After the interviews, the responses were transcribed by one of the researchers. This was part of the process of managing and organising the data. After this process was complete, the responses to each question were collated so that the researchers could compare and contrast these, and identify the emerging codes that were relevant to the research objectives. The codes were organised these into five predetermined themes which were derived from the review of literature. These included: challenges, motivation, benefits, family and delay factors. The additional theme of self-actualisation was added based on the data. These were classified as themes based on their importance to the participants. During the representing and visualising, the researchers developed charts and graphs and examined the findings in light of the literature.

DATA PRESENTATION AND ANALYSIS

This section is organised based on the research objectives.

Demographic data: The participants included two males and eight females. This sample was representative of the gender enrollment by age group within the institution (Campus Office of Planning and Institutional Research, n.d). The ratio of males to females in this research (1:4) was significantly lower than the ratio of males to females in the university population which was one male to three females. However, the male to female ratio in this study is representative of the over cohorts in which females far outnumber males.

The ages of the respondents ranged from 40 to 50 years, with two of the ten participants being 50 years old. Nine of the ten respondents were employed full-time and studied part-time, a finding which concurred with the literature (Merrill, 2015, 1860; Bellare et al., 2021, p. 35; Sayago et al., 2013, p. 532). One of the respondents was employed full-time and was enrolled in college full-time, a situation far from ideal for the traditional student. The sample group members were mostly involved in service-type jobs. Their duties included task such as preparing monthly reports, planning events and meetings, managing documents and circulation of library resources.

There were several reasons they were studying part-time to include: having full-time jobs (70%), attending to family responsibilities, parental duties and caring for aging parents (40%). These respondents were from homes where the parents did not complete secondary education, one of the characteristics of nontraditional students (Delayed entry into higher education, 2016). All the respondents in this study met at least three of the criteria specified by Rutgers University (2024). The most most predominant criteria were graduated from high school for more than four years; being parents and caregivers, and having significant non-academic commitment, in this case their full-time jobs. This profile would make them more vulnerable to dropping out and longer completion times. The high percentage of those studying part-time surpassed the number of students studying part-time in Cummin' et al. (2018) study. The participants were involved in pursuing degrees that aligned to their jobs, similar to the findings of Owusu-Agyeman (2016, p. 6) and Bellare et al. (2021).

MOTIVATIONS TO PURSUE HIGHER EDUCATION

Participants were motivated to enroll in higher education by a variety of factors, and each provided more than one factor. The majority (50%) were pursuing the degree for personal satisfaction including self-actualization (Bellare et al., 2021, p. 30;

Owusu-Agyeman, 2016, p. 9). Another 50% felt that obtaining higher education enabled them to be role models for their children. Within households with parents who have obtained degrees, the likelihood of their children doing the same is greater than in households with parents who did not attain degrees ("Delayed entry into higher education", 2016). Others nontraditional students attended college later in life out of a desire to capitalize off the opportunity which previously did not exist.

Forty percent of the respondents were motivated by the possibility of increased financial benefits (Bellare et al., 2021, p. 30; Oneill & Thomson, 2013, p.166) and as discussed earlier this was due to historical and personal reasons. Twenty percent of the respondents were motivated by family members to continue their education (Aljohani & Alajlan, 2018, p. 38). As expressed by one respondent,

The Lord provided me with the opportunity and setting a good example for the young men I am raising, to gain knowledge, to increase my abilities and skills, while setting a good trajectory towards a career.

In this case, opportunity and motivation were in alignment and so this participant capitalised on both.

It could be concluded that participants were motivated to enter a degree program for intrinsic and extrinsic reasons. The number of reasons they provided speaks to the value of this opportunity to them, and the fact that it was a deliberate and well-thought-out decision. The inclusion of self-actualization as one of the primary reasons indicated that they placed a high value on education and that acquiring the degree would bring great personal satisfaction

CHALLENGES PREVENTING EARLY LIFE COLLEGE ENROLLMENT

As shown in Figure 1, participants experience several challenges which hindered them from pursuing their degrees earlier in life.

Figure 3. Challenges which hindered early entry into higher education

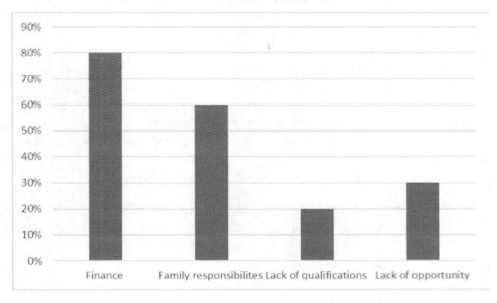

The most significant hindrance to students' early entry into higher education was finances (80%) (Merrill, 2015, p. 1860; Bok 2023, p. 19; Kara et al. 2019, p. 13; Hunter-Johnson & Smith, 2015, 69), and this was followed by family responsibilities (60%) (Bok, 2021, p. 19; Kara et al. 2019, p. 13). In Jamaica, the financial barrier is a critical issue as there is limited access to free tertiary education (Thompson, 2023). Participants therefore joined the job market early with the qualifications they obtained from secondary school. However, they were engaged in jobs that required low qualifications with the resulting low remuneration, so paying tuition was still a challenge more than two decades later.

The financial challenges faced by Jamaican students was acknowledged by the Minister of Education Fayval Williams when she spoke about the inclusion of information on financing tertiary education in the draft higher education policy (Spence, 2023). The issue of financing education in some Caribbean countries is dire. Whereas in Trinidad and Tobago and Barbados, countries with high percentage of enrolment at the tertiary level, higher education is provided free, in Jamaica it is not. Citing the case of The University of the West Indies, Thompson (2023) notes that the government has over the past one and a half decades defaulted on its commitment to pay 80% of the cost of higher education. This has whittled down to some governments pay less than 40%, not even a half of what was agreed on. This is likely to have significant impact on the institutions' ability to deliver quality education at an affordable cost.

The participants who had family obligations indicated, they had child-rearing responsibilities which prevented them from attending school. The findings from this item is telling as to why with students' enroll part-time. Both lack of opportunity and qualifications did not feature much in the literature that was reviewed as factors which hindered access to higher education.

Several researchers mention the difficulty of transitioning back into the learning environment (Panacci, 2015: Oniel & Thomson, 2013; Merrill, 2015; Bozick & Deluca, 2005). Respondents were able to get support from individuals and institutional resources to enable their transition back into the academic environment and these are shown on figure 2.

Figure 4. Sources of assistance for transition into higher education

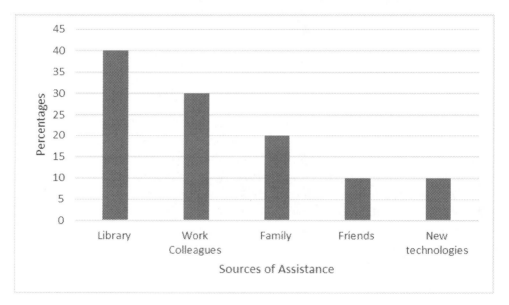

Library resources (40%) was the most popular form of assistance while colleagues ranked next (30%). Work colleagues ranked highly as these non-traditional learners were working in institutions where some of their colleagues at the time pursued degrees in the same specialization they were studying. One respondent expressed:

encouragement from colleagues, support of family and with the new technologies that allows for easy access of resources (such as Databases) made the transition much easier."

Brunton and Buckley (2012) spoke of the importance of social networks in this transitioning phase. While Sayago et al. (2013) refers to the use of technology in the same phase.

RESPONSIBILITIES AND CHALLENGES

The participants were asked to indicate some of the responsibilities they had while attending school. All the respondents indicated that they had work duties. This information was supported with demographic data. In addition to work duties, (80%) of the respondents had to manage family responsibilities (caring for children) while 20% were simultaneously fulfilling church obligations

Given these important responsibilities, it is expected that participants would experience challenges while studying. When asked about the challenges, participants' responses could be categorized into three groups (work, school and family), with a significant level of interplay between them. Some of the same factors which resulted in late entry to tertiary education such as finances also impacted students while they were enrolled in the program, signalling that students were not waiting to resolve all the challenges before beginning their studies. Fifty percent of the respondents experienced challenges balancing three significant life commitments: work, school and family responsibilities (Bellare et al, 2021, p. 32; Merril, 2015, 1860; Baharudin, Murad, and Mat, 2013, p. 772). Based on the severity of the challenges, participants were pursuing degrees at a significant sacrifice to themselves. One explained,

I live out of town, transportation and night classes have limited my time with my family. Finding time to study and balance work is also very challenging.

However, this participant had to discontinue a previous enrolment as she was unable to balance work, family and studies. Bok found work commitment to be the greatest challenge encountered by these students (2021, p. 26).

One respondent who worked a shift job while studying expressed,

I had to work all of the three shifts, at times I had exam and coming off the 10 pm to 6 am shift I had to stay on the campus until the exam starts at 1pm then find somewhere to lay my head until the evening shift starts at 10pm. All this while I have a husband and three children to take care of. Apart from work and the family I had church duties to carry out.

A single mom who also worked at a shift job which required rotation in the schedule while carrying out parental duties expressed,

Being a full-time worker that works on shifts and weekends and a single mom is really tough, because my son has to be at work with me on the night shifts and weekend shifts because I have no support system in order to help with my son.

These responses provide insights into the level of sacrifice required to pursue their studies. However, it points out their tenacity in pursuing their dreams. Many would not be willing to undertake studies with these challenges. One participant summed it up by saying "*Yes, juggling work, school and home gets overwhelming at times.*" Bellare et al. (2021) noted the importance of employer support in mitigating the challenges faced by nontraditional students. Additional support could in terms of flexibility in timetabling could have mitigated some of the challenges noted by participants. Kara et al. made mention of the challenges when schedules for work conflicted with school responsibilities (2019).

One respondent reportedly dropped out of a previous program due to the severity of the challenges. As cited in the literature, non-traditional students tend to have higher incompletion rates or take longer to complete their programs than traditional students (Bozick & DeLuca, 2005; "Non-Traditional Students Not Graduating at Near the Same Rate as Traditional", 2014). However, this did not deter her. She re-enrolled in another program that she was determined to complete. The participants in Merrill's (2015) study experienced severe hardships and just as in this case, they did not drop out the program rather waited until the situation improved. Participants believed the benefits of staying enrolled outweighed the challenges.

COPING AND SELF-EFFICACY

Participants adopted several coping strategies to overcome the challenges they encountered. These strategies included developing time management skills, relying on the support of family members, a factor that some participants in Kara et al's. (2019) study lacked. Also taking leave from work to complete assignments and study for examinations, and setting goals and working towards them. One resilent nontraditional student expressed:

Constantly having a positive mindset and the push to achieve better for myself and my son because I do not want him to have the difficulty I had back then.

Time management (80%) was the most widely used strategy to balance work and school. This was predicted since all study participants worked and studied. Time was managed in several ways. Participants planned, and completed assignments ahead of the due dates, prioritized, used timetables, studied and multi-tasked. Another popular time management strategy was the use of vacation time (30%). Two respondents (20%) spoke of the importance of self-care in successfully balancing school and other priorities. Another respondent who utilized several strategies expressed,

I have accepted all the assistance I have gotten from my family, I have utilized vacation leave to help me study. I also complete assignments in advance to avoid additional stress.

These strategies were not exemplified highly within the literature reviewed. However, given the challenges which participants experienced it is logical that early assignment submission and using vacation to allow long periods of time to study would be employed.

One study respondent indicated she was unable to employ time management solutions. She stating that she was *"lagging behind in all areas of my life."* This suggested that these were personal issues that were impacting her academic pursuits.

None of the study respondents indicated they received any form of preferential treatment, bias or discrimination as a result of their ages. This is because the university treated them in the same manner as traditional students, who made up a majority of the student population.

Given the enormity of the challenges and the high incompletion rates for these older students, it was important for them to remain highly motivated. When asked how they have stayed motivated during the process despite the many challenges, participants had a variety of responses. Of importance was the feeling of achievement to be experienced from degree attainment. Knowing as part-time students, it would take at least five years to complete the degree, it was important for them to remain encouraged. One participant expressed:

I tend to focus on the end result and what I want to achieve professionally as opposed to focusing on the challenges faced in the present.

Another study participant was motivated because school was an enjoyable as she achieved her dream. She expressed:

I enjoy being in school, the lectures are fun and engaging. To gain my degree will be a dream come true. A dream at one time I thought was impossible.

Family members, children and friends were important in keeping participants motivated. One participant who was undeterred by the challenges expressed,

The motivation for me is that yes, I want to at least do and complete something and this is a big break for me because not many have been afforded the opportunity to start university. It was a struggle but I am pulling through by again being positive and thinking of it as something being better for me in the long run.

Family was previously identified as an important source in helping participants transition into the role of students. Again, family is seen as important, this time in helping the participants to remain motivated by providing moral support (Aljohani & Alajlan, 2018, p. 38).

BENEFITS OF DEGREE ATTAINMENT

Benefits of higher education were mentioned among the study respondents. Because of degree attainment, (80%) of the respondents indicated the financial benefits. However, interestingly, no one asserted money as the main motivation for attending college . One participant focused on the professional benefits to be accrued by obtaining a degree stating it would lead to

Self-actualization and professionally being more marketable and the ability to make a greater contribution to whichever organization I am employed.

This concurs with the findings of the literature (Bellare et al. 2021, p. 30; Oneill and Thomson, 2013, p. 166), Another respondent who was pursuing a Bachelor of Arts in Librarianship expressed,

I hope to be a qualified Librarian one who stands out among the rest, one who can satisfy the patrons' information needs, and finally gain much more wisdom, knowledge, understanding and by extension wealth to take care of my family.

Yet another participant, who was highly cognisant of the age factor expressed,

For me personally it was something I never dream I could do at this age but then I remember that there are older people than me who have done this and they have passed the worse. On the professional level it means open more job opportunities for me.

Thirty percent of the respondents used the term "*self-*actualization" in their response to this item. Another captured this same idea in the term "*sense of accomplishment*", while yet another used the term "*respect.*" Attainment of this degree was tied to the respondents' sense of self and self-worth (Owusu-Agyeman, 2016, p. 9). One noted it would result in "*a boost in self-confidence*."

It is clear from the list of expected benefits that these individuals held this degree in high regard. This is understandable given the almost insurmountable challenges that many will have to overcome in order to complete. Their focus on the end product and not necessarily on the challenges that they were experiencing speaks to a mindset that is likely to foster success,

FEEDBACK FROM HIGH-ACHIEVING NONTRADITIONAL STUDENTS

The final interview question asked "What advice would you give to potential adult learners in your age group who desire to pursue further education? Regardless of the challenges that the participants were experiencing responses to the inquiry were overwhelmingly positive. Forty percent of the participants advised potential students to seek higher education by using the term "Go for it". Another 10% stated that potential applicants should "take the first step and begin". The participants did not give the impression that pursuing the degree was going to be easy, as they spoke about the need for dedication, endurance and determination. Others gave advice that had to do with getting through assignments. A comprehensive response was:

Go for it, it might seems hard at the beginning but trust God, He will see you through to the end. Just take it one day at a time. Please complete assignments at all time. Work on any major paper or project as soon as it's made available. Do not rush the major assignments it impacts the quality of your work. Time management is key. You can do it.

Another comprehensive response was,

Always remember it's not too late to go back to school and remember that age does not matter when it comes to education. What you may not have attain when you were younger there is still a chance in achieving it once, you have the motivation and drive to pursue this cause especially when it the long run this will be beneficial to you as the learner.

Students who delayed entry into tertiary education until they were in their forties. However, they were motivated to complete their degree program despite challenges. In addition because of their own experiences on the journey, they believed that others would equally benefit.

CONCLUSION

There were several factors that hindered study participants from enrolling in higher education earlier. The major factors were finances and family responsibilities. These factors were similar to findings within the literature review. Other factors which were not prominent in the literature review included the both the lack of qualifications and opportunities. The major motivating factors for participants to enroll in the degree program were personal factors including the need for self-actualization and the desire to set a good example for their children. Forty percent of the individuals were motivated by the desire to increase their income, while others were extrinsically motivated by family members.

Respondents encountered several challenges with some being severe. These included challenges of balancing work, school, and family responsibilities. They worked full-time, studied part-time and cared for families. These findings were also similar to those founds in the literature (Bellare et al. 2021; Kara et al., 2019; Bok, 2021). Although attempts were made by employers to mitigate some of these issues, other work-related challenges placed them at a distinct disadvantage. Students therefore seemed to lack moral and financial support from employers Bellare et al. (2021)

Respondents found several strategies to cope with these barriers to success. They implemented time management strategies including using weekends and vacation time to study and completing assignments before they were due. Although there were several benefits to be obtained from acquiring a degree, the financial benefits were the overarching theme. Interestingly none of the study respondents were attaining their degree only for monetary gain. Rather, self-actualisation was the primary motivation.

This cohort represents working adults who are desirous of obtaining tertiary qualifications to advance themselves professionally and for self-actualization. Colleges would need to examine the needs of cohorts of non-traditional students in order to provide vital support. In addition to, offering adult learner scholarships and flexible scheduling of classes, colleges can try "open enrolment policies and low tuition", which would ease the barriers of affordability and the integration of college life into regular life by facilitating "financial and temporal flexibility to obtain retraining" (Cummins et al., 2018, p. 25).

The theme of family was very prominent in this study. The majority of participants were mothers and they had child care responsibilities which resulted in several challenges. In addition, family was instrumental in influencing enrolment into higher education. Family was also a source of motivation as these individuals met with and overcome the many challenges associated with serving in multiple roles. Some persons were studying to be role models for their children, while others wanted to be better providers for their families. Furthermore, they believed that their degree would help them fulfil this desire. Institutions wishing to attract and engage these students would do well to keep such factors in mind. According to Panacci (2015), some institutions in Canada have established on-campus childcare facilities. This was reflective of their awareness of this population's challenges with childcare and wanting to provide a solution.

Dauenhauer et al. (2016) recommend that universities develop, promote, and expand lifelong learning opportunities within the multigenerational context (p. 484). Within this context there is the use of intergenerational service learning such as "the application of classroom and community-based learning" built on "well-designed and integrated experiences".. This strategy results in "cognitive benefits, enhanced learning and understanding of subject material, personal and interpersonal development" (Dauenhauer et al., 2016, p. 483). That is, mixing both younger and older learners together so they can work together and learn from each other. For example, the successful St. John's Collaborative for Intergenerational Learning (SCIL) program (Dauenhauer et al., 2016, p. 485). The strategies identified can be used by individuals and universities to enroll and complete multiple cohorts of adult learners.

Given the importance of policies for driving institutional improvements in higher education, there is need for institutional and even national policies to support recruitment and retention of non-traditional students. This is important in light of shrinking enrolment in HEIs in the Caribbean, the competition from overseas universities and the pool of potential candidates who are currently employed in both the public and private sector.

Cox (2023) proposes four strategies to attract and retain non-traditional students which are of value to this discussion. Firstly, scheduling and delivery format is configured for the traditional students who are able to be present on campus for the entire day. Non traditional students do not have this level of flexibility, therefore institutions need to leverage the advantages of technology to serve them whenever they need to be served and wherever they are.

Secondly, there needs to be a flexible approach to helping non traditional students acquire credentials (Cox, 2023). This means breaking down the programmes in smaller portions and allowing students to be able to proceed by stacking up qualifications. This could mean providing students with a certificate after one year, an associate degree and then awarding the degree when all the requirements are met. The system used by the Human Employment and Resource Training Trust/National Service Training Agency is built on this premise as students can pursue their studies up to level 4, but at each level they can choose to terminate with certification. The University of South Florida Counselling Center has a page specifically dedicated to non-traditional students. Small acts like these can bring great rewards in terms of their effectiveness in supporting non-traditional students.

Thirdly, Cox (2024) recommends dedicated support which is targeted to the specific types of challenges that nontraditional students experience. She recommends that this includes both personalised learning experiences as well as dedicated administrative support. Given the many roles that they manage, they should be given the kind of quality service maximises their time and minimises their frustrations. This might mean having personnel specially assigned to assist these persons, or special offices dedicated to meet their needs.

Finally, in order to attract non-traditional students, institutions needs to have targeted recruitment programs (Cox, 2023). Cox concludes that the strategies for college recruitment which focus on traditional students are not attractive to non-traditional students whose life circumstances differ significantly. She therefore advises that advertising to this group should involve information on how the institutions' programs and facilities are relevant to their needs.

Colleges and universities should conduct needs assessments of their enrollment practices and develop creative action plans. Additionally, they need to develop strategic plans to increase recruitment activities aimed at non-traditional students. In light of the challenges being experienced by these students and the high non-completion rates (Delayed entry into higher education, 2016), institutions have to be prepared to institute measures to mitigate the challenges. They must also be willing to develop strategies aimed at removing barriers to access experienced by these individuals. It is clear that non-traditional students have the desire to succeed. Therefore, institutions of higher learning should capitalize on this phenomenon while assisting this vulnerable population improve the quality of life for themselves and their families.

REFERENCES

Aljohani, O. H., & Alajlan, S. M. (2018). Motivating adult learners to learn at adult education schools in Saudi Arabia. *Department of Education*. https://files.eric.ed.gov/fulltext/ED597543.pdf

Baharudin, S., Murad, M., & Mat, N. A. (2013). Challenges of adult learners: A case study of full time postgraduates students. *Procedia – Social and Behavioral Sciences, 90*, 772–781. doi:10.1016/j.sbspro.2013.07.151

Bellare, Y., Smith, A., Cochran, K., & Lopez, S. G. (2023). Motivations and barriers for adult learner achievement: Recommendations for institutions of higher education. *Adult Learning, 34*(1), 30–39. doi:10.1177/10451595211059574

Binkley, C. (2023). *The labor shortage is pushing American colleges into crisis, with the plunge in enrollment the worst ever recorded.* https://fortune.com/2023/03/09/american-skipping-college-huge-numbers-pandemic-turned-them-off-education/

Bok, G. I. (2021). Adult learners' challenges in distance learning: A case study in Universiti Sains Malaysia. *Issues in Educational Research, 31*(1), 19–36. https://www.proquest.com/scholarly-journals/adult-learners-challenges-distance-learning-case/docview/2702191373/se-2

Bozick, R., & DeLuca, S. (2005). Better Late Than Never? Delayed Enrollment in the High School to College Transition. *Social Forces, 84*(1), 531–554. doi:10.1353/sof.2005.0089

Breaking the code: What motivates adult learners. (2021). Shift. Retrieved August 13, 2023, from https://www.shiftelearning.com/blog/what-motivates-adult-learners

Brunton, J., & Buckley, F. (2021). 'You're thrown in the deep end': Adult learner identity formation in higher education. *Studies in Higher Education (Dorchester-on-Thames), 46*(12), 2696-2709. doi:10.1080/03075079.2020.1767049

Campus Office of Planning and Institutional Research. (n.d.). *The University of the West Indies St. Augustine campus student statistical digest 2015/2016 to 2019/2020.* https://sta.uwi.edu/resources/documents/statistics/Student_Statistics_15_16-19_20.pdf

Caribbean consultation held on adult education challenges and opportunities in preparation of CONFINTEA VII. (2021). UNESCO Clearinghouse on Global Citizenship Education. https://www.gcedclearinghouse.org/news/aribbean-consultation-held-adult-education-challenges-and-opportunities-preparation-confinteaCarpenter doi:10.1177/10451595221074731

Caribbean English. (2021). *Oxford English Dictionary.* https://www.oed.com/discover/aribbean-english/?tl=true#:~:text=The%20Anglophone%20Caribbean%20(the%2019,in%20the%20formal%20education%20system

Chisholm, M., & Kennedy, M. (2014). Widening participation in higher education: The case of the UWI, Mona Campus. *UWI Quality Education Forum, 20*, 34 – 61.

Coates, C. O. (2012). *Educational developments in the British West Indies: A historical overview.* https://files.eric.ed.gov/fulltext/ED567093.pdf

Coursera Staff. (2023). *What Is a Nontraditional Student?* Coursera. https://www.coursera.org/articles/nontraditional-student

Cox, S. (2023). *How to serve nontraditional students.* https://moderncampus.com/blog/why-and-how-you-should-serve-non-traditional-students.html

Creswell, J. W., & Poth, C. N. (2018). *Qualitative Inquiry and Research Design Choosing among Five Approaches* (4th ed.). SAGE Publications, Inc.

Cross, J. (2017, October 23). US college recruiter wants more Jamaicans. *The Gleaner.* https://jamaica-gleaner.com/article/news/20171025/us-college-recruiter-wants-more-jamaicans

Cummins, P. A., Brown, J. S., Bahr, P. R., & Mehri, N. (2018). Heterogeneity of Older Learners in Higher Education. *Adult Learning*, *30*(1), 23–33. doi:10.1177/1045159518812077

Dauenhauer, J., Steitz, D. W., & Cochran, L. J. (2016). Fostering a new model of multigenerational learning: Older adult perspectives, community partners, and higher education. *Educational Gerontology*, *42*(7), 483–496. doi:10.1080/03601277.2016.1157419

Defining non-traditional. (2024). Rutgers University. https://transfer.rutgers.edu/admissions/defining-non-traditional

Delayed entry into higher education. (2016). *Intelligence Brief.* https://www.eurostudent.eu/download_files/documents/IB_delayed_transition.pdf

Education in Latin America and the Caribbean at the Crossroad. (n.d.). Regional monitoring report SDG4 – Education 2030. UNESCO. https://repositorio.cepal.org/server/api/core/bitstreams/70fe53c4-9b47-4f64-957b-1adf27c8b1f4/content

Ellis, P., Ramsay, A., & Small, S. (2000). *Adult Education in the Caribbean at the Turn of the Century.* UNESCO. https://uwispace.sta.uwi.edu/server/api/core/bitstreams/76a6bf15-f8a1-4a1e-8b45-861010831b48/content

Fraenkel, J. R., & Warren, N. E. (2000). *How to design and evaluate research in education.* https://books.google.com.jm/books/about/How_to_Design_and_Evaluate_Research_in_E.html?id=vhKvOZ4rqVsC&redir_esc=y

Give Back Policy. (2024). Ministry of Education, Technological and Vocational Training. https://mes.gov.bb/GiveBack/

Higher education. (2021, October 22). *The World Bank.* https://www.worldbank.org/en/topic/tertiaryeducation

Hunter-Johnson, Y., & Smith, S. (2015). *Yes I need help! A day in the journey of adult learners pursuing higher education: A Caribbean perspective.* https://eric.ed.gov/?id=ED570503

Imani Duncan-Price. (2021). Unleashing the multiplier effect of women. *Jamaica Observer.* https://www.jamaicaobserver.com/2021/03/13/unleashing-the-multiplier-effect-of-women/#:~:text=WITH%20just%20over%20410%2C000%20households,the%20average%2C%20with%20more%20children

Inter Q. Research LLC. (2023). *What is the ideal sample size in qualitative research?* https://interq-research.com/what-is-the-ideal-sample-size-in-qualitative-research/

International Students. (2024). *Migration Data Portal.* https://www.migrationdataportal.org/themes/international-students#:~:text=Prominent%20countries%20of%20origin%20of,on%20UIS%2C%202023)

Kara, M., Erdoğdu, F., Kokoç, M., & Cagiltay, K. (2019). Challenges faced by adult learners in online distance education: A literature review. *Open Praxis, 11*(1), 5-22. https://files.eric.ed.gov/fulltext/EJ1213733.pdf

Merrill, B. (2015). Determined to stay or determined to leave? A tale of learner identities, biographies and adult students in higher education. *Studies in Higher Education (Dorchester-on-Thames), 40*(10), 1859-1871. doi:10.1080/03075079.2014.914918

Miller, E. (2008). *Education and social mobility: The case of the Jamaican peasant.* https://errolmiller.com/wp-content/uploads/2018/09/Education-and-Social-Mobility-the-Case-of-the-Jamaican-Peasant-2.pdf?d9dbdd&d9dbdd

Murthi, M., & Bassett, R. M. (2022, November 15). *Higher education: Understanding demand and redefining values.* https://blogs.worldbank.org/education/higher-education-understanding-demand-and-redefining-values

Nietzel, M. T. (2022, October 20). College enrollment losses continue, but at a slower rate, according to new report. *Forbes.* https://www.forbes.com/sites/michaeltnietzel/2022/10/20/college-enrollment-decline-continues-but-at-a-slower-rate-according-to-new-report/?sh=318c13ff3910

Non-Traditional Students Not Graduating at Near the Same Rate as Traditional. (2014, October 15). *College Factual.* https://students.collegefactual.com/blog/are-colleges-supporting-non-traditional-students

Oneill, S., & Thomson, M. M. (2013). Supporting academic persistence in low-skilled adult learners. *Support for Learning, 28*(4), 162–172. doi:10.1111/1467-9604.12038

Owusu-Agyeman, Y. (2016). Investigating the determinants of adults' participation in higher education. *Cogent Education.*, *3*(1), 1–16. doi:10.1080/233118 6X.2016.1194733

Panacci, A. G. (2015). Adult students in higher education: Classroom experiences and needs. *The College Quarterly*, *18*(3).

Perue, C. (2023, June 7). *A librarianship business model for the knowledge economy*. ACURIL 2023 Conference, Kingston, Jamaica.

Radio Jamaica News. (2016, May 30). *Number of students enrolling in tertiary institutions declines.* https://radiojamaicanewsonline.com/local/number-of-students-enrolling-in-tertiary-institutions-declines

Roman, E. (2022). 3 reasons why college enrollments are declining, according to Coursera's CEO. *Yahoo Finance* https://finance.yahoo.com/news/declining-college-enrollments-a-us-phenomenon-coursera-ceo-says-170903514.html?guccounter=1&guce_referrer=aHR0cH M6Ly93d3cuZ29vZ2xlLmNvbS8&guce_referrer_sig=AQAAAGsMO-8PV__qZfRdHJul39YGFT3L1TgVw7ZJ35w0lJixZrZB1-M_ WXhZHj74nmLiueFY4VX29ZVL-JeMP7HLHMzqpDaOmmJXw84MKZ6__YN 5L6fesRvTqg8b71R2bYlfukdRa2c6LZv9LOrTkNAMecJv-yRb_ mb9a4GbmxkqGv-7

Sayago, S., Forbes, P., & Blat, J. (2013). Older people becoming successful ICT learners over time: Challenges and strategies through an ethnographical lens. *Educational Gerontology*, *39*(7), 527–544. doi:10.1080/03601277.2012.703583

Spence, C. (2023). *Draft Higher Education Policy in Final Stage of Review*. Jamaica Information Service. https://jis.gov.jm/draft-higher-education-policy-in-final-stage-of-review/

Steele, D. A. (2016). *The price paid: free higher education in Trinidad and Tobago re-examined* [PhD Dissertation]. Colombia University.

Tatersfield, K. (2022). *How to Address the Struggles of Non-Traditional Students*. https://www.leadsquared.com/industries/education/struggles-of-non-traditional-students/

The University of the West Indies Mona Campus. (n.d.). *Student Statistics 2021 - 2022*. https://www.mona.uwi.edu/principal/sites/default/files/principal/studentstatistics20212022.pdf

Thompson, C. (2023). Right to higher education: A case study of Caribbean countries. In *The right to higher education in Latin America and the Caribbean: Briefing note compendium*, 30 – 32. https://unesdoc.unesco.org/ark:/48223/pf0000387656?posInSet=21&queryId=N-EXPLORE-95f65d07-cdcf-4155-bc78-f28a20b534dd

UNESCO. (2022). Higher education global data report (Summary). *World Higher Education Conference.*

Venezuela, P., & Yáñez, N. (2022). *Trajectory and policies for inclusion in higher education in Latin America and the Caribbean in the context of the pandemic: Two decades of progress and challenges.* https://repositorio.cepal.org/server/api/core/bitstreams/6666262b-754b-4684-a247-8659e96f3fea/content

Vieira, D., Mutize, T., & Chinchilla, J. R. (2020, December 21). Understanding access to higher education in the last two decades. *UNESCO.* https://www.iesalc.unesco.org/en/2020/12/23/understanding-access-to-higher-education-in-the-last-two-decades/

Wilks, A. (2023, March 4). *Student enrolment dips by six per cent at UWI, Mona.* https://jamaica-gleaner.com/article/lead-stories/20230304/student-enrolment-dips-six-cent-uwi-mona

World Bank. (2017). *Higher Education Expanding in Latin America and the Caribbean, but Falling Short of Potential.* https://www.worldbank.org/en/news/press-release/2017/05/17/higher-education-expanding-in-latin-america-and-the-caribbean-but-falling-short-of-potential

Worldwide College Tours. (2018, October 24). *7 benefits of recruiting students in the Caribbean – How can your college or university get involved?* https://www.worldwidecollegetours.com/benefits-recruiting-students-caribbean-college-university

Section 3
Dearth of Positive Ethnic Representation in the Comic Realm

Chapter 7
An Autoethnographic Approach to Adaptations and Limitations in Comics

Jason D. DeHart
The University of Tennessee, Knoxville, USA

ABSTRACT

This chapter explores the experiences of a White male educator in an Appalachian fringe rural setting. Using an Emic perspective, he draws upon autoethnography to explore pedagogy and positionality. In particular, the author focuses on graphic novels and how visual texts can engage readers from underrepresented populations. The medium's limitations are explored, including the lack of some positive representation of minoritized students. Particular texts are named and explored, and the implications of this project include a framing of classroom practice that is both welcoming and text-centered. Further implications point to the necessity for writing and composing with the underrepresented students in mind.

As a literacy scholar who is a White male, I note the threads of this exploration in autoethnography based on the cultural artifactual work of Chang (2016). When considering students' reading lives, I draw upon my own story, as well as the experiences I have in the classroom each day. I do so in order to take steps toward an environment where literacy/literacies can be practiced and honored. While there are experiences that my students have that I will never understand, I seek a foundation of empathy through literature and shared experiences. I arrive at this through the lens of my identity as a long-time resident of Appalachia – a social standing that marks its elements of economic and social minoritization. Because of the first-hand

DOI: 10.4018/979-8-3693-1074-8.ch007

nature of this work, the author uses first-person pronouns to reflect an inextricable link from this research topic. I also approach this work as an educator from a rural and fringe rural community, where social and cultural misconceptions are often assumed to be true. I further approach this work as an educator who seeks inclusive spaces for community and literacy-based dialogue.

This chapter, to this end, will draw upon comics as cultural artifacts and as word and image-based texts for exploring identity and development. I include a particular focus on literacy as a means of connecting with and developing knowledge of underrepresented students whose narratives might otherwise be minoritized. This status of being pushed to the boundaries of experience might stem from several factors – ethnicity, race, gender, political stance, and more. For me, this is work focused on my origins as a rural reader who did not always expect to be a college student, much less a university professor or public school teacher. From these rural beginnings, I became comfortable with the voices of people, as well as moments of silence. While ethnicity and gender were common features that I could locate in common with popular characters, economics and social interactions/connections were an area of difference. I found some community through the authors and artists who created the stories I loved.

As a lone person, I can do little to connect with the experiences of all of my students, but literature allows me to make and see connections that would otherwise be impossible to reach. Moreover, visual literature contains possibilities for additional ways of seeing and exploring both for me as an educator and reader, and for my students. Adaptation is only possible so much as the reader/viewer deems the interpretation worthy and part of what might be considered canonical, and breaches in this sense of honoring characters and worlds. Rather than invite a range of voices, publishers have the responsibility to make space for authentic representations of emic perspectives. What of the broader scope of adaptation when it comes to comics stories? It is not without a sense of comparison that I align this translation work with how I have come to regard the acceptable, or canonical use, of some comic book characters. Translation or adaptation certainly exists in this storytelling work, if nothing else in terms of presentations of stories across multiple strands of media. To further inform this discussion, I draw on Verrone's (2011) work on adaptation as an additional source to guide my thinking.

COMICS FOR UNDERREPRESENTED STUDENTS

Adaptation of ideas constitutes central work for reading comics across languages and locations (Davies, 2016; Tseng & Bateman, 2018; Zanettin, 2014) as popular characters are visually rendered from script form to a fully-fledged multimodal page. These characters are then taken up and shared across media in television and filmic spaces. The presence of a character that resonates with a student in a form of media-based storytelling can be a powerful vehicle for analysis and expression, and building critical awareness of the titles that are available for centering a range of identities is essential work. Comics have been noted to be a potential source for exploring personhood and development to some degree in relationship with some experiences in prior research (Wright, 2016; Yalçınkaya, 2022), and this particular approach takes on the lens of literacy work. In Wright (2016) and Yalçınkaya (2022), in particular, comics have been used to explore the experience of entering academia from minoritized perspectives; yet, there is more work to be done in representing readers more widely through the medium.

In this work of adaptation and representation, some characters tend to stay the same, with little change to their dynamics, while other characters from an improvisational nature. Such popular characters constantly changing to adapt to the needs of the moment. For example, the character of Marvel's Moon Knight begins as an assassin and ends as a hero, with turns both light and dark throughout his narrative journey. Meanwhile, characters like Miles Morales are introduced, but questions continue of authorship and authenticity among authors and artists who contribute to the work. Literacy, in this case, is defined as a multimodal means of considering the world and communicating about one's self, based on the work of Kress (2009) and Gee (2013).

Characters who are non-white and who authentically reflect underrepresented groups have only been piecemeal and even problematic in their inclusion in mainstream comics over the past decade and beyond (Howard & Jackson, 2013). Notable in this regard is the presence of the character who is Black, but who takes the role of villain, as well as the character who is a hero only because they are a reformed villain (Guynes et al., 2020). More recently, autobiographical comics have served as a more fruitful space for sharing from underrepresented perspectives (Køhlert, 2019). While some work is being done to dismantle stereotypes in comics, there is a history of troubling work that might be harmful to a reader whose background and experiences align more closely with problematic character types.

My stance as a teacher as one who includes a wide range of literature stems from what I have seen work at both a practical and theoretical level, and serves as a way of disrupting traditional expectations or definitions of what counts as a complex text. I have experienced moments where students at the post-secondary level examine a text and state, "I can see myself in this." I have also seen the energy in the high school and college classroom when I hand out comics for students to take home. It is an interest and engagement that I do not experience when asking students to open a PDF of the next reading in our curriculum. At the same time, locating characters with agency is an important function for me as a reader, and as a means of working in the classroom. I am always searching for opportunities to share about characters who display empowerment and whose identities are celebrated, rather than shamed. Some examples of this work include canonical texts like *Persepolis* by Marjane Satrapi, as well as more recent titles like *New Kid* by Jerry Craft and *Messy Roots: A Graphic Memoir of a Wuhanese American* by Laura Gao.

I also note the limitations in traditional superhero narratives and the ways that creators are beginning to represent minoritized experiences to a greater degree and in more respectful ways. For example, when I was a young person, engagement with comics was only an honored practice for a limited time and in some spaces. The medium has a long-standing reputation as a lesser form, despite the complex range of work that has been published (Wilson & Shaffer, 1965). The traditional view of comics from decades past is that it is a disposal medium, mostly created for youth, and ready to be discarded when young adulthood arrives. Despite this historical criticism, Moeller (2023) has noted the positive impact of comics on adult readership in terms of lifelong literacy, as has Botzakis (2006). With creators like Alina Chau, Jerry Craft, Maia Kobabe, Betty C. Tang, and more entering the field of comics, there are rich possibilities for wider representation that extend beyond the limitations of my experiences as a rural white male.

In 2008, with the advent of the Marvel Cinematic Universe (MCU) there, some of this seemed to be a shift for my students in their perceptions of comics as a worthy medium for reading, and even for viewing. At an all-new level, adolescents were willing to name and locate themselves as members of fandom, wearing shirts and expressing interest in characters well into young adulthood. While this trend existed to some degree when I was growing up, engagement with comics seems to have found a new level of acceptance. Another shift occurred in 2018, ten years later, when Chadwick Boseman portrayed T'Challa for the MCU, leading as a central Black protagonist. Boseman's performance was so resonant for students from underrepresented backgrounds that I could not mention the Black Panther character without eliciting emotional responses about the actor's death in 2020. To the present time of this writing, my students still use the phrase "Wakanda forever," popularized by the film. Before 2018, the cultural awareness of this phrase would have been limited at best.

Using Comics With Underrepresented Students

In the same way, the person I am and hope to continue to grow, and my sense of welcome continues to grow in my classroom as I become aware of experiences that I have taken for granted, including areas of privilege, and I continue to build my classroom library of resources. At one time, I would have taken for granted the heroic status of a Black hero like Black Lightning from DC Comics, without noting his previous role as a villain. I would not have given closer thought to the role of Marvel hero Luke Cage as a hero, only in terms of a "for hire" status, rather than as an outgrowth of his intrinsic desire to make a better world. I am currently working in a space that is more diverse culturally and linguistically than I have previously practiced in. About ten percent of the student population identifies as Black, and around thirty-three percent of my students identify as Hispanic/Latino/a. As an educator who has advocated for inclusive practices, this is an ideal situation for me. I continue to negotiate my discomforts with the tension that surrounds conversations about race and ethnicity, but I have embraced this challenge. In comics and graphic novels, I have found a way of connecting across languages, and I have an immediate means of centering characters and experiences who do not look like me, either through superhero and science fiction narratives that are popular in the comics form (Hatfield, 2011), or through autobiographical/realistic comics.

I note my identification with comics stories in processing degrees of family trauma. Additionally, I acknowledge the power of authors and artists to speak about trauma I have never experienced. When I was a child, my goals were to become a doctor to, first and foremost, help others, but also to generate enough revenue to finance my career as a superhero. Enrolling in college was a rarity in my family and my larger community. These professional avenues center around the work of helping others, and the limitation I encounter is that I cannot help everyone, nor should I be the person who can meaningfully help everyone. Some of my students do not need my help but rather need me to get out of the way or direct them to someone who can speak, through art, literature, or conversation, to their lives in more pertinent ways. Experiences of trauma can lead to an additional sense of minoritization (marshall.edu), particularly when considering how these experiences are often silenced and seen as a source of social discomfort.

I recognize this is only one character who can represent experiences, and that the character is inherently limited in particular ways, even across reinventions. This focus on branding necessarily draws on Jenkins's (2006) work on participatory culture across media. There are clear budgetary considerations and economic purposes for retelling stories and sharing characters across types of marketing. Without the insistence of the characters themselves, fandom will likely not follow. This is especially salient when considering the presence of a majority of White male heroic characters. Narrative flexibility to allow for more characters of color is essential for readers from underrepresented groups. The central dynamics of certain characters and their tendencies largely remain static so that readers can recognize characters and stories, while lesser elements can be changed. Unfortunately, changing a character's ethnicity or telling a story from an underrepresented cultural perspective is sometimes met with fan backlash.

Questions of representation can apply to the individual and the community. Who are we, and what characters link to our experiences? What are the elements of life that necessarily remain intact, even in the demands and difficulties? Reimaging characters and narrative possibilities across narrative space has been the affordance of comics for some time. In particular with texts I have read, I note the ubiquitous nature of the popular characters from DC and Marvel. The multiple incarnations of popular characters speak to the ongoing narratology that surrounds popular heroes and villains, threads that remain constant in terms of identity for central characters (Jen Tembo, 2017).

A desire to help others and live the best and kindest life possible grew in me, and these are the threads I continue to share. However, my voice can only carry so far. This limitation is why I need students to carry on the story as they become educators. I affirm them, rather than attempt to restructure or even discover their stories and how narratives have inspired their lives. I note the tracing of inspiration from the Harlem Renaissance to the work of Jason Reynolds, whose verse novel, *Long Way Down*, has been adapted as a graphic novel. I note the presence of comic stories around the world and share about the work of Marjane Satrapi and multiple creators in the Manga form.

Play and (Re)Shaping with Comics Stories

As I have already noted, the number of transformations that occur across storytelling and cultural artifacts, no doubt, serves a dedicated economic purpose. Freeman (2015) pointed out this market-based reality in terms of consumerism, yet there are further possibilities for expanding narratives. The benefits of fandom are certainly not one-sided, and the prevalence of the superhero story across media markets in the past decade is clear evidence of this monetary dimension. Beyond film and television, I think of the action figures that populated my childhood bedroom – superhero figures were in full stock, with a variety of nuances. For example, cold weather, heat, skydiving, technology, and other extremes were incorporated into these tiny visions, with molds being easy to reproduce. If there was a potential external challenge, new figures were repainted to meet these demands and the purpose was no doubt realized, at least in part, at the toy store cash register.

For each product line, of three to five figures of the same character, a new villain or supporting character would be introduced with the line. Additional figures could be easily reconfigured with the original mold, cutting production costs for the line. This might be seen as a metaphor for the reproducible nature of some cultural stories, and the treasured and elusive nature of underrepresented stories. This easily replicable set of character designs of course served a purpose on the part of the toy company, yet led me to create my versions of characters that did not exist. I recall

An Autoethnographic Approach to Adaptations and Limitations in Comics

painting and filing action figures into new permutations that were not yet available in the store, reflecting creative ideas and directions, and remaking toys to fit my narrative vision.

Figure 1. Action figure permutations

In the figure above, the central depiction of three characters demonstrates the major players in the action figure story. The figure at far left is a rendition of a character, outfitted for a specific purpose (in this case, "Arctic" conditions). The figure at the far left is my repaint of an original figure, recolored to reflect versions I experienced in media. This redesign was probably done somewhere around the time I was ten years of age. It was not enough to wait for a figure to be developed or redesigned; I engaged in this work on my own. When I was a child, I readily included these figures in play-like storytelling, and combined/reimagined them as I needed to achieve the story demands that I wanted as a young reader and viewer. Often, I wanted the enact and extend the stories I saw in television shows or movies focused on the characters, and the tools I found for this play were reshaped by my artistic resources and abilities. There was a cyclical viewing, reading, and creating/authoring experience going on throughout my childhood, which would go on to include comics-making on notebook pages – a source of tension in my schoolwork. Drawing and creating was not an honored practice in much of my early, formal school life.

Toys were hardly my only way of connecting. Many of my students link music and narrative and engage in texts when streaming media. Some students readily engage in prose that draws from popular media in the 1980s, while others more actively relate to the recent works in comics, like Blue Beetle/Jaime Reyes. Jenkins (2006) has noted the ways that readers express their identification with comic book characters through a set of materials, including clothing, toys, and other cultural artifacts. Such identification with specific brands and ideas is seemingly endemic to the participation of adolescents.

The purposes contained within presenting images of characters are surely varied, depending on the perspective. For the toy company, the economy of mass production of similar molds is part of the rationale for multiple iterations of the same character. Turning from these notions of what saves and makes money, I am reminded of Verrone's (2011) use of adaptation theory, particularly in light of film. Verrone (2011) notes the prominence of adaptation from literary works and has commented on those elements that are changed and those that are retained in the translation. What stays the same and what is changed in the move from one medium to another is a key point here. Will I continue to buy Batman action figures that are applied in new permutations? At what point do I feel enough is enough? Of course, these alternate versions often did not appear in filmed and comic book visions, yet existed on the toy shelf.

From film to television and back to comics, my journey was roundabout, linking to the media-rich literacy experiences of young people. Inspired by Roy Thomas and Mike Mignola's take on the film, *Bram Stoker's Dracula* (1992), I found myself creating a comic book within a notebook, featuring a confrontation between the Batman character and Satan. Images from my memory of what that book looked like, in my childhood scribble, we intended to mirror Mignola's style, while also taking up elements of the film, the Batman books I was reading at the time, and Kelley Jones's artwork in *Batman: Red Rain* (1992). I took up elements of these visual stories to align Batman, a still-heroic character, with my belief in an ultimate good that would triumph over evil. In this case, it is no small wonder that I aligned the notion of evil with the character of Satan, who so often populated discussions of what constituted evil in both reading and talk in my home and, later, in larger social and ritualized circles.

Whitlock (2006) expanded the possibilities for thinking about the ways that comics trouble narrative and cultural constraints by noting how visual narratives can be spaces for viewing cultural and historical contexts and perspectives. In the saga of the Sam Wilson/Captain America character, the African American character who received the "Captain America" role/mantle from the previous White male character, there is an example of a seminal comics character whose is story is re-centered. Sam Wilson simultaneously represents the choice to be heroic, while negative opinions and racism emerge from citizens who do not identify with Captain America as "their" Captain America. This exchange and movement in the narrative points to the reality of racism that punctuates conversations about representations of established characters.

An Autoethnographic Approach to Adaptations and Limitations in Comics

Given the media-based nature of comics, the conversation does not end with the printed page. For film, this attention to a particular incarnation revolves around the year, cast, or production company. For comics, the incarnation of choice may center on the artist's interpretation or the sequence of comic book storytelling. Readers encounter a series, which then transitions to the hands of a new creative team, and the individual reader decides at which point their engagement ends. Is that bound by age? Or is it something else, depending on the character and storytelling? In short, there can never be enough retelling and repositioning of stories that we love. We will always return to the original, and it seems that we will almost always encounter new variations. Some of this greatly depends on the individual, even as fandom retains its collective voice, leading to another kind of pleasure in the process as debates and discussions center around preferred narrative trends.

The Batman storyline has been rebooted and reconfigured in a variety of ways, and will likely continue to be treated with this level of elasticity, with Marvel creator Stan Lee even taking an approach. Some of this narrative work is the passing of the storytelling mantle to a new writer. Some depend on the tone or direction of the storyline. In some comics stories, these narrative moves are intentionally drawn upon to fashion a variety of possibilities for permutations of not only the central character but the villains and supporting cast. When I write and think about comics, it is often difficult for me not to consider this popular character, given the role that these storylines played in my childhood and adolescence. I was a young person at a particular moment in time and within the context of specific cultural movements. This context is reflected in my reading life. As an educator, it is vital to provide a range of texts that can be reflecting points for my students, as well. Without the stories of authors and artists, particularly in comics, I might never have reflected on this necessary work.

There is an essential flexibility in storytelling that still finds boundaries and overlooks some readers and experiences. What happens when Batman finds the ring, instead of Green Lantern? What happens if Batman is the deranged antagonist, and Catwoman is the protagonist? What happens if we transport the Batman character to a historical period and he meets Edgar Allan Poe or is reworked within a vampiric story, or the frame of the Frankenstein story? These permutations have played out across popular media, as well, with animated and live-action adaptations of some comic stories. The notion of "what if," just as explored in Marvel texts, forms the basis of this storytelling. It is a powerful question in all walks of readership and life, including exploring community in classroom practice. Though simplistic, these "what if" scenarios can lead to further thinking about the shape and direction of culture and experiences outside of comics, including larger social questions.

As an effect of ritualized action, "what if" leads us forward into new traditions, and has the potential for implications in light of a social justice framework. What if our work as believers is simply about centering our actions in love? What if my beliefs meet a moment of crisis? I may perhaps redefine them, as I have when I have been wounded by established communities of practice, but I also return to a redefined sense of self, retaining some elements of what I once believed, now mingled with new learning. This is, perhaps, a process of growth and maturity. I acknowledge the pain of those, like myself, who have been rejected and wounded – yet another experience of minoritizing.

As Verrone (2011) noted, the dynamics of both fidelity and narrative play are at work in looking at how characters and stories are shaped across media, and what is striking more so than adherence to narrative tradition is the way that these approaches are taken up and remixed by readers. I am reminded of the student who drew upon the visual elements of Satrapi's work in the graphic novel, *Persepolis*, to share her own story in Spanish, conveying ideas about gender through cartoonish images with words that linked to deeper understandings of adult and adolescent experiences. This linking includes the ways that females are sometimes expected to decorate themselves for the male gaze. This critical view is at once possible by examining the narrative history with all of its problems, including honest evaluations of how stories fall short. Moreover, readers can trace character developments through more recent storytelling practices that either carry on these story issues or address them.

Who has not had the experience of encountering a film and praising the ways that the creators were able to take one story and carry it across to a completely new medium – and who has not had the opposite experience, of encountering a film that failed to do justice to its source material and so changed the story or some aspect of the literary world that the adaptation could hardly be regarded as quality material? In the same way, at what point does a community become a splinter, and at what point does a new group or tradition form? The work of considering representation is critical and necessary.

What is taken, shared, lost, and reworked from one narrative to another speaks to the essential nature of the character, and the ways that character origins are combined speak to the streams that connect the characters, as well. Moreover, the literary tradition is not held in regard for one group of readers and viewers but is an open set of tools. It should always be accessible and practiced by all readers/composers. Creative work and compositional possibility begin with a consideration of what is essential and sanctioned interpretation/application. By including voices beyond the cultural hegemony, educators can make space for students to see themselves as part of the larger literacy conversation.

Origin stories indeed have a particular place in comics lore, and the importance of our origins continues to remind us of who we have been. This an added narrative element pointing to how we have grown and who we ultimately want to become. We may not have power rings or gamma rays, but we all have forces in our lives,

An Autoethnographic Approach to Adaptations and Limitations in Comics

as well as voices, that have shaped us. Moreover, the communal nature of literacy holds implications for thinking about the ways that learning can shape rather than injure one another and be shaped by one another. Policies, in this view, should inclusively and thoughtfully be framed to allow for meaningful encounters with critical questions or the sharing of experiences.

Representing a Range of Experiences

Where does all of this fit in the personal stream of reflection on these materials from an autoethnographic perspective? The truth is I have been adapting since my formative years as a child reading comics. I adapted myself into costumed heroes, as seen in an earlier artifact, but I also took whatever materials were present to me and adapted characters in my forms. Paint, pencil, action figure, notebook paper – it did not matter. Whatever was on hand was useful for my work of storytelling and reflection on characters. To be authentic, this sense of adaptation must be juxtaposed with what is essential about me. My understanding and appreciation of these characters took on multiple forms, and I continued to practice the lines of their formation as I grew older.

Figure 2. Batman rendering

An Autoethnographic Approach to Adaptations and Limitations in Comics

Figure 3. Superman rendering here

The examples above were painted at some point in my childhood and act as two artifacts among many that now only exist in memory of the ways I adapted characters. In this case, the medium was paint on blank puzzle sheets from my local craft store. In another case of assuming identity, I wore a pair of Clark Kent glasses to school in kindergarten and convinced my teachers and classmates they were real. The application of character elements to personal identity was an enactment of who I was and also a glimpse of what I hoped to be. In this way, adaptation took on an embodied form, not unlike cosplay, the engagement in dress that readers explore as a means of considering stories and identity (Rahman et al., 2012).

My uses of adaptations were both externalized in the forms of drawing and other artwork, and they were internalized as I took up the identities of the characters I loved – sometimes with humorous consequences. Any toy or tool I could fashion into an element of superhero attire was quickly seized upon and adapted to my purposes as a reader. This journey, of course, began in the pages of a comic book and then expanded to filmed versions of characters. Gender play was enacted when I took on the role of Catwoman as a child.

I was more than ready to travel with any printed or filmed incarnation of these characters as I was already fashioning an army of my own making. It did not matter if the storylines were consistent, or if the narratives themselves took alternative

An Autoethnographic Approach to Adaptations and Limitations in Comics

forms – the characters were, in some way, real to me. It is no small wonder that I have chosen a profession as an adult that is text-centric and that revolves around flexibility and adaptation.

This sense of adaptation carries its sense of purpose and again depends on the identity and intentions of the reader/fan. In a sense, these texts are vehicles for sharing stories with a wider audience and inviting others to experience the visual medium. The initial medium of storytelling then becomes a space for inspiring further narratives across forms. The limitless nature of this form of storytelling and exploration of self is a potentially fruitful space for thinking about how students can share their stories more actively. Authoring and creating are democratic activities, and using texts by and about authors of color has the potential to invite a wider readership. Students can also more actively see themselves as readers and creators. This is an inclusive vision of literacy that extends beyond comics.

Further Literacy Links

When considering the ways that some stories are composed from emic and etic perspectives, it is an essential and critical function to question the frequency and extent of representation. This was true for me as a youth growing up in a rural space, as a first-generation college student, and as a member of a faith community – it is true for students whose cultural and social identities are even less represented. There is room for all stories, and working from the foundation that students matter and have stories to share is critical.

Kukkoken (2013) shared the idea that, in the affordances of fantasy, we find mirrors for reality outside of that work. Such distortions are often allowed by readers, and even readily embraced for their entertainment value. We find in art the simulacrum of life and individual tastes vary by genre and the degree to which narratives present a realistic representation. Yet, a story finds some connected thread to life events and necessarily entails some sense of realism. This realism might be achievable, if only in the believable and sustainable actions of characters who populate that narrative. We allow flexibility for the ludic possibility of discovering something new, and Black (2005) has examined how these narrative possibilities play out in fanfiction communities. Black (2005) noted particular engagement for students who are learning a second language. Even within this mirroring of reality, there is potential for questioning and critiquing both the representation itself and the reality that is reconstituted for narrative effect.

This use of truth and representation is part of why the science fiction and fantasy genres speak so well to my experience. While graphic novels and comic books, particularly those that feature superhero characters, are often lumped into science fiction and fantasy, Hatfield (2011) has suggested that these books operate with their conventions. Indeed, the tropes of the superhero narrative function uniquely, from capes, cowls, lairs, and nemeses, to alter-egos and the romantic doubles as framed in the books. Hatfield (2011) further suggested that the comic book medium is most known for its use of the superhero story, although comics and graphic novels have featured multiple genres over time, including westerns, romance stories, and tried-and-true science fiction tales that take us to outer space. With so wide a reach, it is unfortunate that political groups have sought to silence underrepresented voices in the medium in recent years. As Dallacqua (2022) has noted, there are harmful implications for students whose identities are banned when found in books.

These story types recall events, reflect reality, and do so in creative ways so that the revelation of their relevance is progressive and illuminating. Superman may be an alien figure but, particularly in the hands of a comics creator like Gene Luen Yang who envisions the ideological possibilities of the character. Yang is the author of both *Superman and Smashes the Klan!* and *American Born Chinese.* Superman's (Kal-El) sense of otherness is wholly relatable to a variety of human experiences. Kal-El, then, becomes an ally, helping an Asian American family tackle racism in their community. The reality of racism is depicted in burning crosses alongside the science fiction affordances of an iron-clad Klansman character. Even in fantasy, Yang brings the reality of hate to vivid life with the artistic work of collaborator Gurihiru.

Kal-El (Superman) is, in so many ways, a character that is unlike us, but how his character has been adapted to be like the humans that he serves is strong enough to help us relate to him. This is likely why I felt comfortable wearing a plastic Superman cape as a child. He represented heroic behavior and superpowers as a set of aspirations, while also embodying my humanity enough to serve as a reflection marker. Batman, on the other hand, acts as a foil. He is human but smart and wealthy.

Batman's pathos-inspired experience speaks to our desire to take hold of fear, wrap ourselves in our greatest challenges, and fight back against the chaos and disorientation that is endemic to experiences of loss. He is the character I wanted to be if anything bad ever happened, a being who could resituate himself in the face of life-shattering experiences. Perhaps that is why my hand was much more quickly drawn to *Detective Comics* on the pharmacy spinner rack, while Superman was more of a substitute character. The student who carries such shattering experiences with them is sometimes underrepresented and minoritized yet a connectedness even if they link to the dominant social group in other ways.

The possibility for transmedia reading and viewing was also somewhat greater with Batman, as I was growing as a young reader at about the same time the 1989 film became popular and issued into a variety of other cultural texts, including clothing, animation, books, and more. Christopher Reeves's incarnation of Superman was present, but less prescient, in my development as a comics fan and reader.

An Autoethnographic Approach to Adaptations and Limitations in Comics

It is the alien and others that we respond to in Superman first, and we are encouraged to keep imagining ourselves as we also consider the enactment of his power. It is the lone figure on the cross who speaks to our moments of pain, and the essential nature of this person as a forgiving and powerful being who continues to invite us to consideration of self and community. Batman, apart from the loss that is central to his origin story, is a maniac in a costume. We allow him to dress up because of his desire for justice. It is an ideation of conquering failures and fears much more so than a recognizable coping mechanism. Even when we find a main character who is an animal or alien, that being is changed for human relatability. This is true of folklore, animated stories, and characters we find in comics. In the case of Spock, readers and viewers find the embodiment of not just what it means to be human, but the extreme of a particular aspect of humanity.

If we are truly good, then how are we like Superman? If we are truly logical, then how are we like Spock? It is through these shades of extremity that we locate some sense of who we are, and perhaps this is why we read stories. Perhaps it is this movement toward a more idealized self that is so essential to the function of a parable that presents an impossible dream. We still press for the enactment of that story. Furthermore, stories from minoritized and underrepresented voices should have presentations and enactments, as well. This is true of representation in curriculum, as well as representation in reading choices from popular literature, including comics.

Comic books also work this way. In the character of the superhero, we can locate our desire for a better world, a striving for what we perceive to be fairness and justice. As Fawaz (2016) noted, these narratives are also replete with enactments of what it means to be masculine, feminine, or even nationalistic. How the narratives are remixed and reapplied act as a dynamic of constraint and flexibility at the same time – and readers/viewers choose to participate in the flow of the narrative, or balk at its presence. In the same way that individuals can resist open and transformative conversations, there have been moves to ban some voices in texts and classrooms. The choice is a dichotomy between silencing and invitation. A text-centered and student-centered approach not only includes a range of texts, but a range of experiences, as well – including those that are underrepresented.

Uses of culturally prioritized texts, for example, have ranged from humanistic efforts to those that are oriented to sustained relationships of hatred and dynamics of divide. Participators in reading and ritualized communities choose to adhere to these applications or decry them as evil. The ways that religiosity, and even the superhero narrative's conceptualization of good and evil, bend and ebb with the flow of time. These changing realities bring with them a series of changes in our understandings and experiences, and we experience concepts of both cosmology and comics through a lens of limited personhood. We are told that God's ways are not our ways, and yet continue to strain our metaphoric understanding of what it means to live an inclusive and informed life.

CONCLUSIONS AND IMPLICATIONS

So, one asks: Do I go there? Am I able to travel with this narrative? Do I attempt to take my students on this journey with me?

In reflecting on this textual journey, my experiences with reading both comic books and other family-honored texts resulted in several interesting works of my participation. These experiences have since inspired my classroom work across spaces, from secondary to post-secondary classroom contexts. When I encountered a hero's story, I often sought to recreate it in my storytelling – and the boundaries of what constituted an authentic narrative and a superhero narrative were sometimes blurry. I note possibilities for thinking about the kinds of stories that can be centered in instruction, particularly at a time when book bans are prevalent. Moreover, I recognize the importance of including a range of genres without making assumptions about what will be connected with readers, and I see possibilities for continuing and expanding honest and critically thoughtful conversations about how texts extend conversations in respectful ways, and how authors sometimes miss this opportunity. Within the troubled tradition of comics representations – including the lack thereof – exists the opportunity for rich and reflective discussions about historical trends. Such discussions can focus on the ways that society can continue to be shaped into a more inclusive and justice-oriented reality. Part of this work can be accomplished through experiences stories and interactions around stories. Having open and critical conversations in respectful ways might help students see one another in new ways.

In the literacy field, this exploration of the ways that stories are taken up over time and across spaces has potential implications. For one, there is a potential impact on the approach educators and theorists take when considering the work of children and adolescents in exploring narrative. For another, there are possibilities for creating appreciation for authors and artists who speak from underrepresented perspectives. Finally, there is space for inviting new possibilities for a younger generation to explore comics as a viable space for storytelling. This work can involve questions of expanding the canon both in terms of the types of works that are celebrated and the identities of authors and illustrators who have been minoritized. Ultimately, a more inclusive treatment of literature means that more student experiences can be celebrated and shared in classrooms.

Yet more implications exist for the ways that popular narratives merge with other aspects of culture, as was the case for me in terms of rural and Appalachian communities, and this is a trend that certainly has room to grow. From my work,

I have concluded that comics and visual stories have great potential as classroom reading material. I have also noted that identity work is made possible by these texts. Creations are made and then inspire recreations in sometimes obvious and sometimes hidden ways and the literacy history continues for readers who explore storytelling as a prioritized or minoritized means of considering reality in educational spaces. The centrality of human experience leads to the centrality of human characters.

REFERENCES

Botzakis, S. (2006). *Reading when they don't have to: Insights from adult comic book readers* [Doctoral dissertation]. University of Georgia.

Chang, H. (2016). *Autoethnography as method*. Routledge. doi:10.4324/9781315433370

Craft, J. (2019). *New kid*. HarperCollins.

Dallacqua, A. K. (2022). "Let me just close my eyes": Challenged and banned books, claimed identities, and comics. *Journal of Adolescent & Adult Literacy*, 66(2), 134–138. doi:10.1002/jaal.1250

Davies, P. F. (2016). Representing experience in comics: Carnet de Voyage. *Journal of Graphic Novels & Comics*, 7(2), 117–133. doi:10.1080/21504857.2015.1131173

Fawaz, R. (2016). *The new mutants*. New York University Press.

Freeman, M. (2015). Branding consumerism: Cross-media characters and storyworlds at the turn of the 20th century. *International Journal of Cultural Studies*, 18(6), 629–644. doi:10.1177/1367877913515868

Gao, L. (2022). *Messy roots: A graphic memoir of a Wuhanese American*. Balzer & Bray.

Gee, J. P. (2017). *Teaching, learning, literacy in our high-risk high-tech world: A framework for becoming human*. Teachers College Press.

Guynes, S., Lund, M., & Berlatsky, N. (Eds.), *Unstable masks: Whiteness and American superhero comics*. Ohio State University Press.

Hatfield, C. (2011). *Hand of fire: the comics art of Jack Kirby*. Univ. Press of Mississippi. doi:10.14325/mississippi/9781617031786.001.0001

Howard, S. C., & Jackson, R. L. II, (Eds.). (2013). *Black comics: Politics of race and representation*. Bloomsbury Publishing.

Jen Tembo, K. D. (2017). Re-theorizing the problem of identity and the onto-existentialism of DC comics' Superman. *Word and Text, A Journal of Literary Studies and Linguistics, 7*(1), 151-167.

Jenkins, H. (2006). *Fans, bloggers, and gamers: Exploring participatory culture.* NYU Press.

Køhlert, F. B. (2019). *Serial selves: Identity and representation in autobiographical comics.* Rutgers University Press.

Kress, G. (2009). *Multimodality: A social semiotic approach to contemporary communication.* Routledge. doi:10.4324/9780203970034

Kukkonen, K. (2013). *Studying comics and graphic novels.* John Wiley & Sons. doi:10.1002/9781394261079

Marshall University. (2023). *Banned books 2022.* https://www.marshall.edu/library/bannedbooks/speak/

Moeller, R. A. (2023). "It's not something I've really thought about 'til now'": The social aspects of US emerging adults' comics reading histories. *Journal of Librarianship and Information Science, 55*(1), 33–42. doi:10.1177/09610006211054213

Moench, D. (1992). *Batman: Red rain.* DC Comics.

Rahman, O., Wing-Sun, L., & Cheung, B. H. M. (2012). "Cosplay": Imaginative self and performing identity. *Fashion Theory, 16*(3), 317–341. doi:10.2752/175174112X13340749707204

Satrapi, M. (2004). *Persepolis: The story of a childhood.* Pantheon.

Spencer, N. (2016). Captain America: Sam Wilson vol. 1: Not my Captain America. Marvel Comics.

Thomas, R. (1992). *Bram stoker's Dracula.* Topps.

Tseng, C. I., & Bateman, J. A. (2018). Cohesion in comics and graphic novels: An empirical comparative approach to transmedia adaptation in City of Glass. *Adaptation, 11*(2), 122–143. doi:10.1093/adaptation/apx027

Verrone, W. E. (2011). *The avant-garde feature film: A critical history.* McFarland.

Wilson, R. C., & Shaffer, E. J. (1965). Reading comics to learn. *The Elementary School Journal, 66*(2), 81–82. doi:10.1086/460267

Wright, R. R. (2016). Comics, kitsch, and class: An autoethnographic exploration of an accidental academic. *International Journal of Qualitative Studies in Education, 29*(3), 426–444. doi:10.1080/09518398.2015.1078518

Yalçınkaya, C. T. (2022). Autographics as autoethnography: Comic book adventures of a migrant academic. *Continuum (Perth), 36*(6), 902–920. doi:10.1080/10304312.2023.2182957

Yang, G.L., & Gurihiru. (2020). *Superman smashes the klan!* DC Comics.

Zanettin, F. (2014). Visual adaptation in translated comics. *Intralinea, 16*, 1–34.

KEY TERMS AND DEFINITIONS

Adaptation: A presentation of a character or world across forms (e.g., from film to comics, from comics to film, etc.).

Comics: A medium that features panels and other features to convey visual and word-based narratives.

Emic Perspective: A narrative told from a cultural insider or one whose experiences authentically link with the experience representation.

Etic Perspective: A narrative told from the perspective of someone who is not an authentic member of the community being represented.

Literacy History: A means of understanding self through tracing interaction with communication methods over time (chiefly, word-based forms, but also including digital works and other forms).

Multimodality: As in the work of Gunther Kress, the way that certain texts work to unite design features across means of communication.

Text: A digital or print-based means of conveying a message.

Transmedia: The practice of storytelling across forms/platforms of communication; specifically, the treatment of the same or similar stories or themes across media.

Compilation of References

Adkins, S. D. H., & Hughes, S. (2020). Back to the future of autoethnography. *Journal of Autoethnography, 1*(3), 297–303. doi:10.1525/joae.2020.1.3.297

Akrani, G., & Trivedi, J. A. (2019). Maslow's hierarchy of needs - theory of human motivation. *International Journal of Research in All Subjects in Multi Languages, 7*(6). https://kalyan-city.blogspot.com/2010/06/maslow-hierarchy-of-needs-theory-of.html?

Aljohani, O. H., & Alajlan, S. M. (2018). Motivating adult learners to learn at adult education schools in Saudi Arabia. *Department of Education*. https://files.eric.ed.gov/fulltext/ED597543.pdf

Allen, C. C., & Alleman, N. F. (2019). A private struggle at a private institution: Effects of student hunger on social and academic experiences. *Journal of College Student Development, 60*(1), 52–69. doi:10.1353/csd.2019.0003

Allen, W. R. (1992). The Color of Success: African-American College Student Outcomes at predominantly White and Historically Black Public Colleges and Universities. *Harvard Educational Review, 62*, 26–44.

American Psychological Association. (2019). APA dictionary of psychology-persistence. *APA Dictionary of Psychology*. https://dictionary.apa.org/persistence

American Psychological Association. (2023). *Attrition*. APA Dictionary of Psychology. https://dictionary.apa.org/attrition

Ames, C., Berman, R., & Casteel, A. (2018). A preliminary examination of doctoral student retention factors in private online workspaces. *International Journal of Doctoral Studies, 13*, 79–107. doi:10.28945/3958

Ampaw, F. D., & Jaeger, A. J. (2011). Completing the Three Stages of Doctoral Education: An Event History Analysis. *Research in Higher Education, 53*(6), 640–660. doi:10.1007/s11162-011-9250-3

Angelou, M. (2008). *Letter to my daughter*. Random House.

Apgar, D. (2022). Linking social work licensure examination pass rates to accreditation: The merits, challenges, and implications for social work education. *Journal of Teaching in Social Work, 42*(4), 335–353. doi:10.1080/08841233.2022.2112809

Compilation of References

Appel, H., & Taylor, A. (2015). Education with a debt sentence: For-Profit colleges as American dream crushers and factories of debt. *New Labor Forum*, *24*(1), 31–36. doi:10.1177/1095796014562860

Arbelo-Marrero, F., & Milacci, F. (2015). A Phenomenological Investigation of the Academic Persistence of Undergraduate Hispanic Nontraditional Students at Hispanic Serving Institutions. *Journal of Hispanic Higher Education*, *15*(1), 22–40. doi:10.1177/1538192715584192

Baharudin, S., Murad, M., & Mat, N. A. (2013). Challenges of adult learners: A case study of full time postgraduates students. *Procedia – Social and Behavioral Sciences, 90*, 772–781. doi:10.1016/j.sbspro.2013.07.151

Bahrainwala, L. (2020). Precarity, citizenship, and the "traditional" student. *Communication Education*, *69*(2), 250–260. doi:10.1080/03634523.2020.1723805

Bandura, A. (1991). Social cognitive theory of self-regulation. *Organizational Behavior and Human Decision Processes*, *50*(2), 248–287. doi:10.1016/0749-5978(91)90022-L

Bardon, E. (2013). *Career goals and decisions: An intersectionality approach* (Publication No. AAT 1570888) [Master's thesis, University of Toronto]. The SAO/NASA Astrophysics Data System.

Battiste, K., & Battiste, K. (2022). *Who Are Today's Nontraditional Students?* AMG Higher Education Marketing. https://www.amghighered.com/who-are-todays-non-traditional-students/

Beckles, H., & Richards-Kennedy, S. (2021). Accelerating the Future into the Present: Re-imagining Higher Education in the Caribbean. In H. van't Land, A. Corcoran, & D. C. Iancu (Eds.), *The Promise of Higher Education*. Springer. doi:10.1007/978-3-030-67245-4_54

Bellare, Y., Smith, A., Cochran, K., & Lopez, S. G. (2023). Motivations and barriers for adult learner achievement: Recommendations for institutions of higher education. *Adult Learning*, *34*(1), 30–39. doi:10.1177/10451595211059574

Bernery, C., Lusardi, L., Marino, C., Philippe-Lesaffre, M., Angulo, E., Bonnaud, E., Guéry, L., Manfrini, E., Turbelin, A., Albert, C., Arbieu, U., & Courchamp, F. (2022). Highlighting the positive aspects of being a PhD student. *eLife*, *11*, e81075. Advance online publication. doi:10.7554/eLife.81075 PMID:35880403

Binkley, C. (2023). *The labor shortage is pushing American colleges into crisis, with the plunge in enrollment the worst ever recorded*. https://fortune.com/2023/03/09/american-skipping-college-huge-numbers-pandemic-turned-them-off-education/

Binkley, C., & Associated Press. (2023). *The labor shortage is pushing American colleges into crisis, with the plunge in enrollment the worst ever recorded*. Retrieved February 5, 2024 from https://fortune.com/2023/03/09/american-skipping-college-huge-numbers-pandemic-turned-them-off-education/

Bitzer, E. (2015). Language of the doctorate: Doctorateness as a threshold concept in doctoral literacy. *Per Linguam*, *30*(3). Advance online publication. doi:10.5785/30-3-585

Bok, G. I. (2021). Adult learners' challenges in distance learning: A case study in Universiti Sains Malaysia. *Issues in Educational Research, 31*(1), 19–36. https://www.proquest.com/scholarly-journals/adult-learners-challenges-distance-learning-case/docview/2702191373/se-2

Boone, S. C., De Charon, L., Hill, M. J., Preiss, A., Ritter-Williams, D., & Young, E. (2020). Doctoral student persistence and progression: A program assessment. *Journal of Applied Research in Higher Education, 12*(4), 753–765. doi:10.1108/JARHE-07-2019-0192

Börgeson, E., Soták, M., Kraft, J., Bagunu, G., Biörserud, C., & Lange, S. (2021). Challenges in PhD education due to COVID-19 - disrupted supervision or business as usual: A cross-sectional survey of Swedish biomedical sciences graduate students. *BMC Medical Education, 21*(1), 294. Advance online publication. doi:10.1186/s12909-021-02727-3 PMID:34022871

Boström, M., Andersson, E., Berg, M., Gustafsson, K., Gustavsson, E., Hysing, E., Lidskog, R., Löfmarck, E., Ojala, M., Olsson, J., Singleton, B., Svenberg, S., Uggla, Y., & Öhman, J. (2018). Conditions for transformative learning for sustainable development: A theoretical review and approach. *Sustainability (Basel), 10*(12), 4479. Advance online publication. doi:10.3390/su10124479

Botzakis, S. (2006). *Reading when they don't have to: Insights from adult comic book readers* [Doctoral dissertation]. University of Georgia.

Boulton, A. B., Durnen, A. K., Boysen, B., Perry, C. L., Bailey, D., Mollner, J., Del La Fosse, K., Sinning, M. W., Guillaume, N. M., Breuninger, R., Jones, S., & Webber, S. (2019). *Doctoral Student Perspectives on Motivation and Persistence*. Academic Press.

Boulton, A. B. (2019). Personal motivation for professional identity: Persistence in the education doctorate. In *Doctoral student perspectives on motivation and persistence: Eye-opening insights into the ideas and thoughts that today's doctoral students have about finishing the doctoral degree* (1st ed., pp. 11–20). Education Doctorate Books. https://openriver.winona.edu/educationeddbooks

Boysen, B. (2016). Realizing imperative motivation: A doctoral student's reflection. In *Doctoral student perspectives on motivation and persistence: Eye-opening insights into the ideas and thoughts that today's doctoral students have about finishing the doctoral degree* (1st ed., pp. 21–26). Education Doctorate Books. https://openriver.winona.edu/educationeddbooks

Bozick, R., & DeLuca, S. (2005). Better Late Than Never? Delayed Enrollment in the High School to College Transition. *Social Forces, 84*(1), 531–554. doi:10.1353/sof.2005.0089

Breaking the code: What motivates adult learners. (2021). Shift. Retrieved August 13, 2023, from https://www.shiftelearning.com/blog/what-motivates-adult-learners

Bringle, R. G., Hatcher, J. A., & Muthiah, R. (2010). The Role of Service-Learning on the Retention of First-Year Students to Second Year. *Michigan Journal of Community Service Learning, 16*(2), 38–49.

Compilation of References

Brown-Rice, K., & Furr, S. (2019). Am I My Peers' Keeper? Problems of Professional Competency in Doctoral Students. *Teaching and Supervision in Counseling*, *1*(1). Advance online publication. doi:10.7290/tsc010104

Brunton, J., & Buckley, F. (2021). 'You're thrown in the deep end': Adult learner identity formation in higher education. *Studies in Higher Education (Dorchester-on-Thames)*, *46*(12), 2696-2709. doi:10.1080/03075079.2020.1767049

Burke, A. (2019). Student Retention Models in Higher Education: A Literature Review. *College and University*, *94*(2), 12–21. https://eric.ed.gov/?id=EJ1216871

Campus Office of Planning and Institutional Research. (n.d.). *The University of the West Indies St. Augustine campus student statistical digest 2015/2016 to 2019/2020.* https://sta.uwi.edu/resources/documents/statistics/Student_Statistics_15_16-19_20.pdf

Caribbean consultation held on adult education challenges and opportunities in preparation of CONFINTEA VII. (2021). UNESCO Clearinghouse on Global Citizenship Education. https://www.gcedclearinghouse.org/news/aribbean-consultation-held-adult-education-challenges-and-opportunities-preparation-confinteaCarpenter doi:10.1177/10451595221074731

Caribbean English. (2021). *Oxford English Dictionary*. https://www.oed.com/discover/aribbean-english/?tl=true#:~:text=The%20Anglophone%20Caribbean%20(the%2019,in%20the%20formal%20education%20system

Carrington, L. G. (2016). *A Qualitative Phenomenological Study of Employee Perceptions of the Impact of Layoffs | Semantic Scholar*. Retrieved September 6, 2022, from https://www.semanticscholar.org/paper/A-Qualitative-Phenomenological-Study-of-Employee-of-Carrington/7804b43498bfb5624a1163ff1634614694f5129d

Caruth, G. D. (2018). Student Engagement, Retention, and Motivation: Assessing Academic success in Today's college students. *Participatory Educational Research*, *5*(1), 17–30. doi:10.17275/per.18.4.5.1

Center for Disease Control and Protection. (2012). *Higher education and income levels keys to better health, according to annual report on nation's health*. Retrieved February 04, 2023 from https://www.cdc.gov/media/releases/2012/p0516_higher_education.html

Chang, H. (2016). *Autoethnography as method*. Routledge. doi:10.4324/9781315433370

Chang, M., Kniola, D., & Olsen, D. (2011). Transformative graduate education programs: An analysis of impact on STEM and non-STEM Ph.D. completion. *Higher Education*, *63*(4), 473–495. doi:10.1007/s10734-011-9453-8

Chen, J. C. (2017). Nontraditional adult learners. *SAGE Open*, *7*(1), 215824401769716. doi:10.1177/2158244017697161

Chisholm, M., & Kennedy, M. (2014). Widening participation in higher education: The case of the UWI, Mona Campus. *UWI Quality Education Forum*, *20*, 34 – 61.

Clark, A. M. (1998). The qualitative-quantitative debate: Moving from positivism and confrontation to post-positivism and reconciliation. *Journal of Advanced Nursing*, 27(6), 1242–1249. doi:10.1046/j.1365-2648.1998.00651.x PMID:9663876

Coates, C. O. (2012). *Educational developments in the British West Indies: A historical overview.* https://files.eric.ed.gov/fulltext/ED567093.pdf

Cohen, S. M. (2011). Doctoral persistence and doctoral program completion among nurses. *Nursing Forum*, 46(2), 64–70. doi:10.1111/j.1744-6198.2011.00212.x PMID:21517879

College Gazette. (2022, March 24). *The 10 best fashion design schools in the us.* https://collegegazette.com/best-fashion-design-schools-in-the-us/#:~:text=With%20such%20high%20accolades%2C%20it%20is%20not%20surprising,the%20list%2C%20with%20an%20acceptance%20rate%20of%2038%25

Coursera Staff. (2023). *What Is a Nontraditional Student?* Coursera. https://www.coursera.org/articles/nontraditional-student

Cox, S. (2023). *How to serve nontraditional students.* https://moderncampus.com/blog/why-and-how-you-should-serve-non-traditional-students.html

Craft, J. (2019). *New kid.* HarperCollins.

Creswell, J. W. (1994). *Research Design: Qualitative, quantitative, and mixed methods approaches.* http://www.revistacomunicacion.org/pdf/n3/resenas/research_design_qualitative_quantitative_and_mixed_methods_approaches.pdf

Creswell, J. W. (2001). *Educational Research: Planning.* Conducting, and Evaluating Quantitative and Qualitative Research.

Creswell, J. W. (2007). *Qualitative inquiry and research design.* SAGE Publications.

Creswell, J. W. (2013). *Qualitative inquiry and research design: Choosing among five approaches.* SAGE Publications.

Creswell, J. W., & Poth, C. N. (2018). *Qualitative Inquiry and Research Design Choosing among Five Approaches* (4th ed.). SAGE Publications, Inc.

Cross, J. (2017, October 23). US college recruiter wants more Jamaicans. *The Gleaner.* https://jamaica-gleaner.com/article/news/20171025/us-college-recruiter-wants-more-jamaicans

Crumb, L., Haskins, N., Dean, L., & Avent Harris, J. (2020). Illuminating social-class identity: The persistence of working-class African American women doctoral students. *Journal of Diversity in Higher Education*, 13(3), 215–227. doi:10.1037/dhe0000109

Cummins, P. A., Brown, J. S., Bahr, P. R., & Mehri, N. (2018). Heterogeneity of Older Learners in Higher Education. *Adult Learning*, 30(1), 23–33. doi:10.1177/1045159518812077

Currid-Halkett, E. (2010). *Starstruck: The business of celebrity.* Farrar, Straus and Giroux.

Compilation of References

Dallacqua, A. K. (2022). "Let me just close my eyes": Challenged and banned books, claimed identities, and comics. *Journal of Adolescent & Adult Literacy, 66*(2), 134–138. doi:10.1002/jaal.1250

Dauenhauer, J., Steitz, D. W., & Cochran, L. J. (2016). Fostering a new model of multigenerational learning: Older adult perspectives, community partners, and higher education. *Educational Gerontology, 42*(7), 483–496. doi:10.1080/03601277.2016.1157419

Davidson, C., & Wilson, K. (2013). Reassessing Tinto's concepts of social and academic integration in student retention. Journal of College Student Retention: Research, Theory &Amp. *Journal of College Student Retention, 15*(3), 329–346. doi:10.2190/CS.15.3.b

Davies, P. F. (2016). Representing experience in comics: Carnet de Voyage. *Journal of Graphic Novels & Comics, 7*(2), 117–133. doi:10.1080/21504857.2015.1131173

Dechter, A. (2009). Facilitating timely completion of a college degree with optimization technology. *AACE Review, 17*(3), 215–299.

Defining non-traditional. (2024). Rutgers University. https://transfer.rutgers.edu/admissions/defining-non-traditional

Delayed entry into higher education. (2016). *Intelligence Brief.* https://www.eurostudent.eu/download_files/documents/IB_delayed_transition.pdf

Dick, A. W., Edlin, A. S., & Emch, E. R. (2003). The savings impact of college financial aid. *Contributions to Economic Analysis & Policy, 2*(1), 1–29. doi:10.2202/1538-0645.1044

Dickinson. (n.d.). *Yellow ribbon program.* Dickson College. https://www.dickinson.edu/info/20046/tuition_and_aid/3312/yellow_ribbon_program#:~:text=While%20the%20VA%20pays%20the%20tuition%20and%20fee,allowance%20stipend%20is%20paid%20monthly%20to%20the%20student

Dictionary, C. (2022). *Doctoral meaning.* Retrieved October 9, 2022, from https://dictionary.cambridge.org/us/dictionary/english/doctoral

Dittman, M. (2002). *The study says Self-esteem based on external sources has mental health consequences.* Retrieved from http://www.apa.org/monitor/ dec02/selfesteem.aspx

Edgar, S., Carr, S., Connaughton, J., & Celenza, A. (2019). Student motivation to learn: Is self-belief the key to transition and first year performance in an undergraduate health professions program? *BMC Medical Education, 19*(1), 111. Advance online publication. doi:10.1186/s12909-019-1539-5 PMID:30999916

Education in Latin America and the Caribbean at the Crossroad. (n.d.). Regional monitoring report SDG4 – Education 2030. UNESCO. https://repositorio.cepal.org/server/api/core/bitstreams/70fe53c4-9b47-4f64-957b-1adf27c8b1f4/content

Edwards, C. W. (2019). Overcoming imposter syndrome and stereotype threat: Reconceptualizing the definition of a scholar. Taboo. *Communications on Stochastic Analysis*, *18*(1). Advance online publication. doi:10.31390/taboo.18.1.03

Elliott, K. E. (2022). *Academic achievement and degree attainment among college students with children* [PhD Dissertation]. University of Louisville.

Ellis, C., Adams, T. E., & Bochner, A. P. (2010). Autoethnography: An overview. *DOAJ (DOAJ: Directory of Open Access Journals)*. https://doaj.org/article/be64f48522e74cadba03b10a6794cb90

Ellis, P., Ramsay, A., & Small, S. (2000). *Adult Education in the Caribbean at the Turn of the Century*. UNESCO. https://uwispace.sta.uwi.edu/server/api/core/bitstreams/76a6bf15-f8a1-4a1e-8b45-861010831b48/content

Ellis, E. M. (2001). The Impact of Race and Gender on Graduate School Socialization, Satisfaction with Doctoral Study, and Commitment to Degree Completion. *The Western Journal of Black Studies*, *25*(1), 30–45. https://eric.ed.gov/?id=EJ646531

Exposito, S., & Bernheimer, S. (2012). Nontraditional students and institutions of higher education: A conceptual framework. *Journal of Early Childhood Teacher Education*, *33*(2), 178–189. doi:10.1080/10901027.2012.675942

Faulk, D. G., & Wang, Z. (2014). Undergraduates with employer-sponsored aid: Comparing group differences. *Journal of Student Financial Aid*, *43*(3), 3. https://ir.library.louisville.edu/jsfa/vol43/iss3/3. doi:10.55504/0884-9153.1043

Fawaz, R. (2016). *The new mutants*. New York University Press.

Feagin, J. R., Vera, H., & Imani, N. (2014). *The agony of education: Black students at a White University*. Routledge.

Feast, L. (2022). Down the brain drain: Searching for doctorateness in all the wrong places. She Ji. *The Journal of Design, Economics, and Innovation*, *8*(1), 147–170. doi:10.1016/j.sheji.2021.11.001

Federal Student Aid. (n.d.-a). *Apply for borrower defense loan discharge*. https://studentaid.gov/borrower-defense/

Federal Student Aid. (n.d.-b). *Sweet v. Cardona settlement*. https://studentaid.gov/announcements-events/sweet-settlement

Federal Student Aid. (n.d.-c). *Who is included in the group of people (the "class") represented by Sweet v. Cardona (formerly Sweet v. Devos)?* https://studentaid.gov/help-center/answers/article/borrower-defense-sweet-v-devos-class

Feenstra, S., Begeny, C. T., Ryan, M. K., Rink, F. A., Stoker, J. I., & Jordan, J. (2020). Contextualizing the impostor "Syndrome." *Frontiers in Psychology*, *11*, 1–6. doi:10.3389/fpsyg.2020.575024 PMID:33312149

Compilation of References

First year definition and meaning: Collins English dictionary. (2023). In *Collins Dictionaries*. https://www.collinsdictionary.com/us/dictionary/english/first-year

Fraenkel, J. R., & Warren, N. E. (2000). *How to design and evaluate research in education*. https://books.google.com.jm/books/about/How_to_Design_and_Evaluate_Research_in_E.html?id=vhKvOZ4rqVsC&redir_esc=y

Frechette, J., Bitzas, V., Aubry, M., Kilpatrick, K., & Lavoie-Tremblay, M. (2020). Capturing Lived Experience: Methodological Considerations for Interpretive Phenomenological Inquiry. *International Journal of Qualitative Methods*, *19*, 160940692090725. doi:10.1177/1609406920907254

Freeman, M. (2015). Branding consumerism: Cross-media characters and story-worlds at the turn of the 20th century. *International Journal of Cultural Studies*, *18*(6), 629–644. doi:10.1177/1367877913515868

Gao, L. (2022). *Messy roots: A graphic memoir of a Wuhanese American*. Balzer & Bray.

Gee, J. P. (2017). *Teaching, learning, literacy in our high-risk high-tech world: A framework for becoming human*. Teachers College Press.

Gibbs, K. D. Jr, & Griffin, K. A. (2013). What Do I Want to Be with My PhD? The Roles of Personal Values and Structural Dynamics in Shaping the Career Interests of Recent Biomedical Science PhD Graduates. *CBE Life Sciences Education*, *12*(4), 711–723. doi:10.1187/cbe.13-02-0021 PMID:24297297

Gill, P. (2008, March 22). Methods of data collection in qualitative research: Interviews and focus groups. *Nature*. https://www.nature.com/articles/bdj.2008.192?error=cookies_not_supported&code=96b76f2d-0608-4b0f-8598-c28c87684671

Gittings, G. L., Bergman, M., Shuck, B., & Rose, K. C. (2018). The Impact of Student Attributes and Program Characteristics on Doctoral Degree Completion. *New Horizons in Adult Education and Human Resource Development*, *30*(3), 3–22. doi:10.1002/nha3.20220

Give Back Policy. (2024). Ministry of Education, Technological and Vocational Training. https://mes.gov.bb/GiveBack/

Glastris, P., & Sweetland, J. (2015). *The Other College Guide: A Roadmap to the Right School for You*. The New Press.

Goodwill A. G. Chen S. A. (2021). Embracing a culture of lifelong learning: The science of lifelong learning. *UNESCO Institute for Lifelong Learning UIL*, 1–11. https://doi.org/ doi:10.31234/osf.io/juefx

Grant, C., & Osanloo, A. (2014). Understanding, selecting, and integrating a theoretical framework in dissertation research: Creating the blueprint for your "House." *Administrative Issues Journal Education Practice and Research, 4*(2). doi:10.5929/2014.4.2.9

Grimes, D. A., & Schulz, K. F. (2002). Cohort studies: Marching towards outcomes. *Lancet*, *359*(9303), 341–345. doi:10.1016/S0140-6736(02)07500-1 PMID:11830217

Guidi, C. (2018). *Experiencing a gap year: Perceptions from students in the united states* (Publication No. 2047) [Doctoral dissertation, Northeastern University]. Northeastern University Library.

Guo, J., Tang, X., Marsh, H. W., Parker, P. D., Basarkod, G., Sahdra, B. K., Ranta, M., & Salmela-Aro, K. (2023). The roles of social–emotional skills in students' academic and life success: A multi-informant and multicohort perspective. *Journal of Personality and Social Psychology*, *124*(5), 1079–1110. doi:10.1037/pspp0000426 PMID:35666915

Guynes, S., Lund, M., & Berlatsky, N. (Eds.), *Unstable masks: Whiteness and American superhero comics*. Ohio State University Press.

Haigler, K., & Nelson, R. (2005). *The gap-year advantage: Helping your child benefit from time off before or during college.* Macmillan.

Hatfield, C. (2011). *Hand of fire: the comics art of Jack Kirby.* Univ. Press of Mississippi. doi:10.14325/mississippi/9781617031786.001.0001

Haynes, R. M. (2008). The impact of financial aid on postsecondary persistence: A review of the literature. *Journal of Student Financial Aid*, *37*(3), 3. doi:10.55504/0884-9153.1047

Herrera, L., Trinh, E., & De Jesús Gómez Portillo, M. (2021). Cultivating calm and stillness at the doctoral level: A Collaborative Autoethnography. *Educational Studies (Ames)*, *58*(2), 121–140. doi:10.1080/00131946.2021.1947817

Higher education. (2021, October 22). *The World Bank.* https://www.worldbank.org/en/topic/tertiaryeducation

Hoggan, C., & Finnegan, F. (2023). Transformative learning theory: Where we are after 45 years. *New Directions for Adult and Continuing Education*, *2023*(177), 5–11. doi:10.1002/ace.20474

Holmes, B. (2016). *Decoding the persistence and engagement patterns of doctoral students who finish.* OpenRiver. https://openriver.winona.edu/educationeddfacultyworks/11

Holmes, B. (2019). *Doctoral student perspectives on motivation and persistence: Eye-Opening insights into the ideas and thoughts that today's doctoral students have about finishing the doctoral degree.* OpenRiver. https://openriver.winona.edu/educationeddbooks/1?utm_source=openriver.winona.edu%2Feducationeddbooks%2F1&utm_medium=PDF&utm_campaign=PDFCoverPages

Holmes, B. D., Birds, K., Seay, A. D., Smith, D. B., & Wilson, K. N. (2010). Cohort learning for graduate students at the dissertation stage. *Journal of College Teaching & Learning (TLC)*, *7*(1), 5–12. doi:10.19030/tlc.v7i1.73

Howard, S. C., & Jackson, R. L. II, (Eds.). (2013). *Black comics: Politics of race and representation.* Bloomsbury Publishing.

Hunter-Johnson, Y., & Smith, S. (2015). *Yes I need help! A day in the journey of adult learners pursuing higher education: A Caribbean perspective.* https://eric.ed.gov/?id=ED570503

Compilation of References

Hurt, S., Woods Ways, E., & Holmes, B. (2022). Wait! Don't quit! Stay with your doctoral program during the global pandemic: Lessons learned from program completers global pandemic: Lessons learned from program completers. *The Journal of Advancing Education Practice*, *3*(1), 2. https://openriver.winona.edu/jaep/vol3/iss1/2

Hyde, B. (2021). Critical discourse and critical reflection in Mezirow's theory of transformative learning: A dialectic between ontology and epistemology (and a subtext of reflexivity mirroring my own Onto-Epistemological movement). *Adult Education Quarterly*, *71*(4), 373–388. doi:10.1177/07417136211003612

Imani Duncan-Price. (2021). Unleashing the multiplier effect of women. *Jamaica Observer*. https://www.jamaicaobserver.com/2021/03/13/unleashing-the-multiplier-effect-of-women/#:~:text=WITH%20just%20over%20410%2C000%20households,the%20average%2C%20with%20more%20children

Inter Q. Research LLC. (2023). *What is the ideal sample size in qualitative research?* https://interq-research.com/what-is-the-ideal-sample-size-in-qualitative-research/

International Students. (2024). *Migration Data Portal*. https://www.migrationdataportal.org/themes/international-students#:~:text=Prominent%20countries%20of%20origin%20of,on%20UIS%2C%202023)

Irwin, V. I., De La Rosa, J., Wang, K. W., Hein, S. H., Zhang, J. Z., Burr, R. B., & Roberts, A. R. (2022). Report on the condition of education 2022. In *National Center for Educational Statistics* (NCES 2022-144). U.S. Department of Education. https://nces.ed.gov/pubsearch/pubsinfo.asp?pubid=2022144

Jack (2019). *The privileged poor: how elite colleges are failing disadvantaged students*. Harvard University Press.

Jackson, J., & Cochran, T. (2021). Approaching the bar: An analysis of post-graduation bar exam study habits. *University of Massachusetts Law Review*, 6(1).

Janse, B. (2022, August 26). *Transformative Learning Theory (Mezirow)*. Toolshero. Retrieved October 9, 2022, from https://www.toolshero.com/personal-development/transformative-learning-theory/

Jen Tembo, K. D. (2017). Re-theorizing the problem of identity and the onto-existentialism of DC comics' Superman. *Word and Text, A Journal of Literary Studies and Linguistics, 7*(1), 151-167.

Jenkins, H. (2006). *Fans, bloggers, and gamers: Exploring participatory culture*. NYU Press.

Jones, S. H., Adams, T. E., & Ellis, C. (2016). *Handbook of autoethnography*. Routledge.

Kang, K. & National Center for Science and Engineering Statistics (NCSES). (2020). *Doctorate recipients from U.S. universities: 2020 NSF - National Science Foundation. Survey of Earned Doctorates*. https://ncses.nsf.gov/pubs/nsf22300/data-tables

Kara, M., Erdoğdu, F., Kokoç, M., & Cagiltay, K. (2019). Challenges faced by adult learners in online distance education: A literature review. *Open Praxis, 11*(1), 5-22. https://files.eric.ed.gov/fulltext/EJ1213733.pdf

Kim, P. Y. (2016). Religious support mediates the racial microaggression-mental health relation among Christian ethnic minority students. *Psychology of Religion and Spirituality*. Advance online publication. 10.1037/rel0000076

Køhlert, F. B. (2019). *Serial selves: Identity and representation in autobiographical comics.* Rutgers University Press.

Kress, G. (2009). *Multimodality: A social semiotic approach to contemporary communication.* Routledge. doi:10.4324/9780203970034

Kucsera, J., & Orfield, G. (2014). *New York State's extreme school segregation: inequality, inaction, and a damaged future.* The UCLA Civil Rights Project.

Kukkonen, K. (2013). *Studying comics and graphic novels.* John Wiley & Sons. doi:10.1002/9781394261079

Kuk, L., & Banning, J. H. (2014). A higher education leadership distance Ph.D. program: An assessment using blocher's ecological learning theory. *Creative Education, 05*(09), 701–712. doi:10.4236/ce.2014.59082

Kundu, A. (2019). Understanding college "burnout" from a social perspective: Reigniting the agency of low-income racial minority strivers towards achievement. *The Urban Review, 51*(5), 677–698. doi:10.1007/s11256-019-00501-w

Lake, E. D., Koper, J., Balayan, A., & Lynch, L. (2016). Cohorts and connections. Journal of College Student Retention: Research, Theory &Amp. *Journal of College Student Retention, 20*(2), 197–214. doi:10.1177/1521025116656386

Lewis, J. A., Mendenhall, R., Harwood, S. A., & Browne Huntt, M. (2013). Coping with Gendered Racial Microaggressions among Black Women College Students. *Journal of African American Studies, 17*(1), 51–73. doi:10.1007/s12111-012-9219-0

Litalien, D. (2020). *Improving PhD completion rates: Where should we start?* doi:10.1016/j.cedpsych.2015.03.004

Litzler & Samuelson, C. (2013). How underrepresented minority engineering students derive a sense of belonging from engineering. *Association for Engineering Education - Engineering Library Division Papers*, 23.674.1

Lively, C. (2021). The emerging scholars issue: Insights on teaching and leading through reshaping policy and practice: Reporting of doctoral student attrition: A policy brief. *Journal of Multicultural Affairs, 7*(3). https://scholarworks.sfasu.edu/jma/vol7/iss3

Compilation of References

Lukate, J. M. (2022). Space, race and identity: An ethnographic study of the Black hair care and beauty landscape and Black women's racial identity constructions in England. *The Journal of Social Issues*, *78*(1), 107–125. doi:10.1111/josi.12433

Marmot, M. G., & Shipley, M. J. (1996). Do socioeconomic differences in mortality persist after retirement? 25 year follow up of civil servants from the first Whitehall study. BMJ (Clinical Research Ed.), 313(7066), 1177–1180. https://doi.org/10.1136/bmj.313.7066.1177

Marmot, M., Ryff, C. D., Bumpass, L. L., Shipley, M., & Marks, N. F. (1997). Social inequalities in health: next questions and converging evidence. *Social Science & Medicine (1982)*, *44*(6), 901–910. https://doi.org/ doi:10.1016/s0277-9536(96)00194-3

Marshall University. (2023). *Banned books 2022*. https://www.marshall.edu/library/bannedbooks/speak/

Martinez-Vogt, E. (2021). Students transitioning to a non-traditional doctoral program: Identifying success factors promoting Doctoral-level Academic Success. *Academia Letters*. Advance online publication. doi:10.20935/AL2285

Maslow, A. H. (1943). A theory of human motivation. *Psychological Review*, *50*(4), 370–396. doi:10.1037/h0054346

Massyn, L. (2021). Persistence in doctoral education: A Part-Time research student perspective in a developing context. Journal of College Student Retention: Research, Theory &Amp. *Practice*, 1–19. doi:10.1177/15210251211007110

Maxfield, R. J. (2017). Epistemology and ontology: The lived experience of Non-Traditional adult students in online and Study-Abroad learning environments. *Journal of Organizational Psychology*, *17*(6). Advance online publication. doi:10.33423/jop.v17i6.1513

McClelland, D. M. (2005). Achievement motivational theory. In *Organizational Behavior*. M.E. Sharpe. https://books.google.com/books?hl=en&lr=&id=kUO5NWwaySYC&oi=fnd&pg=PA46&dq=mcclelland+achievement+motivation+theory&ots=UHcHDcKqEN&sig=luRy4GRDzJMEd_khRWysxm_o-v0

McFarlane, D. (2010). Accreditation discrimination: Impact on school choice, costs, and professional prospects in academia. *Academic Leadership: The Online Journal*, *8*(4), 7. https://scholars.fhsu.edu/alj/vol8/iss4/7

Mechur Karp, M., Hughes, K. L., & O'Gara, L. (2008). *An exploration of Tinto's integration framework for community college students* [PhD Dissertation]. Columbia University.

Mercado, F. M. S., & Shin, S. (2022). Teacher professional development in the 21st century. In IGI Global eBooks (pp. 227–254). doi:10.4018/978-1-6684-5316-2.ch012

Merriam, S. B. (2004). The Role of Cognitive Development in Mezirow's Transformational Learning Theory. *Adult Education Quarterly*, *55*(1), 60–68. doi:10.1177/0741713604268891

Merrill, B. (2015). Determined to stay or determined to leave? A tale of learner identities, biographies and adult students in higher education. *Studies in Higher Education (Dorchester-on-Thames), 40*(10), 1859-1871. doi:10.1080/03075079.2014.914918

Metz, G. W. (2002). Challenges and changes to Tinto's persistence theory. *Annual Meeting of the Mid Western Educational Research Association*, 28. https://eric.ed.gov/?id=ED471529

Mezirow, J. (2008). An overview on transformative learning. *Lifelong Learning*, 40–54. https://doi.org/ doi:10.4324/9780203936207-12

Mezirow, J. (1978). Perspective transformation. *Adult Education, 28*(2), 100–110. doi:10.1177/074171367802800202

Mezirow, J. (1991). *Transformative dimensions of adult learning* (1st ed.). The Jossey-Bass. https://www.umsl.edu/~henschkej/henschke/fostering_transformative_adult_learning

Mezirow, J. (1994). Understanding Transformation Theory. *Adult Education Quarterly, 44*(4), 222–232. doi:10.1177/074171369404400403

Mezirow, J. (1997). Transformative Learning: Theory to Practice. *New Directions for Adult and Continuing Education, 1997*(74), 5–12. doi:10.1002/ace.7401

Mihalache, G. (2019). Heuristic inquiry: Differentiated from descriptive phenomenology and aligned with transpersonal research methods. *The Humanistic Psychologist, 47*(2), 136–157. doi:10.1037/hum0000125

Miller, E. (2008). *Education and social mobility: The case of the Jamaican peasant.* https://errolmiller.com/wp-content/uploads/2018/09/Education-and-Social-Mobility-the-Case-of-the-Jamaican-Peasant-2.pdf?d9dbdd&d9dbdd

Miller, K. (2018). *Persistence*. Routledge Encyclopedia of Philosophy. doi:10.4324/0123456789-N126-1

Moehringer, J. R. (2005). *The tender: A memoir*. Hyperion.

Moeller, R. A. (2023). "It's not something I've really thought about 'til now'": The social aspects of US emerging adults' comics reading histories. *Journal of Librarianship and Information Science, 55*(1), 33–42. doi:10.1177/09610006211054213

Moench, D. (1992). *Batman: Red rain*. DC Comics.

Moran, M. (2021). *Almost 50% of all Doctoral Students Don't Graduate*. Statistics Solutions. https://www.statisticssolutions.com/almost-50-of-all-doctoral-students-dont-graduate/#:~:text=The%20Council%20of%20Graduate%20Schools,program%20remains%20low%20at%2056.6%25

Murthi, M., & Bassett, R. M. (2022, November 15). *Higher education: Understanding demand and redefining values*. https://blogs.worldbank.org/education/higher-education-understanding-demand-and-redefining-values

Compilation of References

National Center for Education Statistics (n.d.) *Nontraditional Undergraduates / Definitions and Data* Retrieved February 04, 2024 from: https://nces.ed.gov/pubs/web/97578e.asp

National Center for Education Statistics (NCES). (n.d.). *Nontraditional undergraduates-definitions and data. Who Is Nontraditional?* Retrieved August 21, 2023, from https://nces.ed.gov/pubs/web/97578e.asp

National Center for Education Statistics. (2019). *Immediate College Enrollment rates.* Retrieved February 04, 2024 from: https://nces.ed.gov/programs/coe/indicator/cpa

Nerstrom, N. (2014). An emerging model for transformative learning. *Adult Education Research Conference*, 325–330.

Neto, M. (2015). Educational motivation meets Maslow: Self- actualisation as contextual driver. *Journal of Student Engagement: Education Matters*, 5(1), 18–27.

Neubauer, B. E., Witkop, C. T., & Varpio, L. (2019). How phenomenology can help us learn from the experiences of others. *Perspectives on Medical Education*, 8(2), 90–97. doi:10.1007/S40037-019-0509-2 PMID:30953335

Nicoletti, M. D. C. (2019). Revisiting the Tinto's theoretical dropout model. *Higher Education Studies*, 9(3), 52. doi:10.5539/hes.v9n3p52

Nietzel, M. T. (2021, October 13). Ten ways U.S. doctoral degrees have changed in the past 20 years. *Forbes*. https://www.forbes.com/sites/michaeltnietzel/2021/10/13/ten-ways-us-doctoral-degrees-have-changed-in-the-past-20-years/?sh=3533ed5a2a71

Nietzel, M. T. (2022, October 20). College enrollment losses continue, but at a slower rate, according to new report. *Forbes*. https://www.forbes.com/sites/michaeltnietzel/2022/10/20/college-enrollment-decline-continues-but-at-a-slower-rate-according-to-new-report/?sh=318c13ff3910

Nimer, M. (2009). The doctoral cohort model: Increasing opportunities for success. *College Student Journal*, 43(4), 1373–1379. https://go.gale.com/ps/i.do?id=GALE%7CA217511799&sid=googleScholar&v=2.1&it=r&linkaccess=abs&issn=01463934&p=AONE&sw=w&userGroupName=tel_oweb#:~:text=The%20cohort%20model%20consists%20of,a%20masters%20or%20doctoral%20degree

Non-Traditional Students Not Graduating at Near the Same Rate as Traditional. (2014, October 15). *College Factual*. https://students.collegefactual.com/blog/are-colleges-supporting-non-traditional-students

Northcentral University. (2016, December 9). *What is a doctorate degree*. Northcentral University. https://www.ncu.edu/student-experience/online-education-guide/doctoral-education/what-is-a-doctorate-degree#gref

Nussbaumer, J., & Johnson, C. (2011). The door to law school. *University of Massachusetts Roundtable Symposium Law Journal*, 6, 1.

O'Herrin, K. T. (2017). *Urban forestry at a crossroads: Development of an emerging profession* (Publication No. 16514) [Doctoral dissertation, Virginia Tech]. VTechWorks.

Oneill, S., & Thomson, M. M. (2013). Supporting academic persistence in low-skilled adult learners. *Support for Learning, 28*(4), 162–172. doi:10.1111/1467-9604.12038

Opacich, K. J. (2019). A cohort model and high impact practices in undergraduate public health education. *Frontiers in Public Health, 7*, 132. Advance online publication. doi:10.3389/fpubh.2019.00132 PMID:31192184

Ortiz, L. G., Clougher, D., Anderson, T., & Maina, M. F. (2021). IDEAS for Transforming Higher Education: An Overview of Ongoing Trends and challenges. *International Review of Research in Open and Distance Learning, 22*(2), 166–184. doi:10.19173/irrodl.v22i2.5206

Owusu-Agyeman, Y. (2016). Investigating the determinants of adults' participation in higher education. *Cogent Education., 3*(1), 1–16. doi:10.1080/2331186X.2016.1194733

Panacci, A. G. (2015). Adult students in higher education: Classroom experiences and needs. *The College Quarterly, 18*(3).

Paprock, K. E. (1992). Mezirow, Jack. (1991) Transformative dimensions of adult learning. San Francisco: Jossey-Bass, 247 pages. $29.95. *Adult Education Quarterly, 42*(3), 195–197. doi:10.1177/074171369204200309

Pemberton, C. L. A., & Akkary, R. K. (2005). A cohort, is a cohort, is a cohort...or is it? *Journal of Research on Leadership Education, 5*(5), 179–208. doi:10.1177/194277511000500501

Perrine, R. (1998). Stress and college persistence as a function of attachment style. *Journal of the First-Year Experience & Students in Transition, 1*(14), 25–38. https://www.ingentaconnect.com/content/fyesit/fyesit/1998/00000011/00000001/art00002

Perseverance. (2022). In *The Merriam-Webster.com Dictionary*. https://www.merriam-webster.com/dictionary/perseverance

Perue, C. (2023, June 7). *A librarianship business model for the knowledge economy.* ACURIL 2023 Conference, Kingston, Jamaica.

PHD Researcher Demographics and Statistics [2022]: Number of PHD Researchers in The US. (2022, September 9). https://www.zippia.com/phd-researcher-jobs/demographics/

Phenomenology (Stanford Encyclopedia of Philosophy). (2013, December 16). https://plato.stanford.edu/entries/phenomenology/

Pierce, C. (1989). Unity in diversity: Thirty-three years of stress. In G. Berry & J. Asamen (Eds.), Black students: Psychosocial issues in academic achievement (pp. 298-3 1 2). Newbury, CA: Sage Publications Inc.

Pierce, C. (1 970). Offensive mechanisms. In F. Barbour (Ed.), *The Black seventies* (pp. 265–282). Porter Sargent.

Compilation of References

Poock, M. C. (1999). Students of Color and Doctoral Programs: Factors Influencing the Application Decision in Higher Education Administration. *College and University, 74*(3), 2–7. https://eric.ed.gov/?id=EJ588129

Poole, B. D. (2015). The rather elusive concept of 'doctorateness': A reaction to Wellington. *Studies in Higher Education, 40*(9), 1507–1522. doi:10.1080/03075079.2013.873026

Postsecondary National Policy Institute. (2021). *Indicator 23: Postsecondary Graduation Rates.* Retrieved February 04, 2024 from: https://nces.ed.gov/programs/raceindicators/indicator_red.asp

Poulos, C. N. (2021). Essentials of autoethnography. In American Psychological Association eBooks. doi:10.1037/0000222-000

Pusser, B., & Ericson, M. (2018). *The impact of the PROSPER act on underrepresented students in for-profit colleges.* https://escholarship.org/uc/item/1k76g8rz

Radio Jamaica News. (2016, May 30). *Number of students enrolling in tertiary institutions declines.* https://radiojamaicanewsonline.com/local/number-of-students-enrolling-in-tertiary-institutions-declines

Rahman, O., Wing-Sun, L., & Cheung, B. H. M. (2012). "Cosplay": Imaginative self and performing identity. *Fashion Theory, 16*(3), 317–341. doi:10.2752/175174112X13340749707204

Rausch, & Buning, M. M. (2022). Student veterans' perspectives of higher education contexts: Beyond the non-traditional student. *College Teaching,* 1–11. doi:10.1080/87567555.2022.2106469

Rhoden, B. J. (2015). *Understanding the impact of academic entry characteristics, remediation requirements, and semester course hour load in the first year on the academic performance and persistence to graduation for Latino students* (Publication No. 2031) [Doctoral dissertation, University of Houston]. University of Houston Libraries.

Rigler, K. L., Jr., Bowlin, L. K., Sweat, K., Watts, S., & Throne, R. (2017). *Agency, socialization, and support: A critical review of doctoral student attrition.* Paper Presented at the 3rd International Conference on Doctoral Education, ED580853. https://www.google.com/url?sa=t&rct=j&q=&esrc=s&source=web&cd=&cad=rja&uact=8&ved=2ahUKEwjF8s2HrNn7AhUymmoFHR2LDGMQFnoECBMQAQ&url=https%3A%2F%2Ffiles.eric.ed.gov%2Ffulltext%2FED580853.pdf&usg=AOvVaw3hwtObTyWn9Mi7ht7QmbLk

Rogers-Shaw, C. A., & Carr-Chellman, D. (2018). Developing care and socio-emotional learning in first year doctoral students: Building capacity for success. *International Journal of Doctoral Studies, 13,* 233–253. doi:10.28945/4064

Roman, E. (2022). 3 reasons why college enrollments are declining, according to Coursera's CEO. *Yahoo Finance* https://finance.yahoo.com/news/declining-college-enrollments-a-us-phenomenon-coursera-ceo-says-170903514.html?guccounter=1&guce_refe rrer=aHR0cHM6Ly93d3cuZ29vZ2xlLmNvbS8&guce_referrer_sig=AQAAAGsMO-8PV__qZfRdHJul39YGFT3L1TgVw7ZJ35w0lJixZrZB1-M_WXhZHj74nmLiueFY4VX29ZVL-JeMP7HLHMzqpDaOmmJXw84MKZ6__YN5L6fesRvTqg8b71R2bYlfukdRa2c6LZv9LOrT kNAMecJv-yRb_mb9a4GbmxkqGv-7

Rowlands, S. L. R. (2010). *Nontraditional students: The impact of role strain on their identity* [PhD Dissertation]. Southern Illinois University Carbondale.

Ruud, C. M., Saclarides, E. S., George-Jackson, C. E., & Lubienski, S. T. (2016). Tipping Points. Journal of College Student Retention: Research, Theory &Amp. *Journal of College Student Retention*, *20*(3), 286–307. doi:10.1177/1521025116666082

Ryan, R. M., & Deci, E. L. (2000). Self-determination theory and the facilitation of intrinsic motivation, social development, and well-being. *The American Psychologist*, *55*(1), 68–78. doi:10.1037/0003-066X.55.1.68 PMID:11392867

Sander, R. H. (2010). Class in American legal education. *Denver University Law Review*, *88*(4), 631.

Santicola, L. (2013). Pressing On: Persistence Through A Doctoral Cohort Program In Education. *Contemporary Issues in Education Research*, *6*(2), 253. doi:10.19030/cier.v6i2.7736

Satrapi, M. (2004). *Persepolis: The story of a childhood.* Pantheon.

Saxena, L. (2022, November 15). *Higher education fails to support non-traditional students – The Statesman*. The Statesman. https://www.sbstatesman.com/2022/11/13/higher-education-fails-to-support-non-traditional-students/

Sayago, S., Forbes, P., & Blat, J. (2013). Older people becoming successful ICT learners over time: Challenges and strategies through an ethnographical lens. *Educational Gerontology*, *39*(7), 527–544. doi:10.1080/03601277.2012.703583

Schaffner, A. K. (2020). Perseverance in psychology: Meaning, importance & books. *PositivePsychology.com*. https://positivepsychology.com/perseverance/#google_vignette

Schiller, C. J. (2018). Teaching concept analysis to graduate nursing students. *Nursing Forum*, *53*(2), 248–254. doi:10.1111/nuf.12233 PMID:29327788

Seniuk Cicek, J., Ingram, S., Friesen, M., & Ruth, D. (2017). Action research: A methodology for transformative learning for a professor and his students in an engineering classroom. *European Journal of Engineering Education*, *44*(1–2), 49–70. doi:10.1080/03043797.2017.1405242

Sheehan, S. (2014). A Conceptual Framework for Understanding Transcendental phenomenology through the lived experiences of biblical leaders. *Emerging Leadership Journeys*, 7. https://www.regent.edu/journal/emerging-leadership-journeys/understanding-transcendental-phenomenology/#:~:text=Transcendental%20phenomenology%20(TPh)%2C%20 largely,experience%20(Moustakas%2C%201994)

Compilation of References

Shokooh, F., & Yazdani, S. (2018). Defining doctorateness: A concept analysis. *International Journal of Doctoral Studies, 13*, 31–48. doi:10.28945/3939

Sonia, VanWye, Schafer, Robertson, & Poore. (2018). Factors Affecting PhD Student Success. *International Journal of Exercise Science, 12*(1), 34–45. PMID:30761191

Soukup. (2014). Looking at, with, and through YouTube. *Communication Research Trends, 33*(3), 3.

Spence, C. (2023). *Draft Higher Education Policy in Final Stage of Review*. Jamaica Information Service. https://jis.gov.jm/draft-higher-education-policy-in-final-stage-of-review/

Spencer, N. (2016). Captain America: Sam Wilson vol. 1: Not my Captain America. Marvel Comics.

Steele, D. A. (2016). *The price paid: free higher education in Trinidad and Tobago re-examined* [PhD Dissertation]. Colombia University.

Stefoff, R., & Zinn, H. (2007a). *A young people's history of the United States*. Seven Stories Press.

Steinmayr, R., Weidinger, A. F., Schwinger, M., & Spinath, B. (2019). The importance of students' motivation for their academic achievement – replicating and extending previous findings. *Frontiers in Psychology, 10*, 1730. Advance online publication. doi:10.3389/fpsyg.2019.01730 PMID:31417459

Stringer, H. (2022). *The nontraditional student*. American Psychological Association. https://www.apa.org/gradpsych/2015/04/nontraditional-student

Sue, D. W., Capodilupo, C. M., Torino, G. C., Bucceri, J. M., Holder, A., Nadal, K. L., & Esquilin, M. (2007). Racial microaggressions in everyday life: Implications for clinical practice. *The American Psychologist, 62*(4), 271–286. doi:10.1037/0003-066X.62.4.271 PMID:17516773

Sverdlik, A., Hall, N. C., McAlpine, L., & Hubbard, K. (2018). The PhD Experience: A Review of the Factors Influencing Doctoral Students' Completion, Achievement, and Well-Being. *International Journal of Doctoral Studies, 13*, 361–388. doi:10.28945/4113

Sweet v. Cardona, 2023 U.S. Dist. LEXIS 31518, 2023 WL 2213610 (United States District Court for the Northern District of California, February 24, 2023, Filed). https://advance-lexis-com.ezproxy.uky.edu/api/document?collection=cases&id=urn:contentItem:67N4-VK01-FGCG-S0D0-00000-00&context=1516831

Tatersfield, K. (2022). *How to Address the Struggles of Non-Traditional Students*. https://www.leadsquared.com/industries/education/struggles-of-non-traditional-students/

The Project on Predatory Student Lending. (2023, April 13). *Sweet v. cardona*. PPSL. https://www.ppsl.org/cases/sweet-v-cardona

The Stanford Encyclopedia of Philosophy. (2013, December 16). Phenomenology. *Stanford Encyclopedia of Philosophy*. https://plato.stanford.edu/entries/phenomenology/

The University of the West Indies Mona Campus. (n.d.). *Student Statistics 2021 - 2022*. https://www.mona.uwi.edu/principal/sites/default/files/principal/studentstatistics20212022.pdf

Thomas, R. (1992). *Bram stoker's Dracula*. Topps.

Thompson, C. (2023). Right to higher education: A case study of Caribbean countries. In *The right to higher education in Latin America and the Caribbean: Briefing note compendium*, 30 – 32. https://unesdoc.unesco.org/ark:/48223/pf0000387656?posInSet=21&queryId=N-EXPLORE-95f65d07-cdcf-4155-bc78-f28a20b534dd

Thompson. (2021). Grade Expectations: The role of first-year grades in predicting the pursuit of STEM majors for first- and continuing-generation students. *The Journal of Higher Education (Columbus)*, *92*(6), 961–985. doi:10.1080/00221546.2021.1907169

Thrower, A. C., Danawi, H., & Lockett, C. (2013). Determinants of High Pre-pregnancy BMI of U.S. Puerto Rican WIC Participants. *The International Journal of Childbirth Education*, *28*(4), 55–61.

Tinto, V. (1993). *Leaving college: Rethinking the causes and cures of student attrition*. University of Chicago Press. https://eric.ed.gov/?id=ED371658

Tinto, V. (2017). Reflections on student persistence. *Student Success*, *8*(2), 1–8. doi:10.5204/ssj.v8i2.376

Tobias, M., Levin, M., & Christopher, B. (2022, March 3). Californians: Here's why your housing costs are so high. *Cal Matters*. https://calmatters.org/explainers/housing-costs-high-california/

Tompsett, J., & Knoester, C. (2023). Family socioeconomic status and college attendance: A consideration of individual-level and school-level pathways. *PLoS One*, *18*(4), e0284188. doi:10.1371/journal.pone.0284188

Trafford, V. (2008). Conceptual Frameworks as a Threshold Concept in Doctorateness. *BRILL eBooks*, 273–288. doi:10.1163/9789460911477_021

Trafford, V., & Leshem, S. (2009). Doctorateness as a threshold concept. *Innovations in Education and Teaching International*, *46*(3), 305–316. doi:10.1080/14703290903069027

Trinidad, J. E. (2024). Positionality in the politics of education: Mapping the strategies and constraints of education reformers. *Educational Policy*, 08959048231220038. Advance online publication. doi:10.1177/08959048231220038

Tseng, C. I., & Bateman, J. A. (2018). Cohesion in comics and graphic novels: An empirical comparative approach to transmedia adaptation in City of Glass. *Adaptation*, *11*(2), 122–143. doi:10.1093/adaptation/apx027

U.S. Department of Education & Institute of Education Sciences. (2022). *Characteristics of postsecondary students: Postbaccalaureate enrollment*. Condition of Education. Retrieved March 19, 2023, from https://nces.ed.gov/programs/coe/indicator/csb

U.S. Department of State. (2015, December). *What is a Graduate Student?* EducationUSA. Retrieved October 9, 2022, from https://educationusa.state.gov/your-5-steps-us-study/research-your-options/graduate/what-graduate-student

Compilation of References

UK Human Resources. (n.d.-a). *Child care resources*. https://hr.uky.edu/work-life-and-well-being/working-parents/child-care-resources

UK Human Resources. (n.d.-b). *Employee education program – frequently asked questions*. University of Kentucky. https://hr.uky.edu/more-great-benefits/employee-education-program-frequently-asked-questions

UK Student Success. (n.d.). *Get help*. https://studentsuccess.uky.edu/get-help

UK Veterans Resource Center. (n.d.). *Resources*. University of Kentucky. https://studentsuccess.uky.edu/veterans-resource-center/resources

UNESCO. (2022). Higher education global data report (Summary). *World Higher Education Conference*.

United States Census Bureau. (2019). *Reports Nearly 77 Million Students Enrolled in U.S. Schools*. Retrieved from https://www.census.gov/newsroom/press-releases/2019/school-enrollment.html

United States Census Bureau. (2022). Improved Race and Ethnicity Measures Reveal U.S. Population Is Much More Multiracial. Retrieved February 04, 2023, from. https://www.census.gov/library/stories/2021/08/improved-race-ethnicity-measures-reveal-united-states-population-much-more-multiracial.html

United States Department of Veterans Affairs. (2023a, March 21). *Post-9/11 gi bill (chapter 33)*. https://www.va.gov/education/about-gi-bill-benefits/post-9-11/

United States Department of Veterans Affairs. (2023b, March 21). *Post-9/11 gi bill (chapter 33) rates*. https://www.va.gov/education/benefit-rates/post-9-11-gi-bill-rates/

University of Nebraska-Lincoln Office of Gr. (2022). *Non-Traditional students graduate connections Nebraska*. Graduate Connections. Retrieved October 9, 2022, from https://graduate.unl.edu/connections/non-traditional-students

Van Der Linden, N., Devos, C., Boudrenghien, G., Frenay, M., Azzi, A., Klein, O., & Galand, B. (2018). Gaining insight into doctoral persistence: Development and validation of doctorate-related need support and need satisfaction short scales. *Learning and Individual Differences*, *65*, 100–111. doi:10.1016/j.lindif.2018.03.008

Van Dijck. (2013). The culture of connectivity: A critical history of social media. Academic Press.

Van Rhijn, T. M., Lero, D. S., Bridge, K., & Fritz, V. A. (2016). Unmet needs: Challenges to success from the perspectives of mature university students. *Canadian Journal for the Study of Adult Education*, *28*(1), 29–47.

Van Rooij, E., Fokkens-Bruinsma, M., & Jansen, E. (2019). Factors that influence PhD candidates' success: The importance of PhD project characteristics. *Studies in Continuing Education*, *43*(1), 48–67. doi:10.1080/0158037X.2019.1652158

Venezuela, P., & Yáñez, N. (2022). *Trajectory and policies for inclusion in higher education in Latin America and the Caribbean in the context of the pandemic: Two decades of progress and challenges.* https://repositorio.cepal.org/server/api/core/bitstreams/6666262b-754b-4684-a247-8659e96f3fea/content

Verrone, W. E. (2011). *The avant-garde feature film: A critical history.* McFarland.

Vieira, D., Mutize, T., & Chinchilla, J. R. (2020, December 21). Understanding access to higher education in the last two decades. *UNESCO.* https://www.iesalc.unesco.org/en/2020/12/23/understanding-access-to-higher-education-in-the-last-two-decades/

Wall, S. (2008). Easier Said than Done: Writing an Autoethnography. *International Journal of Qualitative Methods, 7*(1), 38–53. doi:10.1177/160940690800700103

Wang, V., Torrisi-Steele, G., & Reinsfield, E. (2020). Transformative learning, epistemology and technology in adult education. *Journal of Adult and Continuing Education, 27*(2), 324–340. doi:10.1177/1477971420918602

Wellington, J. (2013). Searching for 'doctorateness.'. *Studies in Higher Education, 38*(10), 1490–1503. doi:10.1080/03075079.2011.634901

Westbrooks, D., Guillaume, N., Jones, S. M., & De La Fosse, K. (2020). Academic residency: Effective engagement and mentorship of doctoral students. *Journal of College Teaching and Learning, 17*(1).

Wilks, A. (2023, March 4). *Student enrolment dips by six per cent at UWI, Mona.* https://jamaica-gleaner.com/article/lead-stories/20230304/student-enrolment-dips-six-cent-uwi-mona

Willis, B., & Carmichael, K. (2014). The Lived Experience of Late-Stage Doctoral Student Attrition in Counselor Education. *The Qualitative Report.* Advance online publication. doi:10.46743/2160-3715/2011.1046

Wilson, R. C., & Shaffer, E. J. (1965). Reading comics to learn. *The Elementary School Journal, 66*(2), 81–82. doi:10.1086/460267

Wollast, R., Boudrenghien, G., Van Der Linden, N., Galand, B., Roland, N., Devos, C., De Clercq, M., Klein, O., Azzi, A. E., & Frenay, M. (2018). Who Are the Doctoral Students Who Drop Out? Factors Associated with the Rate of Doctoral Degree Completion in Universities. *International Journal of Higher Education, 7*(4), 143. doi:10.5430/ijhe.v7n4p143

World Bank. (2017). *Higher Education Expanding in Latin America and the Caribbean, but Falling Short of Potential.* https://www.worldbank.org/en/news/press-release/2017/05/17/higher-education-expanding-in-latin-america-and-the-caribbean-but-falling-short-of-potential

Worldwide College Tours. (2018, October 24). *7 benefits of recruiting students in the Caribbean – How can your college or university get involved?* https://www.worldwidecollegetours.com/benefits-recruiting-students-caribbean-college-university

Compilation of References

Wright, R. R. (2016). Comics, kitsch, and class: An autoethnographic exploration of an accidental academic. *International Journal of Qualitative Studies in Education*, *29*(3), 426–444. doi:10.1080/09518398.2015.1078518

Yalçınkaya, C. T. (2022). Autographics as autoethnography: Comic book adventures of a migrant academic. *Continuum (Perth)*, *36*(6), 902–920. doi:10.1080/10304312.2023.2182957

Yang, G.L., & Gurihiru. (2020). *Superman smashes the klan!* DC Comics.

Young, S. N., & William, R. (2018). Factors affecting PhD student success. *International Journal of Exercise Science, 12*(1), 34–45. https://www.ncbi.nlm.nih.gov/pmc/articles/PMC6355122/

Zanatta, J. A. (2017). *Understanding YouTube culture and how it affects today's media* (Publication No. 83) [Senor Thesis, Dominican University of California]. Dominican Scholar. https://doi.org/doi:10.33015/dominican.edu/2017.CMS.ST.03

Zanettin, F. (2014). Visual adaptation in translated comics. *Intralinea*, *16*, 1–34.

Zhou, E. (2022). Graduate Enrollment and Degrees: 2011 to 2021. In *Graduate Enrollment and Degrees*. Council of Graduate Schools. https://cgsnet.org/wp-content/uploads/2022/11/CGS_GED21_Report_v1-1.pdf

Zhou, E., & Okahana, H. (2016). The role of department supports on doctoral completion and time-to-degree. Journal of College Student Retention: Research, Theory &Amp. *Journal of College Student Retention*, *20*(4), 511–529. doi:10.1177/1521025116682036

Znamenak, K., Lieberth, M., Murphy, J. L., & Sheaffer, A. (2022). Experiences and viewpoints of PhD students completing their dissertations during crises. *New Directions for Adult and Continuing Education*, *2022*(173–174), 33–43. doi:10.1002/ace.20450

Related References

To continue our tradition of advancing academic research, we have compiled a list of recommended IGI Global readings. These references will provide additional information and guidance to further enrich your knowledge and assist you with your own research and future publications.

Aburezeq, I. M., & Dweikat, F. F. (2017). Cloud Applications in Language Teaching: Examining Pre-Service Teachers' Expertise, Perceptions and Integration. *International Journal of Distance Education Technologies*, *15*(4), 39–60. doi:10.4018/IJDET.2017100103

Acharjya, B., & Das, S. (2022). Adoption of E-Learning During the COVID-19 Pandemic: The Moderating Role of Age and Gender. *International Journal of Web-Based Learning and Teaching Technologies*, *17*(2), 1–14. https://doi.org/10.4018/IJWLTT.20220301.oa4

Adams, J. L., & Thomas, S. K. (2022). Non-Linear Curriculum Experiences for Student Learning and Work Design: What Is the Maximum Potential of a Chat Bot? In S. Ramlall, T. Cross, & M. Love (Eds.), *Handbook of Research on Future of Work and Education: Implications for Curriculum Delivery and Work Design* (pp. 299–306). IGI Global. https://doi.org/10.4018/978-1-7998-8275-6.ch018

Adera, B. (2017). Supporting Language and Literacy Development for English Language Learners. In J. Keengwe (Ed.), *Handbook of Research on Promoting Cross-Cultural Competence and Social Justice in Teacher Education* (pp. 339–354). Hershey, PA: IGI Global. doi:10.4018/978-1-5225-0897-7.ch018

Related References

Ahamer, G. (2017). Quality Assurance for a Developmental "Global Studies" (GS) Curriculum. In I. Management Association (Ed.), Educational Leadership and Administration: Concepts, Methodologies, Tools, and Applications (pp. 438-477). Hershey, PA: IGI Global. https://doi.org/ doi:10.4018/978-1-5225-1624-8.ch023

Ahamer, G. (2017). Quality Assurance for a Developmental "Global Studies" (GS) Curriculum. In I. Management Association (Ed.), Educational Leadership and Administration: Concepts, Methodologies, Tools, and Applications (pp. 438-477). Hershey, PA: IGI Global. https://doi.org/ doi:10.4018/978-1-5225-1624-8.ch023

Akayoğlu, S., & Seferoğlu, G. (2019). An Analysis of Negotiation of Meaning Functions of Advanced EFL Learners in Second Life: Negotiation of Meaning in Second Life. In M. Kruk (Ed.), *Assessing the Effectiveness of Virtual Technologies in Foreign and Second Language Instruction* (pp. 61–85). IGI Global. https://doi.org/10.4018/978-1-5225-7286-2.ch003

Akella, N. R. (2022). Unravelling the Web of Qualitative Dissertation Writing!: A Student Reflects. In A. Zimmerman (Ed.), *Methodological Innovations in Research and Academic Writing* (pp. 260–282). IGI Global. https://doi.org/10.4018/978-1-7998-8283-1.ch014

Alegre de la Rosa, O. M., & Angulo, L. M. (2017). Social Inclusion and Intercultural Values in a School of Education. In S. Mukerji & P. Tripathi (Eds.), *Handbook of Research on Administration, Policy, and Leadership in Higher Education* (pp. 518–531). Hershey, PA: IGI Global. doi:10.4018/978-1-5225-0672-0.ch020

Alexander, C. (2019). Using Gamification Strategies to Cultivate and Measure Professional Educator Dispositions. *International Journal of Game-Based Learning*, 9(1), 15–29. https://doi.org/10.4018/IJGBL.2019010102

Anderson, K. M. (2017). Preparing Teachers in the Age of Equity and Inclusion. In I. Management Association (Ed.), Medical Education and Ethics: Concepts, Methodologies, Tools, and Applications (pp. 1532-1554). Hershey, PA: IGI Global. doi:10.4018/978-1-5225-0978-3.ch069

Awdziej, M. (2017). Case Study as a Teaching Method in Marketing. In D. Latusek (Ed.), *Case Studies as a Teaching Tool in Management Education* (pp. 244–263). Hershey, PA: IGI Global. doi:10.4018/978-1-5225-0770-3.ch013

Bakos, J. (2019). Sociolinguistic Factors Influencing English Language Learning. In N. Erdogan & M. Wei (Eds.), *Applied Linguistics for Teachers of Culturally and Linguistically Diverse Learners* (pp. 403–424). IGI Global. https://doi.org/10.4018/978-1-5225-8467-4.ch017

Banas, J. R., & York, C. S. (2017). Pre-Service Teachers' Motivation to Use Technology and the Impact of Authentic Learning Exercises. In L. Tomei (Ed.), *Exploring the New Era of Technology-Infused Education* (pp. 121–140). Hershey, PA: IGI Global. doi:10.4018/978-1-5225-1709-2.ch008

Barton, T. P. (2021). Empowering Educator Allyship by Exploring Racial Trauma and the Disengagement of Black Students. In C. Reneau & M. Villarreal (Eds.), *Handbook of Research on Leading Higher Education Transformation With Social Justice, Equity, and Inclusion* (pp. 186–197). IGI Global. https://doi.org/10.4018/978-1-7998-7152-1.ch013

Benhima, M. (2021). Moroccan English Department Student Attitudes Towards the Use of Distance Education During COVID-19: Moulay Ismail University as a Case Study. *International Journal of Information and Communication Technology Education, 17*(3), 105–122. https://doi.org/10.4018/IJICTE.20210701.oa7

Beycioglu, K., & Wildy, H. (2017). Principal Preparation: The Case of Novice Principals in Turkey. In I. Management Association (Ed.), Educational Leadership and Administration: Concepts, Methodologies, Tools, and Applications (pp. 1152-1169). Hershey, PA: IGI Global. https://doi.org/ doi:10.4018/978-1-5225-1624-8.ch054

Bharwani, S., & Musunuri, D. (2018). Reflection as a Process From Theory to Practice. In M. Khosrow-Pour, D.B.A. (Ed.), Encyclopedia of Information Science and Technology, Fourth Edition (pp. 1529-1539). Hershey, PA: IGI Global. doi:10.4018/978-1-5225-2255-3.ch132

Bhushan, A., Garza, K. B., Perumal, O., Das, S. K., Feola, D. J., Farrell, D., & Birnbaum, A. (2022). Lessons Learned From the COVID-19 Pandemic and the Implications for Pharmaceutical Graduate Education and Research. In C. Ford & K. Garza (Eds.), *Handbook of Research on Updating and Innovating Health Professions Education: Post-Pandemic Perspectives* (pp. 324–345). IGI Global. https://doi.org/10.4018/978-1-7998-7623-6.ch014

Bintz, W., Ciecierski, L. M., & Royan, E. (2021). Using Picture Books With Instructional Strategies to Address New Challenges and Teach Literacy Skills in a Digital World. In L. Haas & J. Tussey (Eds.), *Connecting Disciplinary Literacy and Digital Storytelling in K-12 Education* (pp. 38–58). IGI Global. https://doi.org/10.4018/978-1-7998-5770-9.ch003

Bohjanen, S. L., Cameron-Standerford, A., & Meidl, T. D. (2018). Capacity Building Pedagogy for Diverse Learners. In J. Keengwe (Ed.), *Handbook of Research on Pedagogical Models for Next-Generation Teaching and Learning* (pp. 195–212). Hershey, PA: IGI Global. doi:10.4018/978-1-5225-3873-8.ch011

Related References

Brewer, J. C. (2018). Measuring Text Readability Using Reading Level. In M. Khosrow-Pour, D.B.A. (Ed.), Encyclopedia of Information Science and Technology, Fourth Edition (pp. 1499-1507). Hershey, PA: IGI Global. doi:10.4018/978-1-5225-2255-3.ch129

Brookbanks, B. C. (2022). Student Perspectives on Business Education in the USA: Current Attitudes and Necessary Changes in an Age of Disruption. In A. Zhuplev & R. Koepp (Eds.), *Global Trends, Dynamics, and Imperatives for Strategic Development in Business Education in an Age of Disruption* (pp. 214–231). IGI Global. doi:10.4018/978-1-7998-7548-2.ch011

Brown, L. V., Dari, T., & Spencer, N. (2019). Addressing the Impact of Trauma in High Poverty Elementary Schools: An Ecological Model for School Counseling. In K. Daniels & K. Billingsley (Eds.), *Creating Caring and Supportive Educational Environments for Meaningful Learning* (pp. 135–153). IGI Global. https://doi.org/10.4018/978-1-5225-5748-7.ch008

Brown, S. L. (2017). A Case Study of Strategic Leadership and Research in Practice: Principal Preparation Programs that Work – An Educational Administration Perspective of Best Practices for Master's Degree Programs for Principal Preparation. In V. Wang (Ed.), *Encyclopedia of Strategic Leadership and Management* (pp. 1226–1244). Hershey, PA: IGI Global. doi:10.4018/978-1-5225-1049-9.ch086

Brzozowski, M., & Ferster, I. (2017). Educational Management Leadership: High School Principal's Management Style and Parental Involvement in School Management in Israel. In V. Potocan, M. Ünğan, & Z. Nedelko (Eds.), *Handbook of Research on Managerial Solutions in Non-Profit Organizations* (pp. 55–74). Hershey, PA: IGI Global. doi:10.4018/978-1-5225-0731-4.ch003

Cahapay, M. B. (2020). Delphi Technique in the Development of Emerging Contents in High School Science Curriculum. *International Journal of Curriculum Development and Learning Measurement*, *1*(2), 1–9. https://doi.org/10.4018/IJCDLM.2020070101

Camacho, L. F., & Leon Guerrero, A. E. (2022). Indigenous Student Experience in Higher Education: Implementation of Culturally Sensitive Support. In P. Pangelinan & T. McVey (Eds.), *Learning and Reconciliation Through Indigenous Education in Oceania* (pp. 254–266). IGI Global. https://doi.org/10.4018/978-1-7998-7736-3.ch016

Cannaday, J. (2017). The Masking Effect: Hidden Gifts and Disabilities of 2e Students. In P. Dickenson, P. Keough, & J. Courduff (Eds.), *Preparing Pre-Service Teachers for the Inclusive Classroom* (pp. 220–231). Hershey, PA: IGI Global. doi:10.4018/978-1-5225-1753-5.ch011

Cederquist, S., Fishman, B., & Teasley, S. D. (2022). What's Missing From the College Transcript?: How Employers Make Sense of Student Skills. In Y. Huang (Ed.), *Handbook of Research on Credential Innovations for Inclusive Pathways to Professions* (pp. 234–253). IGI Global. https://doi.org/10.4018/978-1-7998-3820-3.ch012

Cockrell, P., & Gibson, T. (2019). The Untold Stories of Black and Brown Student Experiences in Historically White Fraternities and Sororities. In P. Hoffman-Miller, M. James, & D. Hermond (Eds.), *African American Suburbanization and the Consequential Loss of Identity* (pp. 153–171). IGI Global. https://doi.org/10.4018/978-1-5225-7835-2.ch009

Cohen, M. (2022). Leveraging Content Creation to Boost Student Engagement. In T. Driscoll III, (Ed.), *Designing Effective Distance and Blended Learning Environments in K-12* (pp. 223–239). IGI Global. https://doi.org/10.4018/978-1-7998-6829-3.ch013

Contreras, E. C., & Contreras, I. I. (2018). Development of Communication Skills through Auditory Training Software in Special Education. In M. Khosrow-Pour, D.B.A. (Ed.), Encyclopedia of Information Science and Technology, Fourth Edition (pp. 2431-2441). Hershey, PA: IGI Global. doi:10.4018/978-1-5225-2255-3.ch212

Cooke, L., Schugar, J., Schugar, H., Penny, C., & Bruning, H. (2020). Can Everyone Code?: Preparing Teachers to Teach Computer Languages as a Literacy. In J. Mitchell & E. Vaughn (Eds.), *Participatory Literacy Practices for P-12 Classrooms in the Digital Age* (pp. 163–183). IGI Global. https://doi.org/10.4018/978-1-7998-0000-2.ch009

Cooley, D., & Whitten, E. (2017). Special Education Leadership and the Implementation of Response to Intervention. In F. Topor (Ed.), *Handbook of Research on Individualism and Identity in the Globalized Digital Age* (pp. 265–286). Hershey, PA: IGI Global. doi:10.4018/978-1-5225-0522-8.ch012

Cosner, S., Tozer, S., & Zavitkovsky, P. (2017). Enacting a Cycle of Inquiry Capstone Research Project in Doctoral-Level Leadership Preparation. In I. Management Association (Ed.), Educational Leadership and Administration: Concepts, Methodologies, Tools, and Applications (pp. 1460-1481). Hershey, PA: IGI Global. doi:10.4018/978-1-5225-1624-8.ch067

Crawford, C. M. (2018). Instructional Real World Community Engagement. In M. Khosrow-Pour, D.B.A. (Ed.), Encyclopedia of Information Science and Technology, Fourth Edition (pp. 1474-1486). Hershey, PA: IGI Global. doi:10.4018/978-1-5225-2255-3.ch127

Related References

Crosby-Cooper, T., & Pacis, D. (2017). Implementing Effective Student Support Teams. In P. Dickenson, P. Keough, & J. Courduff (Eds.), *Preparing Pre-Service Teachers for the Inclusive Classroom* (pp. 248–262). Hershey, PA: IGI Global. doi:10.4018/978-1-5225-1753-5.ch013

Curran, C. M., & Hawbaker, B. W. (2017). Cultivating Communities of Inclusive Practice: Professional Development for Educators – Research and Practice. In C. Curran & A. Petersen (Eds.), *Handbook of Research on Classroom Diversity and Inclusive Education Practice* (pp. 120–153). Hershey, PA: IGI Global. doi:10.4018/978-1-5225-2520-2.ch006

Dass, S., & Dabbagh, N. (2018). Faculty Adoption of 3D Avatar-Based Virtual World Learning Environments: An Exploratory Case Study. In I. Management Association (Ed.), Technology Adoption and Social Issues: Concepts, Methodologies, Tools, and Applications (pp. 1000-1033). Hershey, PA: IGI Global. https://doi.org/ doi:10.4018/978-1-5225-5201-7.ch045

Davison, A. M., & Scholl, K. G. (2017). Inclusive Recreation as Part of the IEP Process. In C. Curran & A. Petersen (Eds.), *Handbook of Research on Classroom Diversity and Inclusive Education Practice* (pp. 311–330). Hershey, PA: IGI Global. doi:10.4018/978-1-5225-2520-2.ch013

DeCoito, I. (2018). Addressing Digital Competencies, Curriculum Development, and Instructional Design in Science Teacher Education. In M. Khosrow-Pour, D.B.A. (Ed.), Encyclopedia of Information Science and Technology, Fourth Edition (pp. 1420-1431). Hershey, PA: IGI Global. https://doi.org/ doi:10.4018/978-1-5225-2255-3.ch122

DeCoito, I., & Richardson, T. (2017). Beyond Angry Birds™: Using Web-Based Tools to Engage Learners and Promote Inquiry in STEM Learning. In I. Levin & D. Tsybulsky (Eds.), *Digital Tools and Solutions for Inquiry-Based STEM Learning* (pp. 166–196). Hershey, PA: IGI Global. doi:10.4018/978-1-5225-2525-7.ch007

Delmas, P. M. (2017). Research-Based Leadership for Next-Generation Leaders. In R. Styron Jr & J. Styron (Eds.), *Comprehensive Problem-Solving and Skill Development for Next-Generation Leaders* (pp. 1–39). Hershey, PA: IGI Global. doi:10.4018/978-1-5225-1968-3.ch001

Demiray, U., & Ekren, G. (2018). Administrative-Related Evaluation for Distance Education Institutions in Turkey. In K. Buyuk, S. Kocdar, & A. Bozkurt (Eds.), *Administrative Leadership in Open and Distance Learning Programs* (pp. 263–288). Hershey, PA: IGI Global. doi:10.4018/978-1-5225-2645-2.ch011

Dickenson, P. (2017). What do we Know and Where Can We Grow?: Teachers Preparation for the Inclusive Classroom. In P. Dickenson, P. Keough, & J. Courduff (Eds.), *Preparing Pre-Service Teachers for the Inclusive Classroom* (pp. 1–22). Hershey, PA: IGI Global. doi:10.4018/978-1-5225-1753-5.ch001

Ding, Q., & Zhu, H. (2021). Flipping the Classroom in STEM Education. In J. Keengwe (Ed.), *Handbook of Research on Innovations in Non-Traditional Educational Practices* (pp. 155–173). IGI Global. https://doi.org/10.4018/978-1-7998-4360-3.ch008

Dixon, T., & Christison, M. (2021). Teaching English Grammar in a Hybrid Academic ESL Course: A Mixed Methods Study. In K. Kelch, P. Byun, S. Safavi, & S. Cervantes (Eds.), *CALL Theory Applications for Online TESOL Education* (pp. 229–251). IGI Global. https://doi.org/10.4018/978-1-7998-6609-1.ch010

Donne, V., & Hansen, M. (2017). Teachers' Use of Assistive Technologies in Education. In L. Tomei (Ed.), *Exploring the New Era of Technology-Infused Education* (pp. 86–101). Hershey, PA: IGI Global. doi:10.4018/978-1-5225-1709-2.ch006

Donne, V., & Hansen, M. A. (2018). Business and Technology Educators: Practices for Inclusion. In I. Management Association (Ed.), Business Education and Ethics: Concepts, Methodologies, Tools, and Applications (pp. 471-484). Hershey, PA: IGI Global. https://doi.org/ doi:10.4018/978-1-5225-3153-1.ch026

Dos Santos, L. M. (2022). Completing Student-Teaching Internships Online: Instructional Changes During the COVID-19 Pandemic. In M. Alaali (Ed.), *Assessing University Governance and Policies in Relation to the COVID-19 Pandemic* (pp. 106–127). IGI Global. https://doi.org/10.4018/978-1-7998-8279-4.ch007

Dreon, O., Shettel, J., & Bower, K. M. (2017). Preparing Next Generation Elementary Teachers for the Tools of Tomorrow. In M. Grassetti & S. Brookby (Eds.), *Advancing Next-Generation Teacher Education through Digital Tools and Applications* (pp. 143–159). Hershey, PA: IGI Global. doi:10.4018/978-1-5225-0965-3.ch008

Durak, H. Y., & Güyer, T. (2018). Design and Development of an Instructional Program for Teaching Programming Processes to Gifted Students Using Scratch. In J. Cannaday (Ed.), *Curriculum Development for Gifted Education Programs* (pp. 61–99). Hershey, PA: IGI Global. doi:10.4018/978-1-5225-3041-1.ch004

Egorkina, E., Ivanov, M., & Valyavskiy, A. Y. (2018). Students' Research Competence Formation of the Quality of Open and Distance Learning. In V. Mkrttchian & L. Belyanina (Eds.), *Handbook of Research on Students' Research Competence in Modern Educational Contexts* (pp. 364–384). Hershey, PA: IGI Global. doi:10.4018/978-1-5225-3485-3.ch019

Related References

Ekren, G., Karataş, S., & Demiray, U. (2017). Understanding of Leadership in Distance Education Management. In I. Management Association (Ed.), Educational Leadership and Administration: Concepts, Methodologies, Tools, and Applications (pp. 34-50). Hershey, PA: IGI Global. https://doi.org/ doi:10.4018/978-1-5225-1624-8.ch003

Elmore, W. M., Young, J. K., Harris, S., & Mason, D. (2017). The Relationship between Individual Student Attributes and Online Course Completion. In K. Shelton & K. Pedersen (Eds.), *Handbook of Research on Building, Growing, and Sustaining Quality E-Learning Programs* (pp. 151–173). Hershey, PA: IGI Global. doi:10.4018/978-1-5225-0877-9.ch008

Ercegovac, I. R., Alfirević, N., & Koludrović, M. (2017). School Principals' Communication and Co-Operation Assessment: The Croatian Experience. In I. Management Association (Ed.), Educational Leadership and Administration: Concepts, Methodologies, Tools, and Applications (pp. 1568-1589). Hershey, PA: IGI Global. https://doi.org/ doi:10.4018/978-1-5225-1624-8.ch072

Everhart, D., & Seymour, D. M. (2017). Challenges and Opportunities in the Currency of Higher Education. In K. Rasmussen, P. Northrup, & R. Colson (Eds.), *Handbook of Research on Competency-Based Education in University Settings* (pp. 41–65). Hershey, PA: IGI Global. doi:10.4018/978-1-5225-0932-5.ch003

Farmer, L. S. (2017). Managing Portable Technologies for Special Education. In V. Wang (Ed.), *Encyclopedia of Strategic Leadership and Management* (pp. 977–987). Hershey, PA: IGI Global. doi:10.4018/978-1-5225-1049-9.ch068

Farmer, L. S. (2018). Optimizing OERs for Optimal ICT Literacy in Higher Education. In J. Keengwe (Ed.), *Handbook of Research on Mobile Technology, Constructivism, and Meaningful Learning* (pp. 366–390). Hershey, PA: IGI Global. doi:10.4018/978-1-5225-3949-0.ch020

Ferguson, B. T. (2019). Supporting Affective Development of Children With Disabilities Through Moral Dilemmas. In S. Ikuta (Ed.), *Handmade Teaching Materials for Students With Disabilities* (pp. 253–275). IGI Global. doi:10.4018/978-1-5225-6240-5.ch011

Fındık, L. Y. (2017). Self-Assessment of Principals Based on Leadership in Complexity. In I. Management Association (Ed.), Educational Leadership and Administration: Concepts, Methodologies, Tools, and Applications (pp. 978-991). Hershey, PA: IGI Global. https://doi.org/ doi:10.4018/978-1-5225-1624-8.ch047

Flor, A. G., & Gonzalez-Flor, B. (2018). Dysfunctional Digital Demeanors: Tales From (and Policy Implications of) eLearning's Dark Side. In I. Management Association (Ed.), The Dark Web: Breakthroughs in Research and Practice (pp. 37-50). Hershey, PA: IGI Global. https://doi.org/ doi:10.4018/978-1-5225-3163-0.ch003

Floyd, K. K., & Shambaugh, N. (2017). Instructional Design for Simulations in Special Education Virtual Learning Spaces. In T. Kidd & L. Morris Jr., (Eds.), *Handbook of Research on Instructional Systems and Educational Technology* (pp. 202–215). Hershey, PA: IGI Global. doi:10.4018/978-1-5225-2399-4.ch018

Freeland, S. F. (2020). Community Schools: Improving Academic Achievement Through Meaningful Engagement. In R. Kronick (Ed.), *Emerging Perspectives on Community Schools and the Engaged University* (pp. 132–144). IGI Global. https://doi.org/10.4018/978-1-7998-0280-8.ch008

Ghanbarzadeh, R., & Ghapanchi, A. H. (2019). Applied Areas of Three Dimensional Virtual Worlds in Learning and Teaching: A Review of Higher Education. In I. Management Association (Ed.), *Virtual Reality in Education: Breakthroughs in Research and Practice* (pp. 172-192). IGI Global. https://doi.org/10.4018/978-1-5225-8179-6.ch008

Giovannini, J. M. (2017). Technology Integration in Preservice Teacher Education Programs: Research-based Recommendations. In M. Grassetti & S. Brookby (Eds.), *Advancing Next-Generation Teacher Education through Digital Tools and Applications* (pp. 82–102). Hershey, PA: IGI Global. doi:10.4018/978-1-5225-0965-3.ch005

Good, S., & Clarke, V. B. (2017). An Integral Analysis of One Urban School System's Efforts to Support Student-Centered Teaching. In J. Keengwe & G. Onchwari (Eds.), *Handbook of Research on Learner-Centered Pedagogy in Teacher Education and Professional Development* (pp. 45–68). Hershey, PA: IGI Global. doi:10.4018/978-1-5225-0892-2.ch003

Guetzoian, E. (2022). Gamification Strategies for Higher Education Student Worker Training. In C. Lane (Ed.), *Handbook of Research on Acquiring 21st Century Literacy Skills Through Game-Based Learning* (pp. 164–179). IGI Global. https://doi.org/10.4018/978-1-7998-7271-9.ch009

Hamidi, F., Owuor, P. M., Hynie, M., Baljko, M., & McGrath, S. (2017). Potentials of Digital Assistive Technology and Special Education in Kenya. In C. Ayo & V. Mbarika (Eds.), *Sustainable ICT Adoption and Integration for Socio-Economic Development* (pp. 125–151). Hershey, PA: IGI Global. doi:10.4018/978-1-5225-2565-3.ch006

Related References

Hamim, T., Benabbou, F., & Sael, N. (2022). Student Profile Modeling Using Boosting Algorithms. *International Journal of Web-Based Learning and Teaching Technologies*, *17*(5), 1–13. https://doi.org/10.4018/IJWLTT.20220901.oa4

Henderson, L. K. (2017). Meltdown at Fukushima: Global Catastrophic Events, Visual Literacy, and Art Education. In R. Shin (Ed.), *Convergence of Contemporary Art, Visual Culture, and Global Civic Engagement* (pp. 80–99). Hershey, PA: IGI Global. doi:10.4018/978-1-5225-1665-1.ch005

Hudgins, T., & Holland, J. L. (2018). Digital Badges: Tracking Knowledge Acquisition Within an Innovation Framework. In I. Management Association (Ed.), Wearable Technologies: Concepts, Methodologies, Tools, and Applications (pp. 1118-1132). Hershey, PA: IGI Global. https://doi.org/ doi:10.4018/978-1-5225-5484-4.ch051

Hwang, R., Lin, H., Sun, J. C., & Wu, J. (2019). Improving Learning Achievement in Science Education for Elementary School Students via Blended Learning. *International Journal of Online Pedagogy and Course Design*, *9*(2), 44–62. https://doi.org/10.4018/IJOPCD.2019040104

Jančec, L., & Vodopivec, J. L. (2019). The Implicit Pedagogy and the Hidden Curriculum in Postmodern Education. In J. Vodopivec, L. Jančec, & T. Štemberger (Eds.), *Implicit Pedagogy for Optimized Learning in Contemporary Education* (pp. 41–59). IGI Global. https://doi.org/10.4018/978-1-5225-5799-9.ch003

Janus, M., & Siddiqua, A. (2018). Challenges for Children With Special Health Needs at the Time of Transition to School. In I. Management Association (Ed.), Autism Spectrum Disorders: Breakthroughs in Research and Practice (pp. 339-371). Hershey, PA: IGI Global. doi:10.4018/978-1-5225-3827-1.ch018

Jesus, R. A. (2018). Screencasts and Learning Styles. In M. Khosrow-Pour, D.B.A. (Ed.), Encyclopedia of Information Science and Technology, Fourth Edition (pp. 1548-1558). Hershey, PA: IGI Global. doi:10.4018/978-1-5225-2255-3.ch134

John, G., Francis, N., & Santhakumar, A. B. (2022). Student Engagement: Past, Present, and Future. In S. Ramlall, T. Cross, & M. Love (Eds.), *Handbook of Research on Future of Work and Education: Implications for Curriculum Delivery and Work Design* (pp. 329–341). IGI Global. https://doi.org/10.4018/978-1-7998-8275-6.ch020

Karpinski, A. C., D'Agostino, J. V., Williams, A. K., Highland, S. A., & Mellott, J. A. (2018). The Relationship Between Online Formative Assessment and State Test Scores Using Multilevel Modeling. In M. Khosrow-Pour, D.B.A. (Ed.), Encyclopedia of Information Science and Technology, Fourth Edition (pp. 5183-5192). Hershey, PA: IGI Global. doi:10.4018/978-1-5225-2255-3.ch450

Kats, Y. (2017). Educational Leadership and Integrated Support for Students with Autism Spectrum Disorders. In I. Management Association (Ed.), Educational Leadership and Administration: Concepts, Methodologies, Tools, and Applications (pp. 101-114). Hershey, PA: IGI Global. https://doi.org/ doi:10.4018/978-1-5225-1624-8.ch007

Kaya, G., & Altun, A. (2018). Educational Ontology Development. In M. Khosrow-Pour, D.B.A. (Ed.), Encyclopedia of Information Science and Technology, Fourth Edition (pp. 1441-1450). Hershey, PA: IGI Global. doi:10.4018/978-1-5225-2255-3.ch124

Keough, P. D., & Pacis, D. (2017). Best Practices Implementing Special Education Curriculum and Common Core State Standards using UDL. In P. Dickenson, P. Keough, & J. Courduff (Eds.), *Preparing Pre-Service Teachers for the Inclusive Classroom* (pp. 107–123). Hershey, PA: IGI Global. doi:10.4018/978-1-5225-1753-5.ch006

Kilburn, M., Henckell, M., & Starrett, D. (2018). Factors Contributing to the Effectiveness of Online Students and Instructors. In M. Khosrow-Pour, D.B.A. (Ed.), Encyclopedia of Information Science and Technology, Fourth Edition (pp. 1451-1462). Hershey, PA: IGI Global. doi:10.4018/978-1-5225-2255-3.ch125

Koban Koç, D. (2021). Gender and Language: A Sociolinguistic Analysis of Second Language Writing. In E. Hancı-Azizoglu & N. Kavaklı (Eds.), *Futuristic and Linguistic Perspectives on Teaching Writing to Second Language Students* (pp. 161–177). IGI Global. https://doi.org/10.4018/978-1-7998-6508-7.ch010

Konecny, L. T. (2017). Hybrid, Online, and Flipped Classrooms in Health Science: Enhanced Learning Environments. In I. Management Association (Ed.), Flipped Instruction: Breakthroughs in Research and Practice (pp. 355-370). Hershey, PA: IGI Global. https://doi.org/ doi:10.4018/978-1-5225-1803-7.ch020

Kupietz, K. D. (2021). Gaming and Simulation in Public Education: Teaching Others to Help Themselves and Their Neighbors. In N. Drumhiller, T. Wilkin, & K. Srba (Eds.), *Simulation and Game-Based Learning in Emergency and Disaster Management* (pp. 41–62). IGI Global. https://doi.org/10.4018/978-1-7998-4087-9.ch003

Kwee, C. T. (2022). Assessing the International Student Enrolment Strategies in Australian Universities: A Case Study During the COVID-19 Pandemic. In M. Alaali (Ed.), *Assessing University Governance and Policies in Relation to the COVID-19 Pandemic* (pp. 162–188). IGI Global. https://doi.org/10.4018/978-1-7998-8279-4.ch010

Related References

Lauricella, S., & McArthur, F. A. (2022). Taking a Student-Centred Approach to Alternative Digital Credentials: Multiple Pathways Toward the Acquisition of Microcredentials. In D. Piedra (Ed.), *Innovations in the Design and Application of Alternative Digital Credentials* (pp. 57–69). IGI Global. https://doi.org/10.4018/978-1-7998-7697-7.ch003

Llamas, M. F. (2019). Intercultural Awareness in Teaching English for Early Childhood: A Film-Based Approach. In E. Domínguez Romero, J. Bobkina, & S. Stefanova (Eds.), *Teaching Literature and Language Through Multimodal Texts* (pp. 54–68). IGI Global. https://doi.org/10.4018/978-1-5225-5796-8.ch004

Lokhtina, I., & Kkese, E. T. (2022). Reflecting and Adapting to an Academic Workplace Before and After the Lockdown in Greek-Speaking Cyprus: Opportunities and Challenges. In A. Zhuplev & R. Koepp (Eds.), *Global Trends, Dynamics, and Imperatives for Strategic Development in Business Education in an Age of Disruption* (pp. 126–148). IGI Global. https://doi.org/10.4018/978-1-7998-7548-2.ch007

Lovell, K. L. (2017). Development and Evaluation of Neuroscience Computer-Based Modules for Medical Students: Instructional Design Principles and Effectiveness. In J. Stefaniak (Ed.), *Advancing Medical Education Through Strategic Instructional Design* (pp. 262–276). Hershey, PA: IGI Global. doi:10.4018/978-1-5225-2098-6.ch013

Maher, D. (2019). The Use of Course Management Systems in Pre-Service Teacher Education. In J. Keengwe (Ed.), *Handbook of Research on Blended Learning Pedagogies and Professional Development in Higher Education* (pp. 196–213). IGI Global. https://doi.org/10.4018/978-1-5225-5557-5.ch011

Makewa, L. N. (2019). Teacher Technology Competence Base. In L. Makewa, B. Ngussa, & J. Kuboja (Eds.), *Technology-Supported Teaching and Research Methods for Educators* (pp. 247–267). IGI Global. https://doi.org/10.4018/978-1-5225-5915-3.ch014

Mallett, C. A. (2022). School Resource (Police) Officers in Schools: Impact on Campus Safety, Student Discipline, and Learning. In G. Crews (Ed.), *Impact of School Shootings on Classroom Culture, Curriculum, and Learning* (pp. 53–70). IGI Global. https://doi.org/10.4018/978-1-7998-5200-1.ch004

Marinho, J. E., Freitas, I. R., Leão, I. B., Pacheco, L. O., Gonçalves, M. P., Castro, M. J., Silva, P. D., & Moreira, R. J. (2022). Project-Based Learning Application in Higher Education: Student Experiences and Perspectives. In A. Alves & N. van Hattum-Janssen (Eds.), *Training Engineering Students for Modern Technological Advancement* (pp. 146–164). IGI Global. https://doi.org/10.4018/978-1-7998-8816-1.ch007

McCleskey, J. A., & Melton, R. M. (2022). Rolling With the Flow: Online Faculty and Student Presence in a Post-COVID-19 World. In S. Ramlall, T. Cross, & M. Love (Eds.), *Handbook of Research on Future of Work and Education: Implications for Curriculum Delivery and Work Design* (pp. 307–328). IGI Global. https://doi.org/10.4018/978-1-7998-8275-6.ch019

McCormack, V. F., Stauffer, M., Fishley, K., Hohenbrink, J., Mascazine, J. R., & Zigler, T. (2018). Designing a Dual Licensure Path for Middle Childhood and Special Education Teacher Candidates. In D. Polly, M. Putman, T. Petty, & A. Good (Eds.), *Innovative Practices in Teacher Preparation and Graduate-Level Teacher Education Programs* (pp. 21–36). Hershey, PA: IGI Global. doi:10.4018/978-1-5225-3068-8.ch002

McDaniel, R. (2017). Strategic Leadership in Instructional Design: Applying the Principles of Instructional Design through the Lens of Strategic Leadership to Distance Education. In V. Wang (Ed.), *Encyclopedia of Strategic Leadership and Management* (pp. 1570–1584). Hershey, PA: IGI Global. doi:10.4018/978-1-5225-1049-9.ch109

McKinney, R. E., Halli-Tierney, A. D., Gold, A. E., Allen, R. S., & Carroll, D. G. (2022). Interprofessional Education: Using Standardized Cases in Face-to-Face and Remote Learning Settings. In C. Ford & K. Garza (Eds.), *Handbook of Research on Updating and Innovating Health Professions Education: Post-Pandemic Perspectives* (pp. 24–42). IGI Global. https://doi.org/10.4018/978-1-7998-7623-6.ch002

Meintjes, H. H. (2021). Learner Views of a Facebook Page as a Supportive Digital Pedagogical Tool at a Public South African School in a Grade 12 Business Studies Class. *International Journal of Smart Education and Urban Society*, *12*(2), 32–45. https://doi.org/10.4018/IJSEUS.2021040104

Melero-García, F. (2022). Training Bilingual Interpreters in Healthcare Settings: Student Perceptions of Online Learning. In J. LeLoup & P. Swanson (Eds.), *Handbook of Research on Effective Online Language Teaching in a Disruptive Environment* (pp. 288–310). IGI Global. https://doi.org/10.4018/978-1-7998-7720-2.ch015

Related References

Meletiadou, E. (2022). The Use of Peer Assessment as an Inclusive Learning Strategy in Higher Education Institutions: Enhancing Student Writing Skills and Motivation. In E. Meletiadou (Ed.), *Handbook of Research on Policies and Practices for Assessing Inclusive Teaching and Learning* (pp. 1–26). IGI Global. https://doi.org/10.4018/978-1-7998-8579-5.ch001

Memon, R. N., Ahmad, R., & Salim, S. S. (2018). Critical Issues in Requirements Engineering Education. In I. Management Association (Ed.), Computer Systems and Software Engineering: Concepts, Methodologies, Tools, and Applications (pp. 1953-1976). Hershey, PA: IGI Global. doi:10.4018/978-1-5225-3923-0.ch081

Mendenhall, R. (2017). Western Governors University: CBE Innovator and National Model. In K. Rasmussen, P. Northrup, & R. Colson (Eds.), *Handbook of Research on Competency-Based Education in University Settings* (pp. 379–400). Hershey, PA: IGI Global. doi:10.4018/978-1-5225-0932-5.ch019

Mense, E. G., Griggs, D. M., & Shanks, J. N. (2018). School Leaders in a Time of Accountability and Data Use: Preparing Our Future School Leaders in Leadership Preparation Programs. In E. Mense & M. Crain-Dorough (Eds.), *Data Leadership for K-12 Schools in a Time of Accountability* (pp. 235–259). Hershey, PA: IGI Global. doi:10.4018/978-1-5225-3188-3.ch012

Mense, E. G., Griggs, D. M., & Shanks, J. N. (2018). School Leaders in a Time of Accountability and Data Use: Preparing Our Future School Leaders in Leadership Preparation Programs. In E. Mense & M. Crain-Dorough (Eds.), *Data Leadership for K-12 Schools in a Time of Accountability* (pp. 235–259). Hershey, PA: IGI Global. doi:10.4018/978-1-5225-3188-3.ch012

Mestry, R., & Naicker, S. R. (2017). Exploring Distributive Leadership in South African Public Primary Schools in the Soweto Region. In I. Management Association (Ed.), Educational Leadership and Administration: Concepts, Methodologies, Tools, and Applications (pp. 1041-1064). Hershey, PA: IGI Global. doi:10.4018/978-1-5225-1624-8.ch050

Monaghan, C. H., & Boboc, M. (2017). (Re)Defining Leadership in Higher Education in the U.S. In V. Wang (Ed.), *Encyclopedia of Strategic Leadership and Management* (pp. 567–579). Hershey, PA: IGI Global. doi:10.4018/978-1-5225-1049-9.ch040

Morall, M. B. (2021). Reimagining Mobile Phones: Multiple Literacies and Digital Media Compositions. In C. Moran (Eds.), *Affordances and Constraints of Mobile Phone Use in English Language Arts Classrooms* (pp. 41-53). IGI Global. https://doi.org/10.4018/978-1-7998-5805-8.ch003

Mthethwa, V. (2022). Student Governance and the Academic Minefield During COVID-19 Lockdown in South Africa. In M. Alaali (Ed.), *Assessing University Governance and Policies in Relation to the COVID-19 Pandemic* (pp. 255–276). IGI Global. https://doi.org/10.4018/978-1-7998-8279-4.ch015

Muthee, J. M., & Murungi, C. G. (2018). Relationship Among Intelligence, Achievement Motivation, Type of School, and Academic Performance of Kenyan Urban Primary School Pupils. In M. Khosrow-Pour, D.B.A. (Ed.), Encyclopedia of Information Science and Technology, Fourth Edition (pp. 1540-1547). Hershey, PA: IGI Global. https://doi.org/ doi:10.4018/978-1-5225-2255-3.ch133

Naranjo, J. (2018). Meeting the Need for Inclusive Educators Online: Teacher Education in Inclusive Special Education and Dual-Certification. In D. Polly, M. Putman, T. Petty, & A. Good (Eds.), *Innovative Practices in Teacher Preparation and Graduate-Level Teacher Education Programs* (pp. 106–122). Hershey, PA: IGI Global. doi:10.4018/978-1-5225-3068-8.ch007

Nkabinde, Z. P. (2017). Multiculturalism in Special Education: Perspectives of Minority Children in Urban Schools. In J. Keengwe (Ed.), *Handbook of Research on Promoting Cross-Cultural Competence and Social Justice in Teacher Education* (pp. 382–397). Hershey, PA: IGI Global. doi:10.4018/978-1-5225-0897-7.ch020

Nkabinde, Z. P. (2018). Online Instruction: Is the Quality the Same as Face-to-Face Instruction? In J. Keengwe (Ed.), *Handbook of Research on Digital Content, Mobile Learning, and Technology Integration Models in Teacher Education* (pp. 300–314). Hershey, PA: IGI Global. doi:10.4018/978-1-5225-2953-8.ch016

Nugroho, A., & Albusaidi, S. S. (2022). Internationalization of Higher Education: The Methodological Critiques on the Research Related to Study Overseas and International Experience. In H. Magd & S. Kunjumuhammed (Eds.), *Global Perspectives on Quality Assurance and Accreditation in Higher Education Institutions* (pp. 75–89). IGI Global. https://doi.org/10.4018/978-1-7998-8085-1.ch005

Nulty, Z., & West, S. G. (2022). Student Engagement and Supporting Students With Accommodations. In P. Bull & G. Patterson (Eds.), *Redefining Teacher Education and Teacher Preparation Programs in the Post-COVID-19 Era* (pp. 99–116). IGI Global. https://doi.org/10.4018/978-1-7998-8298-5.ch006

O'Connor, J. R. Jr, & Jackson, K. N. (2017). The Use of iPad® Devices and "Apps" for ASD Students in Special Education and Speech Therapy. In Y. Kats (Ed.), *Supporting the Education of Children with Autism Spectrum Disorders* (pp. 267–283). Hershey, PA: IGI Global. doi:10.4018/978-1-5225-0816-8.ch014

Related References

Okolie, U. C., & Yasin, A. M. (2017). TVET in Developing Nations and Human Development. In U. Okolie & A. Yasin (Eds.), *Technical Education and Vocational Training in Developing Nations* (pp. 1–25). Hershey, PA: IGI Global. doi:10.4018/978-1-5225-1811-2.ch001

Pack, A., & Barrett, A. (2021). A Review of Virtual Reality and English for Academic Purposes: Understanding Where to Start. *International Journal of Computer-Assisted Language Learning and Teaching*, *11*(1), 72–80. https://doi.org/10.4018/IJCALLT.2021010105

Pashollari, E. (2019). Building Sustainability Through Environmental Education: Education for Sustainable Development. In L. Wilson, & C. Stevenson (Eds.), *Building Sustainability Through Environmental Education* (pp. 72-88). IGI Global. https://doi.org/10.4018/978-1-5225-7727-0.ch004

Paulson, E. N. (2017). Adapting and Advocating for an Online EdD Program in Changing Times and "Sacred" Cultures. In I. Management Association (Ed.), Educational Leadership and Administration: Concepts, Methodologies, Tools, and Applications (pp. 1849-1876). Hershey, PA: IGI Global. https://doi.org/doi:10.4018/978-1-5225-1624-8.ch085

Petersen, A. J., Elser, C. F., Al Nassir, M. N., Stakey, J., & Everson, K. (2017). The Year of Teaching Inclusively: Building an Elementary Classroom for All Students. In C. Curran & A. Petersen (Eds.), *Handbook of Research on Classroom Diversity and Inclusive Education Practice* (pp. 332–348). Hershey, PA: IGI Global. doi:10.4018/978-1-5225-2520-2.ch014

Pfannenstiel, K. H., & Sanders, J. (2017). Characteristics and Instructional Strategies for Students With Mathematical Difficulties: In the Inclusive Classroom. In C. Curran & A. Petersen (Eds.), *Handbook of Research on Classroom Diversity and Inclusive Education Practice* (pp. 250–281). Hershey, PA: IGI Global. doi:10.4018/978-1-5225-2520-2.ch011

Phan, A. N. (2022). Quality Assurance of Higher Education From the Glonacal Agency Heuristic: An Example From Vietnam. In H. Magd & S. Kunjumuhammed (Eds.), *Global Perspectives on Quality Assurance and Accreditation in Higher Education Institutions* (pp. 136–155). IGI Global. https://doi.org/10.4018/978-1-7998-8085-1.ch008

Preast, J. L., Bowman, N., & Rose, C. A. (2017). Creating Inclusive Classroom Communities Through Social and Emotional Learning to Reduce Social Marginalization Among Students. In C. Curran & A. Petersen (Eds.), *Handbook of Research on Classroom Diversity and Inclusive Education Practice* (pp. 183–200). Hershey, PA: IGI Global. doi:10.4018/978-1-5225-2520-2.ch008

Randolph, K. M., & Brady, M. P. (2018). Evolution of Covert Coaching as an Evidence-Based Practice in Professional Development and Preparation of Teachers. In V. Bryan, A. Musgrove, & J. Powers (Eds.), *Handbook of Research on Human Development in the Digital Age* (pp. 281–299). Hershey, PA: IGI Global. doi:10.4018/978-1-5225-2838-8.ch013

Rell, A. B., Puig, R. A., Roll, F., Valles, V., Espinoza, M., & Duque, A. L. (2017). Addressing Cultural Diversity and Global Competence: The Dual Language Framework. In L. Leavitt, S. Wisdom, & K. Leavitt (Eds.), *Cultural Awareness and Competency Development in Higher Education* (pp. 111–131). Hershey, PA: IGI Global. doi:10.4018/978-1-5225-2145-7.ch007

Richards, M., & Guzman, I. R. (2020). Academic Assessment of Critical Thinking in Distance Education Information Technology Programs. In I. Management Association (Ed.), *Learning and Performance Assessment: Concepts, Methodologies, Tools, and Applications* (pp. 1-19). IGI Global. https://doi.org/10.4018/978-1-7998-0420-8.ch001

Riel, J., Lawless, K. A., & Brown, S. W. (2017). Defining and Designing Responsive Online Professional Development (ROPD): A Framework to Support Curriculum Implementation. In T. Kidd & L. Morris Jr., (Eds.), *Handbook of Research on Instructional Systems and Educational Technology* (pp. 104–115). Hershey, PA: IGI Global. doi:10.4018/978-1-5225-2399-4.ch010

Roberts, C. (2017). Advancing Women Leaders in Academe: Creating a Culture of Inclusion. In S. Mukerji & P. Tripathi (Eds.), *Handbook of Research on Administration, Policy, and Leadership in Higher Education* (pp. 256–273). Hershey, PA: IGI Global. doi:10.4018/978-1-5225-0672-0.ch012

Rodgers, W. J., Kennedy, M. J., Alves, K. D., & Romig, J. E. (2017). A Multimedia Tool for Teacher Education and Professional Development. In C. Martin & D. Polly (Eds.), *Handbook of Research on Teacher Education and Professional Development* (pp. 285–296). Hershey, PA: IGI Global. doi:10.4018/978-1-5225-1067-3.ch015

Related References

Romanowski, M. H. (2017). Qatar's Educational Reform: Critical Issues Facing Principals. In I. Management Association (Ed.), Educational Leadership and Administration: Concepts, Methodologies, Tools, and Applications (pp. 1758-1773). Hershey, PA: IGI Global. https://doi.org/ doi:10.4018/978-1-5225-1624-8.ch080

Ruffin, T. R., Hawkins, D. P., & Lee, D. I. (2018). Increasing Student Engagement and Participation Through Course Methodology. In M. Khosrow-Pour, D.B.A. (Ed.), Encyclopedia of Information Science and Technology, Fourth Edition (pp. 1463-1473). Hershey, PA: IGI Global. doi:10.4018/978-1-5225-2255-3.ch126

Sabina, L. L., Curry, K. A., Harris, E. L., Krumm, B. L., & Vencill, V. (2017). Assessing the Performance of a Cohort-Based Model Using Domestic and International Practices. In I. Management Association (Ed.), Educational Leadership and Administration: Concepts, Methodologies, Tools, and Applications(pp. 913-929). Hershey, PA: IGI Global. https://doi.org/ doi:10.4018/978-1-5225-1624-8.ch044

Samkian, A., Pascarella, J., & Slayton, J. (2022). Towards an Anti-Racist, Culturally Responsive, and LGBTQ+ Inclusive Education: Developing Critically-Conscious Educational Leaders. In E. Cain-Sanschagrin, R. Filback, & J. Crawford (Eds.), *Cases on Academic Program Redesign for Greater Racial and Social Justice* (pp. 150–175). IGI Global. https://doi.org/10.4018/978-1-7998-8463-7.ch007

Santamaría, A. P., Webber, M., & Santamaría, L. J. (2017). Effective School Leadership for Māori Achievement: Building Capacity through Indigenous, National, and International Cross-Cultural Collaboration. In I. Management Association (Ed.), Educational Leadership and Administration: Concepts, Methodologies, Tools, and Applications (pp. 1547-1567). Hershey, PA: IGI Global. https://doi.org/ doi:10.4018/978-1-5225-1624-8.ch071

Santamaría, L. J. (2017). Culturally Responsive Educational Leadership in Cross-Cultural International Contexts. In I. Management Association (Ed.), Educational Leadership and Administration: Concepts, Methodologies, Tools, and Applications (pp. 1380-1400). Hershey, PA: IGI Global. https://doi.org/ doi:10.4018/978-1-5225-1624-8.ch064

Segredo, M. R., Cistone, P. J., & Reio, T. G. (2017). Relationships Between Emotional Intelligence, Leadership Style, and School Culture. *International Journal of Adult Vocational Education and Technology*, 8(3), 25–43. doi:10.4018/IJAVET.2017070103

Shalev, N. (2017). Empathy and Leadership From the Organizational Perspective. In Z. Nedelko & M. Brzozowski (Eds.), *Exploring the Influence of Personal Values and Cultures in the Workplace* (pp. 348–363). Hershey, PA: IGI Global. doi:10.4018/978-1-5225-2480-9.ch018

Siamak, M., Fathi, S., & Isfandyari-Moghaddam, A. (2018). Assessment and Measurement of Education Programs of Information Literacy. In R. Bhardwaj (Ed.), *Digitizing the Modern Library and the Transition From Print to Electronic* (pp. 164–192). Hershey, PA: IGI Global. doi:10.4018/978-1-5225-2119-8.ch007

Siu, K. W., & García, G. J. (2017). Disruptive Technologies and Education: Is There Any Disruption After All? In I. Management Association (Ed.), Educational Leadership and Administration: Concepts, Methodologies, Tools, and Applications (pp. 757-778). Hershey, PA: IGI Global. https://doi.org/ doi:10.4018/978-1-5225-1624-8.ch037

Slagter van Tryon, P. J. (2017). The Nurse Educator's Role in Designing Instruction and Instructional Strategies for Academic and Clinical Settings. In J. Stefaniak (Ed.), *Advancing Medical Education Through Strategic Instructional Design* (pp. 133–149). Hershey, PA: IGI Global. doi:10.4018/978-1-5225-2098-6.ch006

Slattery, C. A. (2018). Literacy Intervention and the Differentiated Plan of Instruction. In *Developing Effective Literacy Intervention Strategies: Emerging Research and Opportunities* (pp. 41–62). Hershey, PA: IGI Global. doi:10.4018/978-1-5225-5007-5.ch003

Smith, A. R. (2017). Ensuring Quality: The Faculty Role in Online Higher Education. In K. Shelton & K. Pedersen (Eds.), *Handbook of Research on Building, Growing, and Sustaining Quality E-Learning Programs* (pp. 210–231). Hershey, PA: IGI Global. doi:10.4018/978-1-5225-0877-9.ch011

Souders, T. M. (2017). Understanding Your Learner: Conducting a Learner Analysis. In J. Stefaniak (Ed.), *Advancing Medical Education Through Strategic Instructional Design* (pp. 1–29). Hershey, PA: IGI Global. doi:10.4018/978-1-5225-2098-6.ch001

Spring, K. J., Graham, C. R., & Ikahihifo, T. B. (2018). Learner Engagement in Blended Learning. In M. Khosrow-Pour, D.B.A. (Ed.), Encyclopedia of Information Science and Technology, Fourth Edition (pp. 1487-1498). Hershey, PA: IGI Global. doi:10.4018/978-1-5225-2255-3.ch128

Storey, V. A., Anthony, A. K., & Wahid, P. (2017). Gender-Based Leadership Barriers: Advancement of Female Faculty to Leadership Positions in Higher Education. In V. Wang (Ed.), *Encyclopedia of Strategic Leadership and Management* (pp. 244–258). Hershey, PA: IGI Global. doi:10.4018/978-1-5225-1049-9.ch018

Stottlemyer, D. (2018). Develop a Teaching Model Plan for a Differentiated Learning Approach. In *Differentiated Instructional Design for Multicultural Environments: Emerging Research and Opportunities* (pp. 106–130). Hershey, PA: IGI Global. doi:10.4018/978-1-5225-5106-5.ch005

Related References

Stottlemyer, D. (2018). Developing a Multicultural Environment. In *Differentiated Instructional Design for Multicultural Environments: Emerging Research and Opportunities* (pp. 1–27). Hershey, PA: IGI Global. doi:10.4018/978-1-5225-5106-5.ch001

Swagerty, T. (2022). Digital Access to Culturally Relevant Curricula: The Impact on the Native and Indigenous Student. In E. Reeves & C. McIntyre (Eds.), *Multidisciplinary Perspectives on Diversity and Equity in a Virtual World* (pp. 99–113). IGI Global. https://doi.org/10.4018/978-1-7998-8028-8.ch006

Swami, B. N., Gobona, T., & Tsimako, J. J. (2017). Academic Leadership: A Case Study of the University of Botswana. In N. Baporikar (Ed.), *Innovation and Shifting Perspectives in Management Education* (pp. 1–32). Hershey, PA: IGI Global. doi:10.4018/978-1-5225-1019-2.ch001

Swanson, K. W., & Collins, G. (2018). Designing Engaging Instruction for the Adult Learners. In M. Khosrow-Pour, D.B.A. (Ed.), Encyclopedia of Information Science and Technology, Fourth Edition (pp. 1432-1440). Hershey, PA: IGI Global. doi:10.4018/978-1-5225-2255-3.ch123

Swartz, B. A., Lynch, J. M., & Lynch, S. D. (2018). Embedding Elementary Teacher Education Coursework in Local Classrooms: Examples in Mathematics and Special Education. In D. Polly, M. Putman, T. Petty, & A. Good (Eds.), *Innovative Practices in Teacher Preparation and Graduate-Level Teacher Education Programs* (pp. 262–292). Hershey, PA: IGI Global. doi:10.4018/978-1-5225-3068-8.ch015

Taliadorou, N., & Pashiardis, P. (2017). Emotional Intelligence and Political Skill Really Matter in Educational Leadership. In I. Management Association (Ed.), Educational Leadership and Administration: Concepts, Methodologies, Tools, and Applications (pp. 1274-1303). Hershey, PA: IGI Global. https://doi.org/doi:10.4018/978-1-5225-1624-8.ch060

Tandoh, K. A., & Ebe-Arthur, J. E. (2018). Effective Educational Leadership in the Digital Age: An Examination of Professional Qualities and Best Practices. In J. Keengwe (Ed.), *Handbook of Research on Digital Content, Mobile Learning, and Technology Integration Models in Teacher Education* (pp. 244–265). Hershey, PA: IGI Global. doi:10.4018/978-1-5225-2953-8.ch013

Tobin, M. T. (2018). Multimodal Literacy. In M. Khosrow-Pour, D.B.A. (Ed.), Encyclopedia of Information Science and Technology, Fourth Edition (pp. 1508-1516). Hershey, PA: IGI Global. doi:10.4018/978-1-5225-2255-3.ch130

Torres, K. M., Arrastia-Chisholm, M. C., & Tackett, S. (2019). A Phenomenological Study of Pre-Service Teachers' Perceptions of Completing ESOL Field Placements. *International Journal of Teacher Education and Professional Development*, 2(2), 85–101. https://doi.org/10.4018/IJTEPD.2019070106

Torres, M. C., Salamanca, Y. N., Cely, J. P., & Aguilar, J. L. (2020). All We Need is a Boost! Using Multimodal Tools and the Translanguaging Strategy: Strengthening Speaking in the EFL Classroom. *International Journal of Computer-Assisted Language Learning and Teaching*, 10(3), 28–47. doi:10.4018/IJCALLT.2020070103

Torres, M. L., & Ramos, V. J. (2018). Music Therapy: A Pedagogical Alternative for ASD and ID Students in Regular Classrooms. In P. Epler (Ed.), *Instructional Strategies in General Education and Putting the Individuals With Disabilities Act (IDEA) Into Practice* (pp. 222–244). Hershey, PA: IGI Global. doi:10.4018/978-1-5225-3111-1.ch008

Toulassi, B. (2017). Educational Administration and Leadership in Francophone Africa: 5 Dynamics to Change Education. In S. Mukerji & P. Tripathi (Eds.), *Handbook of Research on Administration, Policy, and Leadership in Higher Education* (pp. 20–45). Hershey, PA: IGI Global. doi:10.4018/978-1-5225-0672-0.ch002

Umair, S., & Sharif, M. M. (2018). Predicting Students Grades Using Artificial Neural Networks and Support Vector Machine. In M. Khosrow-Pour, D.B.A. (Ed.), Encyclopedia of Information Science and Technology, Fourth Edition (pp. 5169-5182). Hershey, PA: IGI Global. doi:10.4018/978-1-5225-2255-3.ch449

Vettraino, L., Castello, V., Guspini, M., & Guglielman, E. (2018). Self-Awareness and Motivation Contrasting ESL and NEET Using the SAVE System. In M. Khosrow-Pour, D.B.A. (Ed.), Encyclopedia of Information Science and Technology, Fourth Edition (pp. 1559-1568). Hershey, PA: IGI Global. doi:10.4018/978-1-5225-2255-3.ch135

Wiemelt, J. (2017). Critical Bilingual Leadership for Emergent Bilingual Students. In I. Management Association (Ed.), Educational Leadership and Administration: Concepts, Methodologies, Tools, and Applications (pp. 1606-1631). Hershey, PA: IGI Global. doi:10.4018/978-1-5225-1624-8.ch074

Wolf, F., Seyfarth, F. C., & Pflaum, E. (2018). Scalable Capacity-Building for Geographically Dispersed Learners: Designing the MOOC "Sustainable Energy in Small Island Developing States (SIDS)". In U. Pandey & V. Indrakanti (Eds.), *Open and Distance Learning Initiatives for Sustainable Development* (pp. 58–83). Hershey, PA: IGI Global. doi:10.4018/978-1-5225-2621-6.ch003

Related References

Woodley, X. M., Mucundanyi, G., & Lockard, M. (2017). Designing Counter-Narratives: Constructing Culturally Responsive Curriculum Online. *International Journal of Online Pedagogy and Course Design*, 7(1), 43–56. doi:10.4018/IJOPCD.2017010104

Yell, M. L., & Christle, C. A. (2017). The Foundation of Inclusion in Federal Legislation and Litigation. In C. Curran & A. Petersen (Eds.), *Handbook of Research on Classroom Diversity and Inclusive Education Practice* (pp. 27–52). Hershey, PA: IGI Global. doi:10.4018/978-1-5225-2520-2.ch002

Zinner, L. (2019). Fostering Academic Citizenship With a Shared Leadership Approach. In C. Zhu & M. Zayim-Kurtay (Eds.), *University Governance and Academic Leadership in the EU and China* (pp. 99–117). IGI Global. https://doi.org/10.4018/978-1-5225-7441-5.ch007

About the Contributors

Anika Chanell Thrower earned her B.S. in consumer science/nutrition from Norfolk State University and both her MPH and Ph.D. in public health and community health from Walden University. Dr. Thrower served in Women, Infants, and Children's (WIC) programs nationwide for over 16 years as a health practitioner. Her most valued experiences include serving within a Native American community and the first WIC program in Connecticut. Because of her background, service, and research, she has expertise in utilizing the transtheoretical behavioral health model in underrepresented populations. Serving as a principal researcher and endorsed by the Connecticut Department of Public Health, she completed research within a sample of a WIC clinic investigating health-based variables steeped in VENA. Because of the high quality of her research, she won the Presidential Alumni Research Dissemination Award within her institution of higher learning. Dr. Thrower has published several peer-reviewed scholarly articles. Appointed by the mayor, she co-chaired the New Haven Food Policy Council. Along with others, Dr. Thrower's expertise led to the establishment of the city's first Food Action Plan. She serves as an Assistant Professor within the Health Education department at City University of New York-Borough of Manhattan Community College. Before her current position, Dr. Thrower taught at Springfield College and Southern Connecticut State University. She teaches coursework in stress management and community health education rooted in culturally responsive pedagogy. Dr. Thrower's research interests include investigating mental health, stress, and food security issues that adversely affect the quality of life of women and other members of underrepresented populations. Long-standing, she advocates maternal and child health issues and raising social awareness around health inequalities. As exemplified in her book entitled The Art of Dominating the Winner's Circle of the College-Minded Student, she seeks ways to close gaps in obtaining higher education attainment.

Alex Evangelista (EdD) serves as an Assistant Professor within the Health Education Department at Borough of Manhattan Community College. His academic foundation encompasses education and health, holding a Doctorate of Education

About the Contributors

in Educational Leadership, a Master of Arts in Health Education, and a Bachelor of Science in Physical Education. The scholar's pursuits center on exploring the efficacy of educators' training in collaborative online and technology-based learning environments. This academic interest is reflected in his research endeavors, which have produced notable works such as "Rethinking the Online Environment Through Collaborative Learning" and "Online Collaboration: The Influence of faculty characteristics, training, and presentation mode."Beyond academia, Dr. Evangelista upholds certifications, including Certified Strength & Conditioning Specialist (CSCS) and Basic Life Support (BLS), underscoring his dedication to fitness and first aid standards. Moreover, his entrepreneurial endeavors in health and fitness have been acknowledged through the acquisition of grants, illustrating his multifaceted contributions beyond traditional classroom instruction.

Ruth Baker-Gardner is currently a lecturer and the undergraduate coordinator in the Department of Library and Information Studies at the University of the West Indies, Mona in Jamaica. She obtained her undergraduate degree and Master in Library and Information Studies from that same institution. She earned a PhD in Education Administration at the Northern Caribbean University. Dr. Baker-Gardner has over 35 years of experience in the education sector, having worked at the secondary and the tertiary levels. Her research interests include academic integrity, induction and mentoring, and school librarianship.

Hammed Mogaji holds a First-Class bachelor's degree in Biological Sciences, a master's and PhD in Parasitology all with Distinction. He had additional postdoctoral training in Epidemiology at Institute of Collective Health, Salvador, Brazil, and a Research Scientist position at the Epidemiology at Yale School of Public Health, United States. His research interest revolves around neglected tropical diseases (NTDs), including mapping, exploration of socio-economic and ecological determinants of transmission, and implementation science involving understudying disease control programs to identify and resolve bottlenecks limiting them. Before joining the university as a lecturer, he served as a research scientist with the Spatial Parasitology and Health GIS group and a program/research officer on NTDs with an indigenous non-governmental organization, MITOSATH. He has won several extramural funding for his research, as well as awards and advocacy grants in recognition of his outreach programs on Malaria, NTDs and COVID-19 in Nigeria. He has authored over 60 peer-reviewed articles, and a book chapter with over 500 citations. He also has representations in local and international conferences in over 10 countries including the USA. He reviews for over 10 reputable journals including PLoS NTDs, PLoS ONE, Parasites and Vectors, BMC Public Health, Parasite Epidemiology and Control, Frontier's in Public Health, and Nigerian Journal of

Parasitology to mention a few. He is also a member of some reputable societies including TDR Global, ASTMH, ASTMH, BSP, PPSN, iCHORDS, GSA, ASM and ARNTD. He was recently appointed as a Global Assessor of grants and events abstract for Royal Society of Tropical Medicine and Hygiene (RSTMH) in 2021, and a member of iCHORDS, Canada steering committee. He is one of the winners of the prestigious American Society of Tropical Medicine and Hygiene Young Investigators Award (First Tie Mention) in 2021.

* * *

Suzette Brown is an aspiring librarian and she is currently studying at the University of the West Indies.

Jason D. DeHart is a passionate educator and has served as a middle grades teacher for eight years. He also served as an assistant professor of reading education at Appalachian State University from 2019-2022, and has taught reading education courses at The University of Tennessee, Knoxville and Lee University in Cleveland, Tennessee. DeHart's research interests include multimodal literacy, including film and graphic novels, and literacy instruction with adolescents. His work has recently appeared in SIGNAL Journal, English Journal, and The Social Studies.

Kia Ayana Glimps-Smith is a "lifelong scholar" at the University of the Virgin Islands, in St. Thomas, USVI. She received a bachelor's degree in media arts from Benedict College in Columbia, SC, and her master's degree in special education from Grand Canyon University in Phoenix, Arizona. She has been a special educator in the public school sector for seventeen years in both the elementary, middle, and high school settings. Glimps-Smith's interests include STEAM (science, technology, engineering, arts, and math) education; multicultural education; multicultural children's literature; special education; diversity and inclusion in higher education; creative leadership, innovation, and sensemaking; and curriculum and instruction. She is following in the footsteps of her mother, Dr. Blanche Glimps, a retired professor, and she is motivated my her two daughters.

Musiki Glover, co-writer, is a graduate of Baylor University with a Social Work (BSW) degree. Additionally, Ms. Glover engaged in postgraduate studies in Education from Antioch University, Los Angeles. She has committed her life to social justice practices serving youth, their families, and the community. Musiki, a lay writer, writes widely on topics in education, parents' rights, girl empowerment, and youth preparation for college and careers. She lives in Brownsville, Brooklyn, New York where she too navigates her special needs children through the NYC Educational

About the Contributors

battlegrounds. Musiki and co-author, V. Poleon met and advocated together within their children's Brooklyn elementary school.

Taisha Johnson is a school psychologist and lecturer at the University of LaVerne, USA

Venesta Poleon holds a B.S. in Early Childhood and Special Education from NYU Steinhardt School of Culture, Education, and Human Development graduating with honors. She holds an Associate in Science degree from Borough of Manhattan Community College (BMCC), where she also graduated with honors. Venesta's academic excellence has earned her membership in prestigious professional associations, including the Phi Theta Kappa Society, the National Society of Leadership, and Kappa Delta Pi. In recognition of her exceptional academic achievements, Venesta was named a University Scholar, graduating among the top 40% of her class. Through her personal experience navigating the complex landscape of special education in New York City, Venesta has developed a deep understanding of the challenges facing parents and children with disabilities. She leverages her expertise to advocate for their rights and ensure that they receive appropriate educational opportunities. Venesta's dedication to promoting equity and inclusivity in education makes her a valuable asset to the New York City community. In her personal life, she is a wife, mother of three, and a strong force for her extended family across the globe. In her spare time, she has served as Chair and Vice Chair on the parent's Delegate Agency Policy Committee (DAPC), leading her to join the efforts of the CityWide Head Start Policy Council. In her roles on the council she served as an Area Representative for East New York's Head Start Cluster and a Community Representative Board member for the Administration for Children Services' Head Start Education Policy Council. Venesta's creed is that when you can guide someone in a direction that they want to go, clear the way and lead! The motto that she holds in the greatest value is that of the Borough of Manhattan Community College (where her college journey all began)..."Start Here. Go Anywhere." She hopes the readers of this work will lean into their educational journey one giant step after another and onward to many leaps of faithfulness. You got this and it's Yours!

Nicoleen Saunders-Grant is a Librarian/Media Resource Officer at the HEART NSTA Trust Eastern TVET Institute Stony Hill Campus. Who has been active in the Library and Information sector for 17 years. She holds a Masters in Archives and Records Management (ARCM) along with a Bachelors in Library and Information Studies (LIS).

Melony Smith is at the Arkansas State University, USA.

Christina S. Walker, Esq., J.D., Ph.D. (ABD), is a licensed attorney and doctoral (Ph.D.) student in the College of Communication and Information, University of Kentucky. Her work focuses on pertinent issues at the intersection of communication, law/social justice and culture. Dr. Walker equally studies communication and culture separately, without integrating legal perspectives. Throughout Dr. Walker's career in government, law and policy, and higher education, she has analyzed legal compliance, regulation and policy while advising on best practices in consideration of diversity, equity and inclusion. During 2021-23, Dr. Walker provided over 120 hours of pro bono representation to womxn+ experiencing financial hardship, including representation in areas of probate law, real estate law, contracts, constitutional law and torts. Dr. Walker regularly conducts research on issues disproportionately impacting minority womxn+ individuals, with her recent works focused on sexual harassment policies; stereotypes surrounding intimate partner violence related to race and same-sex couples; sex discrimination in social media policies; and governance of 'Afro-hair'. In Dr. Walker's additional recent works, she's explored audience responses to racial discourse occurring on popular reality tv shows. Further, Dr. Walker is an adjunct faculty member in the Department of Communication at Eastern Kentucky University where she teaches Human Communication while focusing on intercultural and interpersonal communication and public speaking.

Index

A

Adaptation 58, 83, 190-191, 196, 198-201, 206-207
Attrition Rates 66-67, 75-77, 122-123
Autoethnographic Research 57, 70
Autoethnography 57, 59-61, 64-66, 68, 71, 74, 79-82, 85-87, 94, 98, 103, 115, 120, 123-124, 127, 129, 133, 136, 139, 154, 189, 205, 207

B

Black Women 57, 63, 101, 118, 138-145, 148, 154

C

Comics 189-199, 201-207
Composing 189

D

Discrimination 55, 78, 138-140, 153, 177
Diversity 48-49, 72, 74, 84, 95, 104, 109, 115, 117-118, 121-122, 127, 153-154
Doctoral Degrees 35, 68, 75-76, 79, 103-104, 122, 132
Dr. Johnson 1-6, 8-14

E

Emic Perspective 189, 207
Equity 104, 152-153
Ethnography 15, 57, 118-119, 121

Etic Perspective 207

F

Financial Independence 2, 5
Forethought 1, 14

H

Higher Education 12, 15, 24, 26, 35-37, 40-48, 51-52, 54-56, 59-61, 66-68, 70, 72, 74-76, 78-79, 83-84, 90-92, 94, 101, 103-106, 110, 116-118, 121-122, 124-127, 130, 132-134, 136, 139, 145, 155-159, 161, 163-167, 169, 171-174, 178-187

I

Intentionality 14

L

Literacy 125, 189-192, 196, 198-199, 201, 204-205, 207
Literacy History 205, 207

M

Media 6, 38, 56, 62, 150, 190-191, 193-195, 197-198, 207
Microaggression 138-140, 150, 153
Minority Enrollment 15
Multimodality 206-207

N

Non-Traditional Black Women 57
Non-Traditional Students 35, 42, 45, 51, 53, 59-60, 67-69, 71-76, 85-86, 98, 100-103, 107, 110, 113, 122-123, 134-135, 156-160, 162-165, 168-169, 176, 180-182, 185-186

P

Persistence Theory 57, 59, 65, 78, 80, 107-108, 118-119, 121, 123, 131
Purpose 1, 10-12, 14, 17, 27, 31-32, 36, 39, 42, 63, 66, 98-99, 112, 115, 119, 139, 194-195, 201

R

Racism 2, 24, 95, 138-140, 144, 150, 153, 196, 202
Reading 33, 37, 52-53, 65, 111, 123, 142, 170, 189-192, 195-197, 199, 202-206
Representation 116-117, 170, 191-192, 194, 198, 201, 203, 205-207
Resiliency 1

S

Self-Efficacy 1, 14, 107, 176
Stereotypes 6, 14, 49, 191

T

Tertiary Education 155, 157-158, 164, 166-168, 173, 175, 179
Text 53-54, 60, 132, 134, 144, 148, 183, 185, 191, 206-207
Transformative Learning Theory 59, 65-66, 70-71, 77-78, 80, 92-94, 98-99, 104, 106-107, 118-119, 129-130
Transmedia 202, 206-207

U

Undergraduate Programs 155
Underrepresented Students 35, 55, 189-190, 192

V

Values 3, 14, 39, 57, 79, 91, 93, 97, 105, 128, 139, 185
Veteran Students 44, 49

Recommended Reference Books

IGI Global's reference books are available in three unique pricing formats:
Print Only, E-Book Only, or Print + E-Book.
Order direct through IGI Global's Online Bookstore at www.igi-global.com or through your preferred provider.

Online Distance Learning Course Design and Multimedia in E-Learning

ISBN: 9781799897064
EISBN: 9781799897088
© 2022; 302 pp.
List Price: US$ 215

Global and Transformative Approaches Toward Linguistic Diversity

ISBN: 9781799889854
EISBN: 9781799889878
© 2022; 383 pp.
List Price: US$ 215

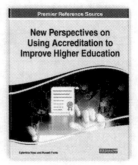

New Perspectives on Using Accreditation to Improve Higher Education

ISBN: 9781668451953
EISBN: 9781668451960
© 2022; 300 pp.
List Price: US$ 215

Impact of School Shootings on Classroom Culture, Curriculum, and Learning

ISBN: 9781799852001
EISBN: 9781799852018
© 2022; 355 pp.
List Price: US$ 215

Modern Reading Practices and Collaboration Between Schools, Family, and Community

ISBN: 9781799897507
EISBN: 9781799897521
© 2022; 304 pp.
List Price: US$ 215

Designing Effective Distance and Blended Learning Environments in K-12

ISBN: 9781799868293
EISBN: 9781799868316
© 2022; 389 pp.
List Price: US$ 215

Do you want to stay current on the latest research trends, product announcements, news, and special offers?
Join IGI Global's mailing list to receive customized recommendations, exclusive discounts, and more.
Sign up at: www.igi-global.com/newsletters.

Publisher of Timely, Peer-Reviewed Inclusive Research Since 1988

Ensure Quality Research is Introduced to the Academic Community

Become an Reviewer for IGI Global Authored Book Projects

The overall success of an authored book project is dependent on quality and timely manuscript evaluations.

Applications and Inquiries may be sent to:
development@igi-global.com

Applicants must have a doctorate (or equivalent degree) as well as publishing, research, and reviewing experience. Authored Book Evaluators are appointed for one-year terms and are expected to complete at least three evaluations per term. Upon successful completion of this term, evaluators can be considered for an additional term.

If you have a colleague that may be interested in this opportunity, we encourage you to share this information with them.

Submit an Open Access Book Proposal

Have Your Work Fully & Freely Available Worldwide After Publication

Seeking the Following Book Classification Types:
Authored & Edited Monographs • Casebooks • Encyclopedias • Handbooks of Research

Gold, Platinum, & Retrospective OA Opportunities to Choose From

Easily Track Your Work in Our Advanced Manuscript Submission System With **Rapid Turnaround Times**

Double-Blind Peer Review by Notable Editorial Boards (*Committee on Publication Ethics* (COPE) Certified

Publications Adhere to All **Current OA Mandates & Compliances**

Affordable APCs *(Often 50% Lower Than the Industry Average)* Including Robust Editorial Service Provisions

Direct Connections with **Prominent Research Funders** & OA Regulatory Groups

Institution Level OA Agreements Available (Recommend or Contact Your Librarian for Details)

Join a **Diverse Community of 150,000+ Researchers Worldwide** Publishing With IGI Global

Content Spread Widely to Leading Repositories (AGOSR, ResearchGate, CORE, & More)

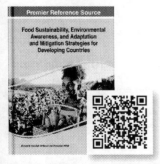

Retrospective Open Access Publishing

You Can Unlock Your Recently Published Work, Including Full Book & Individual Chapter Content to Enjoy All the Benefits of Open Access Publishing

Learn More

Are You Ready to Publish Your Research?

IGI Global offers book authorship and editorship opportunities across 11 subject areas, including business, computer science, education, science and engineering, social sciences, and more!

Benefits of Publishing with IGI Global:

- Free one-on-one editorial and promotional support.
- Expedited publishing timelines that can take your book from start to finish in less than one (1) year.
- Choose from a variety of formats, including Edited and Authored References, Handbooks of Research, Encyclopedias, and Research Insights.
- Utilize IGI Global's eEditorial Discovery® submission system in support of conducting the submission and double-blind peer review process.
- IGI Global maintains a strict adherence to ethical practices due in part to our full membership with the Committee on Publication Ethics (COPE).
- Indexing potential in prestigious indices such as Scopus®, Web of Science™, PsycINFO®, and ERIC – Education Resources Information Center.
- Ability to connect your ORCID iD to your IGI Global publications.
- Earn honorariums and royalties on your full book publications as well as complimentary content and exclusive discounts.

Join Your Colleagues from Prestigious Institutions, Including:

Learn More at: www.igi-global.com/publish
or by Contacting the Acquisitions Department at: acquisition@igi-global.com

Printed in the United States
by Baker & Taylor Publisher Services